Unrestrained
as the
Wind

Unrestrained
as the
Wind

*Releasing the Spirit of
Bahá'í Youth*

Bahá'í Publishing Trust
Wilmette, Illinois

Bahá'í Publishing Trust
415 Linden Avenue, Wilmette, Illinois 60091-2844

Copyright © 1985, 2008 by the National Spiritual Assembly
of the Bahá'ís of the United States
All rights reserved. First edition 1985
Second edition 2008
Printed in the United States of America on acid-free paper ∞

11 10 09 08   4 3 2 1

Library of Congress Cataloging-in-Publication Data

Unrestrained as the wind : releasing the spirit of Bahá'í youth. — New ed.
    p. cm.
    Includes bibliographical references and index.
    ISBN 978-0-87743-283-8 (soft cover : alk. paper) 1. Bahai youth—
Religious life—Quotations, maxims, etc. 2. Bahai Faith—Quotations,
maxims, etc.
    BP380.U54 2007
    297.9'3440835—dc22
                                    2007029629

Extensive quotation from works granted by kind permission of George
Ronald, Publisher. *Some Early Bahá'ís of the West,* by O. Z. Whitehead.
Copyright © 1976 by O. Z. Whitehead. *Some Bahá'ís to Remember,* by
O. Z. Whitehead. Copyright © 1983 by O. Z. Whitehead.

Cover design by Misha Maynerick
Book design by Suni D. Hannan

In memory of the six Bahá'í youth
whose complete love for the Blessed Beauty
resulted in their execution on 18 June 1983 in Shiraz:

Shirin Dalvand
Ruya Ishraqi
Muna Mahmudnizhad
Mahshid Nirumand
Simin Sabiri
Akhtar Thabit

May the Bahá'í youth of the world
be inspired to vindicate these sacrifices
through a renewed sense of dedication and service
to the Cause of Bahá'u'lláh.

London, 9/2/17

Dearest Roya joon,

As you turn 18 years old or young, what
more can I wish you than to be guided
by the unerring 'Lighthouse of His Teaching.
May Baha'u'llah shower His Blessings upon
you and enable you to dedicate your
life to service to humanity & His Cause.
with warmest wishes Dad xx

Contents

Preface to the 2008 Edition

A soul, once it is touched by the breathtaking potency of the Revelation of Bahá'u'lláh, is never the same. Responding to the call of this Revelation, countless Bahá'í youth have arisen throughout the history of the Faith to perform acts of great heroism and distinction that have forever left their mark on the development of the Faith and on the world around them. Those who have arisen have been forever transformed. The Bahá'í Faith was first promulgated by youth, and it remains dependent on the youth of today to carry it forward to even greater heights. When *Unrestrained as the Wind* was first published in 1985, Bahá'í youth around the world were dismayed at the heartbreaking martyrdoms of their fellow youth in Iran. These sacrifices motivated Bahá'í youth worldwide to higher levels of consecration and service. Keenly aware of those who have laid down their lives in the name of Bahá'u'lláh, Bahá'í youth around the world continue to be galvanized by the memory of such heroism.

The youth of today must remember that they are following in the footsteps of the Báb, Who was only twenty-five years old when He declared His Mission; 'Abdu'l-Bahá, Who was only eight years old when Bahá'u'lláh was imprisoned, and Who was called at a young age to shoulder heavy responsibilities for the Faith; Bahíyyih Khánum, who in her teens arose with joy to complete many critical and perilous missions entrusted to her

by her father; Mírzá Mihdí, who at the age of twenty-two sacrificed his life so that visitors to 'Akká would be enabled to attain the presence of Bahá'u'lláh; and Shoghi Effendi, who was
still a university student when called upon to fulfill the role of
Guardianship of the still young worldwide Bahá'í community.
Their lives serve as reminders that youth need not feel they
must wait to be able to perform inestimable acts of service for
the Faith and to become living embodiments of the Faith's precious and sacred teachings.

The degree to which the Bahá'í Faith has progressed in recent years can be seen by the steady growth of the Faith in all
regions of the world, and this process has continued to show
the invaluable role the youth play in its development. The
heightened maturity and wisdom of the Bahá'í youth, their
sense of ownership of their role in the Bahá'í Faith, and the
energy and zeal with which they arise to serve calls to mind the
Master's desire for each to be as "a fearless lion" and the
Guardian's praise of their "enterprising and adventurous spirit,
their alertness, optimism and eagerness." The vitality of the
Bahá'í youth serves to animate the Faith and lead it toward its
unparalleled destiny.

While surveying the growth and progress of the Bahá'í community since 1985, it is impossible not to notice the alarming
effects of the accelerating disintegration of society. Bombarded
by unspeakable acts of school violence; widespread promiscuity; alcohol and drug abuse; environmental degradation; the
pernicious effects of racism, sexism, and materialism; and the
alarming collapse of the family, many young people today suffer
from a numbing sense of complacency and powerlessness. Bahá'í
youth, however, are arising with increasing distinction to overcome the virulent forces around them, and they are working
toward new levels of maturity and service in everything they

do. While society steadily continues to decay, these youth are exerting every effort to build the Kingdom of God on earth through their spiritual discipline, their distinctive service to others, and their courageous willingness to stand out as shining examples of righteousness.

The best tool with which youth can arm themselves in this valiant battle is the Bahá'í writings. In them they will find spiritual sustenance, inspiration, guidance, solace, and comfort. *Unrestrained as the Wind* brings together selections from the Bahá'í writings that provide Bahá'í youth with answers and guidance that address their unique questions and concerns. May it inspire and guide them to overcome the many challenges they face and connect them with the spirit of their heroic spiritual ancestors.

Publisher's Preface to the
2008 Edition

Unrestrained as the Wind was first published in 1985 as a joint project of the Bahá'í National Youth Committee of the United States and the U.S. Bahá'í Publishing Trust. When supplies of the third printing were beginning to run out, the Publishing Trust began consulting about updating the book. The realization that there was a great deal of new guidance from the Universal House of Justice that was not available when the book was first published led to the decision to prepare a new, expanded edition with new material that would make the book even more helpful to today's youth.

The new edition incorporates many changes, primarily in the form of new extracts and updated references. Most chapters include new material, and one chapter—chapter 9—is entirely new.

A foreword has also been added. Chapter 1 of the 1985 edition, titled "Prayers for Spiritual Growth," has been moved to the appendix, and more prayers—including special occasional prayers, prayers for marriage, for youth, and for women, as well as all three of the daily obligatory prayers—have been added. What was formerly chapter 2 has been renamed "Relationship with God and Bahá'u'lláh" and now appears as chapter 1. It includes an entirely new section on the life, station, and revelation of Bahá'u'lláh. Chapter 2 (formerly chapter 3), "The Distinctive Bahá'í Life," includes several new passages on living a distinctive Bahá'í life. Chapter 3 (formerly chapter 4), "Exemplary Lives and Heroic Deeds," has been renamed "Youth on the Forefront," and includes additional passages on the lives of Quddús and Mullá Ḥusayn, an account of the life of Zaynab, and two new sections containing accounts of the lives of contemporary Western Bahá'í youth and young adults and interviews with Bahá'í youth.

Chapter 4 (formerly chapter 5), "Education and a Life of Service," now includes a section on "Pursuing the Arts." Chapter 5 (formerly chapter 6), "Teaching," includes three new sections: "Training Institutes and Core Activities, "College Clubs," and "Youth Year of Service." Chapter 6 (formerly chapter 7), "Purity and Cleanliness," is now titled "Personal Conduct." The section that was titled "Drugs: Hashish, LSD, Marijuana, Opium, Peyote" has been renamed "The Use of Illicit Drugs."

In chapter 7 (formerly chapter 8), "Interpersonal relationships," the section titled "Homosexuality" has been revised to include new material on the subject, and three new sections titled "Divorce," "Violence and Sexual Abuse," and "Loving and Accepting Others" have been added. Chapter 8 (formerly chapter 9), "Social Relationships," includes two new sections: "Freedom" and "The Bahá'í Administrative Order." The section titled "Participation in Social and Economic Development" has been moved to chapter 9.

The new chapter 9 is titled "Social Issues" and includes sections on "Race Unity: Our Most Challenging Issue," "The Equality of Women and Men," "World Peace," "Social and Economic Development" (formerly "Participation in Social and Economic Development" in chapter 8), and "Environmentalism." Chapter 10, "Youth Can Move the World," includes twenty-four new messages from the Universal House of Justice itself or written on its behalf that are either addressed to youth or that deal with issues of direct relevance to Bahá'í youth around the world.

The bibliography has been revised to incorporate references to the new material that has been added and to update existing references. A detailed index has also been added.

The Bahá'í Publishing Trust would like to extend its warmest thanks to the many individuals who were involved in preparing this new edition. We are particularly grateful to Eric Horton, who worked tirelessly in numerous capacities to ensure that the new edition was the best that it could be. We thank Vesal Dini, Anthony Outler, Leili Towfigh, and Nancy Wong for their feedback, vision, thoughtfulness, and for their assistance with the foreword. Thanks are also due to the National Bahá'í Education Task Force, and in particular Barbara Johnson, Saba Ayman-Nolley, and Joanne Yuille, for providing crucial perspective and for helping to ensure the book's usefulness for future generations of Bahá'í youth. We thank Nicole McCoy, Niky Farid, and Serena Fuller for reviewing the first edition and offering suggestions that helped to shape the new edition. Gayle Morrison and Lewis Walker offered helpful suggestions for additional sections in chapter 3, "Youth on the Forefront." Alex Blakeson offered helpful answers on the subject of pioneering and travel teaching. Bart Shull offered many helpful suggestions that led to quite a few important last-minute additions in numerous sections. Charla Edmonstone-Pickens and Manuchehr Derakhshani answered questions and gave helpful advice. We would also like to acknowledge Aaron Emmel for giving permission to reprint interviews with Bahá'í youth. To the many others who offered insight, feedback, wisdom, and encouragement in the course of the project, thereby contributing to its final form, we extend our deep gratitude. Thank you, one and all.

—*U.S. Bahá'í Publishing Trust*

Foreword to the 1985 Edition

In January 1984 the Universal House of Justice addressed a historic message to the Bahá'í youth of the world. Although the immediate concern of the message was with the 1985 International Youth Year, the letter's impact was far greater, as its soul-stirring contents conveyed an exciting vision of the future opportunities and tasks of an entire generation. The response of the Bahá'í youth has subsequently led to plans beyond 1985 and to an upsurge of youth activity in many countries that may well signal the beginning of a movement that, in the words of the Universal House of Justice, has already "caught the imagination of the friends far and wide."

During the many consultations of the youth about the implications of a Bahá'í youth movement that would attract the support of thousands of youth on every continent, it became clear that the greatest challenge to each individual participant would be learning to live according to a spiritual discipline akin to that of the first generation of the youth of this Dispensation—of Mullá Ḥusayn, Ṭáhirih, Quddús, and Badí'. Striving for such a discipline, in turn, would imply achieving a new balance in life, a balance that would be conducive to heroic deeds and to a state of complete devotion. Indeed, each individual youth would have to struggle against the pressures of an environment that at its best interprets as moderation the notion of living comfortably according to the norms of mediocrity and that consistently tries to pull youth away from true spiritual excellence and from com-

mitment to significant social change. The Bahá'í youth would
have to achieve a different vision of moderation and, to do so,
would have to remind themselves constantly of the sacrifices of
their brethren in Iran during the recent years.

It became clear in the deliberations that, in order to rise to
their high destiny, the Bahá'í youth would have to analyze themselves, their potential, and the world with a logic different from
the reasoning they have inherited from a materialistic society;
they would have to see through the eyes of faith and systematically plan and achieve goals that would seem impossible to everyone untouched by the fire of their zeal. Yet practical questions always remained. How would the youth organize their
lives to meet the challenges of their generation and of their
own growth and preparation and, at the same time, follow the
standards of dedication and action required by the special call
of the Universal House of Justice that they "contribute significantly to shaping the societies of the coming century" and that
they "move the world."

The answer clearly lies in the dynamic of a spiritual life
very different from the present life-style fragmented by op-
posing social forces, forces that themselves are in conflict with
the true human spirit. The challenge is to live a spiritual life
that is whole, pure, intense, purposeful, active, and respon-
sive to all the requirements of being a Bahá'í youth in this
moment of history. The present compilation prepared by the
Bahá'í National Youth Committee and the Publishing Trust
of the Bahá'ís of the United States exactly tries to integrate
the many aspects of such a spiritual life of service and dedication to the Cause of Bahá'u'lláh. It is hoped that it will become our close companion in all our endeavors as we participate in the unfoldment of the destiny of the present generation of Bahá'í youth throughout the world.

—*Farzam Arbab*

1

Relationship with God and Bahá'u'lláh

The Covenant of God

1. The first duty prescribed by God for His servants is the recognition of Him Who is the Dayspring of His Revelation and the Fountain of His laws, Who representeth the Godhead in both the Kingdom of His Cause and the world of creation. Whoso achieveth this duty hath attained unto all good. . . . It behooveth everyone who reacheth this most sublime station, this summit of transcendent glory, to observe every ordinance of Him Who is the Desire of the world. These twin duties are inseparable. Neither is acceptable without the other. . . .

They whom God hath endued with insight will readily recognize that the precepts laid down by God constitute the highest means for the maintenance of order in the world and the security of its peoples. . . . Hasten to drink your fill, O men of understanding! They that have violated the Covenant of God by breaking His commandments, and have turned back on their heels, these have erred grievously in the sight of God, the All-Possessing, the Most High.

Bahá'u'lláh

2. This is the Day, O my Lord, which Thou didst announce unto all mankind as the Day whereon Thou wouldst reveal Thy Self, and shed Thy radiance, and shine brightly over all Thy creatures. Thou hast, moreover, entered into a covenant with them, in Thy Books, and Thy Scriptures, and Thy Scrolls, and Thy Tablets, concerning Him Who is the Dayspring of Thy Revelation, and hast appointed the Bayán to be the Herald of this Most Great and all-glorious Manifestation, and this most resplendent and most sublime Appearance.

Bahá'u'lláh

3. The Lord of the universe hath never raised up a prophet nor hath He sent down a Book unless He hath established His covenant with all men, calling for their acceptance of the next Revelation and of the next Book; inasmuch as the outpourings of His bounty are ceaseless and without limit.

The Báb

4. It is evident that the axis of the oneness of the world of humanity is the power of the Covenant and nothing else.

'Abdu'l-Bahá

Knowing and Loving God

5. All praise and glory be to God Who, through the power of His might, hath delivered His creation from the nakedness of nonexistence, and clothed it with the mantle of life. From among all created things He hath singled out for His special favor the pure, the gem-like reality of man, and invested it with a unique capacity of knowing Him and of reflecting the greatness of His glory.

Bahá'u'lláh

6. O Son of Man! Veiled in My immemorial being and in the ancient eternity of My essence, I knew My love for thee; therefore I created thee, have engraved on thee Mine image and revealed to thee My beauty.

Bahá'u'lláh

7. Having created the world and all that liveth and moveth therein, He, through the direct operation of His unconstrained and sovereign Will, chose to confer upon man the unique distinction and capacity to know Him and to love Him—a capacity that must needs be regarded as the generating impulse and the primary purpose underlying the whole of creation.

Bahá'u'lláh

8. O Son of Man! I loved thy creation, hence I created thee. Wherefore, do thou love Me, that I may name thy name and fill thy soul with the spirit of life.

Bahá'u'lláh

Faith and Obedience: Signs of Knowing and Loving God

9. O Son of Being! Walk in my statutes for love of Me and deny thyself that which thou desirest if thou seekest My pleasure.

Bahá'u'lláh

10. Man's highest station . . . is attained through faith in God in every Dispensation and by acceptance of what hath been revealed by Him, and not through learning; inasmuch as in every nation there are learned men who are versed in divers sciences. Nor is it attainable through wealth; for it is similarly

evident that among the various classes in every nation there are those possessed of riches. Likewise are other transitory things.

True knowledge, therefore, is the knowledge of God, and this is none other than the recognition of His Manifestation in each Dispensation. Nor is there any wealth save in poverty in all save God and sanctity from aught else but Him—a state that can be realized only when demonstrated towards Him Who is the Dayspring of His Revelation.

The Báb

11. It is certain that man's highest distinction is to be lowly before and obedient to his God; that his greatest glory, his most exalted rank and honor, depend on his close observance of the Divine commands and prohibitions. Religion is the light of the world, and the progress, achievement, and happiness of man result from obedience to the laws set down in the holy Books.

'Abdu'l-Bahá

Our Relationship with Bahá'u'lláh

THE STATION OF BAHÁ'U'LLÁH

12. He Who in such dramatic circumstances was made to sustain the overpowering weight of so glorious a Mission was none other than the One Whom posterity will acclaim, and Whom innumerable followers already recognize, as the Judge, the Lawgiver and Redeemer of all mankind, as the Organizer of the entire planet, as the Unifier of the children of men, as the Inaugurator of the long-awaited millennium, as the Originator of a new "Universal Cycle," as the Establisher of the Most Great Peace, as the Fountain of the Most Great Justice, as the Proclaimer of the coming of age of the entire human race, as the Creator of a

new World Order, and as the Inspirer and Founder of a world civilization.

Shoghi Effendi

13. The distinguished Orientalist, Prof. E. G. Browne of Cambridge, was granted his four successive interviews with Bahá'u'lláh, during the five days he was His guest at Bahjí (April 15–20, 1890), interviews immortalized by the Exile's historic declaration that "these fruitless strifes, these ruinous wars shall pass away and the 'Most Great Peace' shall come." "The face of Him on Whom I gazed," is the interviewer's memorable testimony for posterity, "I can never forget, though I cannot describe it. Those piercing eyes seemed to read one's very soul; power and authority sat on that ample brow. . . . No need to ask in whose presence I stood, as I bowed myself before one who is the object of a devotion and love which kings might envy and emperors sigh for in vain."

Shoghi Effendi

GLIMPSES INTO THE LIFE OF BAHÁ'U'LLÁH

14. All this generation could offer Us were wounds from its darts, and the only cup it proffered to Our lips was the cup of its venom. On our neck We still bear the scar of chains, and upon Our body are imprinted the evidences of an unyielding cruelty.

Bahá'u'lláh

15. That which hath touched this Wronged One is beyond compare or equal. We have borne it all with the utmost willingness and resignation, so that the souls of men may be edified, and the Word of God be exalted.

Bahá'u'lláh

16. When Bahá'u'lláh was twenty-two years old, His father died, and the Government wished Him to succeed His father's position in the Ministry, as was customary in Persia, but Bahá'u'lláh did not accept the offer. Then the Prime Minister said: "Leave him to himself. Such a position is unworthy of him. He has some higher aim in view. I cannot understand him, but I am convinced that he is destined for some lofty career. His thoughts are not like ours. Let him alone."

'Abdu'l-Bahá

17. He derived His descent, on the one hand, from Abraham (the Father of the Faithful) through his wife Katurah, and on the other from Zoroaster, as well as from Yazdigird, the last king of the Sásáníyán dynasty. He was moreover a descendant of Jesse, and belonged, through His father, Mírzá 'Abbás, better known as Mírzá Buzurg—a nobleman closely associated with the ministerial circles of the Court of Fath-'Alí Sháh—to one of the most ancient and renowned families of Mázindarán.

Shoghi Effendi

18. When Bahá'u'lláh was still a child, the Vazír, His father, dreamed a dream. Bahá'u'lláh appeared to him swimming in a vast, limitless ocean. His body shone upon the waters with a radiance that illumined the sea. Around His head, which could distinctly be seen above the waters, there radiated, in all directions, His long, jet-black locks, floating in great profusion above the waves. As he dreamed, a multitude of fishes gathered round Him, each holding fast to the extremity of one hair. Fascinated by the effulgence of His face, they followed Him in whatever direction He swam. Great as was their number, and however firmly they clung to His locks, not one single hair seemed to have been detached from His head, nor did the least injury

affect His person. Free and unrestrained, He moved above the waters and they all followed Him.

The Vazír, greatly impressed by this dream, summoned a soothsayer, who had achieved fame in that region, and asked him to interpret it for him. This man, as if inspired by a premonition of the future glory of Bahá'u'lláh, declared: "The limitless ocean that you have seen in your dream, O Vazír, is none other than the world of being. Single-handed and alone, your son will achieve supreme ascendancy over it. Wherever He may please, He will proceed unhindered. No one will resist His march, no one will hinder His progress. The multitude of fishes signifies the turmoil which He will arouse amidst the peoples and kindreds of the earth. Around Him will they gather, and to Him will they cling. Assured of the unfailing protection of the Almighty, this tumult will never harm His person, nor will His loneliness upon the sea of life endanger His safety."

Nabíl-i-A'ẓam

THE REVELATION OF BAHÁ'U'LLÁH

19. More grievous became Our plight from day to day, nay, from hour to hour, until they took Us forth from Our prison and made Us, with glaring injustice, enter the Most Great Prison. And if anyone ask them: "For what crime were they imprisoned?" they would answer and say: "They, verily, sought to supplant the Faith with a new religion!" If that which is ancient be what ye prefer, wherefore, then, have ye discarded that which hath been set down in the Torah and the Evangel? Clear it up, O men! By My life! There is no place for you to flee to in this day. If this be My crime, then Muḥammad, the Apostle of God, committed it before Me, and before Him He Who was the Spirit of God (Jesus Christ), and yet earlier He Who conversed with God (Moses). And if My sin be this, that I have exalted the Word of God and

revealed His Cause, then indeed am I the greatest of sinners! Such a sin I will not barter for the kingdoms of earth and heaven.

Bahá'u'lláh

20. The Ancient Beauty hath consented to be bound with chains that mankind may be released from its bondage, and hath accepted to be made a prisoner within this most mighty Stronghold that the whole world may attain unto true liberty. He hath drained to its dregs the cup of sorrow, that all the peoples of the earth may attain unto abiding joy, and be filled with gladness. This is of the mercy of your Lord, the Compassionate, the Most Merciful. We have accepted to be abased, O believers in the Unity of God, that ye may be exalted, and have suffered manifold afflictions, that ye might prosper and flourish. He Who hath come to build anew the whole world, behold, how they that have joined partners with God have forced Him to dwell within the most desolate of cities!

Bahá'u'lláh

21. Praised be Thou, O my God! How can I thank Thee for having singled me out and chosen me above all Thy servants to reveal Thee, at a time when all had turned away from Thy beauty! I testify, O my God, that if I were given a thousand lives by Thee, and offered them up all in Thy path, I would still have failed to repay the least of the gifts which, by Thy grace, Thou hast bestowed upon me.

I lay asleep on the bed of self when lo, Thou didst waken me with the divine accents of Thy voice, and didst unveil to me Thy beauty, and didst enable me to listen to Thine utterances, and to recognize Thy Self, and to speak forth Thy praise, and to extol Thy virtues, and to be steadfast in Thy love. Finally I fell a captive into the hands of the wayward among Thy servants.

Thou beholdest, therefore, the exile which I suffer in Thy days, and art aware of my vehement longing to look upon Thy face, and of mine irrepressible yearnings to enter the court of Thy glory, and of the stirrings of my heart under the influences of the winds of Thy mercy.

I entreat Thee, O Thou Who art the Ruler of the kingdoms of creation and the Author of all names, to write down my name with the names of them who, from eternity, have circled round the Tabernacle of Thy majesty, and clung to the hem of Thy loving-kindness, and held fast the cord of Thy tender mercy.

Thou art, in truth, the Help in Peril, the Self-Subsisting.

Bahá'u'lláh

22. Praised be Thou, O my God! Thou seest me shut up in this Prison, and art well aware that I have entered it solely for Thy sake and for the sake of the glorification of Thy word and the proclamation of Thy Cause. I cry out to Thee, this very moment, O Thou Who art the Lord of all worlds, beseeching Thee, by Thine undoubted Name, to attract the hearts of Thy servants unto the Day-Spring of Thy most excellent titles and the Dawning-Place of Thy most resplendent signs.

But for the troubles that touch me in Thy path, O my God, how else could my heart rejoice in Thy days; and were it not for the blood which is shed for love of Thee, what else could tinge the faces of Thy chosen ones before the eyes of Thy creatures? I swear by Thy might! The ornament that adorneth the countenance of Thy dear ones is the blood which, in their love for Thee, floweth out of their foreheads over their faces.

Thou beholdest, O my God, how every bone in my body soundeth like a pipe with the music of Thine inspiration, revealing the signs of Thy oneness and the clear tokens of Thy unity. I entreat Thee, O my God, by Thy Name which irradiateth all things, to raise up such servants as shall incline their ears to the voice of the melodies that hath ascended from the right hand of the throne of Thy glory. Make them, then, to quaff from the hand of Thy grace the wine of Thy mercy, that it may assure their hearts, and cause them to turn away from the left hand of idle fancies and vain imaginings to the right hand of confidence and certitude.

Now that Thou hast guided them unto the door of Thy grace, O my Lord, cast them not away, by Thy bounty; and now that Thou hast summoned them unto the horizon of Thy Cause, keep them not back from Thee, by Thy graciousness and favor. Powerful art Thou to do as Thou pleasest. No God is there but Thee, the Omniscient, the All-Informed.

Bahá'u'lláh

23. To strive to obtain a more adequate understanding of the significance of Bahá'u'lláh's stupendous Revelation must, it is my unalterable conviction, remain the first obligation and the object of the constant endeavor of each one of its loyal adherents. An exact and thorough comprehension of so vast a system, so sublime a revelation, so sacred a trust, is for obvious reasons beyond the reach and ken of our finite minds. We can, however, and it is our bounden duty to seek to derive fresh inspiration and added sustenance as we labor for the propagation of His Faith through a clearer apprehension of the truths it enshrines and the principles on which it is based.

Shoghi Effendi

24. A Revelation, hailed as the promise and crowning glory of past ages and centuries, as the consummation of all the Dispensations within the Adamic Cycle, inaugurating an era of at least a thousand years' duration, and a cycle destined to last no less than five thousand centuries, signalizing the end

of the Prophetic Era and the beginning of the Era of Fulfillment, unsurpassed alike in the duration of its Author's ministry and the fecundity and splendor of His mission—such a Revelation was, as already noted, born amidst the darkness of a subterranean dungeon in Ṭihrán—an abominable pit that had once served as a reservoir of water for one of the public baths of the city. Wrapped in its stygian gloom, breathing its fetid air, numbed by its humid and icy atmosphere, His feet in stocks, His neck weighed down by a mighty chain, surrounded by criminals and miscreants of the worst order, oppressed by the consciousness of the terrible blot that had stained the fair name of His beloved Faith, painfully aware of the dire distress that had overtaken its champions, and of the grave dangers that faced the remnant of its followers—at so critical an hour and under such appalling circumstances the "Most Great Spirit," as designated by Himself, and symbolized in the Zoroastrian, the Mosaic, the Christian, and Muḥammadan Dispensations by the Sacred Fire, the Burning Bush, the Dove and the Angel Gabriel respectively, descended upon, and revealed itself, personated by a "Maiden," to the agonized soul of Bahá'u'lláh.

Shoghi Effendi

Communing with God*

WHY WE PRAY

25. Intone, O My servant, the verses of God that have been received by thee, as intoned by them who have drawn nigh unto Him, that the sweetness of thy melody may kindle thine

---

* For a selection of Bahá'í prayers, please see the appendix, pp. 377–404.

own soul, and attract the hearts of all men. Whoso reciteth, in the privacy of his chamber, the verses revealed by God, the scattering angels of the Almighty shall scatter abroad the fragrance of the words uttered by his mouth, and shall cause the heart of every righteous man to throb. Though he may, at first, remain unaware of its effect, yet the virtue of the grace vouchsafed unto him must needs sooner or later exercise its influence upon his soul. Thus have the mysteries of the Revelation of God been decreed by virtue of the Will of Him Who is the Source of power and wisdom.

Bahá'u'lláh

26. O thou spiritual friend! Thou hast asked the wisdom of prayer. Know thou that prayer is indispensable and obligatory, and man under no pretext whatsoever is excused from performing the prayer unless he be mentally unsound, or an insurmountable obstacle prevent him. The wisdom of prayer is this: That it causeth a connection between the servant and the True One, because in that state man with all heart and soul turneth his face towards His Highness the Almighty, seeking His association and desiring His love and compassion. The greatest happiness for a lover is to converse with his beloved, and the greatest gift for a seeker is to become familiar with the object of his longing; that is why with every soul who is attracted to the Kingdom of God, his greatest hope is to find an opportunity to entreat and supplicate before his Beloved, appeal for His mercy and grace and be immersed in the ocean of His utterance, goodness and generosity.

Besides all this, prayer and fasting is the cause of awakening and mindfulness and conducive to protection and preservation from tests.

'Abdu'l-Bahá

27. Remembrance of God is like the rain and dew which bestow freshness and grace on flowers and hyacinths, revive them and cause them to acquire fragrance, redolence and renewed charm. . . . Strive thou, then, to praise and glorify God by night and by day, that thou mayest attain infinite freshness and beauty.

'Abdu'l-Bahá

28. The problem with which you are faced is one which concerns and seriously puzzles many of our present-day youth. How to attain spirituality is indeed a question to which every young man and woman must sooner or later try to find a satisfactory answer. It is precisely because no such satisfactory answer has been given or found, that modern youth finds itself bewildered, and is being consequently carried away by the materialistic forces that are so powerfully undermining the foundation of man's moral and spiritual life.

Indeed, the chief reason for the evils now rampant in society is the lack of spirituality. The materialistic civilization of our age has so much absorbed the energy and interest of mankind that people in general do no longer feel the necessity of raising themselves above the forces and conditions of their daily material existence. There is not sufficient demand for things that we should call spiritual to differentiate them from the needs and requirements of our physical existence. The universal crisis affecting mankind is, therefore, essentially spiritual in its causes. The spirit of the age, taken on the whole, is irreligious. Man's outlook on life is too crude and materialistic to enable him to elevate himself into the higher realms of the spirit.

It is this condition, so sadly morbid, into which society has fallen, that religion seeks to improve and transform. For the core of religious faith is that mystic feeling which unites man with God. This state of spiritual communion can be brought about and maintained by means of meditation and prayer. And this is the reason why Bahá'u'lláh has so much stressed the importance of worship. It is not sufficient for a believer merely to accept and observe the teachings. He should, in addition, cultivate the sense of spirituality which he can acquire chiefly by means of prayer. The Bahá'í Faith, like all other Divine Religions, is thus fundamentally mystic in character. Its chief goal is the development of the individual and society, through the acquisition of spiritual virtues and powers. It is the soul of man which has first to be fed. And this spiritual nourishment prayer can best provide. Laws and institutions, as viewed by Bahá'u'lláh, can become really effective only when our inner spiritual life has been perfected and transformed. Otherwise religion will degenerate into a mere organization, and becomes a dead thing.

The believers, particularly the young ones, should therefore fully realize the necessity of praying. For prayer is absolutely indispensable to their inner spiritual development, and this, as already stated, is the very foundation and purpose of the religion of God.

Shoghi Effendi

29. When a person becomes a Bahá'í, actually what takes place is that the seed of the spirit starts to grow in the human soul. This seed must be watered by the outpourings of the Holy Spirit. These gifts of the spirit are received through prayer, meditation, study of the Holy Utterances and service to the Cause of God. The fact of the matter is that service in the Cause is like the plough which ploughs the physical soil when seeds are sown. It is necessary that the soil be ploughed up, so that it can be enriched, and thus cause a stronger growth of the seed. In exactly the same way the evolution of the spirit takes place

through ploughing up the soil of the heart so that it is a constant reflection of the Holy Spirit. In this way the human spirit grows and develops by leaps and bounds.

On behalf of Shoghi Effendi

WHEN TO PRAY

30. At the dawn of every day he should commune with God, and with all his soul persevere in the quest of his Beloved. He should consume every wayward thought with the flame of His loving mention, and, with the swiftness of lightning, pass by all else save Him.

Bahá'u'lláh

31. Although the words "at the hour of dawn" are used in the Book of God, it is acceptable to God at the earliest dawn of day, between dawn and sunrise, or even up to two hours after sunrise.

Bahá'u'lláh

32. Supplication to God at morn and eve is conducive to the joy of hearts, and prayer causes spirituality and fragrance. Thou shouldst necessarily continue therein.

'Abdu'l-Bahá

33. Praise be to God, thy heart is engaged in the commemoration of God, thy soul is gladdened by the glad tidings of God and thou art absorbed in prayer. The state of prayer is the best of conditions, for man is then associating with God. Prayer verily bestoweth life, particularly when offered in private and at times, such as midnight, when freed from daily cares.

'Abdu'l-Bahá

34. We may well emulate Bahá'í youth whose recent surge forward into the van of proclamation and teaching is one of the most encouraging and significant trends in the Faith, and who storm the gates of heaven for support in their enterprises by long-sustained, precedent and continuing prayer. We are all able to call upon Bahá'u'lláh for His Divine, all-powerful aid, and He will surely help us. For He is the Hearer of prayers, the Answerer.

The Universal House of Justice

USING THE OBLIGATORY PRAYERS

35. The daily obligatory prayers are three in number. . . . The believer is entirely free to choose any one of these three prayers, but is under the obligation of reciting one of them, and in accordance with any specific directions with which it may be accompanied.

On behalf of Shoghi Effendi

36. Bahá'u'lláh has reduced all ritual and form to an absolute minimum in His Faith. The few forms that there are—like those associated with the two longer obligatory daily prayers, are only symbols of the inner attitude. There is a wisdom in them, and a great blessing but we cannot force ourselves to understand or feel these things, that is why He gave us also the very short and simple prayer, for those who did not feel the desire to perform the acts associated with the other two.

On behalf of Shoghi Effendi

37. As to the attitude of resentment which the young believers are inclined to assume regarding certain precepts of the Cause such as obligatory prayers; there can and should be no compromise whatever in such matters that are specifically enjoined by Bahá'u'lláh. We should neither have any feeling of shame when

observing such laws and precepts, nor should we over-estimate their value and significance. Just as the friends have no difficulty in recognizing the value of the specific prayers revealed by Bahá'u'lláh, such as the Tablets of Fasting and Healing so also they should recognize that the obligatory prayers are by their very nature of greater effectiveness and are endowed with a greater power than the non-obligatory ones, and as such are essential.

On behalf of Shoghi Effendi

38. You should rest assured that your strict adherence to the laws and observances enjoined by Bahá'u'lláh is the one power that can effectively guide and enable you to overcome the tests and trials of your life, and help you to continually grow and develop spiritually.

The Guardian particularly appreciates the fact that you have been faithfully observing Bahá'u'lláh's injunction regarding the recital of the daily obligatory prayers, and have thereby set such a high example before your Bahá'í fellow-youth. These daily prayers have been endowed with a special potency which only those who regularly recite them can adequately appreciate. The friends should therefore endeavor to make daily use of these prayers, whatever the peculiar circumstances and conditions of their life.

On behalf of Shoghi Effendi

39. The hour of noon should, of course, be observed in accordance with the position of the sun, not in accordance with local time-standards. The short obligatory prayer may be said at any time between noon and sunset.

The Universal House of Justice

40. By "morning," "noon" and "evening," mentioned in connection with the Obligatory Prayers, is meant respectively the

intervals between sunrise and noon, between noon and sunset, and from sunset till two hours after sunset.

Synopsis and Codification of the Kitáb-i-Aqdas

To Whom to Pray

41. It behooveth the servant to pray to and seek assistance from God, and to supplicate and implore His aid. Such becometh the rank of servitude, and the Lord will decree whatsoever He desireth, in accordance with His consummate wisdom.

'Abdu'l-Bahá

42. You have asked whether our prayers go beyond Bahá'u'lláh: It all depends whether we pray to Him directly or through Him to God. We may do both, and also can pray directly to God, but our prayers would certainly be more effective and illuminating if they are addressed to Him through His Manifestation, Bahá'u'lláh.

On behalf of Shoghi Effendi

43. In regard to your question: we must not be rigid about praying; there is not a set of rules governing it; the main thing is we must start out with the right concept of God, the Manifestation, the Master, the Guardian—we can turn, in thought, to any one of them when we pray. For instance you can ask Bahá'u'lláh for something, or thinking of Him, ask God for it. The same is true of the Master or the Guardian. You can turn in thought to either of them and then ask their intercession, or pray direct to God. As long as you don't confuse their stations, and make them all equal, it does not matter much how you orient your thoughts.

On behalf of Shoghi Effendi

WHAT PRAYERS TO USE

44. As to your question about prayer and whether it is necessary to recite the prayers of only the Central Figures of our Faith, we have been asked to quote here the following two excerpts on this subject, from letters written by Shoghi Effendi's secretary on his behalf:

> . . . as the Cause embraces members of all races and religions we should be careful not to introduce into it the customs of our previous beliefs. Bahá'u'lláh has given us the obligatory prayers, also prayers before sleeping, for travelers, etc. We should not introduce a new set of prayers He has not specified, when He has given us already so many, for so many occasions.
>
> He thinks it would be wiser for the Bahá'ís to use the Meditations given by Bahá'u'lláh, and not any set form of meditation recommended by someone else; but the believers must be left free in these details and allowed to have personal latitude in finding their own level of communion with God.

> As to the reading of prayers or selections from the Sacred Writings of other religions such readings are permissible, and indeed from time to time are included in the devotional programs of Bahá'í Houses of Worship, demonstrating thereby the universality of our Faith.

On behalf of the Universal House of Justice

PRAYER AND ACTION

45. O maid-servant of God! Chant the Words of God and, pondering over their meaning, transform them into actions! I ask God to cause thee to attain a high station in the Kingdom of Life forever and ever.

'Abdu'l-Bahá

46. We may well emulate Bahá'í youth . . . who storm the gates
of heaven for support in their enterprises by long sustained,
precedent and continuing prayer. We are all able to call upon
Bahá'u'lláh for His Divine, all-powerful aid, and He will surely
help us. For He is the Hearer of prayers, the Answerer.

The Universal House of Justice

Fasting for Love and Purification

47. Fortunate are ye to have obeyed the commandment of God,
and kept this fast during the holy season. For this material fast is
an outer token of the spiritual fast; it is a symbol of self-restraint,
the withholding of oneself from all appetites of the self, taking
on the characteristics of the spirit, being carried away by the
breathings of heaven and catching fire from the love of God.

'Abdu'l-Bahá

48. Regarding your question concerning the Fast: Travelers are
exempt from fasting, but if they want to fast while they are
traveling, they are free to do so. You are exempt the whole period of your travel, not just the hours you are in a train or car,
etc. If one eats unconsciously during the fasting hours, this is
not breaking the Fast as it is an accident. The age limit is sev-
enty years, but if one desires to fast after the age limit is passed,
and is strong enough to, one is free to do so. If during the Fast
period a person falls ill and is unable to fast, but recovers before
the fast period is over, he can start to fast again and continue
until the end. Of course the Fast, as you know, can only be
kept during the month set aside for that purpose.*

Shoghi Effendi

---

* Additional details on exemptions from the Fast and the like can be
found in *The Kitáb-i-Aqdas.*

49. As regards fasting, it constitutes, together with the obligatory prayers, the two pillars that sustain the revealed Law of
God. They act as stimulants to the soul, strengthen, revive and
purify it, and thus insure its steady development.

The ordinance of fasting is, as is the case with these three
prayers,* a spiritual and vital obligation enjoined by Bahá'u'lláh
upon every believer who has attained the age of fifteen. In the
Aqdas He thus writes: "We have commanded you to pray and
fast from the beginning of maturity; this is ordained by God,
your Lord and the Lord of your forefathers. He has exempted
from this those who are weak from illness or age, as a bounty
from His Presence, and He is the Forgiving, the Generous." And
in another passage He says: "We have enjoined upon you fasting
during a brief period, and at its close have designated for you
Naw-Rúz as a feast. . . . The traveler, the ailing, those who are
with child or giving suck, are not bound by the fast. . . . Abstain
from food and drink, from sunrise to sundown, and beware lest
desire deprive you of this grace that is appointed in the Book."

Also, in the "Questions and Answers" that form an appendix
to the Aqdas, Bahá'u'lláh reveals the following: "Verily, I say
that God has appointed a great station for fasting and prayer.
But during good health its benefit is evident, and when one is
ill, it is not permissible to fulfill them." Concerning the age of
maturity, He reveals in the appendix of that same book: "The
age of maturity is in the fifteenth year; women and men are
alike in this respect." . . .

The fasting period, which lasts nineteen days starting as a
rule from the second of March every year and ending on the
twentieth of the same month, involves complete abstention from

---

* The three obligatory daily prayers, any one of which the believer is free
to choose.

food and drink from sunrise till sunset. It is essentially a period of meditation and prayer, of spiritual recuperation, during which the believer must strive to make the necessary read-
justments in his inner life, and to refresh and reinvigorate the
spiritual forces latent in his soul. Its significance and purpose
are, therefore, fundamentally spiritual in character. Fasting is
symbolic, and a reminder of abstinence from selfish and carnal desires.

On behalf of Shoghi Effendi

50. In one of His Tablets, 'Abdu'l-Bahá, after stating that fasting
consists of abstinence from food and drink, further indicates that
smoking is a form of "drink." In Arabic, the verb "drink" applies
equally to smoking.

The Kitáb-i-Aqdas

Sacrificing Yourself to the Love of God

51. He that giveth up himself wholly to God, God shall,
assuredly, be with him; and he that placeth his complete trust
in God, God shall, verily, protect him from whatsoever may
harm him, and shield him from the wickedness of every evil
plotter.

Bahá'u'lláh

52. O thou faithful one!
   One of the requirements of faithfulness is that thou mayest
sacrifice thyself and, in the divine path, close thine eye to every
pleasure and strive with all thy soul that thou mayest disappear
and be lost, like unto a drop, in the ocean of the love of God.

'Abdu'l-Bahá

53. It is my hope . . . that day by day ye will love God in ever greater measure, and become more tightly bound to the Beauty that abideth forever, to Him Who is the Light of the world. For love of God and spiritual attraction do cleanse and purify the human heart and dress and adorn it with the spotless garment of holiness; and once the heart is entirely attached to the Lord, and bound over to the Blessed Perfection, then will the grace of God be revealed.

This love is not of the body but completely of the soul. And those souls whose inner being is lit by the love of God are even as spreading rays of light, and they shine out like stars of holiness in a pure and crystalline sky. For true love, real love, is the love for God, and this is sanctified beyond the notions and imaginings of men.

'Abdu'l-Bahá

54. Regarding the points you refer to in your letter: the complete and entire elimination of the ego would imply perfection—which man can never completely attain—but the ego can and should be ever-increasingly subordinated to the enlightened soul of man. That is what spiritual progress implies.

On behalf of Shoghi Effendi

55. Regarding the questions you asked: self has really two meanings, or is used in two senses, in the Bahá'í writings; one is self, the identity of the individual created by God. This is the self mentioned in such passages as "he hath known God who hath known himself etc." The other self is the ego, the dark, animalistic heritage each one of us has, the lower nature that can develop into a monster of selfishness, brutality, lust and so on. It is this self we must struggle against, or this side of our natures,

in order to strengthen and free the spirit within us and help it to attain perfection.

Self-sacrifice means to subordinate this lower nature and its desires to the more godly and noble side of our selves. Ultimately, in its highest sense, self-sacrifice means to give our will and our all to God to do with as He pleases. Then He purifies and glorifies our true self until it becomes a shining and wonderful reality.

On behalf of Shoghi Effendi

2

The Distinctive Bahá'í Life

The Call to Spiritual Distinction

1. O My beloved friends! You are the bearers of the name of God in this Day. You have been chosen as the repositories of His mystery. It behoves each one of you to manifest the attributes of God, and to exemplify by your deeds and words the signs of His righteousness, His power and glory. The very members of your body must bear witness to the loftiness of your purpose, the integrity of your life, the reality of your faith, and the exalted character of your devotion. For verily I say, this is the Day spoken of by God in His Book:* "On that day will We set a seal upon their mouths; yet shall their hands speak unto Us, and their feet shall bear witness to that which they shall have done." Ponder the words of Jesus addressed to His disciples, as He sent them forth to propagate the Cause of God. In words such as these, He bade them arise and fulfil their mission: "Ye are even as the fire which in the darkness of the night has been kindled upon the mountain-top. Let your light shine before the eyes of men. Such must be the purity of your character and the degree of your renunciation, that the people of the earth may through you recognize and be

---

* The Qur'án.

drawn closer to the heavenly Father who is the Source of purity
and grace. For none has seen the Father who is in heaven. You
who are His spiritual children must by your deeds exemplify His
virtues, and witness to His glory. You are the salt of the earth, but
if the salt have lost its savor, wherewith shall it be salted? Such
must be the degree of your detachment, that into whatever city
you enter to proclaim and teach the Cause of God, you should
in no wise expect either meat or reward from its people. Nay,
when you depart out of that city, you should shake the dust from
off your feet. As you have entered it pure and undefiled, so must
you depart from that city. For verily I say, the heavenly Father is
ever with you and keeps watch over you. If you be faithful to
Him, He will assuredly deliver into your hands all the treasures
of the earth, and will exalt you above all the rulers and kings of
the world." O My Letters! Verily I say, immensely exalted is this
Day above the days of the Apostles of old. Nay, immeasurable is
the difference! You are the witnesses of the Dawn of the promised Day of God. You are the partakers of the mystic chalice of
His Revelation. Gird up the loins of endeavor, and be mindful of
the words of God as revealed in His Book:* "Lo, the Lord thy
God is come, and with Him is the company of His angels arrayed before Him!" Purge your hearts of worldly desires, and let
angelic virtues be your adorning. Strive that by your deeds you
may bear witness to the truth of these words of God, and beware
lest, by "turning back," He may "change you for another people,"
who "shall not be your like," and who shall take from you the
Kingdom of God. The days when idle worship was deemed sufficient are ended. The time is come when naught but the purest
motive, supported by deeds of stainless purity, can ascend to the
throne of the Most High and be acceptable unto Him. "The
good word riseth up unto Him, and the righteous deed will cause

---

* The Qur'án.

it to be exalted before Him." You are the lowly, of whom God has thus spoken in His Book:* "And We desire to show favor to those who were brought low in the land, and to make them spiritual leaders among men, and to make them Our heirs." You have been called to this station; you will attain to it, only if you arise to trample beneath your feet every earthly desire, and endeavor to become those "honored servants of His who speak not till He hath spoken, and who do His bidding." You are the first Letters that have been generated from the Primal Point,† the first Springs that have welled out from the Source of this Revelation. Beseech the Lord your God to grant that no earthly entanglements, no worldly affections, no ephemeral pursuits, may tarnish the purity, or embitter the sweetness, of that grace which flows through you. I am preparing you for the advent of a mighty Day. . . . Heed not your weaknesses and frailty; fix your gaze upon the invincible power of the Lord, your God, the Almighty. Has He not, in past days, caused Abraham, in spite of His seeming helplessness, to triumph over the forces of Nimrod? Has He not enabled Moses, whose staff was His only companion, to vanquish Pharaoh and his hosts? Has He not established the ascendancy of Jesus, poor and lowly as He was in the eyes of men, over the combined forces of the Jewish people? Has He not subjected the barbarous and militant tribes of Arabia to the holy and transforming discipline of Muḥammad, His Prophet? Arise in His name, put your trust wholly in Him, and be assured of ultimate victory.

The Báb

2. O loved ones of 'Abdu'l-Bahá!

Man's life has its springtime and is endowed with marvelous glory. The period of youth is characterized by strength and vigor

---

* The Qur'án.
† One of the titles of the Báb.

and stands out as the choicest time in human life. Therefore you should strive day and night so that endowed with heavenly strength, inspired with brilliant motives and aided by His celestial power and heavenly grace and confirmation, you may become the ornaments of the world of humanity, and preeminent among those who are initiated into true learning and the love of God. You must be distinguished amidst men by your sanctity and detachment, loftiness of purpose, magnanimity, determination, noble-mindedness, tenacity, the elevation of your aims and your spiritual qualities; that you may become the means of exaltation and glory for the Cause of God and the dawning places of His heavenly bestowals; that you may conduct yourselves in conformity with the counsels and exhortations of the Blessed Beauty—may my life be offered up for His loved ones—and by reflecting Bahá'í qualities and attributes, you may stand out distinguished from others. 'Abdu'l-Bahá eagerly anticipates that each one of you may become even as a fearless lion moving in the pastures of human perfection and a musk-laden breeze wafting over the meads of virtue.

The glory of glories rest upon you.

'Abdu'l-Bahá

3. I desire distinction for you. The Bahá'ís must be distinguished from others of humanity. But this distinction must not depend upon wealth—that they should become more affluent than other people. I do not desire for you financial distinction. It is not an ordinary distinction I desire; not scientific, commercial, industrial distinction. For you I desire spiritual distinction—that is, you must become eminent and distinguished in morals. In the love of God you must become distinguished

from all else. You must become distinguished for loving humanity, for unity and accord, for love and justice. In brief, you must become distinguished in all the virtues of the human world—for faithfulness and sincerity, for justice and fidelity, for firmness and steadfastness, for philanthropic deeds and service to the human world, for love toward every human being, for unity and accord with all people, for removing prejudices and promoting international peace. Finally, you must become distinguished for heavenly illumination and for acquiring the bestowals of God. I desire this distinction for you. This must be the point of distinction among you.

'Abdu'l-Bahá

4. The youth today must show forth a greater maturity than any previous generation, for they are called upon to pass through perhaps the gravest crisis in the history of the world, and they must meet their destiny with faith, steadfastness, assurance and poise.

On behalf of Shoghi Effendi

5. If ever it could be said that a religion belonged to the youth, then surely the Bahá'í Faith today is that religion. The whole world is suffering, it is sunk in misery, crushed beneath its heavy problems. The task of healing its ills and building up its future devolves mainly upon the youth. They are the generation who, after the war, will have to solve the terrible difficulties created by the war and all that brought it about. And they will not be able to upbuild the future except by the laws and principles laid down by Bahá'u'lláh. So their task is very great and their responsibility very grave.

On behalf of Shoghi Effendi

6. We sincerely hope that the forefront of the volunteers, the Bahá'í youth will arise for the sake of God and, through their driving force, their ability to endure inhospitable and arduous conditions, and their contentment with the bare necessities of life, they will offer an inspiring example to the peoples and communities they set out to serve, will exert an abiding influence on their personal lives, and will promote with distinction the vital interests of God's Cause at this crucial stage in the fortunes of the Plan.

The Universal House of Justice

The Importance of a Good Character

7. A good character is, verily, the best mantle for men from God. With it He adorneth the temples of His loved ones. By My life! The light of a good character surpasseth the light of the sun and the radiance thereof. Whoso attaineth unto it is accounted as a jewel among men. The glory and the upliftment of the world must needs depend upon it. A goodly character is a means whereby men are guided to the Straight Path and are led to the Great Announcement. Well is it with him who is adorned with the saintly attributes and character of the Concourse on High.

Bahá'u'lláh

8. The most vital duty, in this day, . . . is to purify your characters, to correct your manners, and improve your conduct. The beloved of the Merciful must show forth such character and conduct among His creatures, that the fragrance of their holiness may be shed upon the whole world, and may quicken the dead, inasmuch as the purpose of the Manifestation of God and the dawning of the limitless lights of the Invisible is to educate the souls of men, and refine the character of every living man.

'Abdu'l-Bahá

9. He hopes that you will develop into Bahá'ís in character as well as in belief. The whole purpose of Bahá'u'lláh is that we should become a new kind of people, people who are upright, kind, intelligent, truthful, and honest and who live according to His great laws laid down for this new epoch in man's development. To call ourselves Bahá'ís is not enough; our inmost being must become ennobled and enlightened through living a Bahá'í life.

On behalf of Shoghi Effendi

10. What can control youth and save it from the pitfalls of the crass materialism of the age is the power of a genuine, constructive and living Faith such as the one revealed to the world by Bahá'u'lláh. Religion, as in the past, is still the world's sole hope, but not that form of religion which our ecclesiastical leaders strive vainly to preach. Divorced from true religion, morals lose their effectiveness and cease to guide and control man's individual and social life. But when true religion is combined with true ethics, then moral progress becomes a possibility and not a mere ideal.

The need of our modern youth is for such a type of ethics founded on pure religious faith. Not until these two are rightly combined and brought into full action can there be any hope for the future of the race.

On behalf of Shoghi Effendi

The Responsibilities of Bahá'í Youth

11. Wherefore, O ye illumined youth, strive by night and by day to unravel the mysteries of the mind and spirit, and to grasp the secrets of the Day of God. Inform yourselves of the evidences that the Most Great Name hath dawned. Open your

lips in praise. Adduce convincing arguments and proofs. Lead those who thirst to the fountain of life; grant ye true health to the ailing. Be ye apprentices of God; be ye physicians directed by God, and heal ye the sick among humankind. Bring those who have been excluded into the circle of intimate friends. Make the despairing to be filled with hope. Waken them that slumber; make the heedless mindful.

Such are the fruits of this earthly life. Such is the station of resplendent glory. Upon you be Bahá'u'l-Abhá.

'Abdu'l-Bahá

12. Life is not easy for the young people of this generation. They enter life with a heart full of hope, but find before themselves nothing but failures, and see in the future nothing but darkness. What they need is the light manifested by Bahá'u'lláh, for that brightens their soul and stimulates their vigor in facing difficulties.

Shoghi Effendi

13. This Cause, although it embraces with equal esteem people of all ages, has a special message and mission for the youth of your generation. It is their charter for their future, their hope, their guarantee of better days to come.

On behalf of Shoghi Effendi

14. The present condition of the world—its economic instability, social dissensions, political dissatisfaction and international distrust—should awaken the youth from their slumber and make them inquire what the future is going to bring. It is surely they who will suffer most if some calamity sweep over the world. They should therefore open their eyes to the existing conditions, study the evil forces that are at play and then with a concerted effort arise and bring about the necessary reforms—

reforms that shall contain within their scope the spiritual as well as social and political phases of human life.

On behalf of Shoghi Effendi

15. The prevailing distress in America and Europe should awaken the youth to the futility of concentrating their whole life on purely material pursuits. They should learn the lesson that spiritual considerations should be the dominating factors of our life, that our guiding purpose should be to enhance our moral life and seek what is eternal and abiding.

Should the different nations continue to go wrong and be guided by the selfish desire of personal aggrandizement, you will be the group that will suffer most. Our present policies bear their fruits only in the future and it is the youth of the present that are the men and women of the future.

On behalf of Shoghi Effendi

16. He urges you to make up your minds to do great, *great* deeds for the Faith; the condition of the world is steadily growing worse, and your generation must provide the saints, heroes, martyrs and administrators of future years. With dedication and will power you can rise to great heights!

On behalf of Shoghi Effendi

17. Shoghi Effendi's greatest hope, and his prayer, is that they may so distinguish themselves in the eyes of their fellow-countrymen that it will become increasingly evident what a Bahá'í is and what he stands for. How wonderful it would be to witness the time when the actions and words of the Bahá'ís will have become so well known that people will say: "Ah! That must be a Bahá'í—they are like that!" and mean it as a compliment.

On behalf of Shoghi Effendi

Meeting the Challenge

18. The responsibility of young believers is very great, as they must not only fit themselves to inherit the work of the older Bahá'ís and carry on the affairs of the Cause in general, but the world which lies ahead of them—as promised by Bahá'u'lláh—will be a world chastened by its sufferings, ready to listen to His Divine Message at last; and consequently a very high character will be expected of the exponents of such a religion. To deepen their knowledge, to perfect themselves in the Bahá'í standards of virtue and upright conduct, should be the paramount duty of every young Bahá'í.

On behalf of Shoghi Effendi

19. For any person, whether Bahá'í or not, his youthful years are those in which he will make many decisions which will set the course of his life. In these years he is most likely to choose his life's work, complete his education, begin to earn his own living, marry, and start to raise his own family. Most important of all, it is during this period that the mind is most questing and that the spiritual values that will guide the person's future behavior are adopted. These factors present Bahá'í youth with their greatest opportunities, their greatest challenges, and their greatest tests—opportunities to truly apprehend the Teachings of their Faith and to give them to their contemporaries, challenges to overcome the pressures of the world and to provide leadership for their and succeeding generations, and tests enabling them to exemplify in their lives the high moral standards set forth in the Bahá'í Writings. Indeed the Guardian wrote of the Bahá'í youth that it is they "who can contribute so decisively to the virility, the purity, and the driv-

ing force of the life of the Bahá'í community, and upon whom must depend the future orientation of its destiny, and the complete unfoldment of the potentialities with which God has endowed it."

The Universal House of Justice

Transforming Society by Individual Example

20. Arise, O people, and, by the power of God's might, resolve to gain the victory over your own selves, that haply the whole earth may be freed and sanctified from its servitude to the gods of its idle fancies—gods that have inflicted such loss upon, and are responsible for the misery of, their wretched worshipers. These idols form the obstacle that impedeth man in his efforts to advance in the path of perfection. We cherish the hope that the Hand of Divine power may lend its assistance to mankind, and deliver it from its state of grievous abasement.

Bahá'u'lláh

21. Our greatest efforts must be directed towards detachment from the things of the world; we must strive to become more spiritual, more luminous, to follow the counsel of the Divine Teaching, to serve the cause of unity and true equality, to be merciful, to reflect the love of the Highest on all men, so that the light of the Spirit shall be apparent in all our deeds, to the end that all humanity shall be united, the stormy sea thereof calmed, and all rough waves disappear from off the surface of life's ocean henceforth unruffled and peaceful. Then will the New Jerusalem be seen by mankind, who will enter through its gates and receive the Divine Bounty.

'Abdu'l-Bahá

22. If we could perceive the true reality of things we could see that the greatest of all battles raging in the world today is the spiritual battle. If the believers like yourself, young and eager and full of life, desire to win laurels for true and undying heroism, then let them join in the spiritual battle—whatever their physical occupation may be—which involves the very soul of man. The hardest and the noblest task in the world today is to be a *true* Bahá'í; this requires that we defeat not only the current evils prevailing all over the world, but the weaknesses, attachments to the past, prejudices, and selfishnesses that may be inherited and acquired within our own characters; that we give forth a shining and incorruptible example to our fellow-men.

On behalf of Shoghi Effendi

Aspects of Bahá'í Character

23. Be generous in prosperity, and thankful in adversity. Be worthy of the trust of thy neighbor, and look upon him with a bright and friendly face. Be a treasure to the poor, an admonisher to the rich, an answerer of the cry of the needy, a preserver of the sanctity of thy pledge. Be fair in thy judgment, and guarded in thy speech. Be unjust to no man, and show all meekness to all men. Be as a lamp unto them that walk in darkness, a joy to the sorrowful, a sea for the thirsty, a haven for the distressed, an upholder and defender of the victim of oppression. Let integrity and uprightness distinguish all thine acts. Be a home for the stranger, a balm to the suffering, a tower of strength for the fugitive. Be eyes to the blind, and a guiding light unto the feet of the erring. Be an ornament to the countenance of truth, a crown to the brow of fidelity, a pillar of the temple of righteousness, a breath of life to the body of mankind, an ensign of

the hosts of justice, a luminary above the horizon of virtue, a dew to the soil of the human heart, an ark on the ocean of knowledge, a sun in the heaven of bounty, a gem on the diadem of wisdom, a shining light in the firmament of thy generation, a fruit upon the tree of humility.

Bahá'u'lláh

24. O ye lovers of this wronged one! Cleanse ye your eyes, so that ye behold no man as different from yourselves. See ye no strangers; rather see all men as friends, for love and unity come hard when ye fix your gaze on otherness. And in this new and wondrous age, the Holy Writings say that we must be at one with every people; that we must see neither harshness nor injustice, neither malevolence, nor hostility, nor hate, but rather turn our eyes toward the heaven of ancient glory. For each of the creatures is a sign of God, and it was by the grace of the Lord and His power that each did step into the world; therefore they are not strangers, but in the family; not aliens, but friends, and to be treated as such.

Wherefore must the loved ones of God associate in affectionate fellowship with stranger and friend alike, showing forth to all the utmost loving-kindness, disregarding the degree of their capacity, never asking whether they deserve to be loved. In every instance let the friends be considerate and infinitely kind. Let them never be defeated by the malice of the people, by their aggression and their hate, no matter how intense. If others hurl their darts against you, offer them milk and honey in return; if they poison your lives, sweeten their souls; if they injure you, teach them how to be comforted; if they inflict a wound upon you, be a balm to their sores; if they sting you, hold to their lips a refreshing cup.

'Abdu'l-Bahá

25. Act in accordance with the counsels of the Lord: that is, rise up in such wise, and with such qualities, as to endow the body of this world with a living soul, and to bring this young child, humanity, to the stage of adulthood. So far as ye are able, ignite a candle of love in every meeting, and with tenderness rejoice and cheer ye every heart. Care for the stranger as for one of your own; show to alien souls the same loving kindness ye bestow upon your faithful friends. Should any come to blows with you, seek to be friends with him; should any stab you to the heart, be ye a healing salve unto his sores; should any taunt and mock at you, meet him with love. Should any heap his blame upon you, praise ye him; should he offer you a deadly poison, give him the choicest honey in exchange; and should he threaten your life, grant him a remedy that will heal him evermore. Should he be pain itself, be ye his medicine; should he be thorns, be ye his roses and sweet herbs. Perchance such ways and words from you will make this darksome world turn bright at last; will make this dusty earth turn heavenly, this devilish prison place become a royal palace of the Lord—so that war and strife will pass and be no more, and love and trust will pitch their tents on the summits of the world. Such is the essence of God's admonitions; such in sum are the teachings for the Dispensation of Bahá.

'Abdu'l-Bahá

26. It is primarily through the potency of noble deeds and character, rather than by the power of exposition and proofs, that the friends of God should demonstrate to the world that what has been promised by God is bound to happen, that it is already taking place and that the divine glad-tidings are clear, evident and complete. For unless some illustrious souls step forth into the arena of service and shine out resplendent in the as-

semblage of men, the task of vindicating the truth of this Cause before the eyes of the enlightened people would be formidable indeed. However, if the friends become embodiments of virtue and good character, words and arguments will be superfluous. Their very deeds will well serve as eloquent testimony, and their noble conduct would ensure the preservation, integrity and glory of the Cause of God.

Shoghi Effendi

3

Youth on the Forefront

The Vital Role of Bahá'í Youth

1. From the very beginning of the Bahá'í Era, youth have played a vital part in the promulgation of God's Revelation. The Báb Himself was but twenty-five years old when He declared His Mission, while many of the Letters of the Living were even younger. The Master, as a very young man, was called upon to shoulder heavy responsibilities in the service of His Father in Iraq and Turkey, and His brother, the Purest Branch, yielded up his life to God in the Most Great Prison at the age of twenty-two that the servants of God might "be quickened, and all that dwell on earth be united." Shoghi Effendi was a student at Oxford when called to the throne of his guardianship, and many of the Knights of Bahá'u'lláh, who won imperishable fame during the Ten Year Crusade, were young people. Let it, therefore, never be imagined that youth must await their years of maturity before they can render invaluable services to the Cause of God.

The Universal House of Justice

2. RECENT MARTYRDOMS COURAGEOUS STEADFAST YOUTH IN SHIRAZ, SCENE INAUGURATION MISSION MARTYR-PROPHET, REMINISCENT ACTS

41

VALOR YOUTHFUL IMMORTALS HEROIC AGE. CONFIDENT BAHÁ'Í YOUTH THIS GENERATION WILL NOT ALLOW THIS FRESH BLOOD SHED ON VERY SOIL WHERE FIRST WAVE PERSECUTION FAITH TOOK PLACE REMAIN UNVINDICATED OR THIS SUBLIME SACRIFICE UNAVAILING. AT THIS HOUR OF AFFLICTION AND GRIEF, AND AS WE APPROACH ANNIVERSARY MARTYRDOM BLESSED BÁB CALL ON BAHÁ'Í YOUTH TO REDEDICATE THEMSELVES TO URGENT NEEDS CAUSE BAHÁ'U'LLÁH. LET THEM RECALL BLESSINGS HE PROMISED THOSE WHO IN PRIME OF YOUTH WILL ARISE TO ADORN THEIR HEARTS WITH HIS LOVE AND REMAIN STEADFAST AND FIRM. LET THEM CALL TO MIND EXPECTATIONS MASTER FOR EACH TO BE A FEARLESS LION, A MUSK-LADEN BREEZE WAFTING OVER MEADS VIRTUE. LET THEM MEDITATE OVER UNIQUE QUALITIES YOUTH SO GRAPHICALLY MENTIONED IN WRITINGS GUARDIAN WHO PRAISED THEIR ENTERPRISING AND ADVENTUROUS SPIRIT, THEIR VIGOR, THEIR ALERTNESS, OPTIMISM AND EAGERNESS, AND THEIR DIVINELY-APPOINTED, HOLY AND ENTHRALLING TASKS. WE FERVENTLY PRAY AT SACRED THRESHOLD THAT ARMY OF SPIRITUALLY AWAKENED AND DETERMINED YOUTH MAY IMMEDIATELY ARISE RESPONSE NEEDS PRESENT HOUR DEVOTE IN EVER GREATER MEASURE THEIR VALUED ENERGIES TO PROMOTE BOTH ON HOMEFRONTS AND IN FOREIGN FIELDS, CAUSE THEIR ALL-WATCHFUL AND EXPECTANT LORD. MAY THEY MANIFEST SAME SPIRIT SO RECENTLY EVINCED THEIR MARTYR BRETHREN CRADLE FAITH, SCALE SUCH HEIGHTS OF ENDEAVOR AS TO BECOME PRIDE THEIR PEERS CONSOLATION HEARTS PERSIAN BELIEVERS, AND DEMONSTRATE THAT THE FLAME HIS OMNIPOTENT HAND HAS KINDLED BURNS EVER BRIGHT AND THAT ITS LIFE-IMPARTING WARMTH AND RADIANCE SHALL SOON ENVELOP PERMEATE WHOLE EARTH.

The Universal House of Justice

'Abdu'l-Bahá, the Perfect Exemplar

3. He ['Abdu'l-Bahá] was only eight years old when—in the wake of a desperate and futile attempt on the life of Náṣiri'd-Dín Sháh, by two half-crazed men—Bahá'u'lláh was imprisoned,

and the Bábís were ferociously persecuted. Bahá'u'lláh's house was pillaged, His lands and goods were confiscated, and His family reduced from opulence to penury. One day, while in Europe, 'Abdu'l-Bahá recalled the sufferings of those bleak times:

> Detachment does not imply lack of means; it is marked by the freedom of the heart. In Ṭihrán, we possessed everything at a nightfall, and on the morrow we were shorn of it all, to the extent that we had no food to eat. I was hungry, but there was no bread to be had. My mother poured some flour into the palm of my hand, and I ate that instead of bread. Yet, we were contented.

And again:

> At that time of dire calamities and attacks mounted by the enemies I was a child of nine.* They threw so many stones into our house that the courtyard was crammed with them. . . . Mother took us for safety to another quarter, and rented a house in a back alley where she kept us indoors and looked after us. But one day our means of subsistence were barely adequate, and mother told me to go to my aunt's house, and ask her to find us a few qiráns.† . . . I went and my aunt did what she could for us. She tied a five-qirán piece in a handkerchief and gave it to me. On my way home someone recognized me and shouted: "Here is a Bábí"; whereupon the children in the street chased me. I found refuge in the entrance to a house. . . . There I stayed until nightfall, and when I came out, I was once again pursued by the children who kept yelling at me and pelted me with stones. . . . When I reached home I was exhausted. Mother wanted to know what had happened to me. I could not utter a word and collapsed. . . .

---

* In the reckoning of the lunar year.

† Iranian silver coin of the period.

One day 'Abdu'l-Bahá, anxious to see His Father, was taken to the dungeon. This is His account of that awesome visit:

> They sent me with a black servant to His blessed presence in the prison. The warders indicated the cell, and the servant carried me in on his shoulders. I saw a dark, steep place. We entered a small, narrow doorway, and went down two steps, but beyond those one could see nothing. In the middle of the stairway, all of a sudden we heard His blessed voice: "Do not bring him in here," and so they took me back. We sat outside, waiting for the prisoners to be led out. Suddenly they brought the Blessed Perfection* out of the dungeon. He was chained to several others. What a chain! It was very heavy. The prisoners could only move it along with great difficulty. Sad and heart-rending it was.
>
> *H. M. Balyuzi*

SACRIFICES AND SERVICES OF 'ABDU'L-BAHÁ

4. That blessed soul ['Abdu'l-Bahá], following the ascension of the sacred Abhá Beauty, may our lives be sacrificed for the dust of His sacred threshold, and until the hour when His own luminous spirit rose up to the realms on high, for a period of thirty years had neither a peaceful day nor a night of quiet rest. Singly and alone, He set about to reform the world, and to educate and refine its peoples. He invited all manner of beings to enter the Kingdom of God; He watered the Tree of the Faith; He guarded the celestial Lote-Tree from the tempest; He defeated the foes of the Faith, and He frustrated the hopes of the malevolent; and always vigilant, He protected God's Cause and defended His Law.

---

* One of the designations of Bahá'u'lláh.

That subtle and mysterious Being, that Essence of eternal glory, underwent trials and sorrows all the days of His life. He was made the target of every calumny and malicious accusation, by foes both without and within. His lot, in all His life, was to be wronged, and be subjected to toil, to pain and grief. Under these conditions, the one and only solace of His sacred heart was to hear good news of the progress of the Faith, and the proclaiming of God's Word, and the spreading of the holy Teachings, and the unity and fervor of the friends, and the staunchness of His loved ones. This news would bring smiles to His countenance; this was the joy of His precious heart.

Meanwhile He trained a number of the faithful and reared them with the hands of His grace, and rectified their character and behavior, and adorned them with the excellence of the favored angels of Heaven—that they might arise today with a new spirit, and stand forth with wondrous power, and confront the forces of idle fancy, and scatter the troops upon troops of darkness with the blazing light of long endurance and high resolve; that they might shine out even as lighted candles, and moth-like, flutter so close about the lamp of the Faith as to scorch their wings.

Bahíyyih Khánum

The Holy Family

BAHÍYYIH KHÁNUM, THE GREATEST HOLY LEAF

5. As far back as the concluding stages of the heroic age of the Cause, which witnessed the imprisonment of Bahá'u'lláh in the Síyáh-Chál of Ṭihrán, the Greatest Holy Leaf, then still in her infancy, was privileged to taste of the cup of woe which the first believers of that Apostolic Age had quaffed.

How well I remember her recall, at a time when her faculties were still unimpaired, the gnawing suspense that ate into the hearts of those who watched by her side, at the threshold of her pillaged house, expectant to hear at any moment the news of Bahá'u'lláh's imminent execution! In those sinister hours, she often recounted, her parents had so suddenly lost their earthly possessions that within the space of a single day from being the privileged member of one of the wealthiest families of Ṭihrán she had sunk to the state of a sufferer from unconcealed poverty. Deprived of the means of subsistence her illustrious mother, the famed Navváb, was constrained to place in the palm of her daughter's hand a handful of flour and to induce her to accept it as a substitute for her daily bread.

And when at a later time this revered and precious member of the Holy Family, then in her teens, came to be entrusted by the guiding hand of her Father with missions that no girl of her age could, or would be willing to, perform, with what spontaneous joy she seized her opportunity and acquitted herself of the task with which she had been entrusted! The delicacy and extreme gravity of such functions as she, from time to time, was called upon to fulfill, when the city of Baghdád was swept by the hurricane which the heedlessness and perversity of Mírzá Yaḥyá had unchained, as well as the tender solicitude which, at so early an age, she evinced during the period of Bahá'u'lláh's enforced retirement to the mountains of Sulaymáníyyih, marked her as one who was both capable of sharing the burden, and willing to make the sacrifice, which her high birth demanded.

How staunch was her faith, how calm her demeanor, how forgiving her attitude, how severe her trials, at a time when the forces of schism had rent asunder the ties that united the little band of exiles which had settled in Adrianople and whose fortunes seemed then to have sunk to their lowest ebb! It was in this period of extreme anxiety, when the rigors of a winter of exceptional severity, coupled with the privations entailed by unhealthy housing accommodation and dire financial distress, undermined once for all her health and sapped the vitality which she had hitherto so thoroughly enjoyed. The stress and storm of that period made an abiding impression upon her mind, and she retained till the time of her death on her beauteous and angelic face evidences of its intense hardships.

Not until, however, she had been confined in the company of Bahá'u'lláh within the walls of the prison-city of 'Akká did she display, in the plenitude of her power and in the full abundance of her love for Him, those gifts that single her out, next to 'Abdu'l-Bahá, among the members of the Holy Family, as the brightest embodiment of that love which is born of God and of that human sympathy which few mortals are capable of evincing.

Banishing from her mind and heart every earthly attachment, renouncing the very idea of matrimony, she, standing resolutely by the side of a Brother whom she was to aid and serve so well, arose to dedicate her life to the service of her Father's glorious Cause. Whether in the management of the affairs of His Household in which she excelled, or in the social relationships which she so assiduously cultivated in order to shield both Bahá'u'lláh and 'Abdu'l-Bahá, whether in the unfailing attention she paid to the everyday needs of her Father, or in the traits of generosity, of affability and kindness, which she manifested, the Greatest Holy Leaf had by that time abundantly demonstrated her worthiness to rank as one of the noblest figures intimately associated with the life-long work of Bahá'u'lláh.

Shoghi Effendi

6. During the period of the sojourn in Baghdád, Bahíyyih Khánum, the Greatest Holy Leaf, was her mother's loving helper,

working always beyond her strength, in the various household tasks. No childish pleasures or companions were hers. Always with eyes on her mother, alert to spare her any fatigue, she rejoiced beyond measure when she could minister in any way to her or her illustrious father.

"My mother," she said, "sometimes gave lessons to my brother 'Abbás; at other times Mírzá Músá would teach Him, and on some occasions he would be taught by His father."

"And *your* lessons?" I asked.

"But I never had any time for studies," she said, in a tone which spoke volumes of absolute self-effacement, and this is the keynote of her whole life, no thought of her unselfishness entered her mind.

Her thoughtfulness and consideration for all who came near her; the countless acts of never-failing kindness, were, in her eyes, all to be taken as a matter of course. Her one joy was to devote every moment of her existence to being of use to her mother and father, to whom she was passionately attached. This loving service was extended, as He grew older, to her brother 'Abbás, Sarkár-i-Áqá, and these three were her being's end and aim.

Her life was spent in prayer to God and service to her loved ones, from the time when, as a small child of six, she cowered in the dark house alone with the tiny Purest Branch, a baby of two, in her little arms, listening in terror to the yells of the infuriated, cruel mob, not knowing if they were murdering her father, or whether they had seized her mother and the little eight-year-old 'Abbás.

After those terrible days in Ṭihrán, and the not less terrible journey to Baghdád, during the sojourn in this city, she grew into a beautiful girl, very much like her lovely mother in grace of body and character, a gentle, slender maiden with large, grey-blue eyes, golden-brown hair, and warm, ivory-colored skin. Her sense of humor was keen and her intelligence remarkable.

As she grew up, she implored her father to allow her to remain unmarried, that she might the better devote herself to her three dearly loved ones.

And so it was.

Lady Blomfield

Mírzá Mihdí, the Purest Branch

7. Mírzá Mihdí was taken to Baghdád to join the Family in the year AH 1276 (*circa* AD 1860). It was in that city that this pure and holy youth, noted for his meekness, came in touch with the Divine Spirit and was magnetized by the energizing forces of Bahá'u'lláh's Revelation. From that time on, he devoted every moment of his life to the service of his heavenly Father. He was Bahá'u'lláh's companion in Baghdád, Adrianople and 'Akká, and served Him as an amanuensis* towards the end of his life, leaving to posterity some Tablets in his handwriting. The last ten years of his life were filled with the hardship and suffering inflicted on Bahá'u'lláh and His companions in the course of the three successive banishments from Baghdád to 'Akká.

The Purest Branch resembled 'Abdu'l-Bahá, and throughout his short and eventful life he displayed the same spiritual qualities which distinguished his illustrious Brother. The believers loved and venerated him as they did 'Abdu'l-Bahá.

Adib Taherzadeh

The Passing of Mírzá Mihdí

8. To the galling weight of these tribulations was now added the bitter grief of a sudden tragedy—the premature loss of the noble, the pious Mírzá Mihdí, the Purest Branch, 'Abdu'l-Bahá's

---

* Although Mírzá Áqá Ján was Bahá'u'lláh's primary amanuensis, there were also others who were engaged in this task from time to time.

twenty-two year old brother, an amanuensis of Bahá'u'lláh and
a companion of His exile from the days when, as a child, he
was brought from Ṭihrán to Ba<u>gh</u>dád to join his Father after
His return from Sulaymáníyyih. He was pacing the roof of the
barracks in the twilight, one evening, wrapped in his customary devotions, when he fell through the unguarded skylight onto
a wooden crate, standing on the floor beneath, which pierced
his ribs, and caused, twenty-two hours later, his death, on the
23rd of Rabí'u'l-Avval 1287 AH (June 23, 1870). His dying
supplication to a grieving Father was that his life might be accepted as a ransom for those who were prevented from attaining the presence of their Beloved.

In a highly significant prayer, revealed by Bahá'u'lláh in
memory of His son—a prayer that exalts his death to the rank
of those great acts of atonement associated with Abraham's intended sacrifice of His son, with the crucifixion of Jesus Christ
and the martyrdom of Imám Ḥusayn—we read the following:
*"I have, O my Lord, offered up that which Thou hast given Me,
that Thy servants may be quickened, and all that dwell on earth
be united."* And, likewise, these prophetic words, addressed to
His martyred son: *"Thou art the Trust of God and His Treasure
in this Land. Erelong will God reveal through thee that which He
hath desired."*

After he had been washed in the presence of Bahá'u'lláh, he
"that was created of the light of Bahá," to whose *"meekness"* the
Supreme Pen had testified, and of the *"mysteries"* of whose ascension that same Pen had made mention, was borne forth,
escorted by the fortress guards, and laid to rest, beyond the city
walls, in a spot adjacent to the shrine of Nabí Sáliḥ.

Shoghi Effendi

9. The death of the Purest Branch must be viewed as Bahá'u'lláh's
own sacrifice, a sacrifice on the same level as the crucifixion of

Christ and the martyrdom of the Báb. Shoghi Effendi, the Guardian of the Faith, states that Bahá'u'lláh has exalted the death of the Purest Branch to the "rank of those great acts of atonement associated with Abraham's intended sacrifice of His son, with the crucifixion of Jesus Christ and the martyrdom of the Imám Ḥusayn . . ." In another instance, Shoghi Effendi states that in the Bábí Dispensation, it was the Báb himself who sacrificed His life for the redemption and purification of mankind. In the Dispensation of Bahá'u'lláh, it was the Purest Branch who gave his life releasing thereby all the forces necessary for bringing about the unity of mankind.

Adib Taherzadeh

10. Lauded be Thy name, O Lord my God! Thou seest me in this day shut up in my prison, and fallen into the hands of Thine adversaries, and beholdest my son (The Purest Branch) lying on the dust before Thy face. He is Thy servant, O my Lord, whom Thou hast caused to be related to Him Who is the Manifestation of Thyself and the Day-Spring of Thy Cause.

At his birth he was afflicted through his separation from Thee, according to what had been ordained for him through Thine irrevocable decree. And when he had quaffed the cup of re-union with Thee, he was cast into prison for having believed in Thee and in Thy signs. He continued to serve Thy Beauty until he entered into this Most Great Prison. Thereupon I offered him up, O my God, as a sacrifice in Thy path. Thou well knowest what they who love Thee have endured through this trial that hath caused the kindreds of the earth to wail, and beyond them the Concourse on high to lament.

I beseech Thee, O my Lord, by him and by his exile and his imprisonment, to send down upon such as loved him what will quiet their hearts and bless their works. Potent art Thou to do as Thou willest. No God is there but Thee, the Almighty, the Most Powerful.

Bahá'u'lláh

11. Upon thee, O Branch of God! be the remembrance of God and His praise, and the praise of all that dwell in the Realm of Immortality, and of all the denizens of the Kingdom of Names. Happy art thou in that thou hast been faithful to the Covenant of God and His Testament, until Thou didst sacrifice thyself before the face of thy Lord, the Almighty, the Unconstrained. Thou, in truth, hast been wronged, and to this testifieth the Beauty of Him, the Self-Subsisting. Thou didst, in the first days of thy life, bear that which hath caused all things to groan; and made every pillar to tremble. Happy is the one that remembereth thee, and draweth nigh, through thee, unto God, the Creator of the Morn.

Bahá'u'lláh

The Letters of the Living

ṬÁHIRIH

12. A woman chaste and holy, a sign and token of surpassing beauty, a burning brand of the love of God, a lamp of His bestowal, was Jináb-i-Ṭáhirih.

'Abdu'l-Bahá

13. She, according to what is related, was skilled in diverse arts, amazed the understandings and thoughts of the most eminent masters by her eloquent dissertations on the exegesis and tradition of the Perspicuous Book, and was a mighty sign in the doctrines of the glorious Shaykh of Aḥsá. At the Supreme Shrines

she borrowed light on matters divine from the lamp of Kázim, and freely sacrificed her life in the way of the Báb. She discussed and disputed with the doctors and sages, loosing her tongue to establish her doctrine. Such fame did she acquire that most people who were scholars or mystics sought to hear her speech and were eager to become acquainted with her powers of speculation and deduction. She had a brain full of tumultuous ideas, and thoughts vehement and restless. In many places she triumphed over the contentious, expounding the most subtle questions.

'Abdu'l-Bahá

14. After the breakup at Bada<u>sh</u>t she was captured, and the oppressors sent her back under guard to Ṭihrán. There she was imprisoned in the house of Maḥmúd <u>Kh</u>án, the Kalántar. But she was aflame, enamored, restless, and could not be still. The ladies of Ṭihrán, on one pretext or another, crowded to see and listen to her. It happened that there was a celebration at the Mayor's house for the marriage of his son; a nuptial banquet was prepared, and the house adorned. The flower of Ṭihrán's ladies were invited, the princesses, the wives of vazírs and other great. A splendid wedding it was, with instrumental music and vocal melodies—by day and night the lute, the bells and songs. Then Ṭáhirih began to speak; and so bewitched were the great ladies that they forsook the cithern and the drum and all the pleasures of the wedding feast, to crowd about Ṭáhirih and listen to the sweet words of her mouth.

Thus she remained, a helpless captive. Then came the attempt on the life of the <u>Sh</u>áh; a farmán was issued; she was sentenced to death. Saying she was summoned to the Prime Minister's, they arrived to lead her away from the Kalántar's house. She bathed her face and hands, arrayed herself in a costly dress, and scented with attar of roses she came out of the house.

They brought her into a garden, where the headsmen waited;
but these wavered and then refused to end her life. A slave was
found, far gone in drunkenness; besotted, vicious, black of heart.
And he strangled Ṭáhirih. He forced a scarf between her lips
and rammed it down her throat. Then they lifted up her unsullied body and flung it in a well, there in the garden, and over it
threw down earth and stones. But Ṭáhirih rejoiced; she had
heard with a light heart the tidings of her martyrdom; she set
her eyes on the supernal Kingdom and offered up her life.

Salutations be unto her, and praise. Holy be her dust, as the
tiers of light come down on it from Heaven.

'Abdu'l-Bahá

QUDDÚS AND MULLÁ ḤUSAYN

15. The first words which, in the company of the assembled
believers, Quddús addressed to Mullá Ḥusayn were the following: "Now, at this very hour, you should arise and, armed
with the rod of wisdom and of might, silence the host of evil
plotters who strive to discredit the fair name of the Faith of
God. You should face that multitude and confound their
forces. You should place your reliance upon the grace of God,
and should regard their machinations as a futile attempt to
obscure the radiance of the Cause. You should interview the
Sa'ídu'l-'Ulamá', that notorious and false-hearted tyrant, and
should fearlessly disclose to his eyes the distinguishing features of this Revelation. From thence you should proceed to
Khurásán. In the town of Mashhad, you should build a house
so designed as both to serve for our private residence and at
the same time afford adequate facilities for the reception of
our guests. Thither we shall shortly journey, and in that house
we shall dwell. To it you shall invite every receptive soul who
we hope may be guided to the River of everlasting life. We

shall prepare and admonish them to band themselves together and proclaim the Cause of God." . . .

Alone and with a heart wholly detached from all else but God, Mullá Ḥusayn set out on his journey to Ma<u>sh</u>had. His only companion, as he trod his way to <u>Kh</u>urásán, was the thought of accomplishing faithfully the wishes of Quddús, and his one sustenance the consciousness of his unfailing promise. He went directly to the home of Mírzá Muḥammad-Báqir-i-Qá'iní, and was soon able to buy, in the neighborhood of that house in Bálá-<u>Kh</u>íyábán, a tract of land on which he began to erect the house which he had been commanded to build, and to which he gave the name of Bábíyyih, a name that it bears to the present day. Shortly after it was completed, Quddús arrived at Ma<u>sh</u>had and abode in that house. A steady stream of visitors, whom the energy and zeal of Mullá Ḥusayn had prepared for the acceptance of the Faith, poured into the presence of Quddús, acknowledged the claim of the Cause, and willingly enlisted under its banner. The all-observing vigilance with which Mullá Ḥusayn labored to diffuse the knowledge of the new Revelation, and the masterly manner in which Quddús edified its ever-increasing adherents, gave rise to a wave of enthusiasm which swept over the entire city of Ma<u>sh</u>had, and the effects of which spread rapidly beyond the confines of <u>Kh</u>urásán. The house of Bábíyyih was soon converted into a rallying center for a multitude of devotees who were fired with an inflexible resolve to demonstrate, by every means in their power, the great inherent energies of their Faith.

Nabíl-i-A'ẓam

16. Mullá Ḥusayn performed his ablutions, clothed himself in new garments, attired his head with the Báb's turban, and pre-

pared for the approaching encounter. An undefinable joy illumined his face. . . . Soon after midnight, as soon as the morning-star had risen, the star that heralded to him the dawning light of eternal reunion with his Beloved, he started to his feet and, mounting his charger, gave the signal that the gate of the fort be opened. As he rode out at the head of three hundred and thirteen of his companions to meet the enemy, the cry of "Yá Ṣáḥibu'z-Zamán!" again broke forth, a cry so intense and powerful that forest, fort, and camp vibrated to its resounding echo. . . .

Dashing forward with the same swiftness and intrepidity, he overcame the resistance of both the second and third barricades, diffusing, as he advanced, despair and consternation among his foes. Undeterred by the bullets which rained continually upon him and his companions, they pressed forward until the remaining barricades had all been captured and overthrown. . . . The steed of Mullá Ḥusayn suddenly became entangled in the rope of an adjoining tent, and ere he was able to extricate himself, he was struck in the breast by a bullet. . . . Mullá Ḥusayn, who was bleeding profusely, dismounted from his horse, staggered a few steps, and, unable to proceed further, fell exhausted upon the ground. Two of his young companions, of Khurásán, Qulí, and Ḥasan, came to his rescue and bore him to the fort.

I have heard the following account from Mullá Ṣádiq and Mullá Mírzá Muḥammad-i-Furúghí: "We were among those who had remained in the fort with Quddús. As soon as Mullá Ḥusayn, who seemed to have lost consciousness, was brought in, we were ordered to retire. 'Leave me alone with him,' were the words of Quddús. . . . 'There are certain confidential matters which I desire him alone to know.'" . . .

"A long time elapsed before Quddús bade Mírzá Muḥammad-Báqir open the door and admit his companions. 'I have bade my last farewell to him,' he said, as we entered the room. 'Things which previously I deemed it unallowable to utter I have now shared with him.' We found on our arrival that Mullá Ḥusayn had expired. A faint smile still lingered upon his face. Such was the peacefulness of his countenance that he seemed to have fallen asleep. Quddús attended to his burial, clothed him in his own shirt, and gave instructions to lay him to rest to the south of, and adjoining, the shrine of <u>Sh</u>ay<u>kh</u> Ṭabarsí. 'Well is it with you to have remained to your last hour faithful to the Covenant of God,' he said, as he laid a parting kiss upon his eyes and forehead. 'I pray God to grant that no division ever be caused between you and me.' He spoke with such poignancy that the seven companions who were standing beside him wept profusely, and wished they had been sacrificed in his stead. Quddús, with his own hands, laid the body in the tomb, and cautioned those who were standing near him to maintain secrecy regarding the spot which served as his resting place, and to conceal it even from their companions. He afterwards instructed them to inter the bodies of the thirty-six martyrs who had fallen in the course of that engagement in one and the same grave on the northern side of the shrine of <u>Sh</u>ay<u>kh</u> Ṭabarsí. 'Let the loved ones of God,' he was heard to remark as he consigned them to their tomb, 'take heed of the example of these martyrs of our Faith. Let them in life be and remain as united as these are now in death.'"

Nabíl-i-Aʻẓam

17. By the testimony of Bahá'u'lláh, that heroic youth [Quddús], who was still on the threshold of his life, was subjected to such tortures and suffered such a death as even Jesus had not faced in

the hour of His greatest agony. The absence of any restraint on the part of the government authorities, the ingenious barbarity which the torture-mongers of Barfurúsh so ably displayed, the fierce fanaticism which glowed in the breasts of its shí'ah inhabitants, the moral support accorded to them by the dignitaries of Church and State in the capital—above all, the acts of heroism which their victim and his companions had accomplished and which had served to heighten their exasperation, all combined to nerve the hand of the assailants and to add to the diabolical ferocity which characterized his martyrdom.

Such were its circumstances that the Báb, who was then confined in the castle of Chihríq, was unable for a period of six months either to write or to dictate. The deep grief which he felt had stilled the voice of revelation and silenced His pen. How deeply He mourned His loss! What cries of anguish He must have uttered as the tale of the siege, the untold sufferings, the shameless betrayal, and the wholesale massacre of the companions of Shaykh Ṭabarsí reached His ears and was unfolded before His eyes! What pangs of sorrow He must have felt when He learned of the shameful treatment which His beloved Quddús had undergone in his hour of martyrdom at the hands of the people of Bárfurúsh; how he was stripped of his clothes; how the turban which He had bestowed upon him had been befouled; how, barefooted, bareheaded, and loaded with chains, he was paraded through the streets, followed and scorned by the entire population of the town; how he was execrated and spat upon by the howling mob; how he was assailed with the knives and axes of the scum of its female inhabitants; how his body was pierced and mutilated, and how eventually it was delivered to the flames!

Amidst his torments, Quddús was heard whispering forgiveness to his foes. "Forgive, O my God," he cried, "the trespasses of this people. Deal with them in Thy mercy, for they know not what we already have discovered and cherish. I have striven to show them the path that leads to their salvation; behold how they have risen to overwhelm and kill me! Show them, O God, the way of Truth, and turn their ignorance into faith." In his hour of agony, the Siyyid-i-Qumí, who had so treacherously deserted the fort, was seen passing by his side. Observing his helplessness, he smote him in the face. "You claimed," he cried in haughty scorn, "that your voice was the voice of God. If you speak the truth, burst your bonds asunder and free yourself from the hands of your enemies." Quddús looked steadfastly into his face, sighed deeply, and said: "May God requite you for your deed, inasmuch as you have helped to add to the measure of my afflictions." Approaching the Sabzih-Maydán, he raised his voice and said: "Would that my mother were with me, and could see with her own eyes the splendor of my nuptials!" He had scarcely spoken these words when the enraged multitude fell upon him and, tearing his body to pieces, threw the scattered members into the fire which they had kindled for that purpose. In the middle of the night, what still remained of the fragments of that burned and mutilated body was gathered by the hand of a devoted friend and interred in a place not far distant from the scene of his martyrdom.

Nabíl-i-Aʿzam

The Dawn-Breakers

BADÍʿ

18. During the latter days [passed] in Adrianople Bahá'u'lláh composed a detailed epistle setting forth all matters clearly and minutely. He unfolded and expounded the main principles of

the sect, and made clear and plain its ethics, manners, course, and mode of conduct: He treated certain political questions in detail, and adduced sundry proofs of His truthfulness: He declared the good intent, loyalty, and sincerity of the sect, and wrote some fragments of prayers, some in Persian, but the greater part in Arabic. He then placed it in a packet and adorned its address with the royal name of His Majesty the King of Persia, and wrote [on it] that some person pure of heart and pure of life, dedicated to God, and prepared for martyr-sacrifice, must, with perfect resignation and willingness, convey this epistle into the presence of the King. A youth named Mírzá Badí', a native of Khurásán, took the epistle, and hastened toward the presence of His Majesty the King. The Royal Train had its abode and station outside Ṭihrán, so he took his stand alone on a rock in a place far off but opposite to the Royal Pavilion, and awaited day and night the passing of the Royal escort or the attainment of admission into the Imperial Presence. Three days did he pass in a state of fasting and vigilance: an emaciated body and enfeebled spirit remained. On the fourth day the Royal Personage was examining all quarters and directions with a telescope when suddenly his glance fell on this man who was seated in the utmost respectful attitude on a rock. It was inferred from the indications [perceived] that he must certainly have thanks [to offer], or some complaint or demand for redress and justice [to prefer]. [The King] commanded one of those in attendance at the court to inquire into the circumstances of this youth. On interrogation [it was found that] he carried a letter which he desired to convey with his own hand into the Royal Presence. On receiving permission to approach, he cried out before the pavilion with a dignity, composure, and respectfulness surpassing description, and in a loud voice, "O King, I have come unto thee from Sheba with a weighty message!" [The King] commanded to take the letter and arrest the bearer. His Majesty the King wished to act with deliberation and desired to discover the truth, but those who were present before him loosed their tongues in violent reprehension, saying, "This person has shown great presumption and amazing audacity, for he hath without fear or dread brought the letter of him against whom all peoples are angered, of him who is banished to Bulgaria and Sclavonia, into the presence of the King. If so be that he do not instantly suffer a grievous punishment there will be an increase of this great presumption." So the ministers of the court signified [that he should suffer] punishment and ordered the torture. As the first torment they applied the chain and rack, saying, "Make known thy other friends that thou mayest be delivered from excruciating punishment, and make thy comrades captive that thou mayest escape from the torment of the chain and the keenness of the sword." But, torture, brand, and torment him as they might, they saw naught but steadfastness and silence, and found naught but dumb endurance [on his part]. So, when the torture gave no result, they [first] photographed him (the executioners on his left and on his right, and he sitting bound in fetters and chains beneath the sword with perfect meekness and composure), and then slew and destroyed him. This photograph I sent for, and found worthy of contemplation, for he was seated with wonderful humility and strange submissiveness, in utmost resignation.

'Abdu'l-Bahá

19. Áqá Buzurg of Khurásán, the illustrious "Badí'" (Wonderful); converted to the Faith by Nabíl; surnamed the "Pride of Martyrs"; the seventeen-year old bearer of the Tablet addressed to Násiri'd-Dín Sháh; in whom, as affirmed by Bahá'u'lláh, *"the spirit of might and power was breathed,"* was arrested, branded

for three successive days, his head beaten to a pulp with the butt of a rifle, after which his body was thrown into a pit and earth and stones heaped upon it. . . . For a space of three years Bahá'u'lláh continued to extol in His writings the heroism of that youth, characterizing the references made by Him to that sublime sacrifice as the *"salt of My Tablets."*

Shoghi Effendi

RÚḤU'LLÁH

20. Rúḥu'lláh, the child-martyr of the Bahá'í Faith, was a prodigy. At the age of twelve, his knowledge of the Holy Scriptures, his powerful arguments in defense of his beloved Faith in the presence of the dreaded religious authorities of Persia, the beautiful poetry he wrote and his sweet, saintly nature won him admirers everywhere he went. Many of the noted enemies of the new Faith were charmed by his eloquence, while others came to look upon him as a living miracle.

At the time when Rúḥu'lláh, his father and Mírzá Ḥusayn had been arrested because of their beliefs and were being taken to Ṭihrán in chains, the soldiers in charge were so attracted by the charm of this child of twelve that they wished to take the heavy chains from round his neck, but he would not have it so. "I am quite happy with these chains," he assured them, "besides, you must be faithful to your trust. You were given orders to take us to Ṭihrán in chains, and it is your duty to obey those orders." He was never heard to complain of the discomforts of that long and arduous journey, but seemed to derive great happiness from the many odes and prayers he chanted to himself as they rode along. . . .

In the prison of Ṭihrán, the Bahá'ís were treated with extreme cruelty. There were four of them there, all chained together with the "black pearl" which was put round their necks.

This chain was so heavy that it was difficult for the men to keep their heads up. Rúḥu'lláh collapsed under its weight and two supports had to be put under the chain on each side of him to keep him in a sitting position. . . .

The account of the incident is recorded by Mírzá Ḥusayn, who was chained with Varqá and Rúḥu'lláh in the prison. The summary of a part of this chronicle is as follows:

". . . Ḥájibu'd-Dawlih entered the prison with a number of executioners clad in their scarlet clothes, and gave orders that all the prisoners should be chained to their places. No one knew what he had in mind and a terrible fear seized everyone. Then the jailer came to us Bahá'ís and said: 'Come with me. You are wanted in court.' We got up to follow him, though we did not believe what he said. 'It is not necessary to put on your 'abás,' he told us, but Rúḥu'lláh insisted on wearing his. As we came out into the prison yard, we were surprised to see armed soldiers standing everywhere and wondered if they had come to shoot us. The executioners too were standing in a row, and Ḥájibu'd-Dawlih had a savage look in his eyes. But there was not a sound from anyone, and the silence was terrifying. At last Ḥájibu'd-Dawlih asked the jailer to open the locks on our chains and send us two by two. The jailer's hands were trembling so badly that he could not open the locks, so another man stepped forward and unlocked our chains. Varqá and Rúḥu'lláh were the first to be taken away. . . .

"Later on I saw one of jailers who had shown us some kindness before. I caught hold of him and begged him to tell me what had happened. I made him swear by the martyred saints of Islám that he would tell me the truth as he had seen it take place. This is what he recounted: '. . . Ḥájibu'd-Dawlih said to Varqá: "Which shall I kill first, you or your son?" Varqá replied: "It makes no difference to me." Then Ḥájibu'd-Dawlih drew his dagger and thrust it into Varqá's heart saying: "How do you feel now?" Varqá's words before he died were: "I am feeling much better than you are. Praise be to God!" Ḥájibu'd-Dawlih ordered four executioners to cut Varqá's body into pieces. The sight of so much blood was horrible to see. Rúḥu'lláh was watching all the time, overcome with grief. He kept on repeating: "Father, father, take me with you!" Ḥájibu'd-Dawlih came to him and said: "Don't weep. I shall take you with me and give you a proper salary. I shall ask the Sh͟áh to give you a position!" But Rúḥu'lláh replied: "I want neither a salary from you, nor a position from the Sh͟áh! I am going to join my father." Ḥájibu'd-Dawlih asked for a piece of rope, but no one could find any rope so they brought the bastinado and put Rúḥu'lláh's neck in it. Two of the jailers lifted the bastinado from either side and held it while Rúḥu'lláh gasped for breath. As soon as his body was still, they put him down and Ḥájibu'd-Dawlih called for the two other Bahá'ís to be brought in. But just then, the child's body made a sudden movement, raised itself from the floor and fell several feet away. Then it was still again. This incident shook Ḥájibu'd-Dawlih so badly that he did not have the nerve to carry on with any more killings.'

"You can imagine how we felt after hearing the details of the martyrdom of Varqá and Rúḥu'lláh. The picture came to life, and I could not put it out of my mind. My heart would not be consoled, and I wept for my beloved friends all through the night. Finally I fell asleep and had a dream. I saw Rúḥu'lláh coming towards me, looking extremely happy. He said: 'Did you see how 'Abdu'l-Bahá's promise came true?' Rúḥu'lláh had often told me with great pride that when he was saying farewell to 'Abdu'l-Bahá after visiting Him in the Holy Land, the Master had patted him on the shoulder and said: 'If God so ordains . . . He will proclaim His Cause through Rúḥu'lláh.'"

Gloria Faizi

ZAYNAB

21. Further evidence of the spirit of sublime renunciation animating those valiant companions [in Zanján] was afforded by the behavior of a village maiden, who, of her own accord, threw in her lot with the band of women and children who had joined the defenders of the fort. Her name was Zaynab, her home a tiny hamlet in the near neighborhood of Zanján. She was comely and fair of face, was fired with a lofty faith, and endowed with intrepid courage. The sight of the trials and hardships which her men companions were made to endure stirred in her an irrepressible yearning to disguise herself in male attire and share in repulsing the repeated attacks of the enemy. Donning a tunic and wearing a head-dress like those of her men companions, she cut off her locks, girt on a sword, and, seizing a musket and a shield, introduced herself into their ranks. No one suspected her of being a maid when she leaped forward to take her place behind the barricade. As soon as the enemy charged, she bared her sword and, raising the cry of "Yá Sáhibu'z-Zamán!"* flung herself with incredible audacity upon the forces arrayed against her. Friend and foe marveled that day at a courage and resourcefulness the equal of which their eyes had scarcely ever beheld. Her enemies pronounced her the curse which an angry Providence had hurled upon them. Overwhelmed with despair and abandoning their barricades, they fled in disgraceful rout before her.

Ḥujjat, who was watching the movements of the enemy from one of the turrets, recognized her and marveled at the prowess which that maiden was displaying. She had set out in pursuit of her assailants, when he ordered his men to bid her return to the

---

* "O Lord of the Age!" one of the titles of the promised Qá'im

fort and give up the attempt. "No man," he was heard to say, as he saw her plunge into the fire directed upon her by the enemy, "has shown himself capable of such vitality and courage." When questioned by him as to the motive of her behavior, she burst into tears and said: "My heart ached with pity and sorrow when I beheld the toil and sufferings of my fellow-disciples. I advanced by an inner urge I could not resist. I was afraid lest you would deny me the privilege of throwing in my lot with my men companions." "You are surely the same Zaynab," Ḥujjat asked her, "who volunteered to join the occupants of the fort?" "I am," she replied. "I can confidently assure you that no one has hitherto discovered my sex. You alone have recognized me. I adjure you by the Báb not to withhold from me that inestimable privilege, the crown of martyrdom, the one desire of my life."

Ḥujjat was profoundly impressed by the tone and manner of her appeal. He sought to calm the tumult of her soul, assured her of his prayers in her behalf, and gave her the name Rustam-'Alí as a mark of her noble courage. "This is the Day of Resurrection," he told her, "the day when 'all secrets shall be searched out.' Not by their outward appearance, but by the character of their beliefs and the manner of their lives, does God judge His creatures, be they men or women. Though a maiden of tender age and immature experience, you have displayed such vitality and resource as few men could hope to surpass." He granted her request, and warned her not to exceed the bounds their Faith had imposed upon them. "We are called upon to defend our lives," he reminded her, "against a treacherous assailant, and not to wage holy war against him."

For a period of no less than five months, that maiden continued to withstand with unrivalled heroism the forces of the enemy. Disdainful of food and sleep, she toiled with fevered earnestness for the Cause she most loved. She quickened, by the example of her splendid daring, the courage of the few who wavered, and reminded them of the duty each was expected to fulfill. The sword she wielded remained, throughout that period, by her side. In the brief intervals of sleep she was able to obtain, she was seen with her head resting upon her sword and her shield serving as a covering for her body. Every one of her companions was assigned to a particular post which he was expected to guard and defend, while that fearless maid alone was free to move in whatever direction she pleased. Always in the thick and forefront of the turmoil that raged round her, Zaynab was ever ready to rush to the rescue of whatever post the assailant was threatening, and to lend her assistance to any one of those who needed either her encouragement or support. As the end of her life approached, her enemies discovered her secret, and continued, despite their knowledge that she was a maid, to dread her influence and to tremble at her approach. The shrill sound of her voice was sufficient to strike consternation into their hearts and to fill them with despair.

One day, seeing that her companions were being suddenly enveloped by the forces of the enemy, Zaynab ran in distress to Ḥujjat and, flinging herself at his feet, implored him, with tearful eyes, to allow her to rush forth to their aid. "My life, I feel, is nearing its end," she added. "I may myself fall beneath the sword of the assailant. Forgive, I entreat you, my trespasses, and intercede for me with my Master, for whose sake I yearn to lay down my life."

Ḥujjat was too much overcome with emotion to reply. Encouraged by his silence, which she interpreted to mean that he consented to grant her appeal, she leaped out of the gate and, raising seven times the cry "Yá Ṣáḥibu'z-Zamán!" rushed to stay the hand that had already slain a number of her companions. "Why befoul by your deeds the fair name of Islám?" she shouted, as she flung herself upon them. "Why flee abjectly from before our face, if you be speakers of truth?" She ran to the barricades which the enemy had erected, routed those who guarded the first three of the defenses, and was engaging in overcoming the fourth, when, beneath a shower of bullets, she dropped dead upon the ground. Not a single voice among her opponents dared question her chastity or ignore the sublimity of her faith and the enduring traits of her character. Such was her devotion that after her death no less than twenty women of her acquaintance embraced the Cause of the Báb. To them she had ceased to be the peasant girl they had known; she was the very incarnation of the noblest principles of human conduct, a living embodiment of the spirit which only a Faith such as hers could manifest.

Nabíl-i-A'zam

Bahá'í Youth and Young Adult Martyrs

22. Bahá'í children and youth have contributed their own significant share to the heroism demonstrated by the believers in Iran. In spite of the difficulties in communication, some accounts of their experiences have been received. Following are a few that have been translated. The names of persons and places have been omitted in most cases so as to protect those who have written the accounts.

On behalf of the Universal House of Justice

SIXTEEN-YEAR-OLD BOY

23. The following report is taken from a letter written by a boy sixteen years of age.

The teacher in my high school was giving a lesson in sociology on the subject of cultural colonialism. As an example, he cited the Bahá'í Faith as a type of cultural colonialism. According to my spiritual obligation, I had to reply. I got permission and to the extent possible for me, I gave a speech on the Faith and countered the statement of my teacher. After a few days the principal called me to his office, accusing me of apostasy, stating that Islám is the last religion of God, etc. One of those present asked me what I believed. I told him I was a Bahá'í. The Hájí, the principal, rose from his chair, agitated and shouting, "You have no place in this school! I thought you were a good boy! Now everything is changed and you have no right to go to your class until your situation is cleared!"

After a week there was a summons from the office of the Imám Jum'ih (High Priest of the town, who is usually appointed by the Central Government to carry out its policy). On the way I was trembling, thinking of what they might ask and what I should reply and what would be my fate. I entered the Imám's office in this condition, but as soon as I was confronted by him I was not the same person anymore. It was as if somebody had taken me by both hands. Not only did I not tremble but I was as erect as a column of steel. In the office of the Imám Jum'ih were eight of the 'Ulamá with turbans, and the bodyguard of the Imám were standing close behind me. After some time the Imám looked at me asking, "Do you have any business?" "No," I replied, "You have business with me."

After asking my name and the name of my father, he asked if I were a Muslim. I told him I was a Bahá'í. He asked what my father did. I told him he was unemployed. The Imám then started saying, "You are against Islám, the Qur'án, and Muhammad."

"No," I responded, "We believe in Islám, in the Qur'án, in Muhammad and the Imáms, and we respect them."

"Now that you say that you are a Muslim and believe in the Qur'án . . ."

I interrupted him with an apology and said, "Sir, I never said that I was a Muslim. I only told you that I believe in Islám. I believe in Islám as you believe in Judaism and Christ and Christianity and believe in the Bible."

Then he said, "All right. Now that you believe in Islám, have you ever read any books of the Imáms?"

"Yes, to the extent possible."

"If you have read these books, tell me where is it written that a wretched woman will give birth to a boy named Siyyid 'Alí Muḥammad, called the Báb, and that he would be the Promised One?"

"First of all, it is not proper that you name a woman in a derogatory manner. We have famous women in history, like Mary, Khadíjih, Fáṭimih, . . ."

He interrupted me saying, "Tell me where is it written in those books about the Báb?"

"It is not written in that way, but you show me in those books where it is written that He is not coming!"

(The report states that there was then a long discussion about the Faith and the writer quoted verses from the Qur'án and the Imáms showing that the Promised One will bring a new religion.)

On this note another Mullá who was present changed the subject. He told me that the Bahá'ís are forces of Russia and that a Russian official called Dolgorouki confessed that he trained Siyyid 'Alí Muḥammad to say first that he was the Promised One, then to claim to be the Light of God, and ultimately to be God, Himself.

I very boldly replied, "The Bahá'í Community does not know what tune to dance to. One says that we are forces of Russia; another says that we are American stooges; still another says we are agents of Britain and recently of Israel. You should know philosophy," I said. "If there is truth then there should be unanimity in the understanding of that truth. Everybody understands that when the water reaches 100 degrees it boils. For boiling water, one doesn't say when it reaches 80 degrees or 120 degrees it boils. Therefore, it is not fair for you to present a false thing."

The Imám suddenly shouted at me, "Be quiet! Islám is the last religion! No religion will come after it! You are not right! You are an apostate!"

I asked, "Sir, do you give me permission to speak?"

He replied, "No."

"Then I am afraid I must speak without your permission. We are not apostates. We are right, and the time for Islám is over."

He interrupted me sharply, shouting, "Islám is eternal!" and he quoted an Arabic verse which I could not understand. Then I quoted a verse from the Qur'án, saying every religion has an end. (Here the writer gives a long discourse about the meaning of this verse and at the end he quotes a verse from a reliable Shí'ih book of traditions to the effect that if Muslims are virtuous, the life of Islám will be 1,000 years and if not, it will be 500.) Then I told him, "You have been virtuous and Islám has lasted 1,000 years. Now is the time for the Faith, and no power on earth can arrest it!"

He shouted, "Shut up! Don't be impudent!" Then he continued to say that the Bahá'ís are aiding Israel. I replied that to do so would be a political act and we are not in politics.

He said that we had buildings in Israel. "You have a Mashriqu'l-Adhkár."

"They are our Holy Places."

"Take your Holy Places out of there!"

"Holy Places cannot be moved. If they could, why don't you bring out the Mosque of Aqṣá from Jerusalem?"

"The Mosque fits that place very well!"

"So do our Holy Places."

Again he shouted, "Shut up!" And then he added, "Get out of the room!"

Throughout the conversation I was very polite and soft-spoken, and then I bade farewell with great politeness, smiled, excused myself, and came out.

On the way out of the room, another Mullá said, "Look, my son, many of us have returned to the bosom of Islám. You have reached the age of maturity (fifteen); you should follow those who have come back to Islám."

I replied, "Yes, I have reached the age of maturity. I have accepted my Faith by my own choice. And to the last breath of my life I will support it. I am prepared to undergo any torture, any difficulty for my Faith! I don't consider my blood to be more red than that of my fellow Bahá'ís who are offering it to God."

The Imám said, "In that case, we have to expel you from school."

"Do whatever your duty demands."

After I left the office of the Imám Jum'ih, to my surprise again I started trembling. I went to my school and said goodbye to my fellow students, got my dismissal order and went back home.

On behalf of the Universal House of Justice

MONA MAHMUDNEZHAD

24. Mona was another young girl eighteen years of age when martyred. She was a teacher of Bahá'í children's classes and served on the Three Members Board and was arrested with her father, Yadollah Mahmudnezhad.

Twice the order for Mona's release was issued, but at the third stage in her trial the religious magistrate, Mr. Qazai, after insulting and humiliating her, said, "Your father and mother have deceived and misled you." In reply Mona said, "Your honor, it is true that I learned about the Bahá'í Faith from my parents, but I have done my own reasoning. In the Bahá'í Faith one adheres to religion after investigation, not by imitation. You have many of our books; you can read and find out for yourself. My father and mother did not insist on my accepting their belief; neither did they force me to become a Bahá'í. If the religious magistrate thinks I should abandon my belief, I will never do so, and prefer submitting to the order of execution." The religious magistrate was astounded and said, "Young girl, what do you know about religion?" Mona exclaimed, "Your honor, I was brought here from the classroom in school; I have been in prison and going through trials for three months. What better proof of my religious certitude than my perseverance and steadfastness in the Faith? It is this Faith that gives me confidence to go through this trial in your presence. . . ." The religious magistrate, impressed by Mona's sincerity, asked her to say a prayer. Mona put away the file and, with the usual respect and humbleness, recited a prayer by 'Abdu'l-Bahá: "O kind Lord, Thou art kinder to me than I am to myself. . . ." The religious magistrate remained silent for a while, then said to Mona, "What harm did you find in Islam that you have turned to Bahaism?" Mona' answer was: "The foundation of all religions is one. From time to time, according to the exigencies of time and place, God sends His Messenger to renew religion and guide the people in the right path. The Bahá'í religion upholds the truth in Islam, but if by Islam you mean the prevailing animosity, murder, and bloodshed in the country, a sample of which I have witnessed in prison, that is the reason I have chosen to be a Bahá'í."

Mona's answer was the subject of conversation among the friends for quite a while in prison. How did Mona dare to talk to the religious magistrate in this way?

Olya Ruhizadegan

ZARRIN MOQIMI

25. When Zarrin was taken to the religious magistrate to recant her Faith, and was told as usual either to recant or to be
prepared for execution, she said in reply, "I have found the way
to reality, and I am not prepared to give it away for any price.
Therefore, I submit to the Court's verdict." On another occasion the judge asked Zarrin, "To what extent are you prepared
to adhere to your belief?" Zarrin answered, "I hope to remain
firm in my belief to the last moment." "But you must give up
your belief!" retorted the judge. Zarrin, annoyed by the repeti-
tion of the same proposal, exclaimed, "Your honor, you have
been conducting my trial for many days, and have asked the
same question, and I have given you a definite and satisfactory
answer. I don't think repeating the same thing is necessary!"
But the judge rudely repeated the same proposal. Dear Zarrin
started crying and with a loud voice said, "In what language do
you want me to tell you? Why don't you leave me alone? My
whole being is Bahá'u'lláh! My love is Bahá'u'lláh! My heart is
dedicated to Bahá'u'lláh!" The infuriated judge shouted, "I will
pull out your heart from your chest!" Zarrin replied, "Then my
heart will call and cry out, 'Bahá'u'lláh! Bahá'u'lláh!'" The judge,
moved by this display of sentiment, left the room.

After Zarrin's martyrdom, dear Mother described the event
for me over the phone: "Saturday, June 18, 1983, I went to visit
Zarrin as usual, taking fresh fruits with me. It was raining, and
the weather was quite warm. At the visiting time Zarrin was
brought behind the glass partition, and we started to talk. Her
countenance seemed to have changed; she said to me, "Mother,
please pray for me and implore God to give me perseverance!"
She did not say good-bye to me when leaving, because she did
not want to see me saddened. Zarrin had always told me not to
hope for her freedom, but it did not occur to me that this was our

last meeting. The friends (Bahá'ís) had been urged to recant for the last time, and most probably they would be executed. Visiting time was over, and I returned home. The following day, Sunday, June 19, early in the morning I found out that ten women prisoners had been hanged during the night. I ran out of the house to inquire from the friends; in the street I met three friends. With tearful eyes they showed me a list; then I realized Zarrin was also martyred. I ran toward Adelabad prison, moaning and crying. This was the place most of our time had been spent the last eight months. I was allowed to go into the cold room. What I went through that day, and what I saw in that historic moment, I cannot describe. I entered the cold room. O, my God! I saw ten angels lying motionless next to each other. I knew all of them; I had been in the same prison with them. Mother and daughter were together. All had a pair of pants and a summer blouse on. Some of them had their chadur (long robe) tied around their waist; others had it thrown on the floor. What force kept me on my feet and breathing I don't know! I looked at all the ten angels, and found Zarrin among them reposed; I embraced her cold body, put my cheek on her delicate and cold cheek, and kissed the mark of rope on her lovely neck on behalf of all of you (Father, who was in prison; myself; and my brother, out of the country). Her face looked natural and composed."

Olya Ruhizadegan

RUYA ISHRAQI

26. The following is an account of what Ruya Ishraqi, a teen-age girl who was martyred with her parents, told a fellow prisoner. The prisoner was later released and conveyed Ruya's story in a letter.

On one of the days of the trial, she said to the judge, "I have not seen my father for the past thirty-two days. If you allow me to turn around and see for a minute the face of my father . . ."

(Before the prisoners were taken to the trial session, they were first blindfolded, then deliberately taken to wrong rooms and zig-zagged through the prison while abuses and insults were heaped upon them. Then they were taken to a wall, their blindfolds were removed, and they were then given their file and required to write a reply to the questions presented.) The judge hesitated for a moment. However, he agreed that Ruya could see her father in the adjoining room for a few minutes.

She kissed her father, telling him how she loved him and encouraging him to be brave and steadfast. Touching the face of her father, she asked why he had not shaved. The reply was they were not allowed to shave.

At the time Ruya was looking at her father with great love and kissing his face, the judge interfered saying, "Isn't it a pity that you refrain from saying only one word—that you are not Bahá'ís—by which you could avoid such trouble. If you say those words, all three of you will be free and all the frozen assets of your father will be given to him."

Ruya, with her customary smile and decisive look, replied, "The love between parents and children is natural, but my love for my Beloved is even greater than my love for my parents."

The judge asked, "Are you holding to this view until the moment of your execution?" And Ruya replied, "I pray and hope that to the last breath, I will stand firm in my love for my Beloved."

On behalf of the Universal House of Justice

Other Examples of Bahá'í Youth and Young Adults

Zikrullah Khadem, Hand of the Cause of God
27. From his early childhood, Dhikru'lláh Khádim [Zikrullah Khadem] demonstrated great spiritual potential. His father ap-

preciated this and felt certain that one day his son would shoulder significant spiritual responsibilities, as alluded to by 'Abdu'l-Bahá in a Tablet.

While still a young boy, Dhikru'lláh was very alert to the needs of the Faith. Thus, when the Central Spiritual Assembly of Persia advised the friends to convey their loyalty to the beloved Guardian of the Bahá'í Faith, Shoghi Effendi, he wholeheartedly followed this recommendation. With tears in his eyes he wrote a letter filled with great love and devotion, professing his loyalty. From that moment, a longing to attain the presence of the beloved Guardian became his consuming and over-riding passion.

His wish was granted in May of 1925 [at the age of 21], and the Guardian asked this ardent pilgrim, eager to perform any service, to convey to the Persian Bahá'í youth his love and encouragement, to ask them to deepen themselves in the Cause and to study English, especially English literature. This request caused Dhikru'lláh to embark on a zealous study of the English language, a study he pursued throughout his life. This was further reinforced on subsequent visits and communications when the Guardian asked him to translate Bahá'í articles from English to Persian. The Guardian sent treasured copies of *The Advent of Divine Justice, The Promised Day Is Come,* and two volumes of *The Bahá'í World* with instructions for Dhikru'lláh to translate portions for distribution to the Bahá'ís of Persia.

The crowning event of that first pilgrimage was the gift of a picture of 'Abdu'l-Bahá with a rose in His hand. The beloved Guardian told him, "I give you a picture of the beloved Master as a souvenir." One cannot describe how deeply he cherished all the gifts the Guardian gave him. His reverence for those objects was evidence of his love and devotion.

After that pilgrimage Dhikru'lláh Khádim was galvanized with a new purpose, propelled in a new direction, infused with a new passion. His only thought, his only desire was to please his beloved.

Jáviddukht Khádím

CATHERINE HEWARD HUXTABLE, KNIGHT OF BAHÁ'U'LLÁH
28. Catherine Huxtable was born in England on January 6, 1932. . . . Following an almost fatal attack of scarlet fever in her tenth year it was discovered that she suffered from muscular dystrophy of a rare type which indicated a rapid decline and a greatly shortened life span which would probably not reach twenty years. She was to be confined to a wheelchair for half her life. At sixteen her worsening condition made it impossible to continue formal schooling. Despite her physical limitations and waning strength Catherine developed into a self-reliant young woman of diversified interests. She attracted to her a widening circle of friends who accompanied her to concerts, ballets, theatres, art galleries, lectures. She became a gifted writer and an accomplished artist in needlepoint. In 1951 she and Clifford Huxtable, by then one of her determined suitors, embraced the Bahá'í Faith; in 1955 they were married.

Catherine served on the Spiritual Assembly of Toronto with dedication and became an extremely effective and informed speaker. She had an unusual capacity for sharing the insights gathered from her intensive study of the Teachings. The intimate "fireside" meetings in her home with Catherine presiding as gracious hostess were a source of confirmation to many; cynicism, doubt and the qualified acceptance of the power of God receded in her presence, so marvelously did she exemplify the Message she presented.

A friend records: "The overpowering combination of Cathy's serenity and saintliness of spirit, her nobility and radiance of character, and the sheer beauty of her physical person—a beauty at one time curiously both regal and winsome—served to almost blind one to her great humanness. Only after being with her did one reflect: she is a truly splendid human being, total and balanced and genuine. She lived to an unusual degree in a condition of consciousness of the presence of God, equally committed to the victory of the spirit and to the joy of a full human life. Perhaps this balance was the source of her power and tranquility. She seemed always to be simultaneously static and meditative, engaged in some higher communion, and soaring in an authoritative, graceful motion that the eye could hardly trace. Wherever she went she was described as a saint, a heroine and a true Bahá'í. . . .

The sensitive observer noting Catherine's special love for the pioneers and her frequent letters to those serving in distant areas would have known that inevitably she would pioneer. The passing of the Guardian whom she loved wholeheartedly crystallized her intention; in response, the Huxtables pioneered to Regina, Saskatchewan, to assist in rebuilding the Spiritual Assembly in 1957. That task successfully accomplished, a more distant and less hospitable goal was selected still father removed from their home base and offering fewer amenities and comforts. The Huxtables founded the first Spiritual Assembly in the Gulf Islands, a virgin territory of the Ten Year Crusade. By this sacrificial service they joined the ranks of the Knights of Bahá'u'lláh. In this remote outpost in the North Pacific Ocean, in 1962, as though in reward for this devoted service, Catherine bore a child, Gavin. Her happiness was complete.

When the call for pioneers in the Nine Year Plan was raised in 1965, again the hearts of Catherine and Clifford Huxtable were touched. They volunteered to settle on the lonely volcanic island of St. Helena. . . . Catherine confided to a friend on the eve of her departure for Africa: "I don't aspire to be a saint; I would rather be one of God's teddy bears. I am really no different from anyone else. It is just that I know I shall have less time than others; I cannot be like the unwary bird Bahá'u'lláh speaks of in *The Hidden Words*. Only by centering myself in the Covenant of God can my life or death have any significance. If I have a private prayer, it's this: Let my life and death count in the Faith!"

Roger White

SHAPOOR (SHÁPÚR) ASPANDIAR ROWHANI,
KNIGHT OF BAHÁ'U'LLÁH

29. Born in Bombay, India, on 15 August 1931, Shápúr was one of a family of seven sisters and two brothers. His father had come to India as a young boy from a village in Írán and, from scratch, had built a successful business in Bombay. In 1953, Shoghi Effendi's clarion call for pioneers to arise during the Ten Year Crusade was echoed in Bombay. Shápúr and another youth, Ardeshir S. Forudi (Ardishír S. Furúdí), volunteered to open to the Faith of Bahá'u'lláh the Kingdom of Bhutan, in the eastern Himalayas. As Shápúr would often recall later, he hadn't the vaguest idea where Bhutan was; he went home that night and discovered its location from an atlas.

In early 1954, Shápúr and Ardishír set out for Calcutta, from whence they proceeded to Kalimpong, and finally to Bhutan. It was not easy for them to enter the country; permission was refused. Then, by fortunate chance, they met the Prime Minister of Bhutan, Jigme Dorji, brother of the Queen, who was intrigued to know why these two young boys had traveled the length of a subcontinent to come to his tiny, and largely unknown, country. He heard of the Bahá'í Faith from them and ultimately granted them permission to enter. As they were being admitted as guests of the Prime Minister, a special pack of mules and provisions were made available to them.

Neither of the young men was prepared for what the journey entailed. They crossed sheer ravines and traversed dense forests, encountering, for the first time in their lives, snakes and blood-sucking leeches. Shápúr recalled that he clung desperately to his copy of *Bahá'u'lláh and the New Era* during that terrifying journey.

When they finally entered Bhutan, in June 1954, they found themselves confronted with age-old traditions and orthodoxy that had remained unchanged during centuries of Buddhist practice and belief in that remote Himalayan Kingdom. Shortly after their arrival, Ardishír received an urgent communication asking him to return to Bombay, and so he had to leave. Shápúr was now alone, facing hostile local monks, a suspicious populace and an almost insurmountable language barrier. Yet, through the unfailing grace of Bahá'u'lláh, he was able to earn his laurel "Knight of Bahá'u'lláh" and open that country to the Faith (see *Messages to the Bahá'í World 1950–1957,* p. 69). Simple villagers, having heard rumors of the purpose of his visit, would surreptitiously visit his wooden hut at night to hear more of the Message he had come to convey and to read laboriously the Bahá'í books in Hindi. He was even enabled to present the Faith to the Bhutanese royal family.

The time soon came, however, when he was gently asked to leave. The Prime Minister, now his fast personal friend, explained that the Queen was soon due to deliver a child and her gynecologist was a European doctor. For years, this doctor had been requesting the Prime Minister to allow a Christian missionary to enter the country, but consent had never been granted. It would now be embarrassing for the Prime Minister if the physician heard of the presence of this Bahá'í youth in Bhutan. Shápúr had no option but to prepare to leave.

The rivers bordering Bhutan were in full spate at the time of his departure. All his belongings, food and other provisions were swept away during the dangerous crossing and he nearly lost his life, too. His eventual arrival in Calcutta was greeted with relief by the brothers of the Prime Minister who had received from the Prime Minister himself several enquiries about his safety.

Mehru S. Rowhani

THOMAS BREAKWELL

30. At the end of her visit, the Master asked May [Bolles Maxwell] to return to Paris and establish a Bahá'í center in that city. Obedient to His instructions she was able to accomplish this task within a few months. May has described an unforgettable event that she experienced during the summer of 1901. Not yet understanding the Bahá'í Cause, her mother disapproved of May's constant service to it, particularly since her journey to 'Akká. Early in the spring of that year, her mother wrote to the Master asking His permission to take May to Brittany for the summer together with her brother. The Master answered that under no account was May to leave Paris. Learning that 'Abdu'l-Bahá's refusal had made Mrs. Bolles most unhappy, the great teacher Mírzá Abu'l-Faḍl wrote to the Master to explain her feelings. But He still did not change His decision.

When her mother and brother left the city, May moved to a small apartment in a charming house belonging to a friend, Edith Jackson. During the first month that May spent there, she held wonderful meetings which led to the conversion of many precious souls. Early in the summer, Mrs. Milner, whom May had got to know some months earlier, met a young Englishman on a ship sailing from the United States to France. Although Mrs. Milner had never shown any apparent interest in the Bahá'í Faith, she still felt moved to invite him to come with her to see "a special friend" in Paris. The day after Mrs. Milner and he had arrived in that city, May found them standing at her door.

She has described her first sight of this young man. "It was like looking at a veiled light. I saw at once his pure heart, his thirsty soul, and over all was cast the veil which is over every soul until it is rent asunder by the power of God in this day." She had described him as "of medium height, slender, erect, and graceful with intense eyes, and an indescribable charm."

May soon learned that although he was English he held an important post in a cotton mill in a southern state of America, where he had been living for some time, and that he usually spent long summer vacations in Europe.

They discussed his work and the trip that he was planning. He spoke of his great interest in theosophy and seemed to think that she shared it. She did not mention the Bahá'í Faith. Even so, she felt that he was studying her carefully. As he was leaving he asked May if he might come to see her again and hear about some teachings that Mrs. Milner had referred to on the steamer, without mentioning what they were. Since he only planned to stay in Paris for a few days she asked him to return on the following morning.

He arrived with "his eyes shining, his face illumined, his voice vibrating under the stress of great emotion." He looked at her very intently and then said: "I have come to you to help me. Yesterday after I left you, I walked alone down the boulevard and suddenly some great force nearly swept me off my feet. I stood still as though awaiting something, and a voice announced to me distinctly, 'Christ has come!'" Then he asked, "What do you think this means?"

In answer she immediately gave him the Bahá'í Message. For the next three days, during many hours which they spent together, she spoke to him about the exalted Mission of His Holiness the Báb, His early martyrdom, the martyrdom of many more who believed in Him, and about "Bahá'u'lláh, the Blessed Beauty Who shone upon the world as the Sun of eternity, Who had given to mankind the law of God for this age—the consummation of all past ages and cycles." She gave him the small amount of Bahá'í literature in her possession. She described to him her visit to the Prison of 'Akká, and the unforgettable days that she had spent there in the presence of the Master. As she taught him, the veil that she had first seen over him disappeared. "He was like a blazing light."

On the third day of their conversation he became entirely transformed. No former ambition remained. He now had only a single passionate longing—to meet the Master. On this same day Thomas Breakwell wrote this supplication to Him: "My Lord! I believe; forgive me, Thy servant, Thos. Breakwell."

Although deeply moved by the depth and simplicity of his words, May did not yet fully understand why he had so urgently asked the Master for forgiveness. Without delay she wrote a letter to Him asking His permission for her young friend to make the pilgrimage and enclosing his supplication. That evening when May went to the concierge of her apartment to get her mail, she found a little blue cablegram from 'Abdu'l-Bahá that had just arrived. It said, "You may leave Paris at any time." May realized that, thanks to her unquestioning obedience to the Master, she had served as "the link in the chain of His mighty purpose." . . .

Breakwell soon left for the prison city of 'Akká. He was the first Englishman to go there as a pilgrim, and went in company with Herbert Hopper, a young American Bahá'í whom May had also taught.

On their arrival at the prison house (of 'Abdu'lláh Páshá), the two young men were ushered into a large room where they expected to meet the Master. At one end of this room stood a group of men from the East. Not impressed with any of them, Breakwell became deeply troubled and was afraid that he had failed to recognize his Lord. "Sorrow and despair filled his heart, when suddenly a door opened, and in that opening he beheld what seemed to him the rising Sun. So brilliant was this orb, so intense the light that he sprang to his feet and saw approaching him out of this dazzling splendor the form of 'Abdu'l-Bahá." Breakwell's mood instantly changed from complete despair to indescribable joy.

In a conversation with the Master he described his position in the cotton mills of the South. Now clearly realizing that such a condition was wrong, he said, "'These mills are run on child labor.' The Master looked at him gravely and sadly for a while, and then said 'Cable your resignation.'" With great relief Breakwell hastened to obey Him. . . .

On his return to Paris, Breakwell, wonderfully influenced by his precious communion with the Master and by the overwhelming experience of his short visit to 'Akká, taught the Faith with increased spiritual power. "He had become the guiding star of our group." . . .

Intensely sympathetic, he had a genuine love for people. Despite any inconvenience to himself he always tried to help them. . . .

Physically frail, Breakwell was stricken with an illness that developed into serious consumption. Although often in great pain, he in no way relaxed in his passionate efforts to serve the Cause throughout the dark city of Paris. In his last letter to Dr. Yúnis Khán, Breakwell wrote: "Suffering is a heady wine; I am prepared to receive that bounty which is the greatest of all; torments of the flesh have enabled me to draw much nearer to my Lord. All agony notwithstanding, I wish life to endure longer, so that I may taste more of pain. That which I desire is the good-pleasure of my Lord; mention me in His presence."

A few days after the doctor had received this letter Breakwell died, a fact which the Master seemed to know without receiving any message. Deeply grieved, He wrote a prayer of visitation for Breakwell and asked Yúnis Khán to "translate it well, so that whoever reads it will weep." . . .

Breakwell had died within a few months of returning from his pilgrimage, probably in the early days of 1902. A year passed before the Master heard any news from his parents. Then one day, as He was examining certain envelopes which He had received from different places, "He, all of a sudden, picked out one and said [to Dr. Yúnis Khán]: 'How pleasing is the fragrance that emanates from this envelope. Make haste, open it and see where it comes from. Make haste.'" The envelope contained a letter and a beautifully coloured postcard with a violet attached to it. On the card was written in gold ink: "He is not dead. He lives on in the Kingdom of God," and at the bottom, "This flower was picked from Breakwell's grave." The enclosed letter said: "Praise be to the Lord that my son left this world for the next with the recognition and love of Abdul-Baha."

As soon as the doctor had translated this letter for the Master, "He at once rose up from His seat, took the card, put it on His blessed brow, and tears flowed down His cheeks."

With his unerring knowledge the Guardian called Thomas Breakwell the first English believer and a luminary in the Cause of God.

O. Z. Whitehead

TABLET REVEALED BY ʿABDUʾL-BAHÁ

31. Grieve thou not over the ascension of my beloved Breakwell, for he hath risen unto a rose garden of splendors within the Abhá Paradise, sheltered by the mercy of his mighty Lord, and he is crying at the top of his voice: "O that my people could know how graciously my Lord hath forgiven me, and made me to be of those who have attained His Presence!"*

---

* Cf. Qurʾán 36:25

O Breakwell, O my dear one!

Where now is thy fair face? Where is thy fluent tongue? Where thy clear brow? Where thy bright comeliness?

O Breakwell, O my dear one!

Where is thy fire, blazing with God's love? Where is thy rapture at His holy breaths? Where are thy praises, lifted unto Him? Where is thy rising up to serve His Cause?

O Breakwell, O my dear one!

Where are thy beauteous eyes? Thy smiling lips? The princely cheek? The graceful form?

O Breakwell, O my dear one!

Thou hast quit this earthly world and risen upward to the Kingdom, thou hast reached unto the grace of the invisible realm, and offered thyself at the threshold of its Lord.

O Breakwell, O my dear one!

Thou hast left the lamp that was thy body here, the glass that was thy human form, thy earthy elements, thy way of life below.

O Breakwell, O my dear one!

Thou hast lit a flame within the lamp of the Company on high, thou hast set foot in the Abhá Paradise, thou hast found a shelter in the shadow of the Blessed Tree, thou hast attained His meeting in the haven of Heaven.

O Breakwell, O my dear one!

Thou art now a bird of Heaven, thou hast quit thine earthly nest, and soared away to a garden of holiness in the kingdom of thy Lord. Thou hast risen to a station filled with light.

O Breakwell, O my dear one!

Thy song is even as birdsong now, thou pourest forth verses as to the mercy of thy Lord; of Him Who forgiveth ever, thou wert a thankful servant, wherefore hast thou entered into exceeding bliss.

O Breakwell, O my dear one!

Thy Lord hath verily singled thee out for His love, and hath led thee into His precincts of holiness, and made thee to enter the garden of those who are His close companions, and hath blessed thee with beholding His beauty.

O Breakwell, O my dear one!

Thou hast won eternal life, and the bounty that faileth never, and a life to please thee well, and plenteous grace.

O Breakwell, O my dear one!

Thou art become a star in the supernal sky, and a lamp amid the angels of high Heaven; a living spirit in the most exalted Kingdom, throned in eternity.

O Breakwell, O my dear one!

I ask of God to draw thee ever closer, hold thee ever faster; to rejoice thy heart with nearness to His presence, to fill thee with light and still more light, to grant thee still more beauty, and to bestow upon thee power and great glory.

O Breakwell, O my dear one!

At all times do I call thee to mind. I shall never forget thee. I pray for thee by day, by night; I see thee plain before me, as if in open day.

O Breakwell, O my dear one!

LEONORA STIRLING ARMSTRONG

32. On 23 June 1895, in a pleasant two-story house, high on a rise overlooking the Hudson River and the Catskill range beyond, a first child was born to Samuel Norris Holsapple and his beautiful wife, Grace Stirling. They named her Leonora. . . . The childhood of Leonora was, however, soon overshadowed with tragedy and sadness, for her mother's health steadily declined. Just after . . . [Leonora's] fifth birthday . . . [her mother] died.

Mrs. Holsapple's untimely death had a profound effect on Leonora and her younger sister, Alethe. They never again had what could truly be called a home. "How we could endure," Leonora herself recounts, "through those years of our child-hood and adolescence, such loneliness, such suffering, even cru-elty, I do not know . . . I can remember how when still a small child, often at night before going to bed, I knelt down at my sister's bedside and in agony of soul, implored God with all the intensity of my being to let us feel His Presence, His nearness, His protection. Little did I then dream in what way, and how specifically, that prayer was later to be answered!" . . .

Though she attended church from an early age, Leonora was somewhat disillusioned by what she experienced there. When she was about thirteen her maternal grandmother, "Mother Stirling," who had by then after long years of spiritual search-ing found and embraced the Bahá'í Faith, first began to teach her granddaughters the truths of the New Day. The example of Mother Stirling's devotion and many efforts to spread the Bahá'í teaching made a lasting impression on Leonora's sensitive na-ture. She was greatly attracted to the new Revelation and began to memorize passages and prayers from the Writings. Already at that time she made her own efforts to share the Message with her classmates and friends. . . .

The desire to pioneer first stirred in Leonora's soul when 'Abdu'l-Bahá's *Tablets of the Divine Plan* were unveiled at the Bahá'í Con-vention held in New York in 1919. Spontaneously, and at once, she wrote to the Master, offering herself in service. *Thou hadst,* was His reply, *expressed thy great wish to be of service to the Divine Threshold and to heal the infirm with the Divine Panacea—the infirm who is afflicted with passion and self. Spiritual malady is more severe than physical illness for it may be that the latter may be converted by the least remedy into health and vigor, while the former will not be cured by a thousand well-known remedies . . . My hope is that thou mayest become a spiritual physician.*

As Leonora recounts it: "This hope of the Master's became my highest aspiration and when, early in 1920, I read His Tablet to Martha Root, commending her teaching work in South America and stressing the importance of its being followed up by others, it at once seemed to me that here there might be a definite task for me. A letter to Martha brought an immediate reply, with all encouragement." Martha Root had opened South America with her historic visit there in 1919. Her response to Leonora was whole-hearted. She shared thrilling accounts of her experiences and gave her young recruit a copy of her own diary notes from that period. Brazil was finally decided on as the best place to go first. . . .

And so it was that on 15 January 1921 she set sail from New York on a divine adventure destined to span no less than sixty years. In doing so, she became one of a handful of valiant souls who arose in response to 'Abdu'l-Bahá's call during His Own lifetime, and the first Bahá'í pioneer to settle permanently in Latin America.

Had not the Master promised confirmation to those souls who, like unto Peter and Paul, would journey to South America with the requisite qualities of "perfect severance, devotion, firmness and steadfastness in the Covenant"? Leonora knew this meant severance "from dearest friends, comforts, profession, from everything . . ." Martha Root had herself impressed this upon her. And now she was to be surrounded and sustained by such divine confirmations. . . .

Life in her land of spiritual adoption was never easy. She often suffered from loneliness, meager means, malnutrition and illness. Gradually as she became proficient in the Portuguese language, she was better able to support herself. Still, it required long working hours, sometimes at several jobs just to keep body and soul together. She found teaching English, which was the main avenue open to her, to be a valuable way of meeting people and interesting them in the Faith. . . .

Providentially, from Bahjí in June 1921, 'Abdu'l-Bahá had revealed a second Tablet for her. This Tablet became a source of great comfort to her not only in that time of tragedy but throughout the long years ahead. The Master had addressed the envelope simply: "Brazil. To the Maidservant of God, Leonora Stirling Holsapple." Amazingly it reached her, as the Master no doubt knew it would. In the text He refers to Leonora as a *Herald of the Kingdom,* calls upon her to *thank God that thou hast enlightened thy sight, and art giving light to the sight of others, too,* refers by name to a number of seekers, and promises that *the intoxicated friends will grow in rapture and ecstasy, begin to break into melodies and harmonies and raise such a tune that will reach the Supreme Concourse and rejoice and exhilarate the holy ones.* He, likewise, advises her to say that *the entering into this Divine Cause is accompanied by everlasting honor and eternal sovereignty.*

"Soon the beloved Guardian's messages began to reach me, urging me never to become discouraged, rather to redouble my efforts, and guiding me with his unfailing wisdom." Indeed, throughout his ministry Shoghi Effendi's esteem for her and her services was clearly evident. His love for her and his warm encouragement of her work lasted till the end of his life and are recorded in the tender words he addressed to her in many letters: "I feel deeply attached to your work." "Your name I assure you will adorn the annals of the Cause and will inspire many a Bahá'í pioneer in future. You cannot realize the splendor and significance of the work you are doing at present." "I will pray that you may be guided and fortified by the spirit of our beloved Master Who I am sure is guiding you, watching over you and sustaining you in your labors. Persevere and never lose heart."

A survey of Leonora Armstrong's tireless pioneer activities must necessarily span six decades of continual service. Her achievements marked a high tide of human endeavor. Whether in her constant teaching of individuals, her historic travels, the publicity she garnered for the Cause wherever she went, her Herculean labor of translating, publishing and disseminating Bahá'í literature both in Portuguese and Spanish, her work in spreading the Message through correspondence, or her eventual material contributions to the community, she stands out eminently distinguished. Through the years she also engaged in social service whenever possible, and became known in the press as the "Nurse of the Poor."

The first decade of these activities is marked by extraordinary travels. . . . she was able to emblazon the Cause of God in city after city up the Brazilian coast, into the heartland of the Amazon basin, and throughout the Caribbean Sea. Between these travels she raised the banner of the Faith in São Paulo, in Rio and particularly in Bahia through extended stays. A number of souls were attracted to the beauty of the Teachings. Alone in Manaus on the Amazon River, to cite one instance, during a short visit she proclaimed the Faith to 3,400 souls in public meetings and school gatherings.

In 1927 she became the first Bahá'í to visit and speak of the Cause in Colombia, Venezuela, Curaçao, Trinidad, Barbados, Haiti, British Guiana and Dutch Guiana, thus complementing and completing Martha Root's unfulfilled intention of raising the Call of God in all the Latin American countries. . . .

During her stay in Santos Leonora began her prodigious and historic task of translating Bahá'í literature into Portuguese; at first it was a simple pamphlet to distribute at her talks—often typed over and over on her small portable typewriter—later, as her skills developed, an intense outpouring of the major works of the Faith. In the end she had rendered into Portuguese a wide range of literature, and for several decades, under the guidance and with the generous assistance of Shoghi Effendi, had personally seen to its publication. . . .

In 1946 she helped form the first Local Spiritual Assembly of Rio itself. During the 1950s she spent much time at their farm outside Rio, and continued her important translation work. At this time she added Braille to her skills and undertook the transcription and distribution of Bahá'í literature in Portuguese Braille.

. . . It was in June of 1973 that the Universal House of Justice appointed her to membership on the Continental Board of Counselors in South America. . . .

Among the joyful events of Leonora's latter years were the visits to Latin America made by the Hand of the Cause, Amatu'l-Bahá Rúḥíyyih Khánum, the Guardian's widow, and the daughter of May and Sutherland Maxwell. . . . On the several occasions that Amatu'l-Bahá visited Brazil, they spent as much time together as possible. Rúḥíyyih Khánum recollects a little of their long association in the following words: "When Leonora went to South America she was over twenty-five years old and I was fifteen years younger. My first vivid recollection of her was when, on one of her return visits to America in the 1920s, she came to the hotel in New York where my mother and I were staying; she was tall and slender with brown hair, a sallow complexion and droopy brown eyes in which was an expression of sincerity, of purpose and purity of spirit. Her personality seemed to have united the tenacity of Martha Root with an unsureness of herself which she constantly overcame through her complete consecration to serving the Faith. I must have seen her many times before this, because she and my mother had a profound bond of love and I loved her too. . . .

"Shoghi Effendi considered Leonora as one of the Faith's outstanding and most distinguished believers in the West, he never forgot the great historic significance of her arising to pioneer in Latin America before the passing of 'Abdu'l-Bahá, and in his letters to her he warmly praised her exemplary and ceaseless services, in which he took a keen interest. . . .

"The study of such a life as Leonora's, a life of complete consecration to Bahá'u'lláh and His teachings, a life of ceaseless work which lasted till a few hours before her passing at the age of eighty-five, a life in which it never even occurred to Leonora that she was sacrificing—such a life is a manual for every generation of Bahá'ís to study and presents an enduring challenge to all those who would follow in her footsteps." . . .

The longing for service came to her young. The vastness of Latin America was the arena of her sacrifice. There she poured forth her life, and having given up the world, she gained the Kingdom. At the end she was incarnate light. Even before she slipped from her earthly vesture, the unearthly radiance of her inner being surrounded those attending her. On 17 October 1980 her precious spirit quietly took flight to its celestial Source.

Hooper C. Dunbar

ROBERT TURNER

33. Some time before 1898, Lua Getsinger (whom 'Abdu'l-Bahá had called Livá, meaning "Banner of the Cause") visited San Francisco. During this trip she called on Mrs. Hearst and spoke to her about the Bahá'í Faith. Even without access to the facts it is not hard to imagine the thrilling scene that ensued. In a sketch, Louis G. Gregory has informed us that Robert Turner, her Negro butler, held a position of some responsibility in her household; he described him as "faithful, dependable, and wise." Robert Turner let Mrs. Getsinger into the house and showed her into a finely furnished sitting-room. After giving her a gracious welcome, Mrs. Hearst asked her guest to sit down next to

her on the sofa. When he had served the tea, Robert stood near to them. In a most moving manner, Mrs. Getsinger spoke to them both about the Bahá'í Faith. Surely on this occasion and those that followed Robert listened eagerly to Mrs. Getsinger and as a result did all that he could to learn about the Faith.

In *God Passes By* Shoghi Effendi has referred to the fact that an American Negro, Robert Turner, was "the first member of his race to embrace the Cause of Bahá'u'lláh in the West." . . .

The Hand of the Cause Louis Gregory has recorded one account of Robert Turner's first meeting with 'Abdu'l-Bahá. "At sight of the Master he dropped upon his knees and exclaimed: 'My Lord! My Lord! I am not worthy to be here!'" 'Abdu'l-Bahá raised him to his feet, and embraced him like a loving father.

A few days later the whole party visited 'Abdu'l-Bahá again in 'Akká, and May Bolles described this meeting. "On the morning of our arrival, after we had refreshed ourselves, the Master summoned us all to Him in a long room overlooking the Mediterranean. He sat in silence gazing out of the window, then looking up He asked if all were present. Seeing that one of the believers was absent, he said, 'Where is Robert?' . . . . In a moment Robert's radiant face appeared in the doorway and the Master rose to greet him, bidding him be seated, and said, 'Robert, your Lord loves you. God gave you a black skin, but a heart white as snow.'"

O. Z. Whitehead

KANICHI YAMAMOTO

34. Kanichi Yamamoto, whom his friends called Moto, was the first Japanese Bahá'í in the world. He came from the village of To-saki in Yamaguchi Province in Japan. According to Marion Yazdi's two valuable appreciations of him, Moto was a serious and independent thinker. Brought up a Buddhist, during his early manhood he became a devout Christian.

Not satisfied with his life at home, in 1901, at the age of twenty-two, he left Japan with the intention of settling in North America. On the way there he stopped over in the Hawaiian Islands and soon found work in Honolulu as a servant in the home of Mr. and Mrs. William Owen Smith.* . . .

On [Elizabeth's] return to the Smith home she felt ready to give him the message. In spite of his imperfect English, he understood and believed what she had told him immediately. When Elizabeth "asked him how he knew it was the Truth, he answered by putting his hand to his heart, and said he knew there." At the close of this conversation, his face radiating joy, Moto said to her: "Oh, Miss Muther, I am so happy! . . . and I can only say, 'Oh God! How hast thou honored me to have made me Thy servant!'"

Moto was now anxious to declare his belief in Bahá'u'lláh and to ask the Master to give him the strength to teach the people of his native land. Mainly for these reasons, he wrote to Him without delay. After four attempts to compose a letter to Him in English, Moto still did not feel that he had given the Master an adequate expression of his thoughts. When he told Elizabeth this, she advised him to write his letter in Japanese and assured Moto that the Master would understand the spirit of his letter just the same.

Before the end of 1902 Moto had the great happiness of receiving the following Tablet revealed for him by the Master:

O thou who art attracted by the Word of God to the Kingdom of God!

Turn with the whole of thy being to God, forget aught else save God, and supplicate God to make thee a sign of guidance in the midst of people who are veiled from God,

* Elizabeth Muther, who knew the Smiths, was a new Bahá'í and had come to know Kanichi through her association with that family.

perchance they may be guided to the Orb of all horizons, enter the Kingdom of Harmony, drink of the cup of the love of God, rejoice at the manifestation of the Kingdom of God, taste the delight of the mention of God and shelter themselves in the shadow of the Tree of Life in the midst of the Paradise of God.

This beseemeth the believers; this is the qualification of the sincere; this is the path of the knowers; and this is the utmost aim of the faithful. Exert thy utmost power that thou mayest share this great bounty.

O. Z. Whitehead.

'ALÍ NAKHJAVÁNÍ AND PHILIP HAINSWORTH

35. Dorothy [Baker, Hand of the Cause of God] attended the All-America Intercontinental Teaching Conference in Chicago, Illinois. There, at the Medinah Temple, she spoke of the Guardian and of his reference to 'Alí Nakhjavání during her pilgrimage:

He told of 'Alí Nakhjavání. He spoke of the fact that this intrepid youth had gone into the jungles of Africa, as you have no doubt been hearing, and, assisted by Philip Hainsworth of Britain, they lived with the Teso people; they ate the food of the Teso people; they slept on straw mats or leaves, or whatever it is that you sleep on among the Teso people. The rain falls on your head and salamanders drop in your tea, if there is tea. And they stayed! And they did not say, "Conditions do not warrant it because these people eat herbs and things that would just kill us." They stayed! Is there an 'Alí Nakhjavání, then, in America? At the present, no. I mean, up to the present. Is there a Philip Hainsworth? Up to the present, no.

Now, the dark skinned people, he [Shoghi Effendi] said, would have an upsurge that is both spiritual and social. The spiritual upsurge will rapidly bring them great gifts because this is an act of God and it was so intended. And all the world's prejudiced forces will not hold it back, one hair's breadth. The Bahá'ís will glorify it and understand it. The social repercussions of race suppressions around the world will increase at the same time, and frightened, the world's forces will see that the dark skinned peoples are really rising to the top—a cream that has latent gifts only to be brought out by Divine bounties. Where do the Bahá'ís stand in this? Again and again he pointed out that the Bahá'ís must be in the vanguard of finding them and giving them the base. For the social repercussions will at times become dreadful, if we do not, and we shall be judged by God.

I thought that I was rather a fanatic on the race question, at least a strong liberal, but I sat judged by my Guardian, and I knew it. My sights were lifted immeasurably and I saw the vistas of these social repercussions, coming because of our spiritual negligence through the years, and I saw the Indian tribes dotted about this continent unredeemed, waiting—waiting for an 'Alí Nakhjavání. Are the African friends going to have to come and awaken us for the dark skinned races in our midst? God forbid, that in even this coming year we fail in this. . . .

God grant that we may raise up our heroes who will dedicate their lives to the Indians, to the great dark skinned races, to the Eskimos, to the Negro peoples so brilliant, so promising in our national life. Which one will be our 'Alí Nakhjavání?

Dorothy Gilstrap

Mohamed Lamin Sumah

36. Mohamed Lamin Sumah (Fallah Sumah), nicknamed Jamil, was born on 28 April 1961. . . . [in] Thadie Village, Sierra Leone. He was from the Susu Tribe. . . . He was a very special youth.

He had a friendly personality and was very honest, reliable and responsible. He was simple yet dignified and respectable.

Sumah was given the Message of Bahá'u'lláh in December 1984 by his aunt, Hawa Kamara, who had first invited the Bahá'ís to Thadie Village. In a little over two years he laid down his life serving the Faith as Sierra Leone's first international pioneer. . . .

In 1984, a number of African countries had received a pioneering call from the Universal House of Justice. The National Spiritual Assembly of the Bahá'ís of Sierra Leone had asked the Universal House of Justice if its community could be given the goal of sending one pioneer to Guinea, to which the House had kindly consented with the condition that the pioneer must know either French or one of the native languages. As soon as the goal was announced Mohamed Lamin Sumah wanted to volunteer. He knew Susu, a widely used local language, and was determined to learn French to teach more effectively.

Sumah first met Friday Ekpe, a member of the Continental Board of Counselors for Africa, in May 1985. Mr. Ekpe traveled to Thadie several times to encourage Sumah to go pioneering.

In June 1985, the Chairman of the National Spiritual Assembly of the Bahá'ís of Sierra Leone, Alusine Kabia, and other friends with the Bahá'ís of Thadie said farewell to Sumah. They were proud that their son was going to serve the Cause. After receiving his letter of credentials in July 1985, he traveled by boat to his pioneering post. It was a difficult trip. He had to spend 48 hours on a small island where he was given no food and had no place to sleep. When he arrived at his pioneering post he contacted the Bahá'ís. He was active in Bahá'í functions and taught the Faith. He earned his living by dyeing lappas (cloth). He always sent money he had saved, no matter how small the amount, to his parents in Thadie because he knew they were old and needed his help. . . .

He loved reading the Bahá'í Scriptures, and studying them made him happy. Sumah said that the reason he became a Bahá'í was because when he read the Holy Writings of the Bahá'í Faith he understood them, but when he read the Holy Writings of other religions he didn't. . . .

On . . . 7 March 1987, he arrived in Conakry . . . with a severe stomach ache and could barely walk. He was examined by a physician who said to take him directly to the hospital. He had acute abdominal pain which was probably appendicitis. They operated on him at midday. At about 7:00 p.m., without ever regaining consciousness, his pure soul went to the Abhá Kingdom. One of the last things he said was to ask if one of the friends, to whom he had taught the Faith, was attending the meetings.

On Sunday seven Bahá'ís met with members of Sumah's family. As one of his cousins stated emphatically that Mohamed was a Bahá'í, it was agreed that he would receive a Bahá'í burial. He was the first pioneer from Sierra Leone to fulfill a goal and also the first Bahá'í to have a Bahá'í burial in Guinea.

Sumah was only 26 years old. We pray that God will bless him and that he helps all of us from the Concourse on High to be firm in the Covenant and that the Faith will grow in Sierra Leone and Guinea.

Sadeh Hakiman and Abdul Karim Sillah

WINNANIK AND MUBARAK

37. Mubarak was born in 1948 in Canga'an village, . . . Indonesia. . . . In 1975 . . . [Mubarak's] family came to know about the Bahá'í Faith and embraced it the following year. Mubarak, . . . became an eager and enthusiastic believer, fearless in spreading the Faith among his friends and neighbors, and in proclaiming it to government officials throughout the district.

In 1970, he married Winnanik, known to her friends as "Nani," who had been born into a Muslim family in Ngawi in about 1959. She also accepted the Faith, and the couple farmed on a small scale. . . .

When, in 1981, Mubarak, his wife and his younger brother, Wahab, as well as 'Abdu'l-Hadi Wibowo and Kurdi, two other local believers, acknowledged themselves as Bahá'ís on their identity cards, the Islámic clergy and others in the village community began to oppose the Bahá'í Faith and to spread abroad false accusations that the Bahá'ís were enemies of Islám. As a result, on 23 November 1982, Mubarak, 'Abdu'l-Hadi, and Kurdi were required to present themselves to the Military Commander in Tanjungkarang where they conducted themselves with equanimity before a trial panel and jury during an intensive interrogation. They explained the principles of the Bahá'í Cause and acknowledged the divine origin of all the great religions of the past, including Islám. They were given a sympathetic hearing and released. However, the 'ulamá continued to make false accusations against the Bahá'ís and stirred up feelings against them among the people by broadcasting false reports over the radio.

On 17 January 1984, Mubarak and three other Bahá'ís had their Bahá'í books seized by the police. Refusing an invitation to recant their belief, they were imprisoned and sentenced to terms ranging from two to five years.

In the difficult circumstance of being forcibly separated from her husband, Nani struggled to keep her family intact. She made a living for herself and the three children by buying chickens in the villages around her home, then selling them in the Panjang City market, 80 kilometers away—an undertaking that required her to use dirty, overcrowded public transport. She would leave her home each day at six o'clock in the morning, depart for Panjang

City about ten, and return home at ten o'clock in the evening, day after day, without cessation, and without complaint. During this time she also visited her husband and the other Bahá'í prisoners regularly, negotiated with a lawyer in Tanjungkarang regarding their case, attended court sessions, initiated solicitations at the office of the court, and made every attempt possible to obtain redress of injustice in the face of implacable official indifference. It is through Nani that the detailed knowledge of the court proceedings in these cases were made known to other Bahá'ís.

At last the great stress of dealing with the authorities, together with the physical strain of working to keep her family together, took their inevitable toll. In her eighth month of pregnancy, Nani suddenly fell ill. She died shortly thereafter on 13 July 1984. She was unstinting in her attempt, on behalf of the four imprisoned Bahá'ís, to wrest justice from a prejudiced and insensitive judiciary. She faced this daunting challenge with remarkable resolution and never failed, on her regular visits, to bring cheer to the hearts of the prisoners who will always be grateful for her valiant efforts.

When informed of his wife's death, Mubarak was inconsolable but he resigned himself to the will of God and entrusted his three children to the care of Bahá'u'lláh. Since his children were also the children of the Bahá'í community, he told his friends, he relied upon the believers to provide them with a Bahá'í education. His steadfastness in the Cause of Bahá'u'lláh remained unshaken despite the added suffering caused by the death of his young wife and his concern about the welfare of his children.

After a two-year confinement, Mubarak was released from prison on 17 January 1986. He and his younger brother, who was released on the same date, went to work for another brother in whose home Mubarak died on 25 May 1986.

M. Samandari and K. H. Payman

CYRUS SAMANDARÍ

38. This radiant young believer received the approval of the beloved Guardian for his pioneer project to Somalia in 1955. Assured by the promise of success which Shoghi Effendi had given him, he arrived in Mogadiscio on Bahá'u'lláh's birthday, and by his warm-heartedness and beautiful chanting endeared himself to . . . all. . . .

He studied hard and learned to speak not only Arabic but sufficient Somali . . . to be able to teach the Faith. He taught with such love, patience and sincerity that he was able to attract many souls. He not only taught the Faith, but mathematics, Arabic and English to the many young men who were unable to study at school. . . .

Most young men would have been bored and complained of the dullness of their life here, but although he lived such a simple, restricted life, he was always radiantly happy, which, combined with his kindly, sympathetic nature, made him not only magnetic but a very successful teacher. . . .

When Cyrus heard of the passing of the beloved Guardian, the radiant light was extinguished, and he said in a broken voice: "There is nothing to live for now. Life without the beloved Guardian has no meaning." Not many days later he became unwell.

At first he was nursed at home, all this time receiving a flow of students and contacts, who came for lessons in Arabic or mathematics, or for "bedside firesides." He continually apologized for giving trouble, though, in fact, he was uncomplaining and undemanding. When his condition suddenly became serious, he was hurried to a hospital. . . .

It was discovered a serious operation would be necessary, and he was sent by air to Nairobi on March 19; with broken hearts his relatives in Mogadiscio helped the now frail and pathetic figure to board the plane—a shadow of the former finely built, handsome young man. The operation proved to be useless, as he was suffering from advanced cancer. Doctors and nurses were all deeply impressed with his gentle and courageous character. He slipped from this life to the next on the evening of April 5, 1958. . . . Although it had been hoped that he could regain sufficient strength to pass his last days with his beloved mother, he was destined by God to serve the Faith in death as in life. The Nairobi friends were able to acquire Bahá'í burial ground and obtain special permission to bury both black and white in the same area. Thus he helped to win another goal.

Medhi and Ursula Samandari

ZLMARIAN STOAKLEY WALKER

39. Peace education has always been implicit in the Bahá'í Cause, but the peace education movement in Brazil and elsewhere owes much to the efforts of Dr. Zlmarian Walker. In the 1980s, when the concept was still new in Europe and practically unknown in Brazil, she grasped its potential for direct and indirect teaching. . . . Zlmarian was born on 15 April 1944 in Washington D.C. She had fond recollections of the dedication of the House of Worship in Wilmette in 1953, to which she was taken by her family, who were Bahá'ís.

When she was 12, Zlmarian pioneered with her family from Batavia, Illinois, to Mississippi. This courageous initiative, involving an unheard-of migration of northern blacks to the heart of the Deep South, won the profound admiration of the friends gathered at the National Convention that year.

In 1967, Zlmarian was married to Robert K. Walker in a beautiful ceremony in the garden of the House of Worship, uniting the extended families of both races. They were to be blessed with two daughters: Shanta Navváb, born 1970; and Leili Leonora, born 1976.

In 1973, Zlmarian and Robert received their Doctor of Education degrees at the University of Massachusetts, where they participated in the development of the Anisa Model of education, under the direction of the late Dr. Daniel Jordan. Zlmarian became an assistant professor at Texas Southern University in Houston, and vice-director of the Multicultural Teacher Corps Program, where she was able to develop principles of multicultural education. These she carried to her pioneering post in Brazil, where she moved with her family in 1974.

As a Latin American Teaching Fellow at the Pontifical Catholic University of Rio Grande do Sul, and subsequently as a visiting professor at the Federal University of Rio Grande do Norte, she was able to combine graduate teaching and research with Bahá'í and family activities. She also lived in Vitória for two years before joining the Escola das Nações in 1981. She served as a member of the National Spiritual Assembly from 1985 until her passing.

Dr. Walker's booklet, "World Peace through World Education," was published in Portuguese in 1986 by the Brazilian Bahá'í Studies Association. An interview with her on the topic was published in the volume, *Perspectives on Peace Education* (Ake Bjerstedt, ed.), published in 1990 by the Malmö School of Education in Sweden. At the time of her death, which occurred 9 July 1989, she was working on a handbook in Portuguese on peace education. . . . The continuing efforts in the field of peace education by the National Spiritual Assembly and Bahá'í communities all over Brazil are another part of her legacy.

Robert Walker

Interviews with Bahá'í Youth

40. Culture Crash: An interview with Soo-Jin Yoon by Aaron Emmel

Soo-Jin Yoon, 27 at the time of this interview, has traveled all over the world and it seems that wherever she goes she immediately impresses and befriends everyone she meets. What is her secret? How is she able to manage so well in such a variety of cultures? These are some questions I asked Soo-Jin at her apartment in Albuquerque, New Mexico.

Aaron: How long have you been a Bahá'í?

Soo-Jin: I've been a Bahá'í for over eight years. I was studying at the University of Illinois in my sophomore year. I had a lot of questions about religion: "How could a just God let a world run like this?" and things like that. The person who taught me—and the way she taught—was perfect for me. Basically, she just slowly introduced me to the Faith without teaching me outright.

Aaron: Was this Layla?

Soo-Jin: Layla, yes. I had been given the *Hidden Words* at a fireside she took me to and in the back was a quotation of 'Abdu'l-Bahá, "Be a lamp, be as a Bahá'í." I started memorizing it, just to keep my mind off my problems. Soon after that I talked with Layla until five in the morning. I asked her all the questions I had left, like, "What about people who drink because it's part of their culture?" In the end, what Layla said was that the most important thing was that you believe in Bahá'u'lláh and the teachings and everything else is secondary. I was like, okay, I guess I don't really have any reason that I shouldn't be a Bahá'í!

Aaron: What made you take that step?

Soo-Jin: I think the thing that touched me the most was realizing how sacred, how important and how special the Bahá'í Faith was to the Bahá'ís I had met.

Aaron: What did the Bahá'í Faith mean to you then?

Soo-Jin: It wasn't that special to me at that point because I had just learned about it and so I felt weird about saying I was a Bahá'í. I was sort of worried about it. I was a matter-of-fact kind of declaration. And then a couple days later, Layla cried and I didn't understand why. A few days after that she gave me a declaration card and I signed it. I was reading about things and I knew a lot of facts. I knew that what I loved about the Bahá'í Faith were the principles. I watched the Bahá'ís striving to meet those standards and their everyday struggles and I really admired them for that. That's what I liked but I don't think I ever truly understood the magnitude of Bahá'u'lláh's Revelation or what the Revelation was until I went teaching, which was about four months after I became a Bahá'í. I went down to Belize.

Aaron: Why did you decide to go travel teaching to another country so soon?

Soo-Jin: I don't really know. When you take that step and sign the declaration card, things start happening. Half the time I didn't know what was going to happen. I couldn't have imagined how I was going to change or what it meant to go travel teaching. I think I was guided, like being enrolled in the Bahá'í school, I guess. I was given crash courses and was pushed along.

At first I wanted to travel and experience something outside of the US, so I started looking at employment because I didn't have money. I paid 30 dollars for a list of places to work and I wrote to them but no one wrote back. Then Layla said, "Why don't you try travel teaching?" And I was like, Oh, okay, all right! I wrote to the National Center and they gave me some information. I picked three or four countries where they spoke English—Botswana, Belize and a couple other countries—and I decided on Belize because it was the closest and the least expensive.

Aaron: Very important considerations.

Soo-Jin: And I had NO idea what the heck I was doing. But I never really worried.

I remember at one point when I was about to leave, my mom asked me, "Well, what are you going to do if no one comes to get you, if no one's there to meet you at the airport?" It never dawned on me to think like that. I didn't even have addresses or phone numbers. I just knew that someone was going to meet me at the airport. I think part of it was me. I wanted to improve myself as far as being a Bahá'í was concerned. But I think there are two ways you can be deepened in knowledge of the Bahá'í Faith—you can have the intellectual deepening and then you have a totally different, almost mysterious, mystical sense of spiritual deepening, where you're guided to the things you need to learn and the stuff you need to have. I think I was definitely pushed in that direction. When I got to Belize, I couldn't have asked for anything better. Now that I've been a Bahá'í for a number of years, I've heard stories of how people go to countries and they're not prepared or there are a lot of difficulties. Obviously I was protected. Belize is one of the most nurturing countries, now that I look at it. The people there just took me in. I call Belize my spiritual mother country because that was where I *really* learned about the Bahá'í Faith.

Aaron: How old were you when you went to Belize?

Soo-Jin: I was 19.

Aaron: So what actually happened when you were there?

Soo-Jin: Well, someone met me at the airport! Bob Hitchcraft. Bob was this jolly, big man who came up to me and just hugged me. It took me by surprise. He's as white as you can get. Then there was a really black lady, Beverly. She was from Jamaica and was travel teaching. They drove me over to Counsellor Ahmadiyeh's house—he and his family lived in Belize City. I had no idea that I was in the presence of a very important person. He passed away a couple years after that. Then we drove to the capital, Belmopan, and went through two or three days of orientation. They taught me how to teach, went through the teaching goals and deepened me. And it was all new to me, I mean, everything was new to me and I was so nervous.

Aaron: How did they "teach you how to teach"?

Soo-Jin: We did role playing with Beverly, pretending that she was teaching me, and I had to try to turn around and do it. I swear, I must have repeated exactly how she taught, every word, every example, every analogy, because I had never heard any of that before. I remember at one point that it came up that Bahá'u'lláh was the return of Christ. See, before that, I had understood the unity of the Manifestations. I had understood that all the Prophets talked about the Prophets of the future but I had never really thought about it—and no one had ever said it to me in those words—that Bahá'u'lláh was the return of Christ. When that came up, since I had been Christian before, it was a big shocker. I didn't say anything to anybody but I was thinking, "My God, what are these people saying? They're saying that He's the return of Christ! Isn't that, like, huge news?"

Aaron: Were you comfortable being so suddenly immersed in such a new environment and new world view?

Soo-Jin: I was going through a lot internally. Especially there. The whole time I didn't say anything but I was very nervous. I thought, these people are so dedicated and they're sacrificing everything. They're out here doing all this stuff and here I am, I'm supposed to be an assistant or help to them. But I am so afraid that I am a burden, that they have to take care of me and that I am imposing and being more of a burden than a help. I really struggled with that—that was the big test for the summer: realizing that whatever effort you put in, no matter how little you know, no matter how inadequate you feel, it's still up to Bahá'u'lláh.

Aaron: So what was it like going out the villages and teaching?

Soo-Jin: Well, when I was 19 I didn't want to be surprised by anything. You think you know everything and you can handle everything, especially around college time, and you want to be adventurous. I just took in everything and thought, "Oh, yeah, that's the way it's supposed to be." I think for some people it might have been a big shock because of the conditions and the physical hardships but at that point nothing fazed me. I think being the age that I was, with everything being so new and me having just become a Bahá'í, I was there to soak everything up. I look back now and think, "Oh my God, how did I do it?"

Aaron: Describe some of these conditions.

Soo-Jin: I remember traveling from town to town. I'd get on these buses—half the time you don't have a seat and the roads are so bumpy. You're standing there and you have nothing to grab onto and you're between all these sweaty people and it's so hot and it's so dusty. When I got off the bus I'd scratch my nails across my skin, my face, and I would have caked-on mud under my nails. It's so humid, you're sweating and everything just sticks to you. It was very dirty. Actually, I struggled with this.

Before we went out to the villages I did a little travel teaching with Beverly. We were partners. We traveled down south and met up with a lot of other people. It was the beginning of the summer and there was a summer institute being held, followed by a teaching project. So we all met up and we had this institute—there were probably 40 or 50 of us. From there, we were all assigned a teacher and a group—teams of teachers went to different towns. A drama and dance group went from town to town. Part of our role as teachers was to prepare for the performances and the teaching, that kind of thing.

There were other goals, like setting up children's classes, training teachers and holding Feasts. I got assigned to this little tiny town, and when I realized where I was assigned, I sort of freaked out because I knew it was going to be hard. I wanted to be with the youth because I was young. I didn't say anything but at one point I was almost teary-eyed and I told myself, "Soo-Jin, just accept it." It just took me five minutes and I totally accepted it.

Then we got there and after the bus ride the first thing I wanted to do was take a shower. Of course there was no running water, no electricity, nothing. Just mosquitoes and sand flies.

Aaron: Mosquitoes seem to be everywhere in Central America.

Soo-Jin: And sand flies like crazy. The first week I was there I had so many sand fly and mosquito bites. Just on one leg, from my knee down to my ankle, I counted over 110 bites. It was horrible. I get very allergic reactions. I was walking around and trying to wear loose clothing. When it gets hot the bites get very irritating, so I was walking around like this the whole time. I still have scars from them. Other people didn't get bitten as badly—for some reason I was being initiated or something.

Anyway, we got there and secured a place to stay but then the guys on the team had to find another place and it was getting late and dark. There was no electricity. Now that I think about it, these are really sweet memories but at the time, you're just like, whoa!

Aaron: "How did I get into this?"

Soo-Jin: Yeah! I remember I had made sure to bring a little cushion to sleep on and one of the guys didn't have one, so I gave mine to him. I said I could sleep on the hammock, which was hanging in the house. All these houses are built on sticks because they are on sand. I tried to sleep in the hammock but couldn't do it, so I ended up on the floor and there were ants crawling all over me, cockroaches crawling all over me. But I was so tired that I just thought, "Okay."

And then they brought us two buckets, one to go to the bathroom in and the other bucket to wash up in; it had water in it. They put it in the kitchen area but by mistake the guys locked the kitchen before they went, so we couldn't even go to the bathroom or wash up. We had to go outside. You couldn't see anything, it was so dark. We just went out and squatted. And then I realized, later, after I'd stayed there for a while, that the local people are so used to having no electricity that they walk around all the time in the dark. So anybody could have been walking around at that time. The next morning, I looked at the water and I was so glad I hadn't bathed in it because it was brown. They said it was only minerals but I thought it was really disgusting.

The people in the village were so different from the people in the bigger towns of Belize. With all these personal struggles, it took me a while to figure out how I was going to relate to them. I had a difficult time until I realized we're all one people, just of different kinds with different cultures. I had to try to change little things, like the way I approached people. It was an experience. I ran into everything from scorpions to chopped-up cat claws.

Aaron: How were you able to relate to the people around you?

Soo-Jin: You just try to find ways. I've seen the materials from the National Spiritual Assembly and National Teaching Committee about how you have to be aware of your own culture and ethnocentrism and how you should try to imagine things from other people's culture, see it from their perspective and not judge. I think those skills are good on one level but the most important thing is love. As long as you feel you love the people you're in contact with, no matter what cultural differences or difficulties you have, people can see it. Especially pure-hearted people from the villages—they can detect sincerity, they can detect condescension, they can sense it much more than we can. But I remember really struggling with it.

I once watched a group of Mayan women, up the river, washing clothes. We had to do all our bathing and washing in the river. I sat there, thinking, "Oh my God, how do I start, what do I say to them, how do I talk to them?" You know? But it's just a matter of getting used to it and being comfortable with yourself. And finding things out about other people which are interesting to you. There's always the commonality of children. You can ask about their children, about their health or what's happening in the community, things like that. But like I said, most important is love. No matter what, you need to sincerely love the person and love the people that you're teaching. You need to have the attitude of service rather than "I'm here to teach you something" because obviously that doesn't work. And I think you need to pray, pray for the station of servitude and pray for love.

41. Transformation: an interview with Houman Vafai

Interviewer: How long have you been a Bahá'í?

Houman: I was born into a Bahá'í family. I grew up in Iran until I was about seven. At that time both my parents were fired from their jobs because we were Bahá'ís. My mom was a doctor, my dad an engineer. We were living a comfortable life. My parents were given the option to recant their faith or leave the country. One of the fundamentals of belief, in my opinion, is that you stick with it, no matter what forces are in opposition.

Interviewer: How old are you now?

Houman: I'm 20 years old. It's been about 13 years that I've been in America. I was born in Isfahan. When we were leaving the country because of religious persecution, I actually didn't know because I was a child. My parents didn't tell me we were leaving. I guess I was too young to understand that I was leaving my friends and going to another country. My parents just said, "We're going on a trip." They were crying but my sister and brother and I didn't know. My brother was only one year old. After a little while, I found out that we were not coming back. Our first stop was Pakistan.

Interviewer: Your brother was one, you were seven and how old was your sister?

Houman: My sister was nine. We went to Pakistan and there we were escorted by a Pakistani tribe. We paid them to take us across the border.

Interviewer: What was the trip like, going from Isfahan to Pakistan? Was there emotional turmoil?

Houman: The whole trip was nothing like a normal trip, where you take a bus and then you take a plane somewhere else. This was an escape, not the normal route people take to get out of Iran. We had to get a truck and that was our main source of transportation. We had to go through back valleys and deserts. I remember that my mom, brother and sister were in the front seat of the truck and my dad and I were in the bed of the pickup. We had to lie down so the officers who were stationed in the mountains and the deserts wouldn't see us. We also had to dress up as members of the tribe. It wasn't pants and shirts; it was a distinct outfit that showed that we were associated with the tribe.

Interviewer: Tell me about the trip from Pakistan. Where did you go from there?

Houman: We spent several weeks there and we got accustomed to the food. From there we went to Austria, where we have family. We have family here in America and we moved here nine months after we arrived in Austria.

Interviewer: Would you say that your experience has helped you to be a stronger person?

Houman: Once I investigated the Bahá'í Faith and understood its history, I understood the significance of the trip. When I read about the early days of the Bahá'í Faith, when Bahá'ís were persecuted and martyred, when the 20,000 Bábís—the early followers—were martyred to initiate the Bahá'í era, the significance kicked in a little more. There was a spiritual significance to it instead of just an escape from the country because we were in trouble.

Interviewer: It seems absurd to many people that you would be killed for your faith or be asked to give it up. Why do you think, even 150 years ago when the Bahá'í Faith started, there was so much persecution?

Houman: It is a question of authority and power for governmental officials and leaders. When they feel that someone is coming in and changing the lifestyle and traditions, it is a threat. Also, at the beginning of every dispensation there is natural opposition. That opposition is what Bahá'u'lláh talks about in the Fire Tablet. He says, "Were it not for the cold, how would the heat of Thy words prevail, O Expounder of the worlds?"

Interviewer: Can you explain that? What does that mean?

Houman: I think the heat and cold refer to the condition of life. When a person is going through struggles and tests, it seems extremely cold, like complete despair. That's when the words of Bahá'u'lláh, or of any Manifestation of God, shine most. When the Bábís were persecuted in Iran, such that 20,000 of them were martyred for their faith, that seems like coldness to me. It makes the heat of Bahá'u'lláh's words much more powerful because these people sacrificed their lives. Other people are confused and caught up in leadership, power, authority and money. These people sacrificed their lives for a spiritual cause.

Interviewer: So could you look to the histories of other faiths, like Christianity, and see similar kinds of opposition?

Houman: A lot of people questioned Christ's faith. They said, "Where's He from, He's not supposed to be from this particular place. I don't believe Him." Then they persecuted Him because of where He was from or the way He looked. Muḥammad was also confronted with religious persecution.

Interviewer: They made Muḥammad flee from His own city, Mecca, to Medina.

Houman: Moses was also persecuted in the early days of the revelation of His teachings. As human beings we have to acknowledge the history evident in each of the dispensations. Still now, in Iran, there are persecutions.

Interviewer: When you came to America, you were in a new country with a new language. What was it like growing up in this new environment?

Houman: I fell into the trends of the American lifestyle, the patterns of American society. I wasn't deep into the Bahá'í Faith; I didn't have any source of guidance within myself. I heard the principles around me—the oneness of humanity and racial unity, for instance—but I didn't have the guiding source within me.

Interviewer: You hadn't discovered those for yourself; you just heard them through the mouth of other people?

Houman: I just followed what the rest of the people were doing. I was like, "Yes, this is fun, so I'm going to do it. Yes, I feel loved, so I'm going to do it." But it wasn't real love; I just went with everyday things with no purposeful approach to life. In my junior or senior year in high school, my sister suggested I say some prayers and she gave me a prayer book. I started saying prayers and then I started going to Bahá'í functions with other youth. With my other friends I would play football or basketball or go to parties. It was a completely different scene with the Bahá'í youth—there was a greater amount of trust. I could definitely sense something, even though at the time I couldn't describe it.

Interviewer: Was there a struggle, like a tug of war, over which direction to go?

Houman: Yes, that was a hard struggle and it's ongoing. When I started hanging out with new people, my other friends would call me and say, "What's going on, how come you're not coming out with us? Why are you conforming to something?" There was a lot of curiosity. I didn't want to say, "Parties are stupid, you guys shouldn't be drinking." It wasn't about forcing my views on other people. It was about going with a natural trend in my life.

Interviewer: Even though you were born into a Bahá'í family and you went through a profound experience as a child, you grew up here and discovered what you believe in your heart. You had to go through your own experience and struggles to reach the realization yourself.

Houman: It's an ongoing thing; it wasn't a one-time discovery. A common point of confusion for people learning about the Bahá'í Faith is thinking that to be a Bahá'í you have to be completely educated and live out every single principle of the religion but that's not true. If that were the case, I wouldn't be able to join the religion. Back then, I was dealing with different issues. In my group of friends, racism would always come up. I was completely blind to it back then but I see what it is now. Back then, we would play some sport and our group was so ignorant that when playing with people of other races, we made racial and ethnic comments that were obviously picked up from other kids in the group or from their parents. I had no idea what those names meant. If I said to myself, "I'm not perfect in the department of racial unity, so I can't become a Bahá'í," then I wouldn't be able to realize my mistakes. The Bahá'í Faith is not about being perfect and then jumping into it.

Interviewer: If two people are both trying to be good, why will one call himself a Bahá'í while someone else will not?

Houman: One reason is faith. It's understanding what this world is all about. My purpose on this earth is to develop myself spiritually. 'Abdu'l-Bahá said that the purpose of human creation is to develop ourselves spiritually. He compares our development to the child growing in the womb of the mother, the child developing his arms, legs and eyes in order to function in this physical world. In a similar sense, I'm trying to do exactly the same thing by following the Manifestation of God for the day, Bahá'u'lláh: following His principles and trying to develop those spiritual arms, legs and eyes. For example, I'm learning humility before God and love for God's creatures on earth, along with principles such as love, submissiveness and general brotherhood and sisterhood.

Interviewer: If there are all these different Manifestations of God, why do you choose to follow the teachings of Bahá'u'lláh?

Houman: It's been prophesied in other religions that this Prophet was going to come. The principles Bahá'u'lláh taught, such as racial unity and the equality of men and women—when you actually put them into practice, they stand out. When you're involved with the principles, they make sense. These things made my heart want to join this Faith and be involved in a process in which I'm helping others, giving a solution to others, being involved in discussions and struggles with others, in order to realize these principles.

Interviewer: So on one level, it just feels like this is right. On another level, Bahá'u'lláh's principles and teachings directly relate to the state of the world today.

Houman: Exactly. There's also trust and faith. I might die soon, or not so soon, but why take the risk of going astray and following the way everything else is going right now when there's eternity waiting for me?

Interviewer: What problem are you working on in particular?

Houman: Race and the equality of men and women are two issues I've learned a lot more about recently. I'm becoming more aware of situations where racism is completely clear or very subtle. Situations where the equality of men and women is just completely not there. Those are the two key things that are directly involved in my life right now.

Interviewer: In our society, there are fundamental problems. You probably have an awareness of certain obstacles and challenges that young people are dealing with.

Houman: Carrying out the principle of the equality of men and women, associating with other males, seeing the treatment of women in particular—I can't describe this in a couple of sentences. It's elaborate but in general it's a pain that men have to feel. I won't say every single man because we're all different but men can't be so scared that they turn and walk away and get caught up in the male ego, which is so subtle sometimes that we don't realize it's there. We have to be willing to accept the pain that's going on. I can think of examples. I'm not saying I've dealt with this in the right way necessarily but I've learned from it. A couple years ago, I went on trips with the Bahá'í Youth Workshop—we do dances, dramatic pieces and performances about the principles of the Bahá'í Faith, such as racial unity, ending violence, the equality of men and women, diversity and things like that. On our trips the issue of the equality of men and women came up. It was often completely painful because I personally didn't understand what was going on. I think it's time for men to feel the pain that women have been feeling for so many years, the oppression even within daily conversations—the complete dominance of men. There are misunderstandings. A lot of men refuse to accept that women are developing characteristics that have been set aside for so many years. It's a pattern we caught into. I know I get caught up in it all the time, following old patterns of behavior. Especially as males, we are peer-pressured by other males into having that macho style, that dominant, in-control thing, not letting in, being careful not to be submissive to a woman. That atmosphere defines society right now. 'Abdu'l-Bahá talked about mental alertness, intuition and the spiritual qualities of love and service that women have.

Interviewer: Would you say that men also have those qualities?

Houman: I think men have those qualities but women, when given a chance to develop them, are stronger than men in those areas. Males and females have two different complementary purposes. We have to develop our own individual roles on this earth. Women bear children and men should complement that process, for example, in a marriage. There are stereotypical roles for males and females now. For example, women staying at home and cleaning the house, doing the dishes, taking care of the children or doing the laundry and the men going out to do the work and coming back home. Those are some behaviors we have to understand and change if necessary. If the family finds, through consultation and unity, that some of those behaviors are the best way for them to be, then fine, but in general I think they've been oppressive and have held back progress. Change requires an attitude of humility, submissiveness to another source—which is God—and also consultation under all conditions. A person should always trust his or her inner feelings, thereby being true to the self. When we feel that something is wrong or something is right, we can go with that feeling.

42. Recite Ye the Verses: An interview with Mojgan Sami by Kalím Armstrong

At the time of this interview Mojgan Sami was 26 and residing in Haifa, Israel, doing volunteer service at the Bahá'í World Center. She has had a pretty interesting life. At the age of 17 she traveled around India, Japan and Hong Kong. She graduated with honors from high school and college. Mojgan attended

Lewis and Clark College in Oregon where she studied International Law and Middle Eastern Studies. She backpacked across Europe for six months after graduating from college, and then came back to Bellingham, Washington to find a job. She ended up working as a journalist for a television station and she wrote and acted in commercials for an advertising agency. When she was interviewed Mojgan had just finished a two-year master's degree program at Johns Hopkins University, one year of which was earned from study in Bologna, Italy. She is a very bright, talented, and knowledgeable woman.

Kalím: You have been traveling since you were 17. Where have you traveled and what was your motivation?

Mojgan: Actually, I've been traveling since I was born. My parents love to travel—it's hereditary. I have traveled to Asia, Europe, North America and Africa. But I've been traveling in the sense of "independent travel" since the age of 16. My motivations stemmed from whatever event I was traveling to, usually a Bahá'í conference or dedication of a Bahá'í temple. I don't look at traveling as a form of vacation. Traveling teaches you to see with your own eyes and hear with your own ears. The world is your classroom and the people are your professors.

Kalím: How have your travels helped to shape your identity?

Mojgan: Before I traveled I considered myself American or Persian depending on my mood. After I started traveling I started thinking of myself as a Bahá'í. I began to understand that Bahá'u'lláh's world order is truly for every single human being, not for just a select few. Bahá'u'lláh wrote, "It is not for him to pride himself who loveth his own country, but rather for him who loveth the whole world. The earth is but one country and mankind its citizens." Traveling led to my desire to serve the Faith in an international setting. When I say serving in an "international setting" I mean serving the institutions that work

for the progress of humanity through education and awareness—institutions that work for social and economic development, human rights and so forth. This is why I studied international relations and specialized in economics and international
law. I wanted to understand the world environment in order to
apply Bahá'í principles.

Kalím: You must have had some difficult situations in your travels. Can you think of an instance where prayer helped you get
through a sticky situation?

Mojgan: Once I was traveling with three other youth from
Strasbourg, France, to the Czech Republic. We had just attended
a Bahá'í youth conference. The car trip went smoothly until we
hit the border of the Czech Republic and were delayed because
of typical customs stuff. By the time we found a youth hostel,
it was midnight. Youth hostels close around 9:30 at night. We
had nowhere to go—the Bahá'í Center was closed and we
couldn't find anyone. So we all said a prayer. All of a sudden, a
group of about five Czech students—not Bahá'ís—came toward the hostel and stared at us. One of them asked in English,
"Where you from?" We replied, "America, Luxembourg and
France." The Czech students were in awe. Mind you, this was
the first year or so that Eastern Europe had seen any Western-
ers! They were so excited to meet us. One of them asked, "Where
you stay?" We told him the hostel was closed and asked if he
knew of another place we could stay. He said, "We have two
rooms, we give girls one room and boys one room. You stay in
our rooms." Not only did the wonderful students give us their
rooms but they offered us food—apples, which are very difficult to find in Eastern Europe!—and they wouldn't let us pay
them for anything. They kept saying, "You're our guest, you're
our guest." Not only did prayer help us out of a difficult situation but it taught me a lot about generosity and kindness.

Kalím: Are attitudes about prayer different in the countries you have traveled through?

Mojgan: Good question. In Asia I noticed that prayer and meditation are mixed. They are not separated. In Europe people pray in churches. In the Middle East and here in Haifa, everyone prays differently—in churches, mosques, synagogues. Bahá'-u'lláh has changed the way people should pray. For example, the Bahá'í obligatory prayers are meant to be said in private and are between you and God, whereas the Muslim obligatory prayer can be said in public and people say them no matter where they are. Also, being close to the Bahá'í shrines here, I notice how important the "pre-prayer" attitude is. Why do you think all the Bahá'í shrines have beautiful gardens around them? To prepare us for entering a sacred spot and offering our prayers to the Beloved. No other religion in the world takes you through a spiritual journey before entering a place of prayer. This has taught me that no matter where I am, I need time to prepare and detach myself from worldly concerns and vain imaginings in order to pray to God.

Kalím: What does prayer mean to you? Why pray?

Mojgan: We should thank God every day for allowing us the bounty of asking for His assistance. What other form of creation can supplicate its creator? Can a chair ask the carpenter for guidance? Can an animal? No. Humanity has been given the distinct honor of being allowed to pray to God. This is an amazing thing to think about. So prayer is a bounty. Prayer is also a way to seek guidance and offer praise and gratitude.

An interesting aspect of the Bahá'í view of prayer is that you could be praying and not even know it. Work done in the spirit of service is considered worship. So if you are working and your intention is service, whether service to your boss, your editor, your teacher or humanity at large, then you are worshipping

God! 'Abdu'l-Bahá stated, "The man who makes a piece of notepaper to the best of his ability, conscientiously, concentrating all his forces on perfecting it, is giving praise to God."

Bahá'u'lláh states in a Hidden Word that He has given us the earth and everything in it—the only thing that He has kept for Himself is the human heart. However, the only way we can feel the love of God is to purify our hearts. This can only be done through prayer and service. Shoghi Effendi wrote to an individual believer in 1936, "It is not sufficient for a believer merely to accept and observe the teachings. He should, in addition, cultivate the sense of spirituality which he can acquire chiefly by the means of prayer." After all, the goal of the Bahá'í Faith is the development of the individual and society through the acquisition of spiritual virtues. How else can you acquire such things if not through prayer?

Kalím: Can you give an explanation of how prayer and meditation are different?

Mojgan: I love to walk in the Bahá'í gardens surrounding the shrines here in Haifa and read holy scriptures or meditate on a particular passage. The gardens are so peaceful, calm and beautiful. They help me become detached from all my problems and concentrate on the Bahá'í writings. Bahá'ís don't have a particular method of meditating. How you meditate is up to you. Every individual must find his own level of communion with God. Bahá'u'lláh asks us to pray and fast from the age of 15, the age of maturity.

You asked me earlier whether I think praying is a chore. If you love someone, do you want to make him happy? Would it be a chore for you to make him happy? If we want to show our love for God, we must fulfill His commands. Praying is one of those commands. It's interesting to note that Bahá'u'lláh also asks us not to pray TOO MUCH! In the Kitáb-i-Aqdas Bahá'u'lláh states, "Read ye the sacred verses in such measure that ye be not overcome by languor and despondency. Lay not upon your souls that which will weary them and weigh them down, but rather what will lighten and uplift them, so that they may soar on the wings of the Divine verses towards to Dawning-place of His manifest signs."

Kalím: What are the Bahá'í obligatory prayers and what is their purpose?

Mojgan: They are specific prayers revealed by Bahá'u'lláh the recitation of which is binding on Bahá'ís from the age of maturity. We can choose among three different ones and recite them in private. Sometimes I think of praying as something we do for ourselves because we are usually asking for something from God, asking for assistance, guidance and so on. However, reciting our obligatory prayer is something we can do for God because we are acknowledging our humble state in comparison to God's power and might.

Kalím: Do you think youth should go to college before doing a year of service?

Mojgan: I have asked myself this question a million times. I've read that one should ask the question, "Will my education assist me in serving the Cause?" Personally, I thought my education was necessary to my serving the Cause. So I got a master's degree before applying for my year of service. But you know what? The service I'm involved in here at the Bahá'í World Center has nothing to do with my studies. This doesn't mean that I studied for nothing. What it's taught me is that serving the Cause has nothing to do with how we want to serve it but, rather, it has to do with how the Cause needs to be served. If you are dealing with this question, you have to pray and pray for guidance. Another thought: who says you can't serve and study at the same time? Of course, there is a balance in all things. Shoghi

Effendi, in a letter written on his behalf, stated that a "good Bahá'í" is "one who so arranges his life as to devote time both to his material needs and also to the service of the Cause."

Kalím: What kind of work are you doing at the Bahá'í World Center?

Mojgan: It would best be described as a photo historian. I am assisting the Audio-Visual Department in the identification and cataloguing of historical photographs. It's the most amazing job in the world. The history of the Bahá'í Faith comes to life in front of my eyes and affords me the opportunity to study the life of early believers.

Kalím: Where and what did you study?

Mojgan: I did my undergraduate degree at Lewis and Clark College in Portland, Oregon, where I majored in International Relations and minored in Middle Eastern Studies. My graduate degree was at Johns Hopkins University School of Advanced International Studies. Since I wanted to learn about the world system and international economics, I chose international relations and international economics as my areas of concentration. It is important to study the Bahá'í writings but one should also study the prevailing non-Bahá'í intellectual theories in order to learn to convey the Bahá'í ideas so others will understand them.

Kalím: Why did you decide to study Middle Eastern Studies?

Mojgan: Mainly to study the region of the world which was first impacted by the coming of Bahá'u'lláh.

Kalím: Living at the Bahá'í World Center, surrounded by people who are serving the Cause of Bahá'u'lláh, an environment where prayer is daily sustenance for all, how is the vibe different? Can you feel the power of prayer and see its results?

Mojgan: Actually, I was talking to my friends about this. There is a "vibe" here, as you call it, that is unexplainable. No matter what you think of, it happens. It's not because we're praying for something in the Holy Land that it happens; it's because being in the Holy Land, we pray for the right things. So they happen. Does that make sense? Bahá'u'lláh says to know thyself. Serving in the Holy Land makes me very aware of my actions and duties to God, so I begin to know myself. And as I know myself better and better, I realize that there are things I need to work on—patience, humility, kindness. So I pray for those things and then I'm tested. If I want patience, I get tested until I develop patience. Tests are a part of prayer.

4

Education and a Life of Service

Transforming Humanity through Education

1. Man is the supreme Talisman. Lack of a proper education hath, however, deprived him of that which he doth inherently possess. Through a word proceeding out of the mouth of God he was called into being; by one word more he was guided to recognize the Source of his education; by yet another word his station and destiny were safeguarded. The Great Being saith: Regard man as a mine rich in gems of inestimable value. Education can, alone, cause it to reveal its treasures, and enable mankind to benefit therefrom.

Bahá'u'lláh

2. Man is said to be the greatest representative of God, and he is the Book of Creation because all the mysteries of beings exist in him. If he comes under the shadow of the True Educator and is rightly trained, he becomes the essence of essences, the light of lights, the spirit of spirits; he becomes the center of the divine appearances, the source of spiritual qualities, the rising-place of heavenly lights, and the receptacle of divine inspirations. If he is deprived of this education, he becomes the

manifestation of satanic qualities, the sum of animal vices, and the source of all dark conditions.

'Abdu'l-Bahá

3. Education is of three kinds: material, human and spiritual. Material education is concerned with the progress and development of the body, through gaining its sustenance, its material comfort and ease. This education is common to animals and man.

Human education signifies civilization and progress—that is to say, government, administration, charitable works, trades, arts and handicrafts, sciences, great inventions and discoveries and elaborate institutions, which are the activities essential to man as distinguished from the animal.

Divine education is that of the Kingdom of God: it consists in acquiring divine perfections, and this is true education; for in this state man becomes the focus of divine blessings, the manifestation of the words, "Let Us make man in Our image, and after Our likeness."* This is the goal of the world of humanity.

'Abdu'l-Bahá

Combining Spiritual Education with Human Education

4. The spiritually learned are lamps of guidance among the nations, and stars of good fortune shining from the horizons of humankind. They are fountains of life for such as lie in the death of ignorance and unawareness, and clear springs of perfections for those who thirst and wander in the wasteland of

---

* Cf. Gen. 1:26.

their defects and errors. They are the dawning places of the emblems of Divine Unity and initiates in the mysteries of the glorious Qur'án. They are skilled physicians for the ailing body of the world, they are the sure antidote to the poison that has corrupted human society. It is they who are the strong citadel guarding humanity, and the impregnable sanctuary for the sorely distressed, the anxious and tormented, victims of ignorance. "Knowledge is a light which God casteth into the heart of whomsoever He willeth."

'Abdu'l-Bahá

5. O ye young Bahá'í children. . . . Ye must . . . put forth a mighty effort, striving by night and day and resting not for a moment, to acquire an abundant share of all the sciences and arts, that the Divine Image, which shineth out from the Sun of Truth, may illumine the mirror of the hearts of men.

It is the longing desire of 'Abdu'l-Bahá to see each one of you accounted as the foremost professor in the academies, and in the school of inner significances, each one becoming a leader in wisdom.

'Abdu'l-Bahá

6. It is incumbent upon Bahá'í children to surpass other children in the acquisition of sciences and arts, for they have been cradled in the grace of God.

Whatever other children learn in a year, let Bahá'í children learn in a month. The heart of 'Abdu'l-Bahá longeth, in its love, to find that Bahá'í young people, each and all, are known throughout the world for their intellectual attainments. There is no question but that they will exert all their efforts, their energies, their sense of pride, to acquire the sciences and arts.

'Abdu'l-Bahá

7. I hope that thou mayest be protected and assisted under the providence of the True One, be occupied always in mentioning the Lord and display effort to complete thy profession. Thou must endeavor greatly so that thou mayest become unique in thy profession and famous in those parts, because attaining perfection in one's profession in this merciful period is considered to be worship of God. And whilst thou art occupied with thy profession, thou canst remember the True One.

'Abdu'l-Bahá

8. Being a Bahá'í you are certainly aware of the fact that Bahá'u'lláh considered education as one of the most fundamental factors of a true civilization. This education, however, in order to be adequate and fruitful, should be comprehensive in nature and should take into consideration not only the physical and intellectual side of man but also his spiritual and ethical aspects. This should be the program of the Bahá'í youth all over the world.

And no doubt the best means through which this educational development can be attained is by joining the different associations and gatherings which intend to promote the ideals of this new international civilization. Although the Guardian prefers that Bahá'ís should join those associations which are within the orbit of Bahá'í activities, he nevertheless approves and even encourages any person who would like to join any non-Bahá'í movements, provided that these movements will not promote any ideal or principle which will harm and check the advance of the Cause.

On behalf of Shoghi Effendi

9. If the Bahá'ís want to be really effective in teaching the Cause they need to be much better informed and able to discuss intelligently, intellectually, the present condition of the world and its problems. We need Bahá'í scholars, not only people far, far

more deeply aware of what our teachings really are, but also well read and well educated people, capable of correlating our teachings to the current thoughts of the leaders of society.

We Bahá'ís should, in other words, arm our minds with knowledge in order to better demonstrate to, especially, the educated classes, the truths enshrined in our Faith.

On behalf of Shoghi Effendi

10. Young men and women in the Faith must be deep and thoughtful scholars of its teachings, so that they can teach in a way that will convince people that all the problems facing them have a remedy. They must grasp the Administration, so that they can wisely and efficiently administer the ever-growing affairs of the Cause; and they must exemplify the Bahá'í way of living. All this is not easy—but the Guardian is always encouraged to see the spirit animating such young believers as yourself. He has high hopes of what your generation will accomplish.

On behalf of Shoghi Effendi

11. The Universal House of Justice . . . regards Bahá'í scholarship as of great potential importance for the development and con-solidation of the Bahá'í community as it emerges from obscurity.

On behalf of the Universal House of Justice

Attaining Spiritual Knowledge

12. With fixed and steady gaze, born of the unerring eye of God, scan for a while the horizon of divine knowledge, and contemplate those words of perfection which the Eternal hath revealed, that haply the mysteries of divine wisdom, hidden ere now beneath the veil of glory and treasured within the taber-nacle of His grace, may be made manifest unto you.

Bahá'u'lláh

13. It is my hope that you may put forth your most earnest endeavor to accomplish this end, that you may investigate and study the Holy Scriptures word by word so that you may attain knowledge of the mysteries hidden therein. Be not satisfied with words, but seek to understand the spiritual meanings hidden in the heart of the words.

Abdu'l-Bahá

14. God has given man the eye of investigation by which he may see and recognize truth. He has endowed man with ears that he may hear the message of reality and conferred upon him the gift of reason by which he may discover things for himself. This is his endowment and equipment for the investigation of reality. Man is not intended to see through the eyes of another, hear through another's ears nor comprehend with another's brain. Each human creature has individual endowment, power and responsibility in the creative plan of God. Therefore, depend upon your own reason and judgment and adhere to the outcome of your own investigation; otherwise, you will be utterly submerged in the sea of ignorance and deprived of all the bounties of God. Turn to God, supplicate humbly at His threshold, seeking assistance and confirmation, that God may rend asunder the veils that obscure your vision. Then will your eyes be filled with illumination, face to face you will behold the reality of God and your heart become completely purified from the dross of ignorance, reflecting the glories and bounties of the Kingdom.

Abdu'l-Bahá

15. I strongly urge you to devote, while you are pursuing your studies, as much time as you possibly can to a thorough study of the history and Teachings of our Beloved Cause. This is the prerequisite of a future successful career of service to the Bahá'í

Faith in which I hope and pray you will distinguish yourself in the days to come.

Shoghi Effendi

16. To deepen in the Cause means to read the writings of Bahá'u'lláh and the Master so thoroughly as to be able to give it to others in its pure form. There are many who have some superficial idea of what the Cause stands for. They, therefore, present it together with all sorts of ideas that are their own. As the Cause is still in its early days we must be most careful lest we fall into this error and injure the Movement we so much adore. There is no limit to the study of the Cause. The more we read the Writings, the more truths we can find in them, the more we will see that our previous notions were erroneous.

Shoghi Effendi

17. It is his fervent hope and his heart's ardent prayer that you may increasingly deepen in your faith, and steadily gain in your understanding and appreciation of the Teachings, and display such earnestness and perseverance in your Bahá'í studies as to gradually acquire the full knowledge, training and experience necessary for active and effective service to the Faith in the future.

Although still young in age, you should endeavor from now, through close association with your fellow-believers, and through your faithful application to your Bahá'í studies, to prepare yourself for that day when you will be called upon, as a grown-up and responsible member of the Community, to take full part in the activities of the Cause, and thus prove yourself worthy of being a member of this world-wide Fellowship created by Bahá'u'lláh.

The Guardian was truly pleased to note that you have already started reading some Bahá'í books, and would specially advise you to endeavor [to] commit to memory certain passages from the Writings of Bahá'u'lláh, and in particular, some of His prayers. This training would undoubtedly be of tremendous help to you in your future studies of the Cause, and would also serve to considerably deepen and enrich your own spiritual life at present.

On behalf of Shoghi Effendi

18. The foundation of all their [young Bahá'ís'] other accomplishments is their study of the teachings, the spiritualization of their lives and the forming of their characters in accordance with the standards of Bahá'u'lláh. As the moral standards of the people around us collapse and decay, whether of the centuries-old civilizations of the East, the more recent cultures of Christendom and Islám, or of the rapidly changing tribal societies of the world, the Bahá'ís must increasingly stand out as pillars of righteousness and forbearance. The life of a Bahá'í will be characterized by truthfulness and decency; he will walk uprightly among his fellowmen, dependent upon none save God, yet linked by bonds of love and brotherhood with all mankind; he will be entirely detached from the loose standards, the decadent theories, the frenetic experimentation, the desperation of present-day society, will look upon his neighbors with a bright and friendly face and be a beacon light and a haven for all those who would emulate his strength of character and assurance of soul.

The Universal House of Justice

Studying the Bahá'í Writings

19. It behooveth us one and all to recite day and night both the Persian and Arabic Hidden Words, to pray fervently and sup-

plicate tearfully that we may be enabled to conduct ourselves in accordance with these divine counsels. These holy Words have not been revealed to be heard but to be practiced.

'Abdu'l-Bahá

20. He is indeed pleased to know that the book of "Prayers and Meditations by Bahá'u'lláh" has been out in time to enable the friends to read it during the Fast, and he has every hope that the perusal of such a precious volume will help to deepen, *more than any other publication*, the spirit of devotion and faith in the friends, and thus charge them with all the spiritual power they require for the accomplishment of their tremendous duties towards the Cause.

On behalf of Shoghi Effendi

21. He is particularly pleased to realize that the book of *Gleanings* is of such a tremendous inspiration to the Bahá'í youth, and that they all are making a careful study of its contents with the view of preparing themselves for proper teaching work. His hope is that this volume will enable them to gain a fuller consciousness of their functions and responsibilities, and to arise and set the example before the rest of the believers, not only in the field of teaching, but in all the other fields of Bahá'í activity as well. He is ardently supplicating Bahá'u'lláh on your behalf, and on behalf of the whole body of young Bahá'ís throughout the States, and especially the National Youth Committee, that you may be given the inspiration, knowledge and guidance to press forward to efficient and loyal service.

On behalf of Shoghi Effendi

22. Some of the younger believers, from letters and reports received here, seem to lack a firm grounding on such matters as

the Will and Testament and the deeper spiritual teachings of the Faith. Whenever the grasp of these fundamentals is weak, the friends are almost sure to pay undue attention to secondary procedures, to quibble over details, to lose themselves in personalities, and to founder in a sea of unnecessary inharmony. This has nothing to do with their devotion, their loyalty, their zeal, their eagerness to serve. It is merely a question of not having received, perhaps through lack of sufficient teachers to carry on the all-important work of deepening the friends in their own faith, a strong enough education in the Covenant before the duties and responsibilities of the Administrative Order were thrust upon them.

On behalf of Shoghi Effendi

23. The Guardian would advise that in their studies of the Will and Testament the young believers should use the "Dispensation," which will undoubtedly help them considerably to grasp the full implications of that sacred and historic Document which he has described as the "Charter of the New World Order."

On behalf of Shoghi Effendi

24. He fully approves the idea of holding study classes, for the deeper the friends go in their understanding of their teachings the more firm and steadfast they will become and the more unwavering in their support of the institutions of the Faith. Books such as the "Íqán," "Some Answered Questions" and "The Dawn-Breakers" should be mastered by every Bahá'í. They should read these books over and over again. The first two books will reveal to them the significance of this divine revelation as well as the unity of all the Prophets of old. The last book will show how the Faith was ushered into the world and how its early adherents heroically faced martyrdom and suffering in their

desire to establish the Cause throughout the world. Knowing the life of those heroes will create in us the urge to follow their footsteps and achieve the same.

On behalf of Shoghi Effendi

25. Shoghi Effendi undertook the translation of *The Dawn-Breakers* only after being convinced that its publication will arouse the friends to greater self-sacrifice and a more determined way of teaching. Otherwise he would not have devoted so much time to it.

On behalf of Shoghi Effendi

26. The Guardian feels that a sound knowledge of history, including religious history, and also of social and economic subjects, is of great help in teaching the Cause to intelligent people; as to what subjects within the Faith you should concentrate on he feels that the young Bahá'ís should gain a mastery of such books as the *Gleanings*, the *Dawn-Breakers*, *God Passes By*, the Íqán, *Some Answered Questions* and the more important Tablets. All aspects of the Faith should be deeply studied.

On behalf of Shoghi Effendi

Acquiring Human Knowledge

27. Look at the world and ponder a while upon it. It unveileth the book of its own self before thine eyes and revealeth that which the Pen of thy Lord, the Fashioner, the All-Informed, hath inscribed therein. It will acquaint thee with that which is within it and upon it and will give thee such clear explanations as to make thee independent of every eloquent expounder.

Bahá'u'lláh

28. All blessings are divine in origin, but none can be compared with this power of intellectual investigation and research, which is an eternal gift producing fruits of unending delight. . . . Therefore, you should put forward your most earnest efforts toward the acquisition of science and arts. The greater your attainment, the higher your standard in the divine purpose. The man of science is perceiving and endowed with vision, whereas he who is ignorant and neglectful of this development is blind. The investigating mind is attentive, alive; the callous and indifferent mind is deaf and dead. A scientific man is a true index and representative of humanity, for through processes of inductive reasoning and research he is informed of all that appertains to humanity, its status, conditions and happenings. He studies the human body politic, understands social problems and weaves the web and texture of civilization. In fact, science may be likened to a mirror wherein the infinite forms and images of existing things are revealed and reflected. It is the very foundation of all individual and national development. Without this basis of investigation, development is impossible. Therefore, seek with diligent endeavor the knowledge and attainment of all that lies within the power of this wonderful bestowal.

'Abdu'l-Bahá

29. Consider carefully: all these highly varied phenomena, these concepts, this knowledge, these technical procedures and philosophical systems, these sciences, arts, industries and inventions—all are emanations of the human mind. Whatever people has ventured deeper into this shoreless sea, has come to excel the rest. The happiness and pride of a nation consist in this, that it should shine out like the sun in the high heaven of knowledge. . . . And the honor and distinction of the individual consist in this, that he among all the world's multitudes should become a source of social good. Is any larger bounty conceiv-

able than this, that an individual, looking within himself, should find that by the confirming grace of God he has become the cause of peace and well-being, of happiness and advantage to his fellow men? No, by the one true God, there is no greater bliss, no more complete delight.

'Abdu'l-Bahá

Studying Disciplines That Will Benefit Humanity

30. Knowledge is as wings to man's life, and a ladder for his ascent. Its acquisition is incumbent upon everyone. The knowledge of such sciences, however, should be acquired as can profit the peoples of the earth, and not those which begin with words and end with words. Great indeed is the claim of scientists and craftsmen on the peoples of the world. . . . In truth, knowledge is a veritable treasure for man, and a source of glory, of bounty, of joy, of exaltation, of cheer and gladness unto him.

Bahá'u'lláh

31. O My Servant! The best of men are they that earn a livelihood by their calling and spend upon themselves and upon their kindred for the love of God, the Lord of all worlds.

Bahá'u'lláh

32. It is enjoined upon every one of you to engage in some form of occupation, such as crafts, trades and the like. We have graciously exalted your engagement in such work to the rank of worship unto God, the True One.

Bahá'u'lláh

33. I hope that you will use *your* understanding to promote the unity and tranquillity of mankind, to give enlightenment and

civilization to the people, to produce love in all around you, and to bring about the universal peace.

Study the sciences, acquire more and more knowledge. Assuredly one may learn to the end of one's life! Use your knowledge always for the benefit of others; so may war cease on the face of this beautiful earth, and a glorious edifice of peace and concord be raised. Strive that your high ideals may be realized in the Kingdom of God on earth, as they will be in Heaven.

'Abdu'l-Bahá

34. The individual should, prior to engaging in the study of any subject, ask himself what its uses are and what fruit and result will derive from it. If it is a useful branch of knowledge, that is, if society will gain important benefits from it, then he should certainly pursue it with all his heart. If not, if it consists in empty, profitless debates and in a vain concatenation of imaginings that lead to no result except acrimony, why devote one's life to such useless hairsplittings and disputes.

'Abdu'l-Bahá

35. Thy letter was received. Praise be to God it imparted the good news of thy health and safety and indicated that thou art ready to enter an agricultural school. This is highly suitable. Strive as much as possible to become proficient in the science of agriculture, for in accordance with the divine teachings the acquisition of sciences and the perfection of arts are considered acts of worship. If a man engageth with all his power in the acquisition of a science or in the perfection of an art, it is as if he has been worshiping God in churches and temples. Thus as thou enterest a school of agriculture and strivest in the acquisition of that science thou art day and night engaged in acts of worship—acts that are accepted at the threshold of the Al-

mighty. What bounty greater than this that science should be considered as an act of worship and art as service to the Kingdom of God.

'Abdu'l-Bahá

36. The Guardian . . . was gratified to learn of the progress of your academic studies, and of your future plans for the study and the teaching of the Cause. The spirit which is moving and sustaining you in the service of the Faith is, indeed, remarkable, and through it you will undoubtedly be moved to render great and imperishable services to the Cause of Bahá'u'lláh. The university training which you are receiving at present will be of immense help to you in your efforts to present the Message in intellectual circles. In these days when people are so skeptical about religion and look with so much contempt towards religious organizations and movements, there seems to be more need than ever for our young Bahá'ís to be well equipped intellectually, so that they may be in a position to present the Message in a befitting way, and in a manner that would convince every unbiased observer of the effectiveness and power of the Teachings.

In view of that Shoghi Effendi would urge you to persevere in your studies, and trusts that as a result you will be greatly assisted in your teaching activities.

On behalf of Shoghi Effendi

37. It is the duty of the children to acquire knowledge of the arts and sciences and to learn a trade or a profession whereby they, in turn, can earn their living and support their families. This, for a Bahá'í youth, is in itself a service to God, a service, moreover, which can be combined with teaching the Faith and often with pioneering. The Bahá'í community will need men

and women of many skills and qualifications; for, as it grows in size the sphere of its activities in the life of society will increase and diversify. Let Bahá'í youth, therefore, consider the best ways in which they can use and develop their native abilities for the service of mankind and the Cause of God, whether this be as farmers, teachers, doctors, artisans, musicians, or any one of the multitude of livelihoods that are open to them.

The Universal House of Justice

Suggestions for Studying Specific Courses

38. The first attribute of perfection is learning and the cultural attainments of the mind, and this eminent station is achieved when the individual combines in himself a thorough knowledge of those complex and transcendental realities pertaining to God, of the fundamental truths of Qur'ánic political and religious law, of the contents of the sacred Scriptures of other faiths, and of those regulations and procedures which would contribute to the progress and civilization of this distinguished country. He should in addition be informed as to the laws and principles, the customs, conditions and manners, and the material and moral virtues characterizing the statecraft of other nations, and should be well versed in all the useful branches of learning of the day, and study the historical records of bygone governments and peoples. For if a learned individual has no knowledge of the sacred Scriptures and the entire field of divine and natural science, of religious jurisprudence and the arts of government and the varied learning of the time and the great events of history, he might prove unequal to an emergency, and this is inconsistent with the necessary qualification of comprehensive knowledge.

'Abdu'l-Bahá

39. I hope thou wilt acquire great proficiency in writing literature, composition, eloquence of tongue and fluency of speech, . . . becoming an esteemed servant in the Threshold of Oneness and partaking of a share of the heavenly gifts, and progressing day by day until thou attain to the apex of the excellencies of this human world.

'Abdu'l-Bahá

40. Public speaking is undoubtedly very important for a person who desires to teach, but this should be learned in schools and classes especially arranged for such training. We should not permit an inferior presentation of the Cause to the public for the sole reason that we desire to learn to do it better in the future. The youth should be encouraged to train themselves in public speaking while they are still pursuing their studies in schools or colleges.

Shoghi Effendi

41. Philosophy, as you will study it and later teach it, is certainly not one of the sciences that begins and ends in words. Fruitless excursions into metaphysical hairsplitting is meant, not a sound branch of learning like philosophy. . . .

As regards your own studies: he would advise you not to devote too much of your time to the abstract side of philosophy, but rather to approach it from a more historical angle. As to correlating philosophy with the Bahá'í teaching; this is a tremendous work which scholars in the future can undertake. We must remember that not only are all the teachings not yet translated into English, but they are not even all collected yet. Many important Tablets may still come to light which are at present owned privately.

Shoghi Effendi

42. Concerning what studies you should specialize in with a view to teaching in the future: He would suggest either History, Economics or Sociology, as these are not only fields in which Bahá'ís take a great interest but also cover subjects which our teachings cast an entirely new light upon.

On behalf of Shoghi Effendi

43. We had heard through various channels the wonderful way your children had grown to speak about the Cause in public. Shoghi Effendi's hope is that they will, the three of them, become able and devoted speakers on the Cause and subjects akin to it. To do this properly they will need a firm foundation of scientific and literary training which fortunately they are obtaining. It is just as important for the Bahá'í young boys and girls to become properly educated in colleges of high standing as it is to be spiritually developed. The mental as well as the spiritual side of the youth has to be developed before he can serve the Cause efficiently.

On behalf of Shoghi Effendi

44. When deciding what course of training to follow, youth can consider acquiring those skills and professions that will be of benefit in education, rural development, agriculture, economics, technology, health, radio and in many other areas of endeavor that are so urgently needed in the developing countries of the world. You can also devote time in the midst of your studies, or other activities, to travel teaching or service projects in the Third World.

The Universal House of Justice

STUDYING THE ARTS

45. The purpose of learning should be the promotion of the welfare of the people, and this can be achieved through crafts.

It hath been revealed and is now repeated that the true worth of artists and craftsmen should be appreciated, for they advance the affairs of mankind. Just as the foundations of religion are made firm through the Law of God, the means of livelihood depend upon those who are engaged in arts and crafts. True learning is that which is conducive to the well-being of the world, not to pride and self-conceit, or to tyranny, violence and pillage.

Bahá'u'lláh

46. The art of music must be brought to the highest stage of development, for this is one of the most wonderful arts and in this glorious age of the Lord of Unity it is highly essential to gain its mastery. However, one must endeavour to attain the degree of artistic perfection and not be like those who leave matters unfinished.

'Abdu'l-Bahá

47. Wherefore, O loved ones of God! Make ye a mighty effort till you yourselves betoken this advancement and all these confirmations, and become focal centers of God's blessings, daysprings of the light of His unity, promoters of the gifts and graces of civilized life. Be ye in that land vanguards of the perfections of humankind; carry forward the various branches of knowledge, be active and progressive in the field of inventions and the arts. Endeavor to rectify the conduct of men, and seek to excel the whole world in moral character. While the children are yet in their infancy feed them from the breast of heavenly grace, foster them in the cradle of all excellence, rear them in the embrace of bounty. Give them the advantage of every useful kind of knowledge. Let them share in every new and rare and wondrous craft and art.

'Abdu'l-Bahá

48. He sincerely hopes that as the Cause grows and talented persons come under its banner, they will begin to produce in art the divine spirit that animates their soul. Every religion has brought with it some form of art—let us see what wonders this Cause is going to bring along. Such a glorious spirit should also give vent to a glorious art. The Temple with all its beauty is only the first ray of an early dawn; even more wondrous things are to be achieved in the future.

On behalf of Shoghi Effendi

49. He wishes to start a new section in "The Bahá'í World" devoted wholly to poems written by Bahá'ís. Though it may be a humble beginning it is a start for great future achievements. Shoghi Effendi wishes thereby to encourage those who are talented to give expression to the wonderful spirit that animates them. We need poets and writers for the Cause and this is undoubtedly one good way to urge them on. Some of the poems are written by very youthful persons yet they ring so true and give expression to such thoughts that one should halt and admire. In Persia the Cause has given birth to poets that even non-Bahá'ís consider as great. We hope before long we will have similar persons arise in the West.

On behalf of Shoghi Effendi

Balancing Human and Spiritual Education

50. In this great dispensation, art (or a profession) is identical with an act of worship and this is a clear text of the Blessed Perfection. Therefore, extreme effort should be made in art and this will not prevent the teaching of the people in that region. Nay, rather, each should assist the other in art and guidance. For instance, when the studying of art is with the intention of

obeying the command of God this study will certainly be done easily and great progress will soon be made therein; and when others discover this fragrance of spirituality in the action itself, this same will cause their awakening. Likewise, managing art with propriety will become the means of sociability and affinity; and sociability and affinity themselves tend to guide others to the Truth.

'Abdu'l-Bahá

51. O thou true friend! Read, in the school of God, the lessons of the spirit, and learn from love's Teacher the innermost truths. Seek out the secrets of Heaven, and tell of the overflowing grace and favor of God.

Although to acquire the sciences and arts is the greatest glory of mankind, this is so only on condition that man's river flow into the mighty sea, and draw from God's ancient source His inspiration. When this cometh to pass, then every teacher is as a shoreless ocean, every pupil a prodigal fountain of knowledge. If, then, the pursuit of knowledge lead to the beauty of Him who is the Object of all Knowledge, how excellent that goal; but if not, a mere drop will perhaps shut a man off from flooding grace, for with learning cometh arrogance and pride, and it bringeth on error and indifference to God.

The sciences of today are bridges to reality; if then they lead not to reality, naught remains but fruitless illusion. By the one true God! If learning be not a means of access to Him, the Most Manifest, it is nothing but evident loss.

It is incumbent upon thee to acquire the various branches of knowledge, and to turn thy face toward the beauty of the Manifest Beauty, that thou mayest be a sign of saving guidance amongst the peoples of the world, and a focal center of understanding in this sphere from which the wise and their wisdom are shut out, except for those who set foot in the Kingdom of lights and become informed of the veiled and hidden mystery, the well-guarded secret.

'Abdu'l-Bahá

52. Concerning the course of study you may follow: Shoghi Effendi prefers you to find what subject you like most and for which you are best fitted. . . . The Cause is such that we can serve it no matter what our profession may be. The only necessity is that we be spiritually minded and not be guided by purely material considerations. We should also not let our studies detain us from deepening our knowledge of the literature of the Cause.

On behalf of Shoghi Effendi

53. The Guardian hopes that along with whatever other studies you take up, you will continually study the teachings and endeavor to acquire a profound knowledge of them. The importance of young Bahá'ís becoming thoroughly steeped in every branch of the teachings cannot be overemphasized, as they have great teaching tasks ahead of them to accomplish.

On behalf of Shoghi Effendi

5

Teaching

Teaching by Word and Example

TALKING ABOUT THE FAITH

1. How vast is the tabernacle of the Cause of God! It hath overshadowed all the peoples and kindreds of the earth, and will, erelong, gather together the whole of mankind beneath its shelter. Thy day of service is now come. Countless Tablets bear the testimony of the bounties vouchsafed unto thee. Arise for the triumph of My Cause, and, through the power of thine utterance, subdue the hearts of men. Thou must show forth that which will ensure the peace and the well-being of the miserable and the downtrodden. Gird up the loins of thine endeavor, that perchance thou mayest release the captive from his chains, and enable him to attain unto true liberty.

Bahá'u'lláh

2. Say: Teach ye the Cause of God, O people of Bahá, for God hath prescribed unto every one the duty of proclaiming His Message, and regardeth it as the most meritorious of all deeds. Such a deed is acceptable only when he that teacheth the Cause

is already a firm believer in God, the Supreme Protector, the Gracious, the Almighty.

Bahá'u'lláh

3. O ye beloved of God! Repose not yourselves on your couches, nay bestir yourselves as soon as ye recognize your Lord, the Creator, and hear of the things which have befallen Him, and hasten to His assistance. Unloose your tongues, and proclaim unceasingly His Cause. This shall be better for you than all the treasures of the past and of the future, if ye be of them that comprehend this truth.

Bahá'u'lláh

4. The Faith of the Blessed Beauty is summoning mankind to safety and love, to amity and peace; it hath raised up its tabernacle on the heights of the earth, and directeth its call to all nations. Wherefore, O ye who are God's lovers, know ye the value of this precious Faith, obey its teachings, walk in this road that is drawn straight, and show ye this way to the people. Lift up your voices and sing out the song of the Kingdom. Spread far and wide the precepts and counsels of the loving Lord, so that this world will change into another world, and this darksome earth will be flooded with light, and the dead body of mankind will arise and live; so that every soul will ask for immortality, through the holy breaths of God.

'Abdu'l-Bahá

5. Rest assured that the breathings of the Holy Spirit will loosen thy tongue. Speak, therefore; speak out with great courage at every meeting. When thou art about to begin thine address, turn first to Bahá'u'lláh, and ask for the confirmations of the

Holy Spirit, then open thy lips and say whatever is suggested to thy heart; this, however, with the utmost courage, dignity and conviction.

'Abdu'l-Bahá

6. It is at such times that the friends of God avail themselves of the occasion, seize the opportunity, rush forth and win the prize. If their task is to be confined to good conduct and advice, nothing will be accomplished. They must speak out, expound the proofs, set forth clear arguments, draw irrefutable conclusions establishing the truth of the manifestation of the Sun of Reality.

'Abdu'l-Bahá

7. To teach the Cause of God, to proclaim its truths, to defend its interests, to demonstrate, by words as well as by deeds, its indispensability, its potency, and universality, should at no time be regarded as the exclusive concern or sole privilege of Bahá'í administrative institutions, be they Assemblies, or committees. All must participate, however humble their origin, however limited their experience, however restricted their means, however deficient their education, however pressing their cares and preoccupations, however unfavorable the environment in which they live.

Shoghi Effendi

8. The individual alone must . . . consult his conscience, prayerfully consider all its aspects, manfully struggle against the natural inertia that weighs him down in his effort to arise, shed, heroically and irrevocably, the trivial and superfluous attachments which hold him back, empty himself of every thought that may tend to obstruct his path, mix, in obedience to the counsels of the Author of His Faith, and in imitation of the One Who is its true Exemplar, with men and women, in all walks of

life, seek to touch their hearts, through the distinction which characterizes his thoughts, his words and his acts, and win them over tactfully, lovingly, prayerfully and persistently, to the Faith he himself has espoused.

Shoghi Effendi

9. Every individual believer—man, woman, youth and child—is summoned to this field of action; for it is on the initiative, the resolute will of the individual to teach and to serve, that the success of the entire community depends. Well-grounded in the mighty Covenant of Bahá'u'lláh, sustained by daily prayer and reading of the Holy Word, strengthened by a continual striving to obtain a deeper understanding of the divine Teachings, illumined by a constant endeavor to relate these Teachings to current issues, nourished by observance of the laws and principles of His wondrous World Order, every individual can attain increasing measures of success in teaching. In sum, the ultimate triumph of the Cause is assured by that "one thing and only one thing" so poignantly emphasized by Shoghi Effendi, namely, "the extent to which our own inner life and private character mirror forth in their manifold aspects the splendor of those eternal principles proclaimed by Bahá'u'lláh."

The Universal House of Justice

BEING AN EXAMPLE

10. O people of God! Do not busy yourselves in your own concerns; let your thoughts be fixed upon that which will rehabilitate the fortunes of mankind and sanctify the hearts and souls of men. This can best be achieved through pure and holy deeds, through a virtuous life and a goodly behavior. Valiant acts will ensure the triumph of this Cause, and a saintly charac-

ter will reinforce its power. Cleave unto righteousness, O people of Bahá! This, verily, is the commandment which this wronged One hath given unto you, and the first choice of His unrestrained Will for every one of you.

Bahá'u'lláh

11. Beware, O people of Bahá, lest ye walk in the ways of them whose words differ from their deeds. Strive that ye may be enabled to manifest to the peoples of the earth the signs of God, and to mirror forth His commandments. Let your acts be a guide unto all mankind, for the professions of most men, be they high or low, differ from their conduct. It is through your deeds that ye can distinguish yourselves from others. Through them the brightness of your light can be shed upon the whole earth. Happy is the man that heedeth My counsel, and keepeth the precepts prescribed by Him Who is the All-Knowing, the All-Wise.

Bahá'u'lláh

12. The Faith of God must be propagated through human perfections, through qualities that are excellent and pleasing, and spiritual behavior. If a soul of his own accord advances toward God he will be accepted at the Threshold of Oneness, for such a one is free of personal considerations, of greed and selfish interests, and he has taken refuge within the sheltering protection of his Lord. He will become known among men as trustworthy and truthful, temperate and scrupulous, high-minded and loyal, incorruptible and God-fearing. In this way the primary purpose in revealing the Divine Law—which is to bring about happiness in the after life and civilization and the refinement of character in this—will be realized.

'Abdu'l-Bahá

13. Is there any deed in the world that would be nobler than service to the common good? Is there any greater blessing conceivable for a man, than that he should become the cause of the education, the development, the prosperity and honor of his fellow-creatures? No, by the Lord God! The highest righteousness of all is for blessed souls to take hold of the hands of the helpless and deliver them out of their ignorance and abasement and poverty, and with pure motives, and only for the sake of God, to arise and energetically devote themselves to the service of the masses, forgetting their own worldly advantage and working only to serve the general good.

'Abdu'l-Bahá

14. The work in which you are engaged is dear and near to my heart and constitutes one of the most vital aspects of the manifold activities of our beloved Faith. The highest standards of purity, of integrity, of detachment and sacrifice must be maintained by the members of your group in order to enable you to play a decisive part in the spread and consolidation of the Faith. A tremendous responsibility has been laid upon you, and nothing short of a pure, a virtuous, an active and truly exemplary life can enable you to fulfill your high destiny. I will pray that you may be guided and strengthened to render the most effective service to the Cause and by your example lend a fresh impetus to the onward march of its new-born institutions.

Shoghi Effendi

15. Every day has certain needs. In those early days the Cause needed Martyrs, and people who would stand all sorts of torture and persecution in expressing their faith and spreading the message sent by God. Those days are, however, gone. The Cause at present does not need martyrs who would die for the faith,

but servants who desire to teach and establish the Cause throughout the world. To live to teach in the present day is like being martyred in those early days. It is the spirit that moves us that counts, not the act through which that spirit expresses itself; and that spirit is to serve the Cause of God with our heart and soul.

On behalf of Shoghi Effendi

16. What is needed now is the awakening of all believers to the immediacy of the challenge so that each may assume his share of the responsibility for taking the Teachings to all humanity. Universal participation . . . must be pressed toward attainment in every continent, country and island of the globe. Every Bahá'í, however humble or inarticulate, must become intent on fulfilling his role as a bearer of the Divine Message. Indeed, how can a true believer remain silent while around us men cry out in anguish for truth, love and unity to descend upon this world?

The Universal House of Justice

17. In addition to teaching every believer can pray. Every believer can strive to make his "own inner life and private character mirror forth in their manifold aspects the splendor of those eternal principles proclaimed by Bahá'u'lláh." Every believer can contribute to the Fund. Not all believers can give public talks, not all are called upon to serve on administrative institutions. But all can pray, fight their own spiritual battles, and contribute to the Fund. If every believer will carry out these sacred duties, we shall be astonished at the accession of power which will result to the whole body, and which in its turn will give rise to further growth and the showering of greater blessings on all of us.

The Universal House of Justice

THE POWER OF LOVE AND FELLOWSHIP

18. Consort with all men, O people of Bahá, in a spirit of friendliness and fellowship. If ye be aware of a certain truth, if ye possess a jewel, of which others are deprived, share it with them in a language of utmost kindliness and good-will. If it be accepted, if it fulfill its purpose, your object is attained. If any one should refuse it, leave him unto himself, and beseech God to guide him. Beware lest ye deal unkindly with him. A kindly tongue is the lodestone of the hearts of men. It is the bread of the spirit, it clotheth the words with meaning, it is the fountain of the light of wisdom and understanding.

Bahá'u'lláh

19. The friends of God should weave bonds of fellowship with others and show absolute love and affection towards them. These links have a deep influence on people and they will listen. When the friends sense receptivity to the Word of God, they should deliver the Message with wisdom. They must first try and remove any apprehensions in the people they teach. In fact, every one of the believers should choose one person every year and try to establish ties of friendship with him, so that all his fear would disappear. Only then, and gradually, must he teach that person. This is the best method.

'Abdu'l-Bahá

20. O ye lovers of God! Be kind to all peoples; care for every person; do all ye can to purify the hearts and minds of men; strive ye to gladden every soul. To every meadow be a shower of grace, to every tree the water of life; be as sweet musk to the sense of humankind, and to the ailing be a fresh, restoring breeze. Be pleasing waters to all those who thirst, a careful guide to all who have lost their way; be father and mother to the

orphan, be loving sons and daughters to the old, be an abundant treasure to the poor. Think ye of love and good fellowship as the delights of heaven, think ye of hostility and hatred as the torments of hell.

Indulge not your bodies with rest, but work with all your souls, and with all your hearts cry out and beg of God to grant you His succor and grace. Thus may ye make this world the Abhá Paradise, and this globe of earth the parade ground of the realm on high. If only ye exert the effort, it is certain that these splendors will shine out, these clouds of mercy will shed down their rain, these life-giving winds will rise and blow, this sweet-smelling musk will be scattered far and wide.

'Abdu'l-Bahá

21. The implications of this principle of the oneness of humanity are many and far-reaching, and it is on these that, the Guardian feels, our Bahá'í youth should dwell in their talks and activities, proving by their deeds as well as through their words, their faithful and whole-hearted adherence to this cornerstone principle of the Faith.

Above all they should strive to get rid of all their ancestral prejudices, whether of race, creed or class, and thus attract through the example of their lives many outsiders to the Cause. At a time when racial prejudice is becoming so widespread and intense, it should be their constant endeavor to associate and mingle with the members of all races, and thereby demonstrate to the world at large the hollowness, nay the stupidity of the racial doctrines and philosophies which are so increasingly poisoning the minds of the individuals, classes and nations throughout the world.

This is the high standard of thought and conduct which the Guardian wishes the Bahá'í youth to strictly and faithfully maintain. May they, each and all, arise and live up to its high and noble ideals!

Shoghi Effendi

22. The love we bear mankind, our conviction that Bahá'u'lláh's Faith contains the only and the Divine remedy for all its ills, must be demonstrated today in action by bringing the Cause before the public. No doubt the majority are not yet able to see its true significance, but they must not be deprived, through our failure in obligation, of the opportunity of hearing of it. And there are many precious souls who are seeking for it and ready to embrace it.

On behalf of Shoghi Effendi

23. Through example, loving fellowship, prayer, and kindness the friends can attract the hearts of such people and enable them to realize that this is the Cause of God in deed, not merely words!

On behalf of Shoghi Effendi

24. The friends must realize their individual responsibility. Each must hold a Fireside in his or her home, once in nineteen days, where new people are invited, and where some phase of the Faith is mentioned and discussed. If this is done with the intent of showing Bahá'í hospitality and love, then there will be results. People will become interested in "what" you are interested in, and then be interested in studying. Individual firesides will bring the knowledge of the Faith to more people, under favorable circumstances, and thus constantly enrich its circle of friends, and finally its members. There is no substitute for the teaching work of the individual.

On behalf of Shoghi Effendi

25. The believers must be encouraged to teach individually in their own homes. Bahá'u'lláh has enjoined upon the Bahá'ís the sacred obligation of teaching. We have no priests, therefore the service once rendered by priests to their religions is the service every single Bahá'í is expected to render individually to his religion. He must be the one who enlightens new souls, confirms them, heals the wounded and the weary upon the road of life, and gives them to quaff from the chalice of everlasting life—the knowledge of the Manifestation of God in His Day.

On behalf of Shoghi Effendi

26. The real secret of universal participation lies in the Master's oft expressed wish that the friends should love each other, constantly encourage each other, work together, be as one soul in one body, and in so doing become a true, organic, healthy body animated and illumined by the spirit. In such a body all will receive spiritual health and vitality from the organism itself, and the most perfect flowers and fruits will be brought forth.

The Universal House of Justice

THE RESPONSIBILITIES OF YOUTH

27. The activities, hopes and ideals of the Bahá'í Youth in America, as well as in all other parts of the world are close and dear to my heart. Upon them rests the supreme and challenging responsibility to promote the interests of the Cause of God in the days to come, to co-ordinate its world-wide activities, to extend its scope, to safeguard its integrity, to exalt its virtues, define its purpose, and translate its ideals and aims into memorable and abiding achievements. Theirs is a mighty task, at once holy, stupendous and enthralling. May the spirit of Bahá'u'lláh protect, inspire and sustain them in the prosecution of their divinely-appointed task!

Shoghi Effendi

28. It is on young and active Bahá'ís, like you, that the Guardian centers all his hopes for the future progress and expansion of the Cause, and it is on their shoulders that he lays the responsibility for the upkeep of the spirit of selfless service among their fellow-believers. Without that spirit no work can be successfully achieved. With it triumph, though hardly won, is but inevitable. You should therefore, try all your best to carry aflame within you the torch of faith, for through it you will surely find guidance, strength and eventual success.

. . . Every one of them is able, in his own measure, to deliver the Message. . . . Everyone is a potential teacher. He has only to use what God has given him and thus prove that he is faithful to his trust.

On behalf of Shoghi Effendi

29. The obligation to teach is essentially the responsibility of young believers. Their whole training should therefore be directed in such a way as to make them competent teachers. It is for this very purpose Bahá'í summer schools, which constitute the very basis upon which the Bahá'í universities of the future will be established, should be widely attended by young believers.

On behalf of Shoghi Effendi

30. The Guardian is looking to the Youth of America to raise the Banner of the Faith to ever higher and more glorious heights.

The Youth should become severed from all things of the world and filled with the dynamic power of The Holy Spirit, arise to spread the Message and quicken the hearts.

On behalf of Shoghi Effendi

31. As to Bahá'í youth, legatees of the heroic early believers and now standing on their shoulders, we call upon them to

redouble their efforts, in this day of widespread interest in the Cause of God, to enthuse their contemporaries with the divine Message and thus prepare themselves for the day when they will be veteran believers able to assume whatever tasks may be laid upon them. We offer them this passage from the Pen of Bahá'u'lláh:

> Blessed is he who in the prime of his youth and the heyday of his life will arise to serve the Cause of the Lord of the beginning and of the end, and adorn his heart with His love. The manifestation of such a grace is greater than the creation of the heavens and of the earth. Blessed are the steadfast and well is it with those who are firm.
>
> *The Universal House of Justice*

32. Not yet having acquired all the responsibilities of a family or a long-established home and job, youth can the more easily choose where they will live and study or work. In the world at large young people travel hither and thither seeking amusement, education and experiences. Bahá'í youth, bearing the incomparable treasure of the Word of God for this Day, can harness this mobility into service for mankind and can choose their places of residence, their areas of travel, and their types of work with the goal in mind of how they can best serve the Faith.

The Universal House of Justice

33. This generation of Bahá'í youth enjoys a unique distinction. You will live your lives in a period when the forces of history are moving to a climax, when mankind will see the establishment of the Lesser Peace, and during which the Cause of God will play an increasingly prominent role in the reconstruction of human society. It is you who will be called upon in the years to come to

stand at the helm of the Cause in face of conditions and developments which can, as yet, scarcely be imagined.

. . . Now is an opportunity to awaken the interest, set afire the hearts and enlist the active support of young people of every nation, class and creed in that continent. The key to success in this endeavor is, firstly, to deepen your understanding of the Teachings of the Cause so that you will be able to apply them to the problems of individuals and society, and explain them to your peers in ways that they will understand and welcome; secondly, to strive to model your behavior in every way after the high standards of honesty, trustworthiness, courage, loyalty, forbearance, purity and spirituality set forth in the Teachings; and, above all, to live in continual awareness of the presence and all-conquering power of Bahá'u'lláh, which will enable you to overcome every temptation and surmount every obstacle.

The Universal House of Justice

Ensuring Success in Teaching

BEING FILLED WITH THE LOVE OF GOD

34. O Friends! You must all be so ablaze in this day with the fire of the love of God that the heat thereof may be manifest in all your veins, your limbs and members of your body, and the peoples of the world may be ignited by this heat and turn to the horizon of the Beloved.

Bahá'u'lláh

35. If he be kindled with the fire of His love, if he forgoeth all created things, the words he uttereth shall set on fire them that hear him.

Bahá'u'lláh

36. By God besides Whom is none other God! Should any one arise for the triumph of our Cause, him will God render victorious though tens of thousands of enemies be leagued against him. And if his love for Me wax stronger, God will establish his ascendancy over all the powers of earth and heaven. Thus have We breathed the spirit of power into all regions.

Bahá'u'lláh

37. With hearts overflowing with the love of God, with tongues commemorating the mention of God, with eyes turned to the Kingdom of God, they must deliver the glad tidings of the manifestation of the Lord of Hosts to all the people. Know ye of a certainty that whatever gathering ye enter, the waves of the Holy Spirit are surging over it, and the heavenly grace of the Blessed Beauty encompasseth that gathering.

'Abdu'l-Bahá

38. The aim is this: The intention of the teacher must be pure, his heart independent, his spirit attracted, his thought at peace, his resolution firm, his magnanimity exalted and in the love of God a shining torch. Should he become as such, his sanctified breath will even affect the rock; otherwise there will be no result whatsoever. As long as a soul is not perfected, how can he efface the defects of others? Unless he is detached from aught else save God, how can he teach severance to others?

'Abdu'l-Bahá

39. When a speaker's brow shineth with the radiance of the love of God, at the time of his exposition of a subject, and he is exhilarated with the wine of true understanding, he becometh the center of a potent force which like unto a magnet will attract the hearts. This is why the expounder must be in the utmost enkindlement.

'Abdu'l-Bahá

40. Many are the souls who, in this Holy Cause, without either worldly means or knowledge, have set ablaze the hearts of others with the divine love and rendered the Faith imperishable services.

On behalf of Shoghi Effendi

DEMONSTRATING LOVE AND FELLOWSHIP

41. O ye beloved of the Lord! Commit not that which defileth the limpid stream of love or destroyeth the sweet fragrance of friendship. By the righteousness of the Lord! Ye were created to show love one to another and not perversity and rancor. Take pride not in love for yourselves but in love for your fellow-creatures. Glory not in love for your country, but in love for all mankind.

Bahá'u'lláh

42. The friends of God must manifest the mercy of the Compassionate Lord in the world of existence and must show forth the bounty of the visible and invisible King. They must purify their sight, and look upon mankind as the leaves, blossoms and fruits of the tree of creation, and must always be thinking of doing good to someone, of love, consideration, affection and assistance to somebody. They must see no enemy and count no one as an ill wisher. They must consider every one on the earth as a friend; regard the stranger as an intimate, and the alien as a companion. They must not be bound by any tie, nay, rather, they should be free from every bond. In this day the one who is favored in the threshold of grandeur is the one who offers the cup of faithfulness and bestows the pearl of gift to the enemies, even to the fallen oppressor, lends a helping hand, and considers every bitter foe as an affectionate friend.

'Abdu'l-Bahá

43. The Guardian feels that the most effective way for the Bahá'ís to teach the Faith is to make strong friends with their neighbors

and associates. When the friends have confidence in the Bahá'ís and the Bahá'ís in their friends, they should give the Message and teach the Cause. Individual teaching of this type is more effective than any other type.

The principle of the fireside meeting, which was established in order to permit and encourage the individual to teach in his own home, has been proven the most effective instrument for spreading the Faith.

On behalf of Shoghi Effendi

44. The Bahá'ís must realize that the success of this work depends upon the individual. The individual must arise as never before to proclaim the Faith of Bahá'u'lláh. The most effective way for them to carry on their work is for the individual to make many contacts, select a few who they feel would become Bahá'ís, develop a close friendship with them, then complete confidence, and finally teach them the Faith, until they become strong supporters of the Cause of God.

On behalf of Shoghi Effendi

DEMONSTRATING THE POWER OF THE FAITH THROUGH
RIGHTEOUS DEEDS AND A DISTINCTIVE CHARACTER

45. Say: O people of God! That which can insure the victory of Him Who is the Eternal Truth, His hosts and helpers on earth, have been set down in the sacred Books and Scriptures, and are as clear and manifest as the sun. These hosts are such righteous deeds, such conduct and character, as are acceptable in His sight. Whoso ariseth, in this Day, to aid Our Cause, and summoneth to his assistance the hosts of a praiseworthy character and upright conduct, the influence from such an action will, most certainly, be diffused throughout the whole world.

Bahá'u'lláh

46. The teaching work should under all conditions be actively pursued by the believers because divine confirmations are dependent upon it. Should a Bahá'í refrain from being fully, vigorously and wholeheartedly involved in the teaching work he will undoubtedly be deprived of the blessings of the Abhá Kingdom. Even so, this activity should be tempered with wisdom— not that wisdom which requireth one to be silent and forgetful of such an obligation, but rather that which requireth one to display divine tolerance, love, kindness, patience, a goodly character, and holy deeds. In brief, encourage the friends individually to teach the Cause of God and draw their attention to this meaning of wisdom mentioned in the writings, which is itself the essence of teaching the Faith—but all this to be done with the greatest tolerance, so that heavenly assistance and divine confirmation may aid the friends.

'Abdu'l-Bahá

47. Of these spiritual prerequisites of success . . . the following stand out as preeminent and vital, which the members of the American Bahá'í community will do well to ponder. Upon the extent to which these basic requirements are met, and the manner in which the American believers fulfill them in their individual lives, administrative activities, and social relationships, must depend the measure of the manifold blessings which the All-Bountiful Possessor can vouchsafe to them all. These requirements are none other than a high sense of moral rectitude in their social and administrative activities, absolute chastity in their individual lives, and complete freedom from prejudice in their dealings with peoples of a different race, class, creed, or color.

Shoghi Effendi

48. The gross materialism that engulfs the entire nation at the present hour; the attachment to worldly things that enshrouds

the souls of men; the fears and anxieties that distract their minds; the pleasure and dissipations that fill their time, the prejudices and animosities that darken their outlook, the apathy and lethargy that paralyze their spiritual faculties—these are among the formidable obstacles that stand in the path of every would-be warrior in the service of Bahá'u'lláh, obstacles which he must battle against and surmount in his crusade for the redemption of his own countrymen.

To the degree that the home front crusader is himself cleansed of these impurities, liberated from these petty preoccupations and gnawing anxieties, delivered from these prejudices and antagonisms, emptied of self, and filled by the healing and the sustaining power of God, will he be able to combat the forces arrayed against him, magnetize the souls of those whom he seeks to convert, and win their unreserved, their enthusiastic and enduring allegiance to the Faith of Bahá'u'lláh.

Delicate and strenuous though the task may be, however arduous and prolonged the effort required, whatsoever the nature of the perils and pitfalls that beset the path of whoever arises to revive the fortunes of a Faith struggling against the rising forces of materialism, nationalism, secularism, racialism, ecclesiasticism, the all-conquering potency of the grace of God, vouchsafed through the Revelation of Bahá'u'lláh, will, undoubtedly, mysteriously and surprisingly, enable whosoever arises to champion His Cause to win complete and total victory.

Shoghi Effendi

DEEPENING IN AND STUDYING THE WRITINGS

49. Whoso ariseth among you to teach the Cause of his Lord, let him, before all else, teach his own self, that his speech may attract the hearts of them that hear him. Unless he teacheth his own self, the words of his mouth will not influence the heart of the seeker. Take heed, O people, lest ye be of them that give

good counsel to others but forget to follow it themselves. The words of such as these, and beyond the words the realities of all things, and beyond these realities the angels that are nigh unto God, bring against them the accusation of falsehood.

Bahá'u'lláh

50. Those who participate in such a campaign, whether in an organizing capacity, or as workers to whose care the execution of the task itself has been committed, must, as an essential preliminary to the discharge of their duties, thoroughly familiarize themselves with the various aspects of the history and teachings of their Faith. In their efforts to achieve this purpose they must study for themselves, conscientiously and painstakingly, the literature of their Faith, delve into its teachings, assimilate its laws and principles, ponder its admonitions, tenets and purposes, commit to memory certain of its exhortations and prayers, master the essentials of its administration, and keep abreast of its current affairs and latest developments.

Shoghi Effendi

51. I wish to urge the necessity of concentrating, at your next summer session, on the systematic study of the early history and principles of the Faith, on public speaking, and on a thorough discussion, both formally and informally, of various aspects of the Cause. These I regard as essential preliminaries to a future intensive campaign of teaching in which the rising generation must engage, if the spread of the Cause is to be assured in that land. May you succeed in your efforts to attain that goal!

Shoghi Effendi

52. If the younger Bahá'í generation, in whom Shoghi Effendi has great hopes, take the pain of studying the Cause deeply and thoroughly, read its history, find its underlying principles and

become both well informed and energetic, they surely can achieve a great deal. It is upon their shoulders that the Master has laid the tremendous work of teaching. They are the ones to raise the call of the Kingdom and arouse the people from slumber. If they fail the Cause is doomed to stagnation.

On behalf of Shoghi Effendi

53. The interests of our beloved Faith require that the youth in particular exert every effort to spread it, while at the same time deepening their own knowledge of the Teachings and perfecting their private lives in accordance with the standards of conduct laid down by Bahá'u'lláh.

On behalf of Shoghi Effendi

CONSECRATION, DEDICATION, AND SERVICE

54. Arise to further My Cause, and to exalt My Word amongst men. We are with you at all times, and shall strengthen you through the power of truth. We are truly almighty. Whoso hath recognized Me, will arise and serve Me with such determination that the powers of earth and heaven shall be unable to defeat his purpose.

Bahá'u'lláh

55. When the friends do not endeavor to spread the message, they fail to remember God befittingly, and will not witness the tokens of assistance and confirmation from the Abhá Kingdom nor comprehend the divine mysteries. However, when the tongue of the teacher is engaged in teaching, he will naturally himself be stimulated, will become a magnet attracting the divine aid and bounty of the Kingdom, and will be like unto the bird at the hour of dawn, which itself becometh exhilarated by its own singing, its warbling and its melody.

'Abdu'l-Bahá

56. The Hosts of the Supreme Concourse are in martial array, poised between Earth and Heaven ready to rush to the assistance of those who arise to teach the Faith. If one seeks the confirmations of the Holy Spirit, they can find it in rich abundance in the Teaching Field. The world is seeking as never before, and if the Friends will arise with new determination, fully consecrated to the noble task ahead of them victory after victory will be won for the Glorious Faith of God.

On behalf of Shoghi Effendi

57. Today, as never before, the magnet which attracts the blessings from on high, is teaching the Faith of God. The Hosts of Heaven are poised between heaven and earth, just waiting, and patiently, for the Bahá'í to step forth, with pure devotion and consecration, to teach the Cause of God, so they may rush to his aid and assistance. It is the Guardian's prayer that the friends may treble their efforts, as the time is short—alas, the workers too few. Let those who wish to achieve immortality, step forth and raise the Divine Call. They will be astonished at the spiritual victories they will gain.

On behalf of Shoghi Effendi

58. What is needed to achieve success in the teaching field is a complete dedication on the part of the individual, consecration to the glorious task of spreading the Faith, and the living of the Bahá'í life, because that creates the magnet for the Holy Spirit, and it is the Holy Spirit which quickens the new soul. Thus the individual should be as a reed, through which the Holy Spirit may flow, to give new life to the seeking soul.

One should search out those who are receptive to the Faith, and then concentrate on these persons in their teaching.

On behalf of Shoghi Effendi

59. Consecration, dedication and enthusiastic service is the Keynote to successful teaching. One must become like a reed through which the Holy Spirit descends to reach the student of the Faith. We give the Message, and explain the Teachings, but it is the Holy Spirit that quickens and confirms.

On behalf of Shoghi Effendi

60. It is not enough for the friends to make the excuse that their best teachers and their exemplary believers have arisen and answered the call to pioneer. A "best teacher" and an "exemplary believer" is ultimately neither more nor less than an ordinary Bahá'í who has consecrated himself to the work of the Faith, deepened his knowledge and understanding of its Teachings, placed his confidence in Bahá'u'lláh, and arisen to serve Him to the best of his ability. This door is one which we are assured will open before the face of every follower of the Faith who knocks hard enough, so to speak. When the will and the desire are strong enough, the means will be found and the way opened either to do more work locally, to go to a new goal town . . . or to enter the foreign pioneer field. . . .

The Bahá'ís are the leaven of God, which must leaven the lump of their nation. In direct ratio to their success will be the protection vouchsafed, not only to them but to their country. These are the immutable laws of God, from which there is no escape: "For unto whomsoever much is given, of him shall be much required."

On behalf of Shoghi Effendi

61. If the friends always waited until they were *fully* qualified to do any particular task, the work of the Cause would be almost at a standstill! But the very act of striving to serve, however unworthy one may feel, attracts the blessings of God and enables one to become more fitted for the task.

Today the need is so great on the part of humanity to hear of the Divine Message, that the believers must plunge into the work, wherever and however they can, heedless of their own shortcomings, but ever heedful of the crying need of their fellowmen to hear of the teachings in their darkest hour of travail.

On behalf of Shoghi Effendi

62. Teaching is the source of Divine Confirmation. It is not sufficient to pray diligently for guidance, but this prayer must be followed by meditation as to the best methods of action and then action itself. Even if the action should not immediately produce results, or perhaps not be entirely correct, that does not make so much difference, because prayers can only be answered through action and if someone's action is wrong, God can use that method of showing the pathway which is right.

On behalf of Shoghi Effendi

63. The Bahá'í teacher must be all confidence. Therein lies his strength and the secret of his success. Though single-handed, and no matter how great the apathy of the people around you may be, you should have faith that the hosts of the Kingdom are on your side, and that through their help you are bound to overcome the forces of darkness that are facing the Cause of God. Persevere, be happy and confident, therefore.

On behalf of Shoghi Effendi

64. Do not feel discouraged if your labors do not always yield an abundant fruitage. For a quick and rapidly-won success is not always the best and the most lasting. The harder you strive to attain your goal, the greater will be the confirmations of Bahá'u'lláh, and the more certain you can feel to attain success. Be cheerful, therefore, and exert yourself with full faith and

confidence. For Bahá'u'lláh has promised His Divine assistance to everyone who arises with a pure and detached heart to spread His holy Word, even though he may be bereft of every human knowledge and capacity, and notwithstanding the forces of darkness and of opposition which may be arrayed against him. The goal is clear, the path safe and certain, and the assurances of Bahá'u'lláh as to the eventual success of our efforts quite emphatic. Let us keep firm, and wholeheartedly carry on the great work which He has entrusted into our hands.

On behalf of Shoghi Effendi

ATTRACTING DIVINE ASSISTANCE

65. Whoso openeth his lips in this day, and maketh mention of the name of his Lord, the hosts of Divine inspiration shall descend upon him from the heaven of My name, the All-Knowing, the All-Wise. On him shall also descend the Concourse on high, each bearing aloft a chalice of pure light. Thus hath it been foreordained in the realm of God's Revelation, by the behest of Him Who is the All-Glorious, the Most Powerful.

Bahá'u'lláh

66. Whosoever quickens one soul in this Cause is like unto one quickening all the servants and the Lord shall bring him forth in the day of resurrection into the Riḍván of oneness, adorned with the Mantle of Himself, the protector, the mighty, the generous! Thus will ye assist your Lord, and naught else save this shall ever be mentioned in this day before God, your Lord and the Lord of your forefathers.

Bahá'u'lláh

67. O my God, aid Thou Thy servant to raise up the Word, and to refute what is vain and false, to establish the truth, to

spread the sacred verses abroad, reveal the splendors, and make the morning's light to dawn in the hearts of the righteous.

Thou art, verily, the Generous, the Forgiving.

'Abdu'l-Bahá

68. Rest ye assured that if a soul arises in the utmost persever-ance and raises the Call of the Kingdom and resolutely pro-mulgates the Covenant—be he an insignificant ant—he shall be enabled to drive away the formidable elephant from the arena, and if he be a feeble moth he shall cut to pieces the plumage of the rapacious vulture.

'Abdu'l-Bahá

Who to Teach

REACHING ALL HUMANITY

69. Be unrestrained as the wind, while carrying the Message of Him Who hath caused the Dawn of Divine Guidance to break. Consider, how the wind, faithful to that which God hath ordained, bloweth upon all the regions of the earth, be they inhabited or desolate. Neither the sight of desolation, nor the evidences of pros-perity, can either pain or please it. It bloweth in every direction, as bidden by its Creator. So should be every one that claimeth to be a lover of the one true God. It behooveth him to fix his gaze upon the fundamentals of His Faith, and to labor diligently for its propagation. Wholly for the sake of God he should proclaim His Message, and with that same spirit accept whatever response his words may evoke in his hearer. He who shall accept and believe, shall receive his reward; and he who shall turn away, shall receive none other than his own punishment.

Bahá'u'lláh

70. The Faith of the Blessed Beauty is summoning mankind to safety and love, to amity and peace; it hath raised up its tabernacle on the heights of the earth, and directeth its call to all nations. Wherefore, O ye who are God's lovers, know ye the value of this precious Faith, obey its teachings, walk in this road that is drawn straight, and show ye this way to the people. Lift up your voices and sing out the song of the Kingdom. Spread far and wide the precepts and counsels of the loving Lord, so that this world will change into another world, and this darksome earth will be flooded with light, and the dead body of mankind will arise and live; so that every soul will ask for immortality, through the holy breaths of God.

'Abdu'l-Bahá

71. The believers ought to give the Message even to those who do not seem to be ready for it, because they can never judge the real extent to which the Word of God can influence the hearts and minds of the people, even those who appear to lack any power of receptivity to the Teachings.

On behalf of Shoghi Effendi

72. The paramount goal of the teaching work at the present time is to carry the message of Bahá'u'lláh to every stratum of human society and every walk of life. An eager response to the teachings will often be found in the most unexpected quarters, and any such response should be quickly followed up, for success in a fertile area awakens a response in those who were at first uninterested.

The Universal House of Justice

TEACHING YOUTH

73. To the Bahá'í youth of America . . . I feel a word should be addressed in particular, as I survey the possibilities which a cam-

paign of such gigantic proportions has to offer to the eager and enterprising spirit that so powerfully animates them in the service of the Cause of Bahá'u'lláh. Though lacking in experience and faced with insufficient resources, yet the adventurous spirit which they possess, and the vigor, the alertness, and optimism they have thus far so consistently shown, qualify them to play an active part in arousing the interest, and in securing the allegiance, of their fellow youth in those countries.

Shoghi Effendi

74. He feels that teaching the Faith to the youth is of the utmost importance in these days, as they will not only become the workers of the future but will be able to widely spread the Message among their own generation.

On behalf of Shoghi Effendi

75. He was . . . very happy to see the Bahá'í youth are holding meetings and making every effort to mingle with other young people, through local clubs and groups, and thus bring the Cause to their notice.

On behalf of Shoghi Effendi

76. He urges you to redouble your efforts during the coming year, to teach the youth this great Message of Bahá'u'lláh. It is indeed the one hope for the spiritual and material security of the world; and although the response may be slow at first, through your perseverance and devotion, you will gradually succeed in attracting a very large group to the Cause of Bahá'u'lláh.

On behalf of Shoghi Effendi

Diverse Populations

77. By all means persevere and associate in a friendly spirit with other groups of young people, particularly of a different race or

minority nationality, for such association will demonstrate your complete conviction of the oneness of mankind and attract others to the Faith, both young and old alike. A spirit of prejudice-free, loving comradeship with others is what will open the eyes of people more than any amount of words. Combined with such deeds you can teach the Faith easily.

On behalf of Shoghi Effendi

78. He urges you all to devote particular attention to the contact with racial minorities. In a country which has such a large element of prejudice against its colored citizens as the United States, it is of the greatest importance that the Bahá'ís—and more especially the youth—should demonstrate actively our complete lack of prejudice and, indeed, our prejudice in favor of minorities.

We cannot very well prosecute a teaching campaign successfully in Africa if we do not in our home communities demonstrate to the fullest extent our love for the people who spring from the African population!

On behalf of Shoghi Effendi

79. The House of Justice feels that the friends, and sometimes the Bahá'í institutions, have tended to over-react to the instructions given from time to time about contacting and teaching Muslims from Iran and other places in the Middle East, and they often take to extremes the cautions given in such instructions. The friends sometimes think they should shun such people entirely or that any contact with them is considered a breach of Bahá'í law. We are asked to point out that the House of Justice has never forbidden the friends to contact Iranian Muslims, as such a general prohibition would be contrary to the spirit of the Faith. However, given the history and the current situation of the Faith in Iran, it has urged the friends in the West to act

toward these people with wisdom and caution. In fact, the House of Justice has clarified the matter on various occasions by stating the following to National Spiritual Assemblies:

> The instructions of the beloved Guardian regarding teaching orientals from the Middle East are to be upheld, even more so at this time because of the present situation in Iran. Iranian Muslims in particular should not be sought out in order to teach them the Faith. It cannot be categorically said, however, that the friends should have no contact with Iranian Muslims. Some of the Bahá'ís have relatives who are Iranian Muslims, some have close Iranian Muslim friends who happen to reside in the West, and they should not relinquish these friendships. At the same time it should be stressed to the Iranian Bahá'ís that while they should not cut themselves off from their Muslim relatives and friends—a step which could create animosity and turn them against the Faith—they should not normally seek out Iranian Muslims in order to initiate friendly contacts with them or teach them the Faith. . . .

> While the House of Justice favors the widest possible dissemination of accurate information about the Faith to Iranian Muslims, the time has not yet come in the West for Bahá'ís, especially Persians, to adopt the general goal of teaching the Cause to Iranian Muslims. As you know, Iranians have a number of societies and organizations; some are admittedly cultural, others are politically oriented, even if seemingly cultural in purpose. These organizations are frequented by people whose standards are not compatible with those of the Faith. Obviously, association with such groups could exert a baneful influence on some of the Bahá'ís, particularly the youth.

> *On behalf of the Universal House of Justice*

SCHOOL AND COLLEGE STUDENTS

80. It is in intellectual circles such as this [a university circle] that the believers should endeavor to teach, confident that no matter how limited their capacity may be, yet their efforts are continually guided and reinforced from on high. This spirit of confident hope, of cheerful courage, and of undaunted enthusiasm in itself, irrespective of any tangible results which it may procure, can alone insure the ultimate success of our teaching efforts.

On behalf of Shoghi Effendi

81. He was greatly pleased and highly encouraged with your slow but progressive work among members of the faculty and the student body in State College. It is high time for the Bahá'ís to try and reach the thinking and educated youth of the country upon whom so much of the future depends, especially the stupendous task of applying the spirit and letter of the Bahá'í teachings to the requirements of the time—a work for which generations of preparation might be necessary.

On behalf of Shoghi Effendi

82. He was deeply interested in your work among the university students and hopes that it will bear much fruit. The youth is open-minded, unhampered by prejudice and ready to accept any message that satisfies his spiritual longings as well as intellectual demands. The work should, however, be both intensive and extensive. It is not sufficient that you should address many student bodies; persons have to be found to follow up that work, pick those who are interested to know more and ground them in the teachings.

On behalf of Shoghi Effendi

83. The account of your work among the foreign students made Shoghi Effendi very happy. Not only will these young people

get a good impression of American families and hospitality, but the spiritual training you try to give them will make their education so much more complete and worthwhile. This is beside the fact that in their heart is planted the seeds of the Bahá'í teachings which in time will germinate and bring forth wondrous fruits. All these young people when they return home will carry the Message with them and even though they do not become confirmed believers, they will remain friends always ready to render a service to the Bahá'í teachers they happen to meet. Shoghi Effendi hopes you will carry on that work but at the same time try to make them true Bahá'ís—in spirit as well as in faith.

On behalf of Shoghi Effendi

THE IMPORTANCE OF THE ARTS IN TEACHING

84. We have to wait only a few years to see how the spirit breathed by Bahá'u'lláh will find expression in the work of the artists. What you and some other Bahá'ís are attempting are only faint rays that precede the effulgent light of a glorious morn. We cannot yet value the part the Cause is destined to play in the life of society. We have to give it time. The material this spirit has to mould is too crude and unworthy, but it will at last give way and the Cause of Bahá'u'lláh will reveal itself in its full splendor.

On behalf of Shoghi Effendi

85. What you could do, and should do, is to use your stories to become a source of inspiration and guidance for those who read them. With such a means at your disposal you can spread the spirit and teachings of the Cause; you can show the evils that exist in society, as well as the way they can be remedied. If you possess a real talent in writing you should consider it as given by God and exert your efforts to use it for the betterment of society.

On behalf of Shoghi Effendi

86. Your understanding that the portrayal of the Báb and Bahá'u'lláh in works of art is forbidden, is correct. The Guardian made it clear that this prohibition refers to all the Manifestations of God; photographs, or reproductions of portraits, of the Master may be used in books, but no attempt should be made to portray Him in dramatic or other works where He would be one of the "dramatis personae." However, there can be no objection to symbolic representations of Holy Figures, provided it does not become a ritual and that the symbol used is not irreverent.

The Universal House of Justice

87. In all their efforts to achieve the aim of the Four Year Plan, the friends are also asked to give greater attention to the use of the arts, not only for proclamation, but also for the work in expansion and consolidation. The graphic and performing arts and literature have played, and can play, a major role in extending the influence of the Cause. At the level of folk art, this possibility can be pursued in every part of the world, whether it be in villages, towns or cities. Shoghi Effendi held high hopes for the arts as a means for attracting attention to the Teachings. A letter written on his behalf to an individual thus conveys the Guardian's view: "The day will come when the Cause will spread like wildfire when its spirit and teachings will be presented on the stage or in art and literature as a whole. Art can better awaken such noble sentiments than cold rationalizing, especially among the mass of the people."

The Universal House of Justice

Training Institutes and Core Activities

88. It is most encouraging to see that the progress of this work is being energized through the training institute process, which

was considerably strengthened last year by the campaigns undertaken in many countries to increase the number of trained
tutors. Where a training institute is well established and constantly functioning, three core activities—study circles, devotional meetings, and children's classes—have multiplied
with relative ease. Indeed, the participation of seekers in these
activities, at the invitation of their Bahá'í friends, has lent a
new dimension to their purposes, consequently effecting new
enrolments. Here, surely, is a direction of great promise for
the teaching work. These core activities, which at the outset
were devised principally to benefit the believers themselves,
are naturally becoming portals for entry by troops. By com-
bining study circles, devotional meetings, and children's classes
within the framework of clusters, a model of coherence in
lines of action has been put in place and is already producing
welcome results. Worldwide application of this model, we feel
confident, holds immense possibilities for the progress of the
Cause in the years ahead.

The Universal House of Justice

89. The coherence thus achieved through the establishment of
study circles, devotional meetings and children's classes provides
the initial impulse for growth in a cluster, an impulse that gathers
strength as these core activities multiply in number. Campaigns
that help a sizeable group of believers advance far enough in the
main sequence of courses to perform the necessary acts of service
lend impetus to this multiplication of activity.

It is evident, then, that a systematic approach to training has
created a way for Bahá'ís to reach out to the surrounding society, share Bahá'u'lláh's message with friends, family, neighbors
and co-workers, and expose them to the richness of His teachings. This outward-looking orientation is one of the finest fruits

of the grassroots learning taking place. The pattern of activity that is being established in clusters around the globe constitutes a proven means of accelerating expansion and consolidation. Yet this is only a beginning.

In many parts of the world, bringing large numbers into the ranks of Bahá'u'lláh's followers has traditionally not been a formidable task. It is therefore encouraging to see that, in some of the more developed clusters, carefully designed projects are being added to the existing pattern of growth to reach receptive populations and lift the rate of expansion to a higher level. Such projects accelerate the tempo of teaching, already on the rise through the efforts of individuals. And, where large-scale enrollment is beginning to result, provision is being made to ensure that a certain percentage of new believers immediately enter the institute program, for, as we have emphasized in several messages, these friends will be called upon to serve the needs of an ever-growing Bahá'í population.

The Universal House of Justice

90. The training institute is effective not only in enhancing the powers of the individual, but also in vitalizing communities and institutions. . . .

Drawing on the wealth of experience now accumulated in this area of endeavor, institutes will have to provide their communities with a constant stream of human resources to serve the process of entry by troops. Elements of a system that can meet the training needs of large numbers of believers have already been tested worldwide and have proven themselves. Study circles, reinforced by extension courses and special campaigns, have shown their ability to lend structure to the process of spiritual education at the grassroots. The value of a sequence of courses, each one following the other in a logical pattern and each one building on the achievements of the previous ones, has become abundantly clear. . . .

With the work of the institutes growing in strength, attention has now been given everywhere to systematizing teaching efforts. . . . As individuals progress through institute courses, they deepen their knowledge of the Faith, gain insights, and acquire skills of service.

The Universal House of Justice

91. Even though children's activities have been a part of past Plans, these have fallen short of the need. Spiritual education of children and junior youth are of paramount importance to the further progress of the community. It is therefore imperative that this deficiency be remedied. Institutes must be certain to include in their programs the training of teachers of children's classes, who can make their services available to local communities. But although providing spiritual and academic education for children is essential, this represents only a part of what must go into developing their characters and shaping their personalities. The necessity exists, too, for individuals and the institutions at all levels, which is to say the community as a whole, to show a proper attitude towards children and to take a general interest in their welfare. Such an attitude should be far removed from that of a rapidly declining order.

The Universal House of Justice

92. The aim of the Five Year Plan, and indeed of the Plan before it and the ones that lie immediately ahead, is to advance the process of entry by troops. In its message of 26 December 1995 to the Conference of the Continental Boards of Counsellors, the House of Justice clearly explained that occasional courses of instruction and the informal activities of commu-

nity life, though important, had not proven sufficient as a means of human resource development. It indicated further that a systematic process for the development of human resources was essential to the sustained large-scale expansion of the Faith. To conceive and nurture an educational process of the magnitude envisioned by the Universal House of Justice is vastly different than thinking about one's own interests. . . .

The present emphasis on the training institute is justified in the light of the extraordinary success it has had in numerous countries of the world, endowing the friends, at long last, with an instrument with which they can address the challenges of large-scale expansion and consolidation of the Faith. To say that the institute is only useful for newly enrolled believers and those who read little is not correct. Many mature and deepened believers are participating in the institute process, both as students and as teachers of various courses, in an effort to contribute directly to the promotion of entry by troops in their respective countries. Through such participation they have furthered their understanding of the requisites of growth and of the action required to maintain it, have caught fresh glimpses of spiritual truths, and have developed their skills and abilities of service. Far from interfering with their own study of the Writings, each according to his or her own capacity and needs, their association with a training institute has enhanced the process.

On behalf of the Universal House of Justice

93. A distinguishing feature of study circles is that in many countries, and across diverse cultures, they have created a new dynamic within the community and have become nuclei of community life and catalysts for teaching, service, and community development. In addition to study of the institute courses, the members of the study circle, both Bahá'ís and non-

Bahá'ís often participate in service and extracurricular activities that bind the group together in fellowship and attract others to this mode of learning. Having experienced the participatory learning style of the courses, the members of the study circle gradually take on a stronger commitment to actively serve and apply the knowledge and skills they are gaining to the work of the Faith. Some members of study circles are eventually trained as tutors and then initiate their own study circles.

After studying one course, many of the members of a study circle will stay together to go on to the next course, but some may drop out until they are ready and able to pursue a subsequent course. As friends move on to higher level courses, and other friends join at various points in the sequence, the membership of a study circle can gradually change. Although members of study circles will often engage in social and service activities together, no feelings of exclusivity should be allowed to develop among them. Furthermore, the study circles should be guided by the spirit of consultation in planning recreation, teaching, and service activities.

The International Teaching Center

College and Campus Clubs

94. The news of the co-operation of the Bahá'í young men and women in Montreal, their establishment of a group for study and discussion, the sane and sober expression of their methods as expressed in the program you had enclosed, and their thoughtful and enthusiastic outlook upon the future, all these have helped to create the liveliest hopes and the deepest satisfaction in the heart of our Guardian. It is indeed with no little pleasure that he welcomes the active co-operation of his young friends in Montreal, and he sincerely trusts that with an adequate study of the proper teachings and their spiritual sig-

nificance coupled with a sufficient knowledge of the problems and perplexities that the world is beset with, you will be able to render great services to the Cause and therefore to humanity.

On behalf of Shoghi Effendi

95. He is very happy to hear of the formation of the new youth groups you mention, as this will not only greatly stimulate the Bahá'í youth and enable them to attract new young people to the Faith, but will also do the general work of the Cause in these cities a great deal of good. He urges your Committee to make every effort to establish youth groups wherever there are Spiritual Assemblies, and circumstances permit.

On behalf of Shoghi Effendi

96. FROM FAR AND NEAR ANGUISHED MULTITUDES CRY FOR PEACE BUT BEING LARGELY IGNORANT HIS LIFE-REDEEMING MISSION THEY FEEL NO HOPE SITUATION THUS PRESENTS BAHÁ'Í YOUTH WITH GREAT OPPORTUNITIES INESCAPABLE CHALLENGE TO RESCUE THEIR PEERS FROM SLOUGH DESPONDENCY POINTING THEM TOWARDS HOPE-RESTORING BANNER MOST GREAT NAME. HOW FITTING THEN THAT YOU SHOULD CONSIDER AT THESE CONFERENCES BEST MEANS EQUIP YOURSELVES SPIRITUALLY TO FULFILL TEACHING MISSION PARTICULARLY SUITED TO YOUR CAPACITIES FOR SERVICE, YOUR ABOUNDING ZEAL AND ENERGY.

The Universal House of Justice

Travel Teaching

97. O that I could travel, even though on foot and in the utmost poverty, to these regions, and, raising the call of "Yá Bahá'u'l-Abhá" in cities, villages, mountains, deserts and oceans, promote the divine teachings! This, alas, I cannot do. How intensely I deplore it! Please God, ye may achieve it.

'Abdu'l-Bahá

98. Now is the time for you to divest yourselves of the garment of attachment to this world that perisheth, to be wholly severed from the physical world, become heavenly angels, and travel to these countries.

'Abdu'l-Bahá

Pioneering

99. They that have forsaken their country for the purpose of teaching Our Cause—these shall the Faithful Spirit strengthen through its power. A company of Our chosen angels shall go forth with them, as bidden by Him Who is the Almighty, the All-Wise. How great the blessedness that awaiteth him that hath attained the honor of serving the Almighty! By My life! No act, however great, can compare with it, except such deeds as have been ordained by God, the All-Powerful, the Most Mighty. Such a service is, indeed, the prince of all goodly deeds, and the ornament of every goodly act. Thus hath it been ordained by Him Who is the Sovereign Revealer, the Ancient of Days.

Whoso ariseth to teach Our Cause must needs detach himself from all earthly things, and regard, at all times, the triumph of Our Faith as his supreme objective. This hath, verily, been decreed in the Guarded Tablet. And when he determineth to leave his home, for the sake of the Cause of his Lord, let him put his whole trust in God, as the best provision for his journey, and array himself with the robe of virtue. Thus hath it been decreed by God, the Almighty, the All-Praised.

If he be kindled with the fire of His love, if he forgoeth all created things, the words he uttereth shall set on fire them that hear him. Verily, thy Lord is the Omniscient, the All-Informed. Happy is the man that hath heard Our voice, and answered Our call. He, in truth, is of them that shall be brought nigh unto Us.

Bahá'u'lláh

100. It is also recorded in the blessed Gospel: Travel ye throughout the world and call ye the people to the Kingdom of God. Now this is the time that you may arise and perform this most great service and become the cause of the guidance of innumerable souls. Thus through this superhuman service the rays of peace and conciliation may illumine and enlighten all the regions and the world of humanity may find peace and composure.

'Abdu'l-Bahá

101. Let this be the paramount and most urgent duty of every Bahá'í. Let us make it the dominating passion of our life. Let us scatter to the uttermost corners of the earth; sacrifice our personal interests, comforts, tastes and pleasures; mingle with the divers kindreds and peoples of the world; familiarize ourselves with their manners, traditions, thoughts and customs; arouse, stimulate and maintain universal interest in the Movement, and at the same time endeavor by all the means in our power, by concentrated and persistent attention, to enlist the unreserved allegiance and the active support of the more hopeful and receptive among our hearers.

Shoghi Effendi

102. Young people, being, for the most part, freer than the older believers, are in a position to arise as pioneers and move to new towns as settlers. A great number of the pioneers in America, who left their native cities, and often their native land, in order to fulfill the Seven Year Plan, were young people—some of them so young that the Spiritual Assemblies they helped to establish, they were themselves not yet old enough to be elected to!

On behalf of Shoghi Effendi

103. He cannot impress too strongly upon the friends the need for action: they must arise in still greater numbers to pioneer . . .

the young people should learn to teach and go forth in the field in the days of their youth and receive this great blessing.

On behalf of Shoghi Effendi

104. This Cause, although it embraces with equal esteem people of all ages, has a special message and mission for the youth of your generation. It is their charter for their future, their hope, their guarantee of better days to come. Therefore the Guardian is especially happy that the young Bahá'ís are active in the pioneer work.

On behalf of Shoghi Effendi

105. Shall I continue my education, or should I pioneer, now? Undoubtedly this same question is in the mind of every young Bahá'í wishing to dedicate his life to the advancement of the Faith. There is no stock answer which applies to all situations; the beloved Guardian gave different answers to different individuals on this question. Obviously circumstances vary with each individual case. Each individual must decide how he can best serve the Cause. In making this decision, it will be helpful to weigh the following factors:

- Upon becoming a Bahá'í one's whole life is, or should become devoted to the progress of the Cause of God, and every talent or faculty he possesses is ultimately committed to this overriding life objective. Within this framework he must consider, among other things, whether by continuing his education now he can be a more effective pioneer later, or alternatively whether the urgent need for pioneers, while possibilities for teaching are still open, outweighs an anticipated increase in effectiveness. This is not an easy decision, since oftentimes the spirit which prompts the pioneering offer is more important than one's academic attainments.
- One's liability for military service may be a factor in timing the offer of pioneer service.

- One may have outstanding obligations to others, including those who may be dependent on him for support.
- It may be possible to combine a pioneer project with a continuing educational program. Consideration may also be given to the possibility that a pioneering experience, even though it interrupts the formal educational program, may prove beneficial in the long run in that studies would later be resumed with a more mature outlook.
- The urgency of a particular goal which one is especially qualified to fill and for which there are no other offers.
- The fact that the need for pioneers will undoubtedly be with us for many generations to come, and that therefore there will be many calls in future for pioneering service.
- The principle of consultation also applies. One may have the obligation to consult others, such as one's parents, one's Local and National Assemblies, and the pioneering committees.
- Finally, bearing in mind the principle of sacrificial service and the unfailing promises Bahá'u'lláh ordained for those who arise to serve His Cause, one should pray and meditate on what his course of action will be. Indeed, it often happens that the answer will be found in no other way.

We assure the youth that we are mindful of the many important decisions they must make as they tread the path of service to Bahá'u'lláh. We will offer our ardent supplications at the Holy Threshold that all will be divinely guided and that they will attract the blessings of the All-Merciful.

The Universal House of Justice

106. In the past, the policy adopted by some National Assemblies was to discourage young Bahá'ís from enrolling to serve in activities sponsored by non-Bahá'í voluntary organizations, as the Assemblies were under the impression that these young people would not be able to engage in direct teaching, nor par-

ticipate, for the most part, in Bahá'í activities while serving abroad in such programs. Perhaps in some instances the Bahá'ís involved were not sure how to function as members of the Bahá'í community in order to give each aspect of their lives its proper due.

In the light of experience, however, it is now clear that we should have no misgivings in encouraging young Bahá'ís to enroll in such voluntary service organization programs as the United Nations Volunteers, United States Peace Corps, Canadian University Services Overseas (CUSO) and similar Canadian agencies, the British Volunteer Programme (BVP) of the Untied Kingdom, and other voluntary service organizations. Other countries such as Germany, the Netherlands, and the Scandinavian lands are understood to have similar service organizations which are compatible with Bahá'í development goals as now tentatively envisaged.

Some of the advantages of such service to the Faith are worth mentioning. Volunteers will receive thorough orientation and sometimes will be taught basic skills which will enable them to help the Bahá'í community in projects undertaken in developing countries. Wherever they serve, these volunteers should be able to participate in Bahá'í activities, and contribute to the consolidation of the Bahá'í community. The freedom to teach is to a large extent dependent upon the local interpretation of the group leader, but even if volunteers do not engage in direct teaching, being known as Bahá'ís and showing the Bahá'í spirit and attitude towards work and service should attract favorable attention and may, in many instances, be instrumental in attracting individuals to the Faith of Bahá'u'lláh. And finally, the period of overseas service often produces a taste for such service, and volunteers may well offer to directly promote the pioneer work either in the same country or in another developing country.

On behalf of the Universal House of Justice

107. On the question of education, we are always thinking–
"education is only in this country or that country." There are
thousands of "best" universities around the world. . . . The youth
must go and study in other areas. . . . and these students . . .
must study the books—what are the possibilities in other countries to study? . . . This student movement must be encouraged
. . . we want the youth to get up and go. Get up and go bravely.
Go to the universities, go to the villages, go to the great teaching areas and do something great and greater. For every movement of a single, young pioneer, oceans of events will happen.

Raḥmatu'lláh Muhájir

Youth Year of Service

108. Bahá'í youth should be encouraged to think of their studies and of their training for a trade or profession as part of their
service to the Cause of God and in the context of a lifetime
that will be devoted to advancing the interests of the Faith. At
the same time, during their years of study, youth are often able
to offer specific periods of weeks or months, or even of a year or
more, during which they can devote themselves to travel teaching or to serving the Bahá'í community in other ways, such as
conducting children's classes in remote villages. They should
be encouraged to offer such service, which will in itself be admirable experience for the future, and the National Assembly
should instruct an appropriate committee to receive such offers
and to organize their implementation so as to derive the greatest possible advantage from them.

The Universal House of Justice

109. It is our hope that in the international travel teaching
program now being launched the youth will assume a major
role by devoting time during their vacations, and particularly

during the long vacation at the end of the academic year, to the promotion of the teaching work in all its aspects, not only within their own national communities but farther afield. Some youth may have financial resources of their own, others may be able and willing to work and save the funds necessary for such projects, still others may have the financial backing of their parents, relatives or friends. In other cases the Bahá'í funds may be able to supplement whatever resources the prospective traveling teacher may be able to supply.

The endurance of youth under arduous conditions, their vitality and vigor, and their ability to adapt themselves to local situations, to meet new challenges, and to impart their warmth and enthusiasm to those they visit, combined with the standard of conduct upheld by Bahá'í youth, make them potent instruments for the execution of the contemplated projects. Indeed, through these distinctive qualities they can become the spearhead of any enterprise and the driving force of any undertaking in which they participate, whether local or national. Our expectant eyes are fixed on Bahá'í youth!

The Universal House of Justice

110. The designation of 1985 by the United Nations as International Youth Year opens new vistas for the activities in which the young members of our community are engaged. The hope of the United Nations in thus focusing on youth is to encourage their conscious participation in the affairs of the world through their involvement in international development and such other undertakings and relationships as may aid the realization of their aspirations for a world without war.

These expectations reinforce the immediate, vast opportunities begging our attention. To visualize, however imperfectly, the challenges that engage us now, we have only to reflect, in the light of our sacred Writings, upon the confluence of favorable circumstances brought about by the accelerated unfolding of the Divine Plan over nearly five decades, by the untold potencies of the spiritual drama being played out in Iran, and by the creative energy stimulated by awareness of the approaching end of the twentieth century. Undoubtedly, it is within your power to contribute significantly to shaping the societies of the coming century; youth can move the world.

How apt, indeed how exciting, that so portentous an occasion should be presented to you, the young, eager followers of the Blessed Beauty, to enlarge the scope of your endeavors in precisely that arena of action in which you strive so conscientiously to distinguish yourselves! For in the theme proposed by the United Nations—"Participation, Development, Peace"—can be perceived an affirmation that the goals pursued by you, as Bahá'ís, are at heart the very objects of the frenetic searchings of your despairing contemporaries.

The Universal House of Justice

111. There is one comment that the Universal House of Justice has asked us to make in relation to a number of points made in the analysis, since this may assist in overcoming the problem of the bewildering range of alternatives that lie before youth in these days. This is the importance of conveying to the youth the awareness that every aspect of a person's life is an element of his or her service to Bahá'u'lláh: the love and respect one has for one's parents; the pursuit of one's education; the nurturing of good health; the acquiring of a trade of profession; one's behavior towards others and the upholding of a high moral standard; one's marriage and the bringing up of one's children; one's activities in teaching the Faith and the building up the strength of the Bahá'í community whether this be in such simple mat-

ters as attending the Nineteen Day Feast or the observance of the Bahá'í Holy Days, or in more demanding tasks required by service in the administration of the Faith; and, not least, to take time each day to read the Writings and say the Obligatory Prayer, which are the source of growing spiritual strength, understanding, and attachment to God. The concept of the Youth Year of Service should be viewed in this context, as a special service that the youth can devote to the Cause, and which should prove to be a highly valuable element in their own spiritual and intellectual development. It is not an alternative to, or in conflict with, the carrying out of the other vital tasks enumerated above, but rather a unique service and privilege which should be combined with them in the way that is best suited to each individual case.

On behalf of the Universal House of Justice

6

Personal Conduct

Purity of Character

1. O ye the beloved of the one true God! Pass beyond the narrow retreats of your evil and corrupt desires, and advance into the vast immensity of the realm of God, and abide ye in the meads of sanctity and of detachment, that the fragrance of your deeds may lead the whole of mankind to the ocean of God's unfading glory.

Bahá'u'lláh

2. A race of men . . . incomparable in character, shall be raised up which, with the feet of detachment, will tread under all who are in heaven and on earth, and will cast the sleeve of holiness over all that hath been created from water and clay.

Bahá'u'lláh

3. Would that ye had the power to perceive the things your Lord, the All-Merciful, doth see—things that attest the excellence of your rank, that bear witness to the greatness of your worth, that proclaim the sublimity of your station! God grant that your desires and unmortified passions may not hinder you from that which hath been ordained for you.

Bahá'u'lláh

4. The choice of clothing and the cut of the beard and its dressing are left to the discretion of men. But beware, O people, lest ye make yourselves the playthings of the ignorant.

Bahá'u'lláh

5. God loveth those who are pure. Naught in the Bayán and in the sight of God is more loved than purity and immaculate cleanliness. . . .

God desireth not to see, in the Dispensation of the Bayán, any soul deprived of joy and radiance. He indeed desireth that under all conditions, all may be adorned with such purity, both inwardly and outwardly, that no repugnance may be caused even to themselves, how much less unto others.

The Báb

6. O Friends of the Pure and Omnipotent God! To be pure and holy in all things is an attribute of the consecrated soul and a necessary characteristic of the unenslaved mind. The best of perfections is immaculacy and the freeing of oneself from every defect. Once the individual is, in every respect, cleansed and purified, then will he become a focal center reflecting the Manifest Light.

First in a human being's way of life must be purity, then freshness, cleanliness, and independence of spirit. First must the stream bed be cleansed, then may the sweet river waters be led unto it. Chaste eyes enjoy the beatific vision of the Lord and know what this encounter meaneth; a pure sense inhaleth the fragrances that blow from the rose gardens of His grace; a burnished heart will mirror forth the comely face of truth. . . .

My meaning is this, that in every aspect of life, purity and holiness, cleanliness and refinement, exalt the human condition and further the development of man's inner reality. Even in the physical realm, cleanliness will conduce to spirituality, as the Holy

Writings clearly state. And although bodily cleanliness is a physical thing, it hath, nevertheless, a powerful influence on the life of the spirit. It is even as a voice wondrously sweet, or a melody played: although sounds are but vibrations in the air which affect the ear's auditory nerve, and these vibrations are but chance phenomena carried along through the air, even so, see how they move the heart. A wondrous melody is wings for the spirit, and maketh the soul to tremble for joy. The purport is that physical cleanliness doth also exert its effect upon the human soul.*

'Abdu'l-Bahá

7. Desire is a flame that has reduced to ashes uncounted lifetime harvests of the learned, a devouring fire that even the vast sea of their accumulated knowledge could never quench. How often has it happened that an individual who was graced with every attribute of humanity and wore the jewel of true understanding, nevertheless followed after his passions until his excellent qualities passed beyond moderation and he was forced into excess. His pure intentions changed to evil ones, his attributes were no longer put to uses worthy of them, and the power of his desires turned him aside from righteousness and its rewards into ways that were dangerous and dark. A good character is in the sight of God and His chosen ones and the possessors of insight, the most excellent and praiseworthy of all things, but always on condition that its center of emanation should be reason and knowledge and its base should be true moderation.

'Abdu'l-Bahá

---

* Bahá'u'lláh, in the Kitáb-i-Aqdas, exhorts the believers "to be the essence of cleanliness." Specifically, one is "to wash one's feet," "to perfume one's self," "to bathe in clean water," "to cut one's nails," "to wash soiled things in clean water," "to be stainless in one's dress," and "to renew the furnishings of one's house" (*Synopsis and Codification of the Kitáb-i-Aqdas,* p. 162).

8. A rectitude of conduct, an abiding sense of undeviating justice, unobscured by the demoralizing influences which a cor-
ruption-ridden political life so strikingly manifests; a chaste,
pure, and holy life, unsullied and unclouded by the indecen-
cies, the vices, the false standards, which an inherently deficient moral code tolerates, perpetuates, and fosters; a fraternity
freed from that cancerous growth of racial prejudice, which is
eating into the vitals of an already debilitated society—these
are the ideals which the American believers must, from now
on, individually and through concerted action, strive to promote, in both their private and public lives, ideals which are
the chief propelling forces that can most effectively accelerate
the march of their institutions, plans, and enterprises, that can
guard the honor and integrity of their Faith, and subdue any
obstacles that may confront it in the future.

This rectitude of conduct, with its implications of justice,
equity, truthfulness, honesty, fair-mindedness, reliability, and
trustworthiness, must distinguish every phase of the life of the
Bahá'í community.

Shoghi Effendi

9. Such a rectitude of conduct must manifest itself, with ever-
increasing potency, in every verdict which the elected representatives of the Bahá'í community, in whatever capacity they may
find themselves, may be called upon to pronounce. It must be
constantly reflected in the business dealings of all its members,
in their domestic lives, in all manner of employment, and in
any service they may, in the future, render their government or
people. It must be exemplified in the conduct of all Bahá'í elec-
tors, when exercising their sacred rights and functions. It must
characterize the attitude of every loyal believer towards non-
acceptance of political posts, nonidentification with political
parties, nonparticipation in political controversies, and non-

membership in political organizations and ecclesiastical institutions. It must reveal itself in the uncompromising adherence of all, whether young or old, to the clearly enunciated and fundamental principles laid down by 'Abdu'l-Bahá in His addresses, and to the laws and ordinances revealed by Bahá'u'lláh in His Most Holy Book. It must be demonstrated in the impartiality of every defender of the Faith against its enemies, in his fair-mindedness in recognizing any merits that enemy may possess, and in his honesty in discharging any obligations he may have towards him. It must constitute the brightest ornament of the life, the pursuits, the exertions, and the utterances of every Bahá'í teacher, whether laboring at home or abroad, whether in the front ranks of the teaching force, or occupying a less active and responsible position.

Shoghi Effendi

10. It must be remembered, however, that the maintenance of such a high standard of moral conduct is not to be associated or confused with any form of asceticism, or of excessive and bigoted puritanism. The standard inculcated by Bahá'u'lláh seeks, under no circumstances, to deny anyone the legitimate right and privilege to derive the fullest advantage and benefit from the manifold joys, beauties, and pleasures with which the world has been so plentifully enriched by an All-Loving Creator. *"Should a man,"* Bahá'u'lláh Himself reassures us, *"wish to adorn himself with the ornaments of the earth, to wear its apparels, or partake of the benefits it can bestow, no harm can befall him, if he alloweth nothing whatever to intervene between him and God, for God hath ordained every good thing, whether created in the heavens or in the earth, for such of His servants as truly believe in Him. Eat ye, O people, of the good things which God hath allowed you, and deprive not yourselves from His wondrous bounties. Render thanks and praise unto Him, and be of them that are truly thankful."*

Shoghi Effendi

Smoking

11. There are ... forbidden things which do not cause immediate harm, and the injurious effects of which are only gradually
produced: such acts are also repugnant to the Lord, and blameworthy in His sight, and repellent. The absolute unlawfulness
of these, however, hath not been expressly set forth in the Text,
but their avoidance is necessary to purity, cleanliness, the preservation of health, and freedom from addiction.

Among these latter is smoking tobacco, which is dirty, smelly,
offensive—an evil habit, and one the harmfulness of which
gradually becometh apparent to all. Every qualified physician
hath ruled—and this hath also been proven by tests—that one
of the components of tobacco is a deadly poison, and that the
smoker is vulnerable to many and various diseases. This is why
smoking hath been plainly set forth as repugnant from the stand-
point of hygiene. . . .

My meaning is that in the sight of God, smoking tobacco is
deprecated, abhorrent, filthy in the extreme; and, albeit by degrees, highly injurious to health. It is also a waste of money and
time, and maketh the user a prey to a noxious addiction. To
those who stand firm in the Covenant, this habit is therefore
censured both by reason and experience, and renouncing it will
bring relief and peace of mind to all men. Furthermore, this
will make it possible to have a fresh mouth and unstained fingers, and hair that is free of a foul and repellent smell. On
receipt of this missive, the friends will surely, by whatever means
and even over a period of time, forsake this pernicious habit.
Such is my hope.

'Abdu'l-Bahá

12. Concerning smoking; it is not forbidden in the Bahá'í teachings and no one can enforce its prohibition. It is strongly dis-

couraged as a habit which is not very clean or very healthy. But it is a matter left entirely to the conscience of the individual and not of major importance, whereas the use of alcohol is definitely forbidden and thus not left optional to the conscience of the believer.

On behalf of Shoghi Effendi

Alcohol

13. O Son of Dust! Turn not away thine eyes from the matchless wine of the immortal Beloved, and open them not to foul and mortal dregs. Take from the hands of the divine Cupbearer the chalice of immortal life, that all wisdom may be thine, and that thou mayest hearken unto the mystic voice calling from the realm of the invisible. Cry aloud, ye that are of low aim! Wherefore have ye turned away from My holy and immortal wine unto evanescent water?

Bahá'u'lláh

14. Fear ye God, O people of the earth, and think not that the wine We have mentioned in Our Tablet is the wine which men drink, and which causeth their intelligence to pass away, their human nature to be perverted, their light to be changed, and their purity to be soiled. Our intention is indeed that wine which intensifieth man's love for God, for His Chosen Ones and for His loved ones, and igniteth in the hearts the fire of God and love for Him, and glorification and praise of Him. So potent is this wine that a drop thereof will attract him who drinketh it to the Court of His sanctity and nearness, and will enable him to attain the presence of God, the King, the Glorious, the Most Beauteous. It is a wine that blotteth out from the hearts of the true lovers all suggestions of limitation, establisheth the truth of the signs of His one-

ness and divine unity, and leadeth them to the Tabernacle of the Well-Beloved, in the presence of God, the Sovereign Lord, the Self-Subsisting, the All-Forgiving, the All-Generous. We meant by this Wine, the River of God, and His favor, the fountain of His living waters, and the Mystic Wine and its divine grace, even as it was revealed in the Qur'án, if ye are of those who understand. He said, and how true is His utterance: "A wine delectable to those who drink it." And He had no purpose in this but the wine We have mentioned to you, O people of certitude!

Beware lest ye exchange the Wine of God for your own wine, for it will stupefy your minds, and turn your faces away from the Countenance of God, the All-Glorious, the Peerless, the Inaccessible. Approach it not, for it hath been forbidden unto you by the behest of God, the Exalted, the Almighty.

Bahá'u'lláh

15. Intellect and the faculty of comprehension are God's gifts whereby man is distinguished from other animals. Will a wise man want to lose this Light in the darkness of intoxication? No, by God! This will not satisfy him! He will, rather, do that which will develop his powers of intelligence and understanding, and not increase his negligence, heedlessness and decline. This is an explicit text in the perspicuous Book, wherein God hath set forth every goodly virtue, and exposed every reprehensible act.

'Abdu'l-Bahá

16. The drinking of wine . . . is, according to the text of the Most Holy Book, forbidden; for it is the cause of chronic diseases, weakeneth the nerves, and consumeth the mind.

'Abdu'l-Bahá

17. With regard to your first question on alcohol and drinking, Bahá'u'lláh, fully aware of the great misery that it brings about, prohibits it as He expressly states that everything that takes away the mind, or in other words makes one drunk, is forbidden.

On behalf of Shoghi Effendi

18. With regard to the question you have raised in connection with the sale of alcoholic liquors by the friends: he wishes me to inform you that dealings with such liquors, in any form, are highly discouraged in the Cause. The believers should, therefore, consider it their spiritual obligation to refrain from undertaking any business enterprise that would involve them in the traffic of alcoholic drinks.

On behalf of Shoghi Effendi

19. With reference to your question whether those foods which have been flavored with alcoholic liquors such as brandy, rum, etc., should be classified under the same category as the intoxicating drinks, and consequently be avoided by believers, the Guardian wished all the friends to know that such foods, or beverages, are strictly prohibited.

On behalf of Shoghi Effendi

20. Under no circumstances should Bahá'ís drink. It is so unambiguously forbidden in the Tablets of Bahá'u'lláh, that there is no excuse for them even touching it in the form of a toast, or in a burning plum pudding; in fact, in any way.

On behalf of Shoghi Effendi

21. On all occasions officially sponsored by Bahá'í Institutions or where the host is acting as a representative of the Cause alcohol should not be served. In private homes or in the course of

business or professional activity it is left to the conscience of Bahá'ís themselves whether they serve alcoholic drinks to non-Bahá'ís but the obligation is very strong to observe the prohibition enjoined by Bahá'u'lláh.

The Universal House of Justice

22. The fact that Bahá'ís themselves must not drink alcohol is abundantly clear and needs no comment here. With regard to the serving of alcohol to non-Bahá'ís:

1. No Bahá'í institution should serve alcohol to non-Bahá'ís under any circumstances.
2. If an individual Bahá'í entertaining an individual guest or a small group of guests as an official representative of the Bahá'í community, he should not serve alcohol in his own home, but must use his discretion whether or not to do so if the entertaining is taking place in a restaurant.
3. No Bahá'í should serve alcohol at any function or reception given by him, such as a wedding reception or a party to which a number of people are invited.
4. When a Bahá'í is privately entertaining a non-Bahá'í or a small group of guests in his own home, he must himself judge whether or not to serve alcohol. This will depend to a great degree on the customs of the country in which he is living, the individuals concerned, and the host's relationship to his guests. Obviously it is better for the Bahá'í not to serve alcohol if possible, but against this he must weigh the probable reaction of the guest in the circumstances which prevail and in the particular situation. In some countries there would be no problem in failing to provide alcohol to a guest; in others it would be regarded as extremely peculiar and anti-social and would immedi-

ately raise a barrier to further contact. It is not desirable to
make a major issue of the matter.

5. When such private entertaining of an individual or small
   group of non-Bahá'ís taking place in a restaurant the same
   general principles as in point 4 above apply, except that in
   such a public place a failure to provide alcoholic drinks
   would be less easily understood than in a private home,
   and the Bahá'í must use his discretion accordingly.

6. Alcohol must not be served in a restaurant or other business which is wholly owned by Bahá'ís.

7. If a Bahá'í is employed by others in a job which involves
   the serving of alcohol, he is not obliged to change that
   employment. This is a matter left to each individual to
   decide in the light of his own conscience. Obviously such
   kind of employment vary widely from bartending to serving in a grocery in which wine is retailed. If the job requires a great deal of involvement with the serving of
   alcohol it is better for the Bahá'í to obtain other employment if he can.

On behalf of the Universal House of Justice

Use of Illicit Drugs

23. As to opium, it is foul and accursed. God protect us from
the punishment He inflicteth on the user. According to the explicit Text of the Most Holy Book, it is forbidden, and its use is
utterly condemned. Reason showeth that smoking opium is a
kind of insanity, and experience attesteth that the user is completely cut off from the human kingdom. May God protect all
against the perpetration of an act so hideous as this, an act which
layeth in ruins the very foundation of what it is to be human,
and which causeth the user to be dispossessed for ever and ever.

For opium fasteneth on the soul, so that the user's conscience dieth, his mind is blotted away, his perceptions are eroded. It turneth the living into the dead. It quencheth the natural heat. No greater harm can be conceived than that which opium inflicteth. Fortunate are they who never even speak the name of it; then think how wretched is the user.

O ye lovers of God! In this, the cycle of Almighty God, violence and force, constraint and oppression, are one and all condemned. It is, however, mandatory that the use of opium be prevented by any means whatsoever, that perchance the human race may be delivered from this most powerful of plagues. And otherwise, woe and misery to whoso falleth short of his duty to his Lord.

'Abdu'l-Bahá

24. Bahá'ís should not use hallucinogenic agents, including LSD, peyote and similar substances, except when prescribed for medical treatment. Neither should they become involved in experiments with such substances.

Although we have found no direct reference to marijuana in the Bahá'í writings, since this substance is derived from what is considered to be a milder form of cannabis, the species used to produce ḥashísh, we can share with you a translation from the Persian of a Tablet of 'Abdu'l-Bahá on ḥashísh:

> Regarding ḥashísh you had pointed out that some Persians have become habituated to its use. Gracious God! This is the worst of all intoxicants, and its prohibition is explicitly revealed. Its use causeth the disintegration of thought and the complete torpor of the soul. How could anyone seek this fruit of the infernal tree, and by partaking of it, be led to exemplify the qualities of a monster? How could one use this forbidden drug, and thus deprive himself of the blessings of the All-Merciful? . . .

Alcohol consumeth the mind and causeth man to commit acts of absurdity, but . . . this wicked ḥashísh extinguisheth the mind, freezeth the spirit, petrifieth the soul, wasteth the body and leaveth man frustrated and lost.

The Universal House of Justice

25. Concerning the so-called "spiritual" virtues of the hallucinogens. . . . spiritual stimulation should come from turning one's heart to Bahá'u'lláh, and not through physical means such as drugs and agents.

From the description given in your letter it appears that hallucinogenic agents are a form of intoxicant. As the friends, including the youth, are required strictly to abstain from all forms of intoxicants, and are further expected conscientiously to obey the civil law of their country, it is obvious that they should refrain from using these drugs.

A very great responsibility for the future peace and well-being of the world is borne by the youth of today. Let the Bahá'í youth by the power of the Cause they espouse be the shining example for their companions.

The Universal House of Justice

26. Anyone involved in the use of peyote should be told that in the Bahá'í Faith spiritual stimulation comes from turning one's heart to Bahá'u'lláh and not through any physical means. They should therefore be encouraged to give up the use of peyote.

The Universal House of Justice

Gambling and Lotteries

27. The trials of man are of two kinds. (a) The consequences of his own actions. If a man eats too much, he ruins his digestion; if he takes poison he becomes ill or dies. If a person gambles

lose his money; if he drinks too much he will lose his equilibrium. All these sufferings are caused by the man himself, it is quite clear therefore that certain sorrows are the result of our own deeds.

'Abdu'l-Bahá

28. Although we have not found any text which forbids the owning of race horses, horse racing as a means of winning the prize money and betting at race courses, we quote the translation of a Tablet of 'Abdu'l-Bahá on horse racing:

> Betting on horse racing is a pernicious disease. It hath been seen in Europe what distress this hath caused. Thousands have become afflicted and distraught. The friends of God must engage in work which is lawful and attracteth blessings, so that God's aid and bounty may always surround them.

The Universal House of Justice

29. Although we may have written to you previously commenting on the question as to whether lotteries and betting, such as betting on football games, bingo, etc., are included under the prohibition of gambling, we repeat that this is a matter that is to be considered in detail by the Universal House of Justice. In the meantime, your National Assembly should not make an issue of these matters and should leave it to the consciences of the individual friends who ask to decide for themselves in each case.

The Universal House of Justice

Being Distinguished for Purity and Sanctity

30. Make ye then a mighty effort, that the purity and sanctity which, above all else, are cherished by 'Abdu'l-Bahá, shall distinguish the people of Bahá; that in every kind of excellence

the people of God shall surpass all other human beings; that both outwardly and inwardly they shall prove superior to the rest; that for purity, immaculacy, refinement, and the preservation of health, they shall be leaders in the vanguard of those who know. And that by their freedom from enslavement, their knowledge, their self-control, they shall be first among the pure, the free and the wise.

'Abdu'l-Bahá

31. O Divine Providence! Bestow Thou in all things purity and cleanliness upon the people of Bahá. Grant that they be freed from all defilement, and released from all addictions. Save them from committing any repugnant act, unbind them from the chains of every evil habit, that they may live pure and free, wholesome and cleanly, worthy to serve at Thy Sacred Threshold and fit to be related to their Lord. Deliver them from intoxicating drinks and tobacco, save them, rescue them, from this opium that bringeth on madness, suffer them to enjoy the sweet savors of holiness, that they may drink deep of the mystic cup of heavenly love and know the rapture of being drawn ever closer unto the Realm of the All-Glorious. For it is even as Thou hast said: "All that thou hast in thy cellar will not appease the thirst of my love—bring me, O cupbearer, of the wine of the spirit a cup full as the sea!"

'Abdu'l-Bahá

7

Interpersonal Relationships

The Relationship of Children to Parents

1. The fruits of the tree of existence are trustworthiness, loyalty, truthfulness and purity. After the recognition of the oneness of the Lord, exalted be He, the most important of all duties is to have due regard for the rights of one's parents. This matter hath been mentioned in all the Books of God.

Bahá'u'lláh

2. Say, O My people! Show honor to your parents and pay homage to them. This will cause blessings to descend upon you from the clouds of the bounty of your Lord, the Exalted, the Great. . . .

Beware lest ye commit that which would sadden the hearts of your fathers and mothers. Follow ye the path of Truth which indeed is a straight path. Should anyone give you a choice between the opportunity to render a service to Me and a service to them, choose ye to serve them, and let such service be a path leading you to Me. This is My exhortation and command unto thee. Observe therefore that which thy Lord, the Mighty, the Gracious, hath prescribed unto thee.

Bahá'u'lláh

3. It is seemly that the servant should, after each prayer, supplicate God to bestow mercy and forgiveness upon his parents. Thereupon God's call will be raised: "Thousand upon thousand of what thou hast asked for thy parents shall be thy recompense!" Blessed is he who remembereth his parents when communing with God. There is, verily, no God but Him, the Mighty, the Well-Beloved.

The Báb

4. If thou wouldst show kindness and consideration to thy parents so that they may feel generally pleased, this would also please Me, for parents must be highly respected and it is essential that they should feel contented, provided they deter thee not from gaining access to the Threshold of the Almighty, nor keep thee back from walking in the way of the Kingdom. Indeed it behooveth them to encourage and spur thee on in this direction.

'Abdu'l-Bahá

5. The son . . . must show forth the utmost obedience towards his father, and should conduct himself as a humble and a lowly servant. Day and night he should seek diligently to ensure the comfort and welfare of his loving father and to secure his good-pleasure. He must forgo his own rest and enjoyment and constantly strive to bring gladness to the hearts of his father and mother, that thereby he may attain the good-pleasure of the Almighty and be graciously aided by the hosts of the unseen.

'Abdu'l-Bahá

6. Also a father and mother endure the greatest troubles and hardships for their children; and often when the children have reached the age of maturity, the parents pass on to the other world. Rarely does it happen that a father and mother in this

world see the reward of the care and trouble they have undergone for their children. Therefore, children, in return for this care and trouble, must show forth charity and beneficence, and must implore pardon and forgiveness for their parents. So you ought, in return for the love and kindness shown you by your father, to give to the poor for his sake, with greatest submission and humility implore pardon and remission of sins, and ask for the supreme mercy.

'Abdu'l-Bahá

7. The Guardian, in his remarks to . . . about parents' and children's, wives' and husbands' relations in America, meant that there is a tendency in that country for children to be too independent of the wishes of their parents and lacking in the respect due to them.

On behalf of Shoghi Effendi

8. Although Bahá'í services should be undertaken with a spirit of sacrifice, one cannot lose sight of the importance given in our Holy Writings to the responsibilities placed on parents in relationship to their children, as well as to the duties of children towards their parents.

The Universal House of Justice

The Bond of Marriage

THE RELATIONSHIP BETWEEN HUSBAND AND WIFE

9. And when He desired to manifest grace and beneficence to men, and to set the world in order, He revealed observances and created laws; among them He established the law of marriage, made it as a fortress for well-being and salvation, and enjoined it

upon us in that which was sent down out of the heaven of sanctity in His Most Holy Book. He saith, great is His glory: "Enter into wedlock, O people, that ye may bring forth one who will make mention of Me amid My servants. This is My bidding unto you; hold fast to it as an assistance to yourselves."

Bahá'u'lláh

10. O peerless Lord! In Thine almighty wisdom Thou hast enjoined marriage upon the peoples, that the generations of men may succeed one another in this contingent world, and that ever, so long as the world shall last, they may busy themselves at the Threshold of Thy oneness with servitude and worship, with salutation, adoration and praise.

'Abdu'l-Bahá

11. Marriage, among the mass of the people, is a physical bond, and this union can only be temporary, since it is foredoomed to a physical separation at the close.

Among the people of Bahá, however, marriage must be a union of the body and of the spirit as well, for here both husband and wife are aglow with the same wine, both are enamored of the same matchless Face, both live and move through the same spirit, both are illumined by the same glory. This connection between them is a spiritual one, hence it is a bond that will abide forever. Likewise do they enjoy strong and lasting ties in the physical world as well, for if the marriage is based both on the spirit and the body, that union is a true one, hence it will endure. If, however, the bond is physical and nothing more, it is sure to be only temporary, and must inexorably end in separation.

When, therefore, the people of Bahá undertake to marry, the union must be a true relationship, a spiritual coming together as well as a physical one, so that throughout every phase of life, and in all the worlds of God, their union will endure; for this real oneness is a gleaming out of the love of God.

In the same way, when any souls grow to be true believers, they will attain a spiritual relationship with one another, and show forth a tenderness which is not of this world. They will, all of them, become elated from a draft of divine love, and that union of theirs, that connection, will also abide forever. Souls, that is, who will consign their own selves to oblivion, strip from themselves the defects of humankind, and unchain themselves from human bondage, will beyond any doubt be illumined with the heavenly splendors of oneness, and will all attain unto real union in the world that dieth not.

'Abdu'l-Bahá

12. O ye two believers in God! The Lord, peerless is He, hath made woman and man to abide with each other in the closest companionship, and to be even as a single soul. They are two helpmates, two intimate friends, who should be concerned about the welfare of each other.

If they live thus, they will pass through this world with perfect contentment, bliss, and peace of heart, and become the object of divine grace and favor in the Kingdom of heaven. But if they do other than this, they will live out their lives in great bitterness, longing at every moment for death, and will be shamefaced in the heavenly realm.

Strive, then, to abide, heart and soul, with each other as two doves in the nest, for this is to be blessed in both worlds.

'Abdu'l-Bahá

13. Of course, under normal circumstances, every person should consider it his moral duty to marry. And this is what Bahá'u'lláh has encouraged the believers to do. But marriage is by no means

an obligation. In the last resort it is for the individual to decide whether he wishes to lead a family life or live in a state of celibacy.

On behalf of Shoghi Effendi

14. A truly Bahá'í home is a true fortress upon which the Cause can rely while planning its campaigns. If . . . and . . . love each other and would like to marry, Shoghi Effendi does not wish them to think that by doing so they are depriving themselves of the privilege of service; in fact such a union will enhance their ability to serve. There is nothing more beautiful than to have young Bahá'ís marry and found truly Bahá'í homes, the type Bahá'u'lláh wishes them to be. Please give them both the Guardian's loving greetings.

On behalf of Shoghi Effendi

15. It should, moreover, be borne in mind that although to be married is highly desirable, and Bahá'u'lláh has strongly recommended it, it is not the central purpose of life. If a person has to wait a considerable period before finding a spouse, or if ultimately, he or she must remain single, it does not mean that he or she is thereby unable to fulfill his or her life's purpose.

The Universal House of Justice

CHOOSING A SPOUSE

16. Bahá'í marriage is the commitment of the two parties one to the other, and their mutual attachment of mind and heart. Each must, however, exercise the utmost care to become thoroughly acquainted with the character of the other, that the binding covenant between them may be a tie that will endure forever. Their purpose must be this: to become loving companions and comrades and at one with each other for time and eternity. . . .

The true marriage of Bahá'ís is this, that husband and wife should be united both physically and spiritually, that they may ever improve the spiritual life of each other, and may enjoy everlasting unity throughout all the worlds of God. This is Bahá'í marriage.

Abdu'l-Bahá

17. As for the question regarding marriage under the Law of God: first thou must choose one who is pleasing to thee, and then the matter is subject to the consent of father and mother. Before thou makest thy choice, they have no right to interfere.

Abdu'l-Bahá

18. O ye two who have believed in Him!

Your letter was received and its contents were noted, I pray God that ye may at all times be in the utmost love and harmony, and be a cause for the spirituality of the human world. This union will unquestionably promote love and affection between the black and the white, and will affect and encourage others. These two races will unite and merge together, and there will appear and take root a new generation sound in health and beauteous in countenance.

Abdu'l-Bahá

19. He realizes your desire to get married is quite a natural one, and he will pray that God will assist you to find a suitable companion with whom you can be truly happy and united in the service of the Faith. Bahá'u'lláh has urged marriage upon all people as the natural and rightful way of life. He has also, however, placed strong emphasis on its spiritual nature, which, while in no way precluding a normal physical life, is the most essential aspect of marriage. That two people should live their lives

...love and harmony is of far greater importance than that they should be consumed with passion for each other. The one is a great rock of strength on which to lean in time of need; the other a purely temporary thing which may at any time die out.

On behalf of Shoghi Effendi

20. Bahá'í law places the responsibility for ascertaining knowledge of the character of those entering into the marriage contract on the two parties involved, and on the parents, who must give consent to the marriage.

The obligation of the Spiritual Assembly is to ascertain that all requirements of civil and Bahá'í law have been complied with, and, having done so, the Assembly may neither refuse to perform the marriage ceremony nor delay it.

The Universal House of Justice,

ENGAGEMENT

21. Bahá'í marriage is union and cordial affection between the two parties. They must, however, exercise the utmost care and become acquainted with each other's character. This eternal bond should be made secure by a firm covenant, and the intention should be to foster harmony, fellowship and unity and to attain everlasting life.

'Abdu'l-Bahá

22. The law of the Kitáb-i-Aqdas that the lapse of time between engagement and marriage should not exceed ninety-five days is binding on Persian believers wherever they reside, if both parties are Persian. This law is not applicable, however, if one of the parties is a western believer.

The Universal House of Justice

23. The laws of the Kitáb-i-Aqdas regarding the period of engagement have not been made applicable to believers in the West, and therefore there is no requirement that the parties to a marriage obtain consent of the parents before announcing their engagement. However, there is no objection to informing the believers that it would be wise for them to do so in order to avoid later embarrassment if consents are withheld.

The Universal House of Justice

THE LAW OF CONSENT

24. Bahá'u'lláh has clearly stated the consent of all living parents is required for a Bahá'í marriage. This applies whether the parents are Bahá'ís or non-Bahá'ís, divorced for years, or not. This great law He has laid down to strengthen the social fabric, to knit closer the ties of the home, to place a certain gratitude and respect in the hearts of children for those who have given them life and sent their souls out on the eternal journey towards their Creator. We Bahá'ís must realize that in present-day society the exact opposite process is taking place: young people care less and less for their parents' wishes, divorce is considered a natural right, and obtained on the flimsiest and most unwarrantable and shabby pretexts. People separated from each other, especially if one of them has had full custody of the children, are only too willing to belittle the importance of the partner in marriage also responsible as a parent for bringing those children into this world. The Bahá'ís must, through rigid adherence to the Bahá'í laws and teachings, combat those corrosive forces which are so rapidly destroying home life and the beauty of family relationships, and tearing down the moral structure of society.

On behalf of Shoghi Effendi

25. Regarding the question whether it is necessary to obtain the consent of the parents of a non-Bahá'í participant in a marriage with a Bahá'í; as Bahá'u'lláh has stated that the consent of the parents of both parties is required in order to promote unity and avoid friction, and as the Aqdas does not specify any exceptions to this rule, the Guardian feels that under all circumstances the consent of the parents of both parties is required.

On behalf of Shoghi Effendi

26. I notice that I have neglected to answer your question concerning Mrs. . . . consent to her daughter's marriage: this must be given in order to be a Bahá'í Marriage. Bahá'u'lláh requires this and makes no provision about a parent changing his or her mind. So they are free to do so. Once the written consent is given and the marriage takes place, the parents have no right to interfere any more.

On behalf of Shoghi Effendi

27. All too often nowadays . . . consent [of parents for Bahá'í marriage] is withheld by non-Bahá'í parents for reasons of bigotry and racial prejudice; yet we have seen again and again the profound effect on those very parents of the firmness of the children in the Bahá'í law, to the extent that not only is the consent ultimately given in many cases, but the character of the parents can be affected and their relationship with their child greatly strengthened.

The Universal House of Justice

28. It is perfectly true that Bahá'u'lláh's statement that the consent of all living parents is required for marriage places a grave responsibility on each parent. When the parents are Bahá'ís they should, of course, act objectively in withholding or granting

their approval. They cannot evade this responsibility by merely acquiescing in their child's wish, nor should they be swayed by prejudice; but, whether they be Bahá'í or non-Bahá'í, the parents' decision is binding, whatever the reason that may have motivated it. Children must recognize and understand that this act of consenting is the duty of a parent. They must have respect in their hearts for those who have given them life, and whose good pleasure they must at all times strive to win.

The Universal House of Justice

THE CEREMONY

29. The pledge of marriage, the verse to be spoken individually by the bride and the bridegroom in the presence of at least two witnesses acceptable to the Spiritual Assembly is, as stipulated in the Kitáb-i-Aqdas (The Most Holy Book):

"We will, all, verily, abide by the Will of God."

Bahá'í Prayers

30. Bahá'í marriage should at present not be pressed into any kind of a uniform mold. What is absolutely essential is what Bahá'u'lláh stipulated in the Aqdas: the friends can add to these selected writings if they please.

On behalf of Shoghi Effendi

31. If a Bahá'í marries a non-Bahá'í who wishes to have the religious ceremony of his own sect carried out, it must be quite clear that, first, the Bahá'í partner is understood to be a Bahá'í by religion, and not to accept the religion of the other party to the marriage through having his or her religious ceremony; and second, the ceremony must be of a nature which does not commit the Bahá'í to any declaration of faith in a religion other

than his own. Under these circumstances the Bahá'í can partake of the religious ceremony of his non-Bahá'í partner.

The Bahá'í should insist on having the Bahá'í ceremony carried out before or after the non-Bahá'í one, on the same day.

Shoghi Effendi

DIVORCE

32. Truly, the Lord loveth union and harmony and abhorreth separation and divorce. Live ye one with another, O people, in radiance and joy. By My life! All that are on earth shall pass away, while good deeds alone shall endure; to the truth of My words God doth Himself bear witness. Compose your differences, O My servants; then heed ye the admonition of Our Pen of Glory and follow not the arrogant and wayward.

Bahá'u'lláh

33. The friends . . . must strictly refrain from divorce unless something ariseth which compelleth them to separate because of their aversion for each other, in that case with the knowledge of the Spiritual Assembly they may decide to separate. They must then be patient and wait one complete year. If during this year harmony is not re-established between them, then their divorce may be realized. It should not happen that upon the occurrence of a slight friction of displeasure between husband and wife, the husband would think of union with some other woman or, God forbid, the wife also think of another husband. This is contrary to the standard of heavenly value and true chastity. The friends of God must so live and conduct themselves, and evince such excellence of character and conduct, as to make others astonished. The love between husband and wife should not be purely physical, nay rather it must be

spiritual and heavenly. These two souls should be considered as one soul. How difficult it would be to divide a single soul! Nay, great would be the difficulty!

'Abdu'l-Bahá

Family Relationships

HAVING CHILDREN

34. O ye my two beloved children! The news of your union, as soon as it reached me, imparted infinite joy and gratitude. Praise be to God, those two faithful birds have sought shelter in one nest. I beseech God that He may enable them to raise an honored family, for the importance of marriage lieth in the bringing up of a richly blessed family, so that with entire gladness they may, even as candles, illuminate the world. For the enlightenment of the world dependeth upon the existence of man. If man did not exist in this world, it would have been like a tree without fruit. My hope is that you both may become even as one tree, and may, through the outpourings of the cloud of loving-kindness, acquire freshness and charm, and may blossom and yield fruit, so that your line may eternally endure.

Upon ye be the Glory of the Most Glorious.

'Abdu'l-Bahá

35. Both Bahá'u'lláh and the Báb emphasize the need of children in marriage. The latter, for example, states that to beget children is the highest physical fruit of man's existence. But neither say whether the number of children should be limited or not. Or if it is to be limited what is the proper method to be used.

On behalf of Shoghi Effendi

36. As to the problem of birth control. Neither Bahá'u'lláh nor 'Abdu'l-Bahá has revealed anything direct or explicit regarding this question. But the Bahá'í Teachings, when carefully studied imply that such current conceptions like birth control, if not necessarily wrong and immoral in principle, have nevertheless to be discarded as constituting a real danger to the very foundations of our social life. For Bahá'u'lláh explicitly reveals in His Book of laws that the very purpose of marriage is the procreation of children who, when grown up, will be able to know God and to recognize and observe His Commandments and Laws as revealed through His Messengers. Marriage is thus, according to the Bahá'í Teachings, primarily a social and moral act. It has a purpose which transcends the immediate personal needs and interests of the parties.

On behalf of Shoghi Effendi

37. We, as Bahá'ís, are not therefore in a position either to condemn the practice of birth control or to confirm it.

Birth control, however, when exercised in order to deliberately prevent the procreation of any children is against the Spirit of the Law of Bahá'u'lláh, which defines the primary purpose of marriage to be the rearing of children and their spiritual training in the Cause. The Universal House of Justice will have to consider this issue and give its verdict upon it.

On behalf of Shoghi Effendi

38. Basically the deliberate taking of human life is forbidden in the Cause, but the Sacred Text envisages certain possible exceptions to this rule and allows for the Universal House of Justice to legislate upon them. One such possible exception is the matter of abortion. It is clear that it is absolutely forbidden for a woman to have an abortion merely because she wants to have

one, but there may be circumstances in which an abortion might be justified. However, at the present time we do not wish to legislate on whether or in what circumstances abortion may be permitted, and therefore the whole matter is left to the consciences of those concerned who must carefully weigh the medical advice on the case in the light of the general guidance given in the Teachings.

The Universal House of Justice

39. We have not discovered any specific reference in the texts to the problem of population explosion in its relation to birth control. This question, of course, is a matter which is currently a subject of concern and speculation by many. A study of our teachings, however, indicates that in the future there will no doubt be a general improvement of standards of life and of health, but there will also be the full exploitation of unused and as yet unsuspected resources of the planet along with the control and tapping of its sources of raw material, with a great increase in productivity.

The Universal House of Justice

40. As to the use of intrauterine devices, we understand that there is a difference of professional opinion as to how they work, i.e., whether they prevent conception or whether they prevent the fertilized ovum from attaching to the wall of the uterus. However, the Guardian has stated that the individual life begins at conception. In using such devices, therefore, Bahá'ís will have to be guided by the best professional advice available and their own consciences. There is nothing in the Kitáb-i-Aqdas, however, concerning the placing of foreign materials in the body for preventing birth.

On behalf of the Universal House of Justice

41. It is clear that to have a surgical operation merely to avoid unwanted children is not acceptable. However, as in the case of abortion, circumstances might exist in which such an operation would be justified. Individual believers called upon to make such a decision must be guided by the Bahá'í principles involved, the best professional advice available to them and their own consciences. In arriving at a decision the parties must also take into consideration the availability, reliability and reversibility of all contraceptive methods.

On behalf of the Universal House of Justice

42. Abortion and surgical operations for the purpose of preventing the birth of unwanted children are forbidden in the Cause unless there are circumstances which justify such actions on medical grounds, in which case the decision, at present, is left to the consciences of those concerned who must carefully weigh the medical advice in the light of the general guidance given in the Teachings. Beyond this nothing has been found in the Writings concerning specific methods or procedures to be used in family planning. It should be pointed out, however, that the Teachings state that the soul appears at conception, and that therefore it would be improper to use such a method, the effect of which would be to produce an abortion after conception has taken place.

On behalf of the Universal House of Justice

43. As to birth control methods, the House of Justice does not wish to comment on the effectiveness or possible hazards of present-day contraceptive agents, and leaves it to individuals to decide what course of action they will take in light of the teachings and the best medical advice available.

On behalf of the Universal House of Justice

44. There is nothing in the Sacred Writings specifically on the subjects of birth control, abortion or sterilization, but Bahá'u'lláh did state that the primary purpose of marriage was the procreation of children, and it is to this primary purpose that the beloved Guardian alludes in many of the letters which are quoted in the compilation. This does not imply that a couple are obliged to have as many children as they can; the Guardian's secretary clearly stated on his behalf, in answer to an enquiry, that it was for the husband and wife to decide how many children they would have. A decision to have no children at all would vitiate the primary purpose of marriage unless, of course, there were some medical reason why such a decision would be required.

On behalf of the Universal House of Justice

RELATIONSHIPS AMONG HUSBAND, WIFE, AND CHILDREN

45. According to the teachings of Bahá'u'lláh the family, being a human unit, must be educated according to the rules of sanctity. All the virtues must be taught the family. The integrity of the family bond must be constantly considered, and the rights of the individual members must not be transgressed. The rights of the son, the father, the mother—none of them must be transgressed, none of them must be arbitrary. Just as the son has certain obligations to his father, the father, likewise, has certain obligations to his son. The mother, the sister and other members of the household have their certain prerogatives. All these rights and prerogatives must be conserved, yet the unity of the family must be sustained. The injury of one shall be considered the injury of all; the comfort of each, the comfort of all; the honor of one, the honor of all.

'Abdu'l-Bahá

46. The education and training of children is among the most meritorious acts of humankind and draweth down the grace and favor of the All-Merciful, for education is the indispensable foundation of all human excellence and alloweth man to work his way to the heights of abiding glory. If a child be trained from his infancy, he will, through the loving care of the Holy Gardener, drink in the crystal waters of the spirit and of knowledge, like a young tree amid the rilling brooks. And certainly he will gather to himself the bright rays of the Sun of Truth, and through its light and heat will grow ever fresh and fair in the garden of life. . . .

If, in this momentous task, a mighty effort be exerted, the world of humanity will shine out with other adornings, and shed the fairest light. Then will this darksome place grow luminous, and this abode of earth turn into Heaven. The very demons will change to angels then, and wolves to shepherds of the flock, and the wild-dog pack to gazelles that pasture on the plains of oneness, and ravening beasts to peaceful herds; and birds of prey, with talons sharp as knives, to songsters warbling their sweet native notes.

'Abdu'l-Bahá

47. While the children are yet in their infancy feed them from the breast of heavenly grace, foster them in the cradle of all excellence, rear them in the embrace of bounty. Give them the advantage of every useful kind of knowledge. Let them share in every new and rare and wondrous craft and art. Bring them up to work and strive, and accustom them to hardship. Teach them to dedicate their lives to matters of great import, and inspire them to undertake studies that will benefit mankind.

'Abdu'l-Bahá

48. A family . . . is a very special kind of "community." The Research Department has not come across any statements which specifically name the father as responsible for the "security, progress and unity of the family" . . . but it can be inferred from a number of the responsibilities placed upon him, that the father can be regarded as the "head" of the family. The members of a family all have duties and responsibilities towards one another and to the family as a whole, and these duties and responsibilities vary from member to member because of their natural relationships. The parents have the inescapable duty to educate their children—but not vice versa; the children have the duty to obey their parents—the parents do not obey the children; the mother—not the father—bears the children, nurses them in babyhood, and is thus their first educator; hence daughters have a prior right to education over sons and, as the Guardian's secretary has written on his behalf, "The task of bringing up a Bahá'í child, as emphasized time and again in Bahá'í Writings, is the chief responsibility of the mother, whose unique privilege is indeed to create in her home such conditions as would be most conducive to both his material and spiritual welfare and advancement. The training which a child first receives through his mother constitutes the strongest foundation for his future development. . . ." A corollary of this responsibility of the mother is her right to be supported by her husband—a husband has no explicit right to be supported by his wife. This principle of the husband's responsibility to provide for and protect the family can be seen applied also in the law of intestacy which provides that the family's dwelling place passes, on the father's death, not to his widow, but to his eldest son; the son at the same time has the responsibility to care for his mother.

It is in this context of mutual and complementary duties, and responsibilities that one should read the Tablet in which 'Abdu'l-Bahá gives the following exhortation:

> O Handmaids of the All-Sufficing God!
>
> Exert yourselves, that haply ye may be enabled to acquire such virtues as shall honor and distinguish you amongst all women. Of a surety, there is no greater pride and glory for a woman than to be a handmaid in God's Court of Grandeur; and the qualities that shall merit her this station are an alert and wakeful heart; a firm conviction of the unity of God, the Peerless; a heartfelt love for all His maidservants; spotless purity and chastity; obedience to and consideration for her husband; attention to the education and nurturing of her children; composure, calmness, dignity and self-possession; diligence in praising God, and worshipping Him both night and day; constancy and firmness in His holy Covenant; and the utmost ardor, enthusiasm, and attachment to His Cause.
>
> *On behalf of the Universal House of Justice*

49. These are all relationships within the family, but there is a much wider sphere of relationships between men and women than in the home, and this too we should consider in the context of Bahá'í society, not in that of past or present social norms. For example, although the mother is the first educator of the child, and the most important formative influence in his development, the father also has the responsibility of educating his children, and this responsibility is so weighty that Bahá'u'lláh has stated that a father who fails to exercise it forfeits his rights of fatherhood. Similarly, although the primary responsibility for supporting the family financially is placed upon the husband, this does not by any means imply that the place of women is confined to the home. On the contrary, 'Abdu'l-Bahá has stated:

In the Dispensation of Bahá'u'lláh, women are advancing side by side with men. There is no area or instance where they will lag behind: they have equal rights with men, and will enter, in the future, into all branches of the administration of society. Such will be their elevation that, in every area of endeavor, they will occupy the highest levels in the human world.*

and again:

So it will come to pass that when women participate fully and equally in the affairs of the world, when they enter confidently and capably the great arena of laws and politics, war will cease; . . . (*The Promulgation of Universal Peace*, p. 135)

In the Tablet of the World, Bahá'u'lláh Himself has envisaged that women as well as men would be breadwinners in stating:

Everyone, whether man or woman, should hand over to a trusted person a portion of what he or she earneth through trade, agriculture or other occupation, for the training and education of children, to be spent for this purpose with the knowledge of the Trustees of the House of Justice. (*Tablets of Bahá'u'lláh Revealed after the Kitáb-i-Aqdas*, p. 90)

A very important element in the attainment of such equality is Bahá'u'lláh's provision that boys and girls must follow essentially the same curriculum in schools. *(28 December 1980 to the National Spiritual Assembly of the Bahá'ís of New Zealand)*
On behalf of the Universal House of Justice

---

* The quotation in the original letter which was taken from *Paris Talks*, no. 59.5, has been replaced by this revised translation.

FOSTERING HARMONY IN THE FAMILY

50. Treat all thy friends and relatives, even strangers, with a spirit of utmost love and kindliness.

'Abdu'l-Bahá

51. When you love a member of your family or a compatriot, let it be with a ray of the Infinite Love! Let it be in God, and for God! Wherever you find the attributes of God love that person, whether he be of your family or of another.

'Abdu'l-Bahá

52. If love and agreement are manifest in a single family, that family will advance, become illumined and spiritual; but if enmity and hatred exist within it, destruction and dispersion are inevitable.

'Abdu'l-Bahá

53. Note ye how easily, where unity existeth in a given family, the affairs of that family are conducted; what progress the members of that family make, how they prosper in the world. Their concerns are in order, they enjoy comfort and tranquility, they are secure, their position is assured, they come to be envied by all. Such a family but addeth to its stature and its lasting honor, as day succeedeth day.

'Abdu'l-Bahá

54. It is one of the essential teachings of the Faith that unity should be maintained in the home. Of course this does not mean that any member of the family has a right to influence the faith of any other member; and if this is realized by all the members, then it seems certain that unity would be feasible.

On behalf of Shoghi Effendi

55. It made him very happy to know of the recent confirmation of your . . . friend, and of her earnest desire to serve and promote the Faith. He will certainly pray on her behalf that she may, notwithstanding the opposition of her parents and relatives, increasingly gain in knowledge and in understanding of the Teachings, and become animated with such a zeal as to arise, and bring into the Cause a large number of her former co-religionists.

Under no circumstances, however, should she allow her parents to become completely alienated from her, but it is her bounden duty to strive, through patient, continued and loving effort, to win their sympathy for the Faith, and even perhaps, to bring about their confirmation.

On behalf of Shoghi Effendi

56. She should certainly not grieve if she finds that her family are not receptive to the teachings—for not every soul is spiritually enlightened. Indeed, many members of the families of the Prophets themselves have remained unconverted even in face of the example and persuasion of the Manifestation of God; therefore, the friends should not be distressed by such things but rather leave the future of those they love in the hand of God, and by their services and devotion to the Faith, win the right to plead for their ultimate spiritual re-birth.

On behalf of Shoghi Effendi

57. Deep as are family ties, we must always remember that the spiritual ties are far deeper; they are everlasting and survive death, whereas physical ties, unless supported by spiritual bonds, are confined to this life. You should do all in your power, through prayer and example, to open the eyes of your family to the Bahá'í Faith, but do not grieve too much over their actions.

On behalf of Shoghi Effendi

USING CONSULTATION TO FOSTER HARMONY

58. The Great Being saith: The heaven of divine wisdom is illumined with the two luminaries of consultation and compassion. Take ye counsel together in all matters, inasmuch as consultation is the lamp of guidance which leadeth the way, and is the bestower of understanding.

Bahá'u'lláh

59. Man must consult on all matters, whether major or minor, so that he may become cognizant of what is good. Consultation giveth him insight into things and enableth him to delve into questions which are unknown. The light of truth shineth from the faces of those who engage in consultation. Such consultation causeth the living waters to flow in the meadows of man's reality, the rays of ancient glory to shine upon him, and the tree of his being to be adorned with wondrous fruit. The members who are consulting, however, should behave in the utmost love, harmony and sincerity towards each other. The principle of consultation is one of the most fundamental elements of the divine edifice. Even in their ordinary affairs the individual members of society should consult.

'Abdu'l-Bahá

60. Settle all things, both great and small, by consultation. Without prior consultation, take no important step in your own personal affairs. Concern yourselves with one another. Help along one another's projects and plans. Grieve over one another. Let none in the whole country go in need. Befriend one another until ye become as a single body, one and all.

'Abdu'l-Bahá

61. A Bahá'í who has a problem may wish to make his own decision upon it after prayer and after weighing all the aspects of it in his own mind; he may prefer to seek the counsel of individual friends or of professional counselors such as his doc-

tor or lawyer so that he can consider such advice when making his decision; or in a case where several people are involved, such as a family situation, he may want to gather together those who are affected so that they may arrive at a collective decision.

The Universal House of Justice

62. Bahá'u'lláh came to bring unity to the world, and a fundamental unity is that of the family. Therefore, one must believe that the Faith is intended to strengthen the family, not weaken it, and one of the keys to the strengthening of unity is loving consultation. The atmosphere within a Bahá'í family as within the community as a whole should express "the keynote of the Cause of God" which, the beloved Guardian has stated, "is not dictatorial authority but humble fellowship, not arbitrary power, but the spirit of frank and loving consultation."

The Universal House of Justice.

Violence and Sexual Abuse

63. If the health and well-being of the body be expended in the path of the Kingdom, this is very acceptable and praiseworthy; and if it be expended to the benefit of the human world in general—even though it be to their material benefit—and be a means of doing good, that is also acceptable. But if the health and welfare of man be spent in sensual desires, in a life on the animal plane, and in devilish pursuits—then disease were better than such health; nay, death itself were preferable to such a life. If thou art desirous of health, wish thou health for serving the Kingdom. I hope that thou mayest attain perfect insight, inflexible resolution, complete health, and spiritual and physical strength in order that thou mayest drink from the fountain of eternal life and be assisted by the spirit of divine confirmation.

'Abdu'l-Bahá

64. The Universal House of Justice has now completed its consideration of your letter . . . in which you raised a number of questions pertaining to violence and to the sexual abuse of women and children. We have been instructed to provide the following response to your questions.

As you know, the principle of the oneness of mankind is described in the Bahá'í Writings as the pivot round which all the Teachings of Bahá'u'lláh revolve. It has widespread implications which affect and remold all dimensions of human activity. It calls for a fundamental change in the manner in which people relate to each other, and the eradication of those age-old practices which deny the intrinsic human right of every individual to be treated with consideration and respect.

Within the family setting, the rights of all members must be respected. 'Abdu'l-Bahá stated: *"The integrity of the family bond must be constantly considered and the rights of the individual members must not be transgressed. The rights of the son, the father, the mother—none of them must be transgressed, none of them must be arbitrary. Just as the son has certain obligations to his father, the father, likewise, has certain obligations to his son. The mother, the sister and all other members of the household have their certain prerogatives. All these rights and prerogatives must be conserved. . . ."*

The use of force by the physically strong against the weak, as a means of imposing one's will and fulfilling one's desires, is a flagrant transgression of the Bahá'í Teachings. There can be no justification for anyone compelling another, through the use of force or through the threat of violence, to do that which the other person is not inclined. 'Abdu'l-Bahá has written: *"O ye lovers of God! In this, the cycle of Almighty God, violence and force, constraint and oppression, are one and all condemned."*

Let those who, driven by their passions or by their inability to exercise discipline in the control of their anger, might be tempted to inflict violence on another human being, be mindful of the condemnation of such disgraceful behavior by the Revelation of Bahá'u'lláh.

Among the signs of moral downfall in the declining social order are the high incidence of violence within the family, the increase in degrading and cruel treatment of spouses and children, and the spread of sexual abuse. It is essential that the members of the community of the Greatest Name take the utmost care not to be drawn into acceptance of such practices because of their prevalence. They must be ever mindful of their obligation to exemplify a new way of life distinguished by its respect for the dignity and rights of all people, by its exalted moral tone, and by its freedom from oppression and from all forms of abuse.

Consultation has been ordained by Bahá'u'lláh as the means by which agreement is to be reached and a collective course of action defined. It is applicable to the marriage partners and within the family, and indeed, in all areas where believers participate in mutual decision-making. It requires all participants to express their opinions with absolute freedom and without apprehension that they will be censured or their views belittled; these prerequisites for success are unattainable if the fear of violence or abuse is present.

A number of your questions pertain to the treatment of women, and are best considered in light of the principle of the equality of the sexes which is set forth in the Bahá'í Teachings. This principle is far more than the enunciation of admirable ideas; it has profound implications on all aspects of human relations and must be an integral element of Bahá'í domestic and community life. The application of this principle gives rise to changes in habits and practices which have prevailed for many centuries. An example of this is found in the response provided on behalf of Shoghi Effendi to a question about whether the traditional practice whereby the man proposes marriage to the woman is altered by the Bahá'í Teachings to permit the woman to issue a marriage proposal to the man; the response is, "The Guardian wishes to state that there is absolute equality between the two, and that no distinction or preference is permitted. . . ." With the passage of time, during which Bahá'í men and women endeavor to apply more fully the principle of the equality of the sexes, will come a deeper understanding of the far-reaching ramifications of this vital principle. As 'Abdu'l-Bahá has stated, *"Until the reality of equality between man and woman is fully established and attained, the highest social development of mankind is not possible."*

The Universal House of Justice has in recent years urged that encouragement be given to Bahá'í women and girls to participate in greater measure in the social, spiritual and administrative activities of their communities, and has appealed to Bahá'í women to arise and demonstrate the importance of their role in all fields of service to the Faith.

For a man to use force to impose his will on a woman is a serious transgression of the Bahá'í Teachings. 'Abdu'l-Bahá has stated that: *"The world in the past has been ruled by force, and man has dominated over woman by reason of his more forceful and aggressive qualities of body and mind. But the balance is already shifting; force is losing its dominance, and mental alertness, intuition, and the spiritual qualities of love and service, in which woman is strong, are gaining ascendancy."*

Bahá'í men have the opportunity to demonstrate to the world around them a new approach to the relationship between the sexes, where aggression and the use of force are eliminated and replaced by cooperation and consultation. The Universal House of Justice has pointed out in response to questions addressed to it that, in a marriage relationship, neither husband nor wife should ever unjustly dominate the other, and that there are times when the husband and the wife should defer to the wishes of the other. If agreement cannot be reached through consultation, each couple should determine exactly under what circumstances deference is to take place.

From the Pen of Bahá'u'lláh Himself has come the following statement on the subject of the treatment of women: *"The friends of God must be adorned with the ornament of justice, equity, kindness and love. As they do not allow themselves to be the object of cruelty and transgression, in like manner they should not allow such tyranny to visit the handmaidens of God. He, verily, speaketh the truth and commandeth that which befiteth His servants and handmaidens. He is the Protector of all in this world and the next."*

No Bahá'í husband should ever beat his wife, or subject her to any form of cruel treatment; to do so would be an unacceptable abuse of the marriage relationship and contrary to the Teachings of Bahá'u'lláh.

The lack of spiritual values in society leads to a debasement of the attitudes which should govern the relationship between the sexes, with women being treated as no more than objects for sexual gratification and being denied the respect and courtesy to which all human beings are entitled. Bahá'u'lláh has warned: "They that follow their lusts and corrupt inclinations, have erred and dissipated their efforts. They, indeed, are of the lost." Believers might well ponder the exalted standard of conduct to which they are encouraged to aspire in the statement of Bahá'u'lláh concerning His *"true follower,"* that: *"And if he met the fairest and most comely of women, he would not feel his heart seduced by the least shadow of desire for her beauty. Such an one, indeed, is the creation of spotless chastity. Thus instructeth you the Pen of the Ancient of Days, as bidden by your Lord, the Almighty, the All-Bountiful."*

One of the most heinous of sexual offenses is the crime of rape. When a believer is a victim, she is entitled to the loving aid and support of the members of her community, and she is free to initiate action against the perpetrator under the law of the land should she wish to do so. If she becomes pregnant as a consequence of this assault, no pressure should be brought upon her by the Bahá'í institutions to marry. As to whether she should continue or terminate the pregnancy, it is left to her to decide on the course of action she should follow, taking into consideration medical and other relevant factors, and in the light of the Bahá'í Teachings. If she gives birth to a child as a result of the rape, it is left to her discretion whether to seek financial support for the maintenance of the child from the father; however, his claim to any parental rights would, under Bahá'í law, be called into question, in view of the circumstances.

The Guardian has clarified, in letters written on his behalf, that "The Bahá'í Faith recognizes the value of the sex impulse" and that "The proper use of the sex instinct is the natural right of every individual, and it is precisely for this very purpose that the institution of marriage has been established."

In this aspect of the marital relationship, as in all others, mutual consideration and respect should apply. If a Bahá'í woman suffers abuse or is subjected to rape by her husband, she has the right to turn to the Spiritual Assembly for assistance or counsel, or to seek legal protection. Such abuse would gravely jeopardize the constitution of the marriage, and could well lead to a condition of irreconcilable antipathy.

You have raised several questions about the treatment of children. It is clear from the Bahá'í Writings that a vital component of the education of children in the exercise of discipline. Shoghi Effendi has stated, in a letter written on his behalf about the education of children, that:

"Discipline of some sort, whether physical, moral or intellectual, is indeed indispensable, and no training can be said to be complete and fruitful if it disregards this element. The child when born is far from perfect. It is not only helpless, but actually is imperfect, and even is naturally inclined toward evil. He should be trained, his natural inclinations harmonized, adjusted and controlled, and if necessary suppressed or regulated, so as to ensure his healthy physical and moral development. Bahá'í parents cannot simply adopt an attitude of non-resistance toward their children, particularly those who are unruly and violent by nature. It is not even sufficient that they should pray on their behalf. Rather they should endeavor to inculcate, gently and patiently, into their youthful minds such principles of moral conduct and initiate them into the principles and teachings of the Cause with such tactful and loving care as would enable them to become 'true sons of God' and develop into loyal and intelligent citizens of His Kingdom. . . ."

While the physical disciplining of children is an acceptable part of their education and training, such actions are to be carried out "gently and patiently" and with "loving care," far removed from the anger and violence with which children are beaten and abused in some parts of the world. To treat children in such an abhorrent manner is a denial of their human rights, and a betrayal of the trust which the weak should have in the strong in a Bahá'í community.

It is difficult to imagine a more reprehensible perversion of human conduct than the sexual abuse of children, which finds its most debased form in incest. At a time in the fortunes of humanity when, in the words of the Guardian, "The perversion of human nature, the degradation of human conduct, the corruption and dissolution of human institutions, reveal themselves . . . in their worst and most revolting aspects," and when "the voice of human conscience is stilled," when "the sense of decency and shame is obscured," the Bahá'í institutions must be uncompromising and vigilant in their commitment to the protection of children entrusted to their care, and must not allow either threats or appeals to expediency to divert them from their duty. A parent who is aware that the marriage partner is subjecting a child to such sexual abuse should not remain silent, but must take all necessary measures, with the assistance of the Spiritual Assembly or civil authorities if necessary, to bring about an immediate cessation of such grossly immoral behavior, and to promote healing and therapy.

Bahá'u'lláh has placed great emphasis on the duties of parents toward their children, and He has urged children to have gratitude in their hearts for their parents, whose good pleasure they should strive to win as a means of pleasing God Himself. However, He has indicated that under certain circumstances, the parents could be deprived of the right of parenthood as a consequence of their actions. The Universal House of Justice has the right to legislate on this matter. It has decided for the present that all cases should be referred to it in which the conduct or character of the parent appears to render him unworthy of having such parental rights as that of giving consent to marriage. Such questions could arise, for example, when a parent has committed incest, or when the child was conceived as a consequence of rape, and also when a parent consciously fails to protect the child from flagrant sexual abuse.

As humanity passes through the age of transition in its evolution to a world civilization which will be illumined by spiritual values and will be distinguished by its justice and its unity, the role of the Bahá'í community is clear: it must accomplish a spiritual transformation of its members, and must offer to the world a model of the society destined to come into being through the power of the Revelation of Bahá'u'lláh. Membership in the Bahá'í community is open to all who accept Bahá'u'lláh as the Manifestation of God, and who thereupon embark on the process of changing their conduct and refining their character. It is inevitable that this community will, at times, be subject to delinquent behavior of members whose actions do not conform to the standards of the Teachings. At such times, the institutions of the Faith must not hesitate to apply Bahá'í law with justice and fairness, in full confidence that this Divine Law is the means for the true happiness of all concerned.

However, it should be recognized that the ultimate solution to the problems of humanity lies not in penalties and punishments, but rather in spiritual education and illumination. 'Abdu'l-Bahá has written: *"It is incumbent upon human society to expend all its forces on the education of the people, and to copiously water men's hearts with the sacred streams that pour down from the Realm of the All-Merciful, and to teach them the manners of Heaven and spiritual ways of life, until every member of the community of man will be schooled, refined, and exalted to such a degree of perfection that the very committing of a shameful act will seem in itself the direst infliction of the most agonizing of punishments, and man will fly in terror and seek refuge in his God from the very idea of crime, as something far harsher and more grievous than the punishment assigned to it."*

It is toward this goal that the community of the Greatest Name is striving, aided and reinforced by the limitless power of the Holy Spirit.

On behalf of the Universal House of Justice

Chastity and Sex

A CHASTE AND HOLY LIFE

65. O friends! Be not careless of the virtues with which ye have been endowed, neither be neglectful of your high destiny. Suffer not your labors to be wasted through the vain imaginations which certain hearts have devised. Ye are the stars of the heaven of understanding, the breeze that stirreth at the break of day, the soft-flowing waters upon which must depend the very life of all men, the letters inscribed upon His sacred scroll.

Bahá'u'lláh

66. And if he met the fairest and most comely of women, he would not feel his heart seduced by the least shadow of desire for her beauty. Such a one, indeed, is the creation of spotless chastity. Thus instructeth you the Pen of the Ancient of Days, as bidden by your Lord, the Almighty, the All-Bountiful.

Bahá'u'lláh

67. Ye are forbidden to commit adultery, sodomy and lechery. Avoid them, O concourse of the faithful. By the righteousness of God! Ye have been called into being to purge the world from the defilement of evil passions. This is what the Lord of all mankind hath enjoined upon you, could ye but perceive it. He who relateth himself to the All-Merciful and committeth satanic deeds, verily he is not of Me. Unto this beareth witness every atom, pebble, tree and fruit, and beyond them this ever-proclaiming, truthful and trustworthy Tongue.

Bahá'u'lláh

68. A chaste and holy life, with its implications of modesty, purity, temperance, decency, and clean-mindedness, involves no

less than the exercise of moderation in all that pertains to dress, language, amusements, and all artistic and literary avocations. It demands daily vigilance in the control of one's carnal desires and corrupt inclinations. It calls for the abandonment of a frivolous conduct, with its excessive attachment to trivial and often misdirected pleasures. It requires total abstinence from all alcoholic drinks, from opium, and from similar habit-forming drugs. It condemns the prostitution of art and of literature, the practices of nudism and of companionate marriage, infidelity in marital relationships, and all manner of promiscuity, of easy familiarity, and of sexual vices. It can tolerate no compromise with the theories, the standards, the habits, and the excesses of a decadent age. Nay rather it seeks to demonstrate, through the dynamic force of its example, the pernicious character of such theories, the falsity of such standards, the hollowness of such claims, the perversity of such habits, and the sacrilegious character of such excesses.

Shoghi Effendi

69. It must be remembered, however, that the maintenance of such a high standard of moral conduct is not to be associated or confused with any form of asceticism, or of excessive and bigoted puritanism. The standard inculcated by Bahá'u'lláh seeks, under no circumstances, to deny anyone the legitimate right and privilege to derive the fullest advantage and benefit from the manifold joys, beauties, and pleasures with which the world has been so plentifully enriched by an All-Loving Creator.

Shoghi Effendi

70. What Bahá'u'lláh means by chastity certainly does not include the kissing that goes on in modern society. It is detrimental to the morals of young people, and often leads them to go

too far, or arouses appetites which they cannot perhaps at the time satisfy legitimately through marriage, and the suppression of which is a strain on them.

The Bahá'í standard is very high, more particularly when compared with the thoroughly rotten morals of the present world. But this standard of ours will produce healthier, happier, nobler people, and induce stabler marriages.

Shoghi Effendi

71. Briefly stated the Bahá'í conception of sex is based on the belief that chastity should be strictly practiced by both sexes, not only because it is in itself highly commendable ethically, but also due to its being the only way to a happy and successful marital life. Sex relationships of any form, outside marriage, are not permissible therefore, and whoso violates this rule will not only be responsible to God, but will incur the necessary punishment from society.

The Bahá'í Faith recognizes the value of the sex impulse, but condemns its illegitimate and improper expressions such as free love, companionate marriage and others, all of which it considers positively harmful to man and to the society in which he lives. The proper use of the sex instinct is the natural right of every individual, and it is precisely for this very purpose that the institution of marriage has been established. The Bahá'ís do not believe in the suppression of the sex impulse but in its regulation and control.

On behalf of Shoghi Effendi

72. The question you raise as to the place in one's life that a deep bond of love with someone we meet other than our husband or wife can have is easily defined in view of the teachings. Chastity implies both before and after marriage an unsullied,

chaste sex life. Before marriage absolutely chaste, after marriage absolutely faithful to one's chosen companion. Faithful in all sexual acts, faithful in word and in deed.

On behalf of Shoghi Effendi

73. In the teachings there is nothing against dancing, but the friends should remember that the standard of Bahá'u'lláh is modesty and chastity. The atmosphere of modern dance halls, where so much smoking and drinking and promiscuity goes on, is very bad, but decent dances are not harmful in themselves. There is certainly no harm in classical dancing or learning dancing in school. There is also no harm in taking part in dramas. Likewise in cinema acting. The harmful thing, nowadays, is not the art itself but the unfortunate corruption which often surrounds these arts. As Bahá'ís we need avoid none of the arts, but acts and the atmosphere that sometimes go with these professions we should avoid.

On behalf of Shoghi Effendi

74. The Guardian has urged over and over again, the paramount necessity for Bahá'í Youth to exemplify the Teachings, most particularly the *moral* aspect of them. If they are not distinguished for their high conduct they cannot expect other young people to take the Cause very seriously.

He heartily agrees with you that unless we practice the Teachings we cannot possibly expect the Faith to grow, because the fundamental purpose of all religions—including our own—is to bring man nearer to God, and to change his character, which is of the utmost importance. Too much emphasis is often laid on the social and economic aspects of the Teachings; but the moral aspect cannot be over-emphasized.

On behalf of Shoghi Effendi

75. He feels that the youth, in particular, must constantly and determinedly strive to exemplify a Bahá'í life. In the world around us we see moral decay, promiscuity, indecency, vulgarity, bad manners—the Bahá'í young people must be the opposite of these things, and, by their chastity, their uprightness, their decency, their consideration and good manners, attract others, old and young, to the Faith. The world is tired of words; it wants example, and it is up to the Bahá'í youth to furnish it.

On behalf of Shoghi Effendi

76. The young Bahá'ís in every city should make a point of keeping in touch with local youth activities and clubs, and endeavoring to make their views known to as many young people in as many ways as possible. Above all they should set a high example to them; chastity, politeness, friendliness, hospitality, joyous optimism about the ultimate future happiness and well being of mankind, should distinguish them and win over to them the love and admiration of their fellow youth. The thing which is most conspicuously lacking in modern life is a high standard of conduct and good character; the young Bahá'ís must demonstrate both, if they hope to seriously win over to the Faith members of their own generation, so sorely disillusioned and so contaminated by the laxity war gives rise to.

On behalf of Shoghi Effendi

77. In considering the effect of obedience to the laws on individual lives, one must remember that the purpose of this life is to prepare the soul for the next. Here one must learn to control and direct one's animal impulses, not to be a slave to them. Life in this world is a succession of tests and achievements, of falling short and of making new spiritual advances. Sometimes the course may seem very hard, but one can witness, again and

again, that the soul who steadfastly obeys the law of Bahá'u‸ however hard it may seem, grows spiritually, while the one ‸ ‿ compromises with the law for the sake of his own apparent happiness is seen to have been following a chimera: he does not attain the happiness he sought, he retards his spiritual advance and often brings new problems upon himself.

The Universal House of Justice

78. We have considered your several letters and have noted your questions, and your view that many Bahá'í youth in . . . are confused, and are pleading for guidance in simple clear language on how to meet daily situations, particularly those involving sex.

It is neither possible nor desirable for The Universal House of Justice to set forth a set of rules covering every situation. Rather is it the task of the individual believer to determine, according to his own prayerful understanding of the Writings, precisely what his course of conduct should be in relation to situations which he encounters in his daily life. If he is to fulfill his true mission in life as a follower of the Blessed Perfection, he will pattern his life according to the Teachings. The believer cannot attain this objective merely by living according to a set of rigid regulations. When his life is oriented toward service to Bahá'u'lláh, and when every conscious act is performed within this frame of reference, he will not fail to achieve the true purpose of his life.

The Universal House of Justice

MASTURBATION

79. We have found in the Holy Writings no explicit references to masturbation, but there are a number of principles and teachings which can guide a Bahá'í to the correct attitude towards it.

In a letter to an individual believer, written by the Guardian's secretary on his behalf, it is pointed out that,

"The Bahá'í Faith recognizes the value of the sex impulse, but condemns its illegitimate and improper expressions such as free love, companionate marriage and others, all of which it considers positively harmful to man and to the society in which he lives. The proper use of the sex instinct is the natural right of every individual, and it is precisely for this very purpose that the institution of marriage has been established. The Bahá'ís do not believe in the suppression of the sex impulse but in its regulation and control."

In response to another letter enquiring if there were any legitimate way in which a person could express the sex instinct if, for some reason, he were unable to marry or if outer circumstances such as economic factors were to cause him to delay marriage, the Guardian's secretary wrote on his behalf:

"Concerning your question whether there are any legitimate forms of expression of the sex instinct outside of marriage; according to the Bahá'í Teachings no sexual act can be considered lawful unless performed between lawfully married persons. Outside of marital life there can be no lawful or healthy use of the sex impulse. The Bahá'í youth should, on the one hand, be taught the lesson of self-control which, when exercised, undoubtedly has a salutary effect on the development of character and of personality in general, and on the other should be advised, nay even encouraged, to contract marriage while still young and in full possession of their physical vigor. Economic factors, no doubt, are often a serious hindrance to early marriage but in most cases are only an excuse, and as such should not be over stressed."

In another letter on the Guardian's behalf, also to an individual believer, the secretary writes:

"Amongst the many other evils afflicting society in this spiritual low water mark in history, is the question of immorality, and overemphasis of sex. . . ."

This indicates how the whole matter of sex and the problems related to it have assumed far too great an importance in the thinking of present-day society.

Masturbation is clearly not a proper use of the sex instinct, as this is understood in the Faith. Moreover it involves, as you have pointed out, mental fantasies, while Bahá'u'lláh, in the Kitáb-i-Aqdas, has exhorted us not to indulge our passions and in one of His well-known Tablets 'Abdu'l-Bahá encourages us to keep our "secret thoughts pure." Of course many wayward thoughts come involuntarily to the mind and these are merely a result of weakness and are not blameworthy unless they become fixed or even worse, are expressed in improper acts. In "The Advent of Divine Justice," when describing the moral standards that Bahá'ís must uphold both individually and in their community life, the Guardian wrote:

"Such a chaste and holy life, with its implications of modesty, purity, temperance, decency, and clean-mindedness, involves no less than the exercise of moderation in all that pertains to dress, language, amusements, and all artistic and literary avocations. It demands daily vigilance in the control of one's carnal desires and corrupt inclinations."

Your problem, therefore, is one against which you should continue to struggle, with determination and with the aid of prayer. You should remember, however, that it is only one of the many temptations and faults that a human being must strive to overcome during his lifetime, and you should not increase the difficulty you have by over-emphasizing its importance. We suggest you try to see it within the whole spectrum of the qualities that a Bahá'í must develop in his character. Be vigilant against temptation, but do not allow it to claim too great a share of your attention. You should concentrate, rather, on the virtues that you should develop, the services you should strive to render, and, above all, on God and His attributes, and devote your energies to living a full Bahá'í life in all its many aspects.

The Universal House of Justice

HOMOSEXUALITY

80. The Universal House of Justice has considered your letters of August 27, 1993, and September 19, 1994, in which you describe the impact of the changing sexual mores and the public debate on homosexuality on some of the members of the American Bahá'í community who are homosexuals.

We are instructed to provide the following guidance in response to the National Spiritual Assembly's requests for a clarification of the Bahá'í law on homosexual practices and for assistance in guiding the believers.

It is important to understand that there is a difference between the Bahá'í attitude toward, on the one hand, the condition of homosexuality and those who are affected by it and, on the other, the practice of homosexual relations by members of the Bahá'í community.

As you know, the Bahá'í Faith strongly condemns all blatant acts of immorality, and it includes among them the expression of sexual love between individuals of the same sex. With regard to homosexual practices, Bahá'u'lláh, in the Kitáb-i-Aqdas, paragraph 107, and Questions and Answers, number 49, forbids pederasty and sodomy. The following extract from one of His Tablets reveals the strength of His condemnation:

"Ye are forbidden to commit adultery, sodomy and lechery. Avoid them, O concourse of the faithful. By the righteousness of God! Ye have been called into being to purge the world from the defilement of evil passions. This is what the Lord of all mankind hath enjoined upon you, could ye but perceive it. He who relateth himself to the All-Merciful and committeth satanic deeds, verily he is not of Me. Unto this beareth witness every atom, pebble, tree and fruit, and beyond them this ever-proclaiming, truthful and trustworthy Tongue."

In a letter dated March 26, 1950, written on his behalf, Shoghi Effendi, the authorized interpreter of the Bahá'í Teachings, further explicates the Bahá'í attitude toward homosexuality. It should be noted that the Guardian's interpretation of this subject is based on his infallible understanding of the Texts. It represents both a statement of moral principle and unerring guidance to Bahá'ís who are homosexuals. The letter states:

"No matter how devoted and fine the love may be between people of the same sex, to let it find expression in sexual acts is wrong. To say that it is ideal is no excuse. Immorality of every sort is really forbidden by Bahá'u'lláh, and homosexual relationships He looks upon as such, besides being against nature.

"To be afflicted this way is a great burden to a conscientious soul. But through the advice and help of doctors, through a strong and determined effort, and through prayer, a soul can overcome this handicap."

It is evident, therefore, that the prohibition against Bahá'ís engaging in homosexual behavior is an explicit teaching in the Cause. The Universal House of Justice is authorized to change or repeal its own legislation as conditions change, thus providing Bahá'í law with an essential element of flexibility, but it cannot abrogate or change any of the laws which are explicitly laid down in the sacred Texts. It follows, then, that the House of Justice has no authority to change this clear teaching on homosexual practice.

You mention that concern has been expressed by some of the friends that the unique identity of homosexual Bahá'ís is not sufficiently appreciated by the Bahá'í community. It is important to reflect on the fact that the Writings of the Faith not only acknowledge that each individual has a God-given identity, but they also set out the means by which this identity can achieve its highest development and fulfillment.

Bahá'u'lláh attests that through the Teachings of the Manifestations of God "every man will advance and develop until he attaineth the station at which he can manifest all the potential forces with which his inmost true self hath been endowed." 'Abdu'l-Bahá observes that should man's "natural qualities . . . be used and displayed in an unlawful way, they become blameworthy."

Shoghi Effendi, in a letter dated May 25, 1936, written on his behalf, identifies man's "true self" with "his soul." In describing the nature of "man's inner spiritual self or reality," he notes that the "two tendencies for good or evil are but manifestations of a single reality or self," and that the self "is capable of development in either way." Underlining the importance of education to the actualization of man's potential, the Guardian concludes:

"All depends fundamentally on the training or education which man receives. Human nature is made up of possibilities both for good and evil. True religion can enable it to soar in the highest realm of the spirit, while its absence can, as we already witness around us, cause it to fall to the lowest depths of degradation and misery."

As a framework within which to consider the subject of homosexuality, it is important to acknowledge, with all due humility, that basic to the Bahá'í Teaching is the concept that it is only God Who knows the purpose of human life, and Who can convey this to us through His Manifestations.

A distinguishing feature of human existence is that we have been given the capacity to know and love God and to consciously obey Him. Thus we also have the converse: the ability to turn away from God, to fail to love Him and to disobey Him. Indeed, left to himself, man is naturally inclined toward evil. Human beings need not only assistance in defining acceptable behavior of one person toward another, but also guidance which will help them to refrain from doing that which is spiritually damaging to themselves.

By responding to the Message of the Manifestation of God we learn how we should live and draw on the spiritual strength which comes with it. Through studying the Word of God and training ourselves to follow His commandments, we rise to the full stature that He has designed for us.

The material world, in relation to the spiritual world, is a world of imperfections. It is full of dangers and difficulties which have been greatly aggravated by man's neglect and misuse of his responsibilities. Human society itself, which exists in the material world, is in disastrous disarray.

Our appetites and inclinations are strongly influenced by the condition of our physical makeup, and our bodies are in varying degrees of health, depending upon factors such as heredity, environment, nourishment and our own treatment of them. Genetic variations occur, producing conditions which can create problems for the individual. Some conditions are of an emotional or psychological nature, producing such imbalances as quickness to anger, recklessness, timorousness, and so forth; others involve purely physical characteristics, resulting not only in unusual capacities but also in handicaps or diseases of various kinds.

Whether deficiencies are inborn or are acquired, our purpose in this life is to overcome them and to train ourselves in accordance with the pattern that is revealed to us in the divine Teachings.

The view that homosexuality is a condition that is not amenable to change is to be questioned by Bahá'ís. There are, of course, many kinds and degrees of homosexuality, and overcoming extreme conditions is sure to be more difficult than overcoming others. Nevertheless, as noted earlier, the Guardian has stated that "through the advice and help of doctors, through a strong and determined effort, and through prayer, a soul can overcome this handicap."

The statistics which indicate that homosexuality is incurable are undoubtedly distorted by the fact that many of those who overcome the problem never speak about it in public, and others solve their problems without even consulting professional counselors.

Nevertheless there are undoubtedly cases in which the individual finds himself (or herself) unable to eliminate a physical attraction to members of the same sex, even though he succeeds in controlling his behavior. This is but one of the many trials and temptations to which human beings are subject in this life. For Bahá'ís, it cannot alter the basic concept taught by Bahá'u'lláh, that the kind of sexuality purposed by God is the love between a man and a woman, and that its primary (but not its only) purpose is the bringing of children into this world and providing them with a loving and protective environment in which they can be reared to know and love God.

If, therefore, a homosexual cannot overcome his or her condition to the extent of being able to have a heterosexual marriage, he or she must remain single, and abstain from sexual relations. These are the same requirements as for a heterosexual person who does not marry. While Bahá'u'lláh encourages the believers to marry, it is important to note that marriage is by no means an obligation. It is for the individual to decide whether he or she wishes to lead a family life or to live in a state of celibacy.

The condition of being sexually attracted to some object other than a mature member of the opposite sex, a condition of which homosexuality is but one manifestation, is regarded by the Faith as a distortion of human nature, as a problem to be overcome, no matter what specific physical or psychological condition may be the immediate cause. Any Bahá'í who suffers from such a disability should be treated with understanding, and should be helped to control and overcome it. All of us suffer from imperfections which we must struggle to overcome, and we all need one another's understanding and patience.

To regard homosexuals with prejudice and disdain would be entirely against the spirit of Bahá'í Teachings. The doors are open for all of humanity to enter the Cause of God, irrespective of their present circumstances; this invitation applies to homosexuals as well as to any others who are engaged in practices contrary to the Bahá'í Teachings.

Associated with this invitation is the expectation that all believers will make a sincere and persistent effort to eradicate those aspects of their conduct which are not in conformity with Divine Law. It is through such adherence to the Bahá'í Teachings that a true and enduring unity of the diverse elements of the Bahá'í community is achieved and safeguarded.

When a person wishes to join the Faith and it is generally known that he or she has a problem such as drinking, homosexuality, taking drugs, adultery, etc., the individual should be told in a patient and loving way of the Bahá'í Teachings on these matters. If it is later discovered that a believer is violating Bahá'í standards, it is the duty of the Spiritual Assembly to determine whether the immoral conduct is flagrant and can bring the name of the Faith into disrepute, in which case the Assembly must take action to counsel the believer and require him or her to make every effort to mend his ways.

If the individual fails to rectify his conduct in spite of repeated warnings, sanctions should be imposed. Assemblies, of course, must exercise care not to pry into the private lives of the believers to ensure that they are behaving properly, but should not hesitate to take action in cases of blatant misbehavior.

The Spiritual Assemblies should, to a certain extent, be forbearing in the matter of people's moral conduct, such as homosexuality, in view of the terrible deterioration of society in general. The Assemblies must also bear in mind that while awareness of contemporary social and moral values may well enhance their understanding of the situation of the homosexual, the standard which they are called upon to uphold is the Bahá'í standard. A flagrant violation of this standard disgraces the Bahá'í community in its own eyes even if the surrounding society finds the transgression tolerable.

With regard to the organized network of homosexual Bahá'ís mentioned in your letter, the Universal House of Justice has instructed us to say that, while there is an appropriate role in the Bahá'í community for groups of individuals to come together to help each other to understand or to deal with certain problem situations, according to the Bahá'í Teachings there can be no place in our community for groups which actively promote a style of life that is contrary to the teachings of the Cause.

It should be understood that the homosexual tendencies of some individuals do not entitle them to an identity setting them apart from others. Such individuals share with every other Bahá'í the responsibility to adhere to the laws and principles of the Faith as well as the freedom to exercise their administrative rights.

The Universal House of Justice will pray that, armed with the guidance contained in this letter, the National Spiritual Assembly will act with love, sensitivity and firmness to assist the believers both to gain a deeper understanding of their true and ennobling purpose in life and to make a strong and determined effort to overcome every handicap to their spiritual development.

On the behalf of the Universal House of Justice

81. As to chastity, this is one of the most challenging concepts to get across in this very permissive age, but Bahá'ís must make the utmost effort to uphold Bahá'í standards, no matter how difficult they may seem at first. Such efforts will be made easier if the youth will understand that the laws and standards of the Faith are meant to free them from untold spiritual and moral difficulties in the same way that a proper appreciation of the laws of nature enables one to live in harmony with the forces of the planet.

On behalf of the Universal House of Justice

Loving and Accepting Others

82. It is Our wish and desire that every one of you may become a source of all goodness unto men, and an example of uprightness to mankind. Beware lest ye prefer yourselves above your neighbors. Fix your gaze upon Him Who is the Temple of God amongst men. He, in truth, hath offered up His life as a ransom for the redemption of the world. He, verily, is the All-Bountiful, the Gracious, the Most High. If any differences arise amongst you, behold Me standing before your face, and overlook the faults of one another for My name's sake and as a token of your love for My manifest and resplendent Cause. We love to see you at all times consorting in amity and concord within the paradise of My good-pleasure, and to inhale from your acts the fragrance of friendliness and unity, of loving-kindness and fellowship. Thus counseleth you the All-Knowing, the Faithful. We shall always be with you; if We inhale the perfume of your fellowship, Our heart will assuredly rejoice, for naught else can satisfy Us. To this beareth witness every man of true understanding.

Bahá'u'lláh

83. This is certain, that the divine policy is justice and kindness toward all mankind. For all the nations of the world are the sheep of God, and God is the kind shepherd. He has created these sheep. He has protected them, sustained and trained them. What greater kindness than this? And every moment we must render a hundred thousand thanksgivings that, praise be to God, we are freed from all the ignorant prejudices, are kind to all the sheep of God, and our utmost hope is to serve each and all, and like unto a benevolent father educate every one.

'Abdu'l-Bahá

84. Beware lest ye offend the feelings of anyone, or sadden the heart of any person, or move the tongue in reproach of and finding fault with anybody. . . . Beware, beware that any one rebuke or reproach a soul, though he may be an ill-wisher and an ill-doer.

'Abdu'l-Bahá

85. Do not be satisfied until each one with whom you are concerned is to you as a member of your family. Regard each one either as a father, or as a brother, or as a sister, or as a mother, or as a child. If you can attain to this, your difficulties will vanish, you will know what to do.

'Abdu'l-Bahá

86. When you love a member of your family or a compatriot, let it be with a ray of the Infinite Love! Let it be in God, and for God! Wherever you find the attributes of God love that person, whether he be of your family or of another. Shed the light of a boundless love on every human being whom you meet.

'Abdu'l-Bahá

8

Social Relationships

Our Relationship to the Old World Order

FREEDOM

1. Freedom of thought, freedom of expression, freedom of action are among the freedoms which have received the ardent attention of social thinkers across the centuries. The resulting outflow of such profound thought has exerted a tremendous liberating influence in the shaping of modern society. Generations of the oppressed have fought and died in the name of freedom. Certainly the want of freedom from oppression has been a dominant factor in the turmoil of the times: witness the plethora of movements which have resulted in the rapid emergence of new nations in the latter part of the twentieth century. A true reading of the teachings of Bahá'u'lláh leaves no doubt as to the high importance of these freedoms to constructive social processes. Consider, for instance, Bahá'u'lláh's proclamation to the kings and rulers. Can it not be deduced from this alone that attainment of freedom is a significant purpose of His Revelation? His denunciations of tyranny and His urgent appeals on behalf of the oppressed provide unmistakable proof.

But does not the freedom foreshadowed by His Revelation imply nobler, ampler manifestations of human achievement? Does it not indicate an organic relationship between the internal and external realities of man such as has not yet been attained?

The Universal House of Justice

2. The quality of freedom and of its expression—indeed, the very capacity to maintain freedom in a society—undoubtedly depends on the knowledge and training of individuals and on their abilities to cope with the challenges of life with equanimity. As the beloved Master has written: "And the honor and distinction of the individual consist in this, that he among all the world's multitudes should become a source of social good. Is any larger bounty conceivable than this, than an individual, looking within himself, should find that by the confirming grace of God he has become the cause of peace and well-being, of happiness and advantage to his fellowmen? No, by the one true God, there is no greater bliss, no more complete delight."

The Universal House of Justice

3. The spirit of liberty which in recent decades has swept over the planet with such tempestuous force is a manifestation of the vibrancy of the Revelation brought by Bahá'u'lláh. His own words confirm it. "The Ancient Beauty," He wrote in a soul-stirring commentary on His sufferings, "hath consented to be bound with chains that mankind may be released from its bondage, and hath accepted to be made a prisoner within this most mighty Stronghold that the whole world may attain unto true liberty."

Might it not be reasonably concluded, then, that "true liberty" is His gift of love to the human race? Consider what Bahá'u'lláh has done: He revealed laws and principles to guide the free; He established an Order to channel the actions of the free; He proclaimed a Covenant to guarantee the unity of the free.

Thus, we hold to this ultimate perspective: Bahá'u'lláh came to set humanity free. His Revelation is, indeed, an invitation to freedom—freedom from want, freedom from war, freedom to unite, freedom to progress, freedom in peace and joy.

You who live in a land where freedom is so highly prized have not, then, to dispense with its fruits, but you are challenged and do have the obligation to uphold and vindicate the distinction between the license that limits your possibilities for genuine progress and the moderation that ensures the enjoyment of true liberty.

The Universal House of Justice

OBEDIENCE TO GOVERNMENT

4. In every country where any of this people reside, they must behave towards the government of that country with loyalty, honesty and truthfulness. This is that which hath been revealed at the behest of Him Who is the Ordainer, the Ancient of Days.

Bahá'u'lláh

5. Now, as the government of America is a republican form of government, it is necessary that all the citizens shall take part in the elections of officers and take part in the affairs of the republic.

'Abdu'l-Bahá

6. The attitude of the Bahá'ís must be two-fold, complete obedience to the government of the country they reside in, and no interference *whatsoever* in political matters or questions. What the Master's statement really means is obedience to a duly constituted government, whatever that government may be in form.

We are not the ones, as individual Bahá'ís, to judge our government as just or unjust—for each believer would be sure to hold a different viewpoint, and within our own Bahá'í fold a hotbed of dissension would spring up and destroy our unity. We must build up our Bahá'í system, and leave the faulty systems of the world to go their way. We cannot change them through becoming involved in them; on the contrary, they will destroy us.

Shoghi Effendi

Avoiding Political Affairs and Activities

7. O ye the beloved of the one true God! Pass beyond the narrow retreats of your evil and corrupt desires, and advance into the vast immensity of the realm of God, and abide ye in the meads of sanctity and of detachment, that the fragrance of your deeds may lead the whole of mankind to the ocean of God's unfading glory. Forbear ye from concerning yourselves with the affairs of this world and all that pertaineth unto it, or from meddling with the activities of those who are its outward leaders.

Bahá'u'lláh

8. O handmaid of the Lord! Speak thou no word of politics; thy task concerneth the life of the soul, for this verily leadeth to man's joy in the world of God. Except to speak well of them, make thou no mention of the earth's kings, and the worldly governments thereof. Rather, confine thine utterance to spreading the blissful tidings of the Kingdom of God, and demonstrating the influence of the Word of God, and the holiness of the Cause of God. Tell thou of abiding joy and spiritual delights, and godlike qualities, and of how the Sun of Truth hath risen above the earth's horizons: tell of the blowing of the spirit of life into the body of the world.

'Abdu'l-Bahá

9. We should—every one of us—remain aloof, in heart and in mind, in words and in deeds, from the political affairs and disputes of the Nations and of Governments. We should keep ourselves away from such thoughts. We should have no political connection with any of the parties and should join no faction of these different and warring sects.

Absolute impartiality in the matter of political parties should be shown by words and by deeds, and the love of the whole humanity, whether a Government or a nation, which is the basic teaching of Bahá'u'lláh, should also be shown by words and by deeds. . . .

According to the exhortations of the Supreme Pen and the confirmatory explanations of the Covenant of God, Bahá'ís are in no way allowed to enter into political affairs under any pretense or excuse; since such an action brings about disastrous results and ends in hurting the Cause of God and its intimate friends.

Shoghi Effendi

Nonparticipation, Not Indifference

10. It should be made unmistakably clear that such an attitude [of nonparticipation in politics] implies neither the slightest indifference to the cause and interests of their own country, nor involves any insubordination on their part to the authority of recognized and established governments. Nor does it constitute a repudiation of their sacred obligation to promote, in the most effective manner, the best interests of their government and people. It indicates the desire cherished by every true and loyal follower of Bahá'u'lláh to serve, in an unselfish, unostentatious and patriotic fashion, the highest interests of the country to which he belongs, and in a way that would entail no departure from the high standards of integrity and truthfulness associated with the teachings of his Faith.

Shoghi Effendi

11. Let there be no misgivings as to the animating purpose of the world-wide Law of Bahá'u'lláh. Far from aiming at the subversion of the existing foundations of society, it seeks to broaden its basis, to remold its institutions in a manner consonant with the needs of an ever-changing world. It can conflict with no legitimate allegiances, nor can it undermine essential loyalties. Its purpose is neither to stifle the flame of a sane and intelligent patriotism in men's hearts, nor to abolish the system of national autonomy so essential if the evils of excessive centralization are to be avoided. It does not ignore, nor does it attempt to suppress, the diversity of ethnical origins, of climate, of history, of language and tradition, of thought and habit, that differentiate the peoples and nations of the world. It calls for a wider loyalty, for a larger aspiration than any that has animated the human race. It insists upon the subordination of national impulses and interests to the imperative claims of a unified world. It repudiates excessive centralization on one hand, and disclaims all attempts at uniformity on the other. Its watchword is unity in diversity.

Shoghi Effendi

VIOLENCE AND SELF-DEFENSE

12. Say: Fear God, O people, and refrain from shedding the blood of anyone. Contend not with your neighbor, and be ye of them that do good. Beware that ye commit no disorders on the earth after it hath been well ordered, and follow not the footsteps of them that are gone astray.

Bahá'u'lláh

13. It is better to be killed than kill.

Bahá'u'lláh

14. Vengeance, according to reason, is also blameworthy, because through vengeance no good result is gained by the avenger.

So if a man strikes another, and he who is struck takes revenge by returning the blow, what advantage will he gain? Will this be a balm for his wound or a remedy for his pain? No, God forbid! In truth the two actions are the same: both are injuries; the only difference is that one occurred first, and the other afterward. Therefore, if he who is struck forgives, nay, if he acts in a manner contrary to that which has been used toward him, this is laudable. The law of the community will punish the aggressor but will not take revenge. This punishment has for its end to warn, to protect and to oppose cruelty and transgression so that other men may not be tyrannical.

But if he who has been struck pardons and forgives, he shows the greatest mercy. This is worthy of admiration.

'Abdu'l-Bahá

15. A hitherto untranslated Tablet from 'Abdu'l-Bahá . . . points out that in the case of attack by robbers and highwaymen, a Bahá'í should not surrender himself, but should try, as far as circumstances permit, to defend himself, and later on lodge a complaint with the government authorities. In a letter written on behalf of the Guardian, he also indicates that in an emergency when there is no legal force at hand to appeal to, a Bahá'í is justified in defending his life. In another letter the Guardian has further pointed out that the assault of an irresponsible assailant upon a Bahá'í should be resisted by the Bahá'í, who would be justified, under such circumstances, in protecting his life.

The House of Justice does not wish at the present time to go beyond the guidelines given in the above-mentioned statements. The question is basically a matter of conscience, and in each case the Bahá'í involved must use his judgment in determining when to stop in self-defense lest his action deteriorate into retaliation.

The Universal House of Justice

WAR AND MILITARY DUTY

16. O people! Spread not disorder in the land, and shed not
the blood of any one, and consume not the substance of others
wrongfully, neither follow every accursed prattler.

Bahá'u'lláh

17. Today there is no greater glory for man that that of service
in the cause of the Most Great Peace. Peace is light, whereas
war is darkness. Peace is life; war is death. Peace is guidance;
war is error. Peace is the foundation of God; war is a satanic
institution. Peace is the illumination of the world of humanity;
war is the destroyer of human foundations. When we consider
outcomes in the world of existence, we find that peace and fellowship are factors of upbuilding and betterment, whereas war
and strife are the causes of destruction and disintegration. . . .
Consider the restlessness and agitation of the human world today because of war. Peace is health and construction; war is
disease and dissolution. When the banner of truth is raised,
peace becomes the cause of the welfare and advancement of
the human world. In all cycles and ages war has been a factor of
derangement and discomfort, whereas peace and brotherhood
have brought security and consideration of human interests.

'Abdu'l-Bahá

18. Bahá'ís should continue to apply, under all circumstances,
for exemption from any military duties that necessitate the taking of life. There is no justification for any change of attitude
on our part at the present time.

Shoghi Effendi

19. It is still his firm conviction that the believers, while expressing their readiness to unreservedly obey any directions that
the authorities may issue in time of war, should also, and while

there is yet no outbreak of hostilities, appeal to the government for exemption from active military service in a combatant capacity, stressing the fact that in doing so they are not prompted by any selfish considerations but by the sole and supreme motive of upholding the Teachings of their Faith, which makes it a moral obligation for them to desist from any act that would involve them in direct warfare with their fellow-humans of any other race or nation. There are many other avenues through which the believers can assist in times of war by enlisting in services of a non-combatant nature—services that do not involve the direct shedding of blood—such as ambulance work, air raid precaution service, office and administrative works, and it is for such types of national service that they should volunteer.

It is immaterial whether such activities would still expose them to dangers, either at home or in the front, since their desire is not to protect their lives, but to desist from any acts of willful murder.

On behalf of Shoghi Effendi

20. We have considered your letter of July 15, 1965 concerning Bahá'ís and military service. Reference is made to the statements of your National Assembly as reported in Bahá'í News for April, 1943:

> The National Assembly records its understanding of the Guardian's instructions concerning the duty of Bahá'ís in time of war as obligating each believer called under the draft to apply for noncombatant status, in which status he gives full obedience to the military authority of his country; that this obligation does not mean he is a conscientious objector who refuses obedience to military authority, but on the other hand it makes it incumbent upon the Bahá'í to apply for and

maintain the noncombatant status without regard to its consequences upon his personal safety, his convenience, the type of activity he must discharge or the rank to which he may be assigned.

With this statement in mind, we think that Bahá'ís should be discouraged from seeking or continuing a career in the military, and that in any event they must, in obedience to the Guardian's clear instructions, apply for exemption from military duty which necessitates the taking of human life.

When the law imposes an obligation upon citizens to fulfill a term of military service, as the U.S. Selective Service Act does, and a Bahá'í may fulfill this term of service by enlisting, re-enlisting or by being commissioned as an officer, he may do so provided he does not in any way jeopardize his right to "apply for and maintain the noncombatant status" within the spirit of the above principle. We make no judgement as to whether the law in fact permits him to do this. This is for the believer to determine.*

The Universal House of Justice

21. There is no objection to a Bahá'í enlisting voluntarily in the armed forces of a country in order to obtain a training in some trade or profession, provided he can do so without making himself liable to undertake combatant service.

On behalf of the Universal House of Justice

22. The Universal House of Justice has considered your letter of 8 July 1982 concerning the decision you have taken in regard to service in the military, and the doubts which are now

---

* Bahá'í youth living outside the United States should consult their own National Spiritual Assemblies for specific guidance on serving in their countries' armed forces.

troubling you about whether your enlistment in the Army's flight school is in violation of the teachings of the Faith.

We are instructed to say that your action in requesting guidance from your National Spiritual Assembly was correct. The National Assembly in its reply to you of 7 June stated that it was up to you to decide whether or not to enlist, keeping in mind the guidance already given in its previous letter. Now that you have enlisted, the House of Justice is confident that you will do all you can to ensure that you are not required to undertake combatant status.

On behalf of the Universal House of Justice

Membership in Non-Bahá'í Religious and Other Organizations

23. Concerning membership in non-Bahá'í religious associations, the Guardian wishes to re-emphasize the general principle already laid down in his communications to your Assembly and also to the individual believers that no Bahá'í who wishes to be a wholehearted and sincere upholder of the distinguishing principles of the Cause can accept full membership in any non-Bahá'í ecclesiastical organization. For such an act would necessarily imply only a partial acceptance of the Teachings and laws of the Faith, and an incomplete recognition of its independent status, and would thus be tantamount to an act of disloyalty to the verities it enshrines. For it is only too obvious that in most of its fundamental assumptions the Cause of Bahá'u'lláh is completely at variance with outworn creeds, ceremonies and institutions. To be a Bahá'í and at the same time accept membership in another religious body is simply an act of contradiction that no sincere and logically minded person can possibly accept. To follow Bahá'u'lláh does not mean accepting some of His teachings and rejecting the rest.

On behalf of Shoghi Effendi

24. Generally speaking, the friends should not enter secret societies. It is certainly much better for the believers to dissociate themselves from such organizations.

On behalf of Shoghi Effendi

25. Here are a few general guidelines that individual Bahá'ís should consider before joining any organization. When in doubt they should consult their local Spiritual Assembly or even the National Spiritual Assembly.

The Guardian did not elaborate on what is meant by "secret organizations," but the term certainly applies to all those organizations whose aims and objects are not available to everyone who wishes to know them and whose membership is not open to all persons without regard to race or religion. Furthermore, the organization must not engage in partisan politics. Neither should it be one that would not be acceptable anywhere in the world. . . .

As for fraternities and sororities, membership in these is permissible provided membership does not exclude persons because of race, religion, or social position.

Membership in the League of Women Voters is permissible unless and until it becomes involved in partisan politics. Discussion of political issues in itself is not forbidden to Bahá'ís but they cannot support any particular party.

As for membership in the Grange, we assume this is permissible for Bahá'ís so long as it remains the educational and social movement we understand it to be.

The chief criteria for membership in any organization are: Are its aims or objects compatible with the Bahá'í laws and principles? Is membership open to persons of all racial and religious backgrounds? Is it free of partisan politics?

If any Bahá'í is in doubt about a particular organization, he can consult the administrative institutions. In doing so he should supply all possible information so that a decision can be based on facts.

National Spiritual Assembly of the Bahá'ís of the United States

ASSOCIATING WITH SOCIAL MOVEMENTS

26. Fully aware of the repeated statements of 'Abdu'l-Bahá that universality is of God, Bahá'ís in every land are ready, nay anxious, to associate themselves by word and deed with any association of men which, after careful scrutiny, they feel satisfied is free from every tinge of partisanship and politics and is wholly devoted to the interests of all mankind. In their collaboration with such associations they would extend any moral and material assistance they can afford, after having fulfilled their share of support to those institutions that affect directly the interests of the Cause. They should always bear in mind, however, the dominating purpose of such a collaboration which is to secure in time the recognition by those with whom they are associated of the paramount necessity and the true significance of the Bahá'í Revelation in this day.

Shoghi Effendi

27. Membership in nonpolitical organizations . . . is, indeed, the best method of teaching indirectly the Message by making useful and frequent contacts with well-known and influential persons who, if not completely won to the Faith, can at least become of some effective use to it.

On behalf of Shoghi Effendi

28. It is surely very necessary that the friends should keep in touch with the modern social movements, but their main objective should be to draw more people to the spirit and teachings of the Cause. They should learn from the experience of

others and not permit themselves to go (off) at a tangent, and finally be so absorbed in other movements as to forget the Cause of God.

On behalf of Shoghi Effendi

Our Relationship to the New World Order

THE BAHÁ'Í ADMINISTRATIVE ORDER

29. The administrative order which lies embedded in the Teachings of Bahá'u'lláh, and which the American believers have championed and are now establishing, should, under no circumstances, be identified with the principles underlying present-day democracies. Nor is it identical with any purely aristocratic or autocratic form of government. The objectionable features inherent in each of these political systems are entirely avoided. It blends, as no system of human polity has as yet achieved, those salutary truths and beneficial elements which constitute the valuable contributions which each of these forms of government have made to society in the past.

Shoghi Effendi

30. It should be noted . . . that this Administrative Order is fundamentally different from anything that any Prophet has previously established, inasmuch as Bahá'u'lláh has Himself revealed its principles, established its institutions, appointed the person to interpret His Word and conferred the necessary authority on the body designed to supplement and apply His legislative ordinances. Therein lies the secret of its strength, its fundamental distinction, and the guarantee against disintegration and schism. Nowhere in the sacred scriptures of any of the world's religious systems, nor even in the writings of the Inaugurator of the Bábí Dispensation, do we find any provisions

establishing a covenant or providing for an administrative order that can compare in scope and authority with those that lie at the very basis of the Bahá'í Dispensation.

Shoghi Effendi

FORGING BAHÁ'Í COMMUNITIES

31. It behooveth all the beloved of God to become as one, to gather together under the protection of a single flag, to stand for a uniform body of opinion, to follow one and the same pathway, to hold fast to a single resolve. Let them forget their divergent theories and put aside their conflicting views since, God be praised, our purpose is one, our goal is one. We are the servants of one Threshold, we all draw our nourishment from the same one Source, we all are gathered in the shade of the same high Tabernacle, we all are sheltered under the one celestial Tree.

'Abdu'l-Bahá

32. It is incumbent upon every one not to take any step without consulting the Spiritual Assembly, and they must assuredly obey with heart and soul its bidding and be submissive unto it, that things may be properly ordered and well arranged. Otherwise every person will act independently and after his own judgment, will follow his own desire, and do harm to the Cause.

'Abdu'l-Bahá

33. It is of the utmost importance that in accordance with the explicit text of the Kitáb-i-Aqdas, the Most Holy Book, in every locality, be it city or hamlet, where the number of adult (21 years and above) declared believers exceeds nine,* a local "Spiri-

---

* When the number of believers is exactly nine, they constitute themselves as the Local Spiritual Assembly by joint declaration.

tual Assembly" be forthwith established. To it all local matters pertaining to the Cause must be directly and immediately referred for full consultation and decision. The importance, nay the absolute necessity of these local Assemblies is manifest when we realize that in the days to come they will evolve into the local Houses of Justice.

Shoghi Effendi

34. The divinely ordained institution of the Local Spiritual Assembly operates at the first levels of human society and is the basic administrative unit of Bahá'u'lláh's World Order. It is concerned with individuals and families whom it must constantly encourage to unite in a distinctive Bahá'í society, vitalized and guarded by the laws, ordinances and principles of Bahá'u'lláh's Revelation. It protects the Cause of God; it acts as the loving shepherd of the Bahá'í flock.

The Universal House of Justice

SUPPORTING BAHÁ'Í COMMUNITIES

35. And now as I look into the future, I hope to see the friends at all times, in every land, and of every shade of thought and character, voluntarily and joyously rallying round their local and in particular their national centers of activity, upholding and promoting their interests with complete unanimity and contentment, with perfect understanding, genuine enthusiasm, and sustained vigor. This indeed is the one joy and yearning of my life, for it is the fountainhead from which all future blessings will flow, the broad foundation upon which the security of the Divine Edifice must ultimately rest. May we not hope that now at last the dawn of a brighter day is breaking upon our beloved Cause?

Shoghi Effendi

36. His brotherly advice to you, and to all loyal and ardent young believers like you, is that you should deepen your knowledge of the history and of the tenets of the Faith, not merely by means of careful and thorough study, but also through active, whole-hearted and continued participation in all the activities, whether administrative or otherwise, of your community. The Bahá'í community life provides you with an indispensable laboratory where you can translate into living and constructive action the principles which you imbibe from the Teachings. By becoming a real part of that living organism you can catch the real spirit which runs throughout the Bahá'í teachings. To study the principles, and to try to live according to them, are, therefore, the two essential mediums through which you can ensure the development and progress of your inner spiritual life and of your outer existence as well. May Bahá'u'lláh enable you to attain this high station, and may He keep the torch of faith for ever burning in your hearts!

On behalf of Shoghi Effendi

37. The friends are called upon to give their wholehearted support and cooperation to the Local Spiritual Assembly, first by voting for the membership and then by energetically pursuing its plans and programs, by turning to it in time of trouble or difficulty, by praying for its success and taking delight in its rise to influence and honor. This great prize, this gift of God within each community must be cherished, nurtured, loved, assisted, obeyed and prayed for.

Such a firmly founded, busy and happy community life as is envisioned when Local Spiritual Assemblies are truly effective, will provide a firm home foundation from which the friends may derive courage and strength and loving support in bearing the Divine Message to their fellowmen and conforming their lives to its benevolent rule.

The Universal House of Justice

38. Paralleling the growth of his inner life through prayer, meditation, service and study of the teachings, Bahá'í youth have the opportunity to learn in practice the very functioning of the Order of Bahá'u'lláh. Through taking part in conferences and summer schools as well as Nineteen Day Feasts, and in service on committees, they can develop the wonderful skill of Bahá'í consultation, thus tracing new paths of human corporate action.

The Universal House of Justice

39. Youth may demonstrate the efficiency, the vigor, the access of unity which arise from true consultation and, by contrast, demonstrate the futility of partisanship, lobbying, debate, secret diplomacy and unilateral action which characterize modern affairs. Youth also take part in the life of the Bahá'í community as a whole and promote a society in which all generations—elderly, middle-aged, youth, children—are fully integrated and make up an organic whole. By refusing to carry over the antagonisms and mistrust between the generations which perplex and bedevil modern society they will again demonstrate the healing and life-giving nature of their religion.

The Universal House of Justice

40. Wherever a Bahá'í community exists, whether large or small, let it be distinguished for its abiding sense of security and faith, its high standard of rectitude, its complete freedom from all forms of prejudice, the spirit of love among its members and for the closely knit fabric of its social life. The acute distinction between this and present-day society will inevitably arouse the

interest of the more enlightened, and as the world's gloom deepens the light of Bahá'í life will shine brighter and brighter until its brilliance must eventually attract the disillusioned masses and cause them to enter the haven of the Covenant of Bahá'u'lláh, Who alone can bring them peace and justice and an ordered life.

The Universal House of Justice

FOSTERING UNITY IN THE COMMUNITY

41. O handmaid of God, peace must first be established among individuals, until it leadeth in the end to peace among nations. Wherefore, O ye Bahá'ís, strive ye with all your might to create, through the power of the Word of God, genuine love, spiritual communion and durable bonds among individuals. This is your task.

'Abdu'l-Bahá

42. The great and fundamental teachings of Bahá'u'lláh are the oneness of God and unity of mankind. This is the bond of union among Bahá'ís all over the world. They become united among themselves, then unite others. It is impossible to unite unless united. Christ said, "Ye are the salt of the earth; but if the salt has lost its savour, wherewith shall it be salted?" This proves there were dissensions and lack of unity among His followers. Hence His admonition to unity of action.

Now must we, likewise, bind ourselves together in the utmost unity, be kind and loving to each other, sacrificing all our possessions, our honor, yea, even our lives for each other. Then will it be proved that we have acted according to the teachings of God, that we have been real believers in the oneness of God and unity of mankind.

'Abdu'l-Bahá

43. How good it is if the friends be as close as sheaves of light, if they stand together side by side in a firm unbroken line. For now have the rays of reality from the Sun of the world of existence, united in adoration all the worshipers of this light; and these rays have, through infinite grace, gathered all peoples together within this wide-spreading shelter; therefore must all souls become as one soul, and all hearts as one heart. Let all be set free from the multiple identities that were born of passion and desire, and in the oneness of their love for God find a new way of life.

'Abdu'l-Bahá

44. In their relations amongst themselves as fellow-believers, let them not be content with the mere exchange of cold and empty formalities often connected with the organizing of banquets, receptions, consultative assemblies, and lecture-halls. Let them rather, as equal co-sharers in the spiritual benefits conferred upon them by Bahá'u'lláh, arise and, with the aid and counsel of their local and national representatives, supplement these official functions with those opportunities which only a close and intimate social intercourse can adequately provide. In their homes, in their hours of relaxation and leisure, in the daily contact of business transactions, in the association of their children, whether in their study-classes, their playgrounds, and club-rooms, in short under all possible circumstances, however insignificant they appear, the community of the followers of Bahá'u'lláh should satisfy themselves that in the eyes of the world at large and in the sight of their vigilant Master they are the living witnesses of those truths which He fondly cherished and tirelessly championed to the very end of His days. If we relax in our purpose, if we falter in our faith, if we neglect the varied opportunities given us from time to time by an all-wise and gracious Master, we are not merely failing in what is our

most vital and conspicuous obligation, but are thereby insensibly retarding the flow of those quickening energies which can alone insure the vigorous and speedy development of God's struggling Faith.

Shoghi Effendi

45. The believers have not yet fully learned to draw on each other's love for strength and consolation in time of need. The Cause of God is endowed with tremendous powers, and the reason the believers do not gain more from it is because they have not learned to duly draw these mighty forces of love and strength and harmony generated by the Faith.

Shoghi Effendi

46. What impressed him most in the account of your services was the statement that the old and the young Bahá'ís are firmly united and co-operating in bearing the burdens of the Faith in that locality. Nothing will attract God's blessings and grace more than the unity of the friends, and nothing is more destructive of their highest purpose than divisions and misunderstandings. Cling therefore to unity if you desire to succeed and abide by the will of your Lord Bahá'u'lláh; for that is the true objective of His Mission in this world.

On behalf of Shoghi Effendi

47. As humanity plunges deeper into that condition of which Bahá'u'lláh wrote, "to disclose it now would not be meet and seemly," so must the believers increasingly stand out as assured, orientated and fundamentally happy beings, conforming to a standard which, in direct contrast to the ignoble and amoral attitudes of modern society, is the source of their honor, strength and maturity. It is this marked contrast between the vigor, unity

and discipline of the Bahá'í community on the one hand, and the increasing confusion, despair and feverish tempo of a doomed society on the other, which, during the turbulent years ahead will draw the eyes of humanity to the sanctuary of Bahá'u'lláh's world-redeeming Faith.

The Universal House of Justice

Supporting and Strengthening Bahá'í Youth

48. The winds of test and trial have blown upon our Faith more than once, and he strongly feels that old believers like yourself should do everything in their power to protect the younger Bahá'ís, to strengthen their faith, deepen them in the Covenant, and enable them to take full refuge in the Will and Testament of the beloved Master, that impregnable fortress He built for our safety when He Himself should have gone from our sight.

On behalf of Shoghi Effendi

49. Give great attention and support to youth participation in community life and to their teaching the Cause to their own generation in high schools, colleges and elsewhere; encourage and offer guidance to Bahá'í youth to plan their lives to be of greatest service to the Faith, and provide the means whereby their offers of specific periods of teaching and other service beyond normal teaching activities can be organized and used to the best advantage.

The Universal House of Justice

Supporting the Bahá'í Funds

50. All the friends of God . . . should contribute to the extent possible, however modest their offering may be. God doth not burden a soul beyond its capacity. Such contributions must come from all centers and all believers. . . . O Friends of God! Be ye assured that in place of these contributions, your agriculture,

your industry, and your commerce will be blessed by manifold increases, with goodly gifts and bestowals. He who cometh with one goodly deed will receive a tenfold reward. There is no doubt that the living Lord will abundantly confirm those who expend their wealth in His path.

'Abdu'l-Bahá

51. The institutions of the local and national Funds, that are now the necessary adjuncts to all local and national spiritual assemblies, have not only been established by 'Abdu'l-Bahá in the Tablets He revealed to the Bahá'ís of the Orient, but their importance and necessity have been repeatedly emphasized by Him in His utterances and writings.

Shoghi Effendi

52. As to the idea of "giving what one can afford": this does by no means put a limit or even exclude the possibility of self-sacrifice. There can be no limit to one's contributions to the national fund. The more one can give the better it is, especially when such offerings necessitate the sacrifice of other wants and desires on the part of the donor. The harder the sacrifice the more meritorious will it be, of course, in the sight of God. For after all it is not so much the quantity of one's offerings that matters, but rather the measure of deprivation that such offerings entail. It is the spirit, not the mere fact of contributing, that we should always take into account when we stress the necessity for a universal and whole-hearted support of the various funds of the Cause.

Shoghi Effendi

53. We must be like the fountain or spring that is continually emptying itself of all that it has and is continually being re-filled from an invisible source. To be continually giving out for

the good of our fellows undeterred by the fear of poverty and reliant on the unfailing bounty of the Source of all wealth and all good—this is the secret of right living.

On behalf of Shoghi Effendi

54. As to the material sacrifices towards the welfare of the Cause, he wishes you to understand that the general interests of the Cause take precedence over the interests of particular individuals. For instance contributions to the welfare of individuals are secondary to contributions towards the National and Local Funds and that of the Temple.

This is a general instruction. Of course helping the individuals in case one is able to help, is also desirable and merits appreciation.

On behalf of Shoghi Effendi

55. Regarding the question you raised: in the first place every believer is free to follow the dictates of his own conscience as regards the manner in which he should spend his own money. Secondly, we must always bear in mind that there are so few Bahá'ís in the world, relative to the world's population, and so many people in need, that even if all of us gave all we had, it would not alleviate more than an infinitesimal amount of suffering. This does not mean we must not help the needy, we should; but our contributions to the Faith are the surest way of lifting once and for all time the burden of hunger and misery from mankind, for it is only through the System of Bahá'u'lláh— Divine in origin—that the world can be gotten on its feet and want, fear, hunger, war, etc., be eliminated. Non-Bahá'ís cannot contribute to our work or do it for us; so really our first obligation is to support our own teaching work, as this will lead to the healing of the nations.

On behalf of Shoghi Effendi

56. He wishes you . . . to stress the importance of the institution of the national Bahá'í Fund, which, in these early days of the administrative development of the Faith, is the indispensable medium for the growth and expansion of the Movement. Contributions to this fund constitute, in addition, a practical and effective way whereby every believer can test the measure and character of his faith, and prove in deeds the intensity of his devotion and attachment to the Cause.

On behalf of Shoghi Effendi

57. Most urgently, may every believer give sacrificially of his substance, each in accordance with his means, to the funds of the Cause, local, national, continental and international, so that the material resources—the lifeblood of all activities—will be adequate to the tremendous work that we have to perform in the months and years immediately ahead. It requires a concentration of effort, a unity of purpose and a degree of self-sacrifice to match the heroic exertions of the victors of past plans in the progress of the Cause.

The Universal House of Justice

Achieving God's Holy Purpose for Humanity

58. The Ancient Beauty was ever, during His sojourn in this transitory world, either a captive bound with chains, or living under a sword, or subjected to extreme suffering and torment, or held in the Most Great Prison. Because of His physical weakness, brought on by His afflictions, His blessed body was worn away to a breath; it was light as a cobweb from long grieving. And His reason for shouldering this heavy load and enduring all this anguish, which was even as an ocean that hurleth its waves to high heaven—His reason for putting on the heavy iron chains and for becoming the very embodiment of utter resignation and

meekness, was to lead every soul on earth to concord, to fellow feeling, to oneness; to make known amongst all peoples the sign of the singleness of God, so that at last the primal oneness deposited at the heart of all created things would bear its destined fruit, and the splendor of "No difference canst thou see in the creation of the God of Mercy,"* would cast abroad its ray.

Now is the time, O ye beloved of the Lord, for ardent endeavor. Struggle ye, and strive. And since the Ancient Beauty was exposed by day and night on the field of martyrdom, let us in our turn labor hard, and hear and ponder the counsels of God; let us fling away our lives, and renounce our brief and numbered days. Let us turn our eyes away from empty fantasies of this world's divergent forms, and serve instead this pre-eminent purpose, this grand design.

'Abdu'l-Bahá

59. O ye believers of God! Be not concerned with the smallness of your numbers, neither be oppressed by the multitude of an unbelieving world. Five grains of wheat will be endued with heavenly blessing, whereas a thousand tons of tares will yield no results or effect. One fruitful tree will be conducive to the life of society, whereas a thousand forests of wild trees offer no fruits. The plain is covered with pebbles, but precious stones are rare. One pearl is better than a thousand wildernesses of sand, especially this pearl of great price, which is endowed with divine blessing. Erelong thousands of other pearls will be born from it. When that pearl associates and becomes the intimate of the pebbles, they also all change into pearls.

'Abdu'l-Bahá

---

* Qur'án 67:3.

60. Humanity, torn with dissension and burning with hate, is crying at this hour for a fuller measure of that love which is born of God, that love which in the last resort will prove the one solvent of its incalculable difficulties and problems. Is it not incumbent upon us, whose hearts are aglow with love for Him, to make still greater effort, to manifest that love in all its purity and power in our dealings with our fellow-men? May our love of our beloved Master, so ardent, so disinterested in all its aspects, find its true expression in love for our fellow-brethren and sisters in the faith as well as for all mankind. I assure you, dear friends, that progress in such matters as these is limitless and infinite, and that upon the extent of our achievements along this line will ultimately depend the success of our mission in life.

Shoghi Effendi

61. By the sublimity of their principles, the warmth of their love, the spotless purity of their character, and the depth of their devoutness and piety, let them demonstrate to their fellow-countrymen the ennobling reality of a power that shall weld a disrupted world.

We can prove ourselves worthy of our Cause only if in our individual conduct and corporate life we sedulously imitate the example of our beloved Master, Whom the terrors of tyranny, the storms of incessant abuse, the oppressiveness of humiliation, never caused to deviate a hair's breadth from the revealed Law of Bahá'u'lláh.

Such is the path of servitude, such is the way of holiness He chose to tread to the very end of His life. Nothing short of the strictest adherence to His glorious example can safely steer our course amid the pitfalls of this perilous age, and lead us on to fulfill our high destiny.

Shoghi Effendi

62. Ours, dearly-beloved co-workers, is the paramount duty to continue, with undimmed vision and unabated zeal, to assist in the final erection of that Edifice the foundations of which Bahá'u'lláh has laid in our hearts, to derive added hope and strength from the general trend of recent events, however dark their immediate effects, and to pray with unremitting fervor that He may hasten the approach of the realization of that Wondrous Vision which constitutes the brightest emanation of His Mind and the fairest fruit of the fairest civilization the world has yet seen.

Shoghi Effendi

63. The champion builders of Bahá'u'lláh's rising World Order must scale nobler heights of heroism as humanity plunges into greater depths of despair, degradation, dissension and distress. Let them forge ahead into the future serenely confident that the hour of their mightiest exertions and the supreme opportunity for their greatest exploits must coincide with the apocalyptic upheaval marking the lowest ebb in mankind's fast-declining fortunes.

Shoghi Effendi

64. We are told by Shoghi Effendi that two great processes are at work in the world: the great Plan of God, tumultuous in its progress, working through mankind as a whole, tearing down barriers to world unity and forging humankind into a unified body in the fires of suffering and experience. This process will produce, in God's due time, the Lesser Peace, the political unification of the world. Mankind at that time can be likened to a body that is unified but without life. The second process, the task of breathing life into this unified body—of creating true unity and spirituality culminating in the Most Great Peace—is

that of the Bahá'ís, who are laboring consciously, with detailed instructions and continuing divine guidance, to erect the fabric of the Kingdom of God on earth, into which they call their fellowmen, thus conferring upon them eternal life.

The working out of God's Major Plan proceeds mysteriously in ways directed by Him alone, but the Minor Plan that He has given us to execute, as our part in His grand design for the redemption of mankind, is clearly delineated. It is to this work that we must devote all our energies, for there is no one else to do it.

The Universal House of Justice

65. You are a community of victors; you occupy the front ranks of Bahá'u'lláh's invincible army of light; indeed, you must remain in the vanguard of its thrust. The soul-shaking events transpiring at this very moment in the motherland of our Faith make even more urgent than ever the necessity of multiplying the size of your community on which rest inescapable God-given responsibilities towards the world community, no less than towards itself. All your accomplishments proclaim your ability to excel in the fundamental goal of expanding your membership. The progress of the Cause in your country undoubtedly depends upon such expansion.

It is, of course, the individual believer who bears primary responsibility for securing this goal; therefore, it is primarily to the individual believer "on whom," as the beloved Guardian averred, "in the last resort, depends the fate of the entire community," that our concern in this instance is addressed. For it is the individual who possesses the will to act as a teacher or not. No Spiritual Assembly, no teaching committee, no group of well-intentioned Bahá'ís, however much it exerts itself, may usurp the position occupied by the individual in this fundamental activity. Recognizing that the Spiritual Assemblies and

their designated committees have devoted much to proclaiming the Faith through the mass media and sundry other means,
that the enormous resources poured into such proclamation
represent an investment in the teaching work which paves the
way for the action of the individual teacher, and that publicity,
however much it may arouse public interest in the Cause, is
incapable of replacing personal teaching efforts, let the individual Bahá'í renew his resolve to "arise and respond to the call
of teaching." Let him, acting on Shoghi Effendi's advice, "survey the possibilities which the particular circumstances in which
he lives offer him, evaluate their advantages, and proceed intelligently and systematically to utilize them for the achievement
of the object he has in mind." Let him also strive to obtain
adequate knowledge of the Teachings and reflect the virtues of
that knowledge in his daily life. Finally, let him waste no time,
forfeit no further opportunity.

The Universal House of Justice

66. The rising sun of Bahá'u'lláh's Revelation is having its visible effect upon the world and upon the Bahá'í community itself. Opportunities, long dreamed of for teaching, attended by
showering confirmations, now challenge in ever-increasing numbers, every individual believer, every Local and National Spiritual
Assembly. The potent seeds sown by 'Abdu'l-Bahá are beginning
to germinate within the divinely-ordained Order expounded and
firmly laid by the beloved Guardian. Humanity is beaten almost
to its knees, bewildered and shepherdless, hungry for the bread
of life. This is our day of service; we have that heavenly food to
offer. The peoples are disillusioned with deficient political theories, social systems and orders; they crave, knowingly or unknow-
ingly, the love of God and reunion with Him. Our response to
this growing challenge must be a mighty upsurge of effective

teaching, imparting the divine fire which Bahá'u'lláh has kindled in our hearts until a conflagration arising from millions of souls on fire with His love shall at last testify that the Day for which the Chief Luminaries of our Faith so ardently prayed has at last dawned.

The Universal House of Justice

9

Social Issues

Race Unity: Our Most Challenging Issue

1. Ye observe how the world is divided against itself, how many a land is red with blood and its very dust is caked with human gore. The fires of conflict have blazed so high that never in early times, not in the Middle Ages, not in recent centuries hath there ever been such a hideous war, a war that is even as millstones, taking for grain the skulls of men. Nay, even worse, for flourishing countries have been reduced to rubble, cities have been leveled with the ground, and many a once prosperous village hath been turned into ruin. Fathers have lost their sons, and sons their fathers. Mothers have wept away their hearts over dead children. Children have been orphaned, women left to wander, vagrants without a home. From every aspect, humankind hath sunken low. Loud are the piercing cries of fatherless children; loud the mothers' anguished voices, reaching to the skies.

And the breeding-ground of all these tragedies is prejudice: prejudice of race and nation, of religion, of political opinion; and the root cause of prejudice is blind imitation of the past—imitation in religion, in racial attitudes, in national bias, in politics. So long as this aping of the past persisteth, just so long will the foundations of the social order be blown to the four winds, just so long will humanity be continually exposed to direst peril.

'Abdu'l-Bahá

2. In this day, the one favored at the Threshold of the Lord is he who handeth round the cup of faithfulness; who bestoweth, even upon his enemies, the jewel of bounty, and lendeth, even to his fallen oppressor, a helping hand; it is he who will, even to the fiercest of his foes, be a loving friend. These are the Teachings of the Blessed Beauty, these are the counsels of the Most Great Name.

O ye dear friends! The world is at war and the human race is in travail and mortal combat. The dark night of hate hath taken over, and the light of good faith is blotted out. The peoples and kindreds of the earth have sharpened their claws, and are hurling themselves one against the other. It is the very foundation of the human race that is being destroyed. It is thousands of households that are vagrant and dispossessed, and every year seeth thousands upon thousands of human beings weltering in their lifeblood on dusty battlefields. The tents of life and joy are down. The generals practice their generalship, boasting of the blood they shed, competing one with the next in inciting to violence. "With this sword," saith one of them, "I beheaded a people!" And another: "I toppled a nation to the ground!" And yet another: "I brought a government down!" On such things do men pride themselves, in such do they glory! Love— righteousness—these are everywhere censured, while despised are harmony, and devotion to the truth.

The Faith of the Blessed Beauty is summoning mankind to safety and love, to amity and peace; it hath raised up its tabernacle on the heights of the earth, and directeth its call to all nations. Wherefore, O ye who are God's lovers, know ye the value of this precious Faith, obey its teachings, walk in this road that is drawn straight, and show ye this way to the people. Lift up your voices and sing out the song of the Kingdom. Spread far and wide the precepts and counsels of the loving Lord, so that this world will change into another world, and this darksome earth will be flooded with light, and the dead body of mankind will arise and live; so that every soul will ask for immortality, through the holy breaths of God.

Soon will your swiftly-passing days be over, and the fame and riches, the comforts, the joys provided by this rubbish-heap, the world, will be gone without a trace. Summon ye, then, the people to God, and invite humanity to follow the example of the Company on high. Be ye loving fathers to the orphan, and a refuge to the helpless, and a treasury for the poor, and a cure for the ailing. Be ye the helpers of every victim of oppression, the patrons of the disadvantaged. Think ye at all times of rendering some service to every member of the human race. Pay ye no heed to aversion and rejection, to disdain, hostility, injustice: act ye in the opposite way. Be ye sincerely kind, not in appearance only. Let each one of God's loved ones center his attention on this: to be the Lord's mercy to man; to be the Lord's grace. Let him do some good to every person whose path he crosseth, and be of some benefit to him. Let him improve the character of each and all, and reorient the minds of men. In this way, the light of divine guidance will shine forth, and the blessings of God will cradle all mankind: for love is light, no matter in what abode it dwelleth; and hate is darkness, no matter where it may make its nest. O friends of God! That the hidden Mystery may stand revealed, and the secret essence of all things may be disclosed, strive ye to banish that darkness for ever and ever.

'Abdu'l-Bahá

3. The principle of the Oneness of Mankind—the pivot round which all the teachings of Bahá'u'lláh revolve—is no mere outburst of ignorant emotionalism or an expression of vague and pious hope. Its appeal is not to be merely identified with a reawakening of the spirit of brotherhood and good-will among men, nor does it aim solely at the fostering of harmonious coöperation among individual peoples and nations. Its implications are deeper, its claims greater than any which the Prophets of old were allowed to advance. Its message is applicable not only to the individual, but concerns itself primarily with the nature of those essential relationships that must bind all the states and nations as members of one human family. It does not constitute merely the enunciation of an ideal, but stands inseparably associated with an institution adequate to embody its truth, demonstrate its validity, and perpetuate its influence. It implies an organic change in the structure of present-day society, a change such as the world has not yet experienced. It constitutes a challenge, at once bold and universal, to outworn shibboleths of national creeds—creeds that have had their day and which must, in the ordinary course of events as shaped and controlled by Providence, give way to a new gospel, fundamentally different from, and infinitely superior to, what the world has already conceived. It calls for no less than the reconstruction and the demilitarization of the whole civilized world—a world organically unified in all the essential aspects of its life, its political machinery, its spiritual aspiration, its trade and finance, its script and language, and yet infinite in the diversity of the national characteristics of its federated units.

It represents the consummation of human evolution—an evolution that has had its earliest beginnings in the birth of family life, its subsequent development in the achievement of tribal solidarity, leading in turn to the constitution of the city-state, and expanding later into the institution of independent and sovereign nations.

The principle of the Oneness of Mankind, as proclaimed by Bahá'u'lláh, carries with it no more and no less than a solemn assertion that attainment to this final stage in this stupendous evolution is not only necessary but inevitable, that its realization is fast approaching, and that nothing short of a power that is born of God can succeed in establishing it.

Shoghi Effendi

4. Racism, one of the most baneful and persistent evils, is a major barrier to peace. Its practice perpetrates too outrageous a violation of the dignity of human beings to be countenanced under any pretext. Racism retards the unfoldment of the boundless potentialities of its victims, corrupts its perpetrators, and blights human progress. Recognition of the oneness of mankind, implemented by appropriate legal measures, must be universally upheld if this problem is to be overcome.

The Universal House of Justice

5. Evidence of the negative effect of racial and ethnic conflict on the economy has prompted a number of businesses and corporations to institute educational programs that teach conflict resolution and are designed to eliminate racial and ethnic tensions from the workplace. These are important steps and should be encouraged. If, however, they are intended primarily to save the economy, no enduring solution will be found to the disastrous consequences of racism. For it cannot suffice to offer academic education and jobs to people while at the same time shutting them out because of racial prejudice from normal social intercourse based on brotherly love and mutual respect. The fundamental solution—the one that will reduce violence,

regenerate and focus the intellectual and moral energy of minorities, and make them partners in the construction of a progressive society—rests ultimately on the common recognition of the oneness of humankind.

It is entirely human to fail if that which is most important to people's self-perception is denied them—namely, the dignity they derive from a genuine regard by others for their stature as human beings. No educational, economic, or political plan can take the place of this essential human need; it is not a need that business and schools, or even governments, can provide in isolation from the supportive attitude of society as a whole. Such an attitude needs to be grounded in a spiritual and moral truth that all acknowledge and accept as their own and that, like the oxygen that serves all equally, breathes life into their common effort to live in unity and peace. Absence of the genuine regard for others fostered by such truth causes hopelessness in those discriminated against; and in a state of hopelessness, people lose the coherent moral powers to realize their potential. This vitalizing truth, we are convinced, is summarized in the phrase: the oneness of humankind. . . . .

The responsibility for the achievement of racial peace and unity in the United States rests upon both Black and White Americans. To build a society in which the rights of all its members are respected and guaranteed, both races must be animated with the spirit of optimism and faith in the eventual realization of their highest aspirations. Neither White nor Black Americans should assume that the responsibility for the elimination of prejudice and of its effects belongs exclusively to the other. Both must recognize that unity is essential for their common survival. Both must recognize that there is only one human species. Both must recognize that a harmoniously functioning society that permits the full expression of the potential of all persons can resolve the social and economic problems now confounding a society racked with disunity. . . .

From its inception in 1863 the Bahá'í community was dedicated to the principle of the unity of humankind. Bahá'ís rely upon faith in God, daily prayer, meditation, and study of sacred texts to effect the transformation of character necessary for personal growth and maturity; however, their aim is to create a world civilization that will in turn react upon the character of the individual. Thus the concept of personal salvation is linked to the salvation, security, and happiness of all the inhabitants of the earth and stems from the Bahá'í belief that "the world of humanity is a composite body" and that "when one part of the organism suffers all the rest of the body will feel its consequences."

The National Spiritual Assembly of the Bahá'ís of the United States

The Equality of Women and Men

6. In the sight of Bahá [Bahá'u'lláh], women are accounted the same as men, and God hath created all humankind in His own image, and after His own likeness. That is, men and women alike are the revealers of His names and attributes, and from the spiritual viewpoint there is no difference between them. Whosoever draweth nearer to God, that one is the most favored, whether man or woman. How many a handmaid, ardent and devoted, hath, within the sheltering shade of Bahá, proved superior to the men, and surpassed the famous of the earth.

'Abdu'l-Bahá

7. The world in the past has been ruled by force, and man has dominated over woman by reason of his more forceful and aggressive qualities both of body and mind. But the balance is already shifting; force is losing its dominance, and mental alert-

ness, intuition, and the spiritual qualities of love and service, in which woman is strong, are gaining ascendancy. Hence the new age will be an age less masculine and more permeated with the feminine ideals, or, to speak more exactly, will be an age in which the masculine and feminine elements of civilization will be more evenly balanced.

'Abdu'l-Bahá

8. The world of humanity is possessed of two wings: the male and the female. So long as these two wings are not equivalent in strength, the bird will not fly. Until womankind reaches the same degree as man, until she enjoys the same arena of activity, extraordinary attainment for humanity will not be realized; humanity cannot wing its way to heights of real attainment. When the two wings or parts become equivalent in strength, enjoying the same prerogatives, the flight of man will be exceedingly lofty and extraordinary. Therefore, woman must receive the same education as man and all inequality be adjusted. Thus, imbued with the same virtues as man, rising through all the degrees of human attainment, women will become the peers of men, and until this equality is established, true progress and attainment for the human race will not be facilitated.

The evident reasons underlying this are as follows: Woman by nature is opposed to war; she is an advocate of peace. Children are reared and brought up by the mothers who give them the first principles of education and labor assiduously in their behalf. Consider, for instance, a mother who has tenderly reared a son for twenty years to the age of maturity. Surely she will not consent to having that son torn asunder and killed in the field of battle. Therefore, as woman advances toward the degree of man in power and privilege, with the right of vote and control in human government, most assuredly war will cease; for woman is naturally the most devoted and staunch advocate of international peace.

'Abdu'l-Bahá

9. From the beginning of existence until the Promised Day men retained superiority over women in every respect. It is revealed in the Qur'án: "Men have superiority over women." But in this wondrous Dispensation, the supreme outpouring of the Glorious Lord became the cause of manifest achievements by women. Some handmaidens arose who excelled men in the arena of knowledge. They arose with such love and spirituality that they became the cause of the outpouring of the bounty of the Sovereign Lord upon mankind, and with their sanctity, purity and attributes of the spirit led a great many to the shore of unity. They became a guiding torch to the wanderers in the wastes of bewilderment, and enkindled the despondent in the nether world with the flame of the love of the Lord. This is a bounteous characteristic of this wondrous Age which hath granted strength to the weaker sex and hath bestowed masculine might upon womanhood.

'Abdu'l-Bahá

10. O handmaid of God! In this wondrous dispensation in which the Ancient Beauty and the Manifest Light—may my spirit be sacrificed for His loved ones—hath risen from the horizon of age-old hopes, women have assumed the attributes of men in showing forth steadfastness in the Cause of God, and revealing the heroism and might of fearless men. They invaded the arena of mystic knowledge and hoisted aloft the banner on the heights of certitude. Thou, too, must make a mighty

effort and show forth supreme courage. Exert thyself and taste of the sweetness of a heavenly draught, for the sweet taste of the love of God will linger on to the end that hath no end.

'Abdu'l-Bahá

11. The Lord, peerless is He, hath made woman and man to abide with each other in the closest companionship, and to be even as a single soul. They are two helpmates, two intimate friends, who should be concerned about the welfare of each other.

If they live thus, they will pass through this world with perfect contentment, bliss, and peace of heart, and become the object of divine grace and favor in the Kingdom of heaven. But if they do other than this, they will live out their lives in great bitterness, longing at every moment for death, and will be shamefaced in the heavenly realm.

Strive, then, to abide, heart and soul, with each other as two doves in the nest, for this is to be blessed in both worlds.

'Abdu'l-Bahá

12. In brief, the assumption of superiority by man will continue to be depressing to the ambition of woman, as if her attainment to equality was creationally impossible; woman's aspiration toward advancement will be checked by it, and she will gradually become hopeless. On the contrary, we must declare that her capacity is equal, even greater than man's. This will inspire her with hope and ambition, and her susceptibilities for advancement will continually increase. She must not be told and taught that she is weaker and inferior in capacity and qualification. If a pupil is told that his intelligence is less than his fellow pupils, it is a very great drawback and handicap to his progress. He must be encouraged to advance by the statement,

"You are most capable, and if you endeavor, you will attain the highest degree."

'Abdu'l-Bahá

13. The emancipation of women, the achievement of full equality between the sexes, is one of the most important, though less acknowledged prerequisites of peace. The denial of such equality perpetrates an injustice against one-half the world's population and promotes in men harmful attitudes and habits that are carried from the family to the workplace, to political life, and ultimately to international relations. There are no grounds, moral, practical, or biological, upon which such denial can be justified. Only as women are welcomed into full partnership in all fields of human endeavor will the moral and psychological climate be created in which international peace can emerge.

The Universal House of Justice

14. Concerning your questions about the equality of men and women, this, as 'Abdu'l-Bahá has often explained, is a fundamental principle of Bahá'u'lláh; therefore the Laws of the "Aqdas" should be studied in the light of it. Equality between men and women does not, indeed physiologically it cannot, mean identity of functions. In some things women excel men, for others men are better fitted than women, while in very many things the difference of sex is of no effect at all. The differences of function are most apparent in family life. The capacity for motherhood has many far-reaching implications which are recognized in Bahá'í Law. For example, when it is not possible to educate all one's children, daughters receive preference over sons, as mothers are the first educators of the next generation. Again, for physiological reasons, women are granted certain exemptions from fasting that are not applicable to men.

The Universal House of Justice

15. The damaging effects of gender prejudice are a fault line beneath the foundation of our national life. The gains for women rest uneasily on unchanged, often unexamined, inherited assumptions. Much remains to be done. The achievement of full equality requires a new understanding of who we are, what is our purpose in life, and how we relate to one another—an understanding that will compel us to reshape our lives and thereby our society. . . .

Asserting that women and men share similar "station and rank" and "are equally the recipients of powers and endowments from God," the Bahá'í teachings offer a model of equality based on the concept of partnership. Only when women become full participants in all domains of life and enter the important arenas of decision-making will humanity be prepared to embark on the next stage of its collective development. . . .

The elimination of discrimination against women is a spiritual and moral imperative that must ultimately reshape existing legal, economic, and social arrangements. Promoting the entry of greater numbers of women into positions of prominence and authority is a necessary but not sufficient step in creating a just social order. Without fundamental changes in the attitudes and values of individuals and in the underlying ethos of social institutions full equality between women and men cannot be achieved. A community based on partnership, a community where aggression and the use of force are supplanted by cooperation and consultation, requires the transformation of the human heart. . . .

Men have an inescapable duty to promote the equality of women. The presumption of superiority by men thwarts the ambition of women and inhibits the creation of an environment in which equality may reign. The destructive effects of inequality prevent men from maturing and developing the qualities necessary to meet the challenges of the new millennium. "As long as women are prevented from attaining their highest possibilities," the Bahá'í Writings state, "so long will men be unable to achieve the greatness which might be theirs." It is essential that men engage in a careful, deliberate examination of attitudes, feelings, and behavior deeply rooted in cultural habit that block the equal participation of women and stifle the growth of men. The willingness of men to take responsibility for equality will create an optimum environment for progress: "When men own the equality of women there will be no need for them to struggle for their rights!"

The National Spiritual Assembly of the Bahá'ís of the United States

World Peace

16. Chaos and confusion are daily increasing in the world. They will attain such intensity as to render the frame of mankind unable to bear them. Then will men be awakened and become aware that religion is the impregnable stronghold and the manifest light of the world, and its laws, exhortations and teachings the source of life on earth.

Bahá'u'lláh

17. In cycles gone by, though harmony was established, yet, owing to the absence of means, the unity of all mankind could not have been achieved. Continents remained widely divided, nay even among the peoples of one and the same continent association and interchange of thought were well nigh impossible. Consequently intercourse, understanding and unity amongst all the peoples and kindreds of the earth were unattainable. In this day, however, means of communication have multiplied, and the five continents of the earth have virtually

merged into one. . . . In like manner all the members of the human family, whether peoples or governments, cities or villages, have become increasingly interdependent. For none is self-sufficiency any longer possible, inasmuch as political ties unite all peoples and nations, and the bonds of trade and industry, of agriculture and education, are being strengthened every day. Hence the unity of all mankind can in this day be achieved. Verily this is none other but one of the wonders of this wondrous age, this glorious century. Of this past ages have been deprived, for this century—the century of light—has been endowed with unique and unprecedented glory, power and illumination. Hence the miraculous unfolding of a fresh marvel every day. Eventually it will be seen how bright its candles will burn in the assemblage of man.

Behold how its light is now dawning upon the world's darkened horizon. The first candle is unity in the political realm, the early glimmerings of which can now be discerned. The second candle is unity of thought in world undertakings, the consummation of which will ere long be witnessed. The third candle is unity in freedom which will surely come to pass. The fourth candle is unity in religion which is the corner-stone of the foundation itself, and which, by the power of God, will be revealed in all its splendor. The fifth candle is the unity of nations—a unity which in this century will be securely established, causing all the peoples of the world to regard themselves as citizens of one common fatherland. The sixth candle is unity of races, making of all that dwell on earth peoples and kindreds of one race. The seventh candle is unity of language, i.e., the choice of a universal tongue in which all peoples will be instructed and converse. Each and every one of these will inevitably come to pass, inasmuch as the power of the Kingdom of God will aid and assist in their realization.

Bahá'u'lláh

18. Rest thou assured that in this era of the spirit, the Kingdom of Peace will raise up its tabernacle on the summits of the world, and the commandments of the Prince of Peace will so dominate the arteries and nerves of every people as to draw into His sheltering shade all the nations on earth. From springs of love and truth and unity will the true Shepherd give His sheep to drink.

O handmaid of God, peace must first be established among individuals, until it leadeth in the end to peace among nations. Wherefore, O ye Bahá'ís, strive ye with all your might to create, through the power of the Word of God, genuine love, spiritual communion and durable bonds among individuals. This is your task.

'Abdu'l-Bahá

19. The grandeur of their task is indeed commensurate with the mortal perils by which their generation is hemmed in. As the dusk creeps over a steadily sinking society the radiant outlines of their redemptive mission become sharper every day. The present world unrest, symptom of a worldwide malady, their world religion has already affirmed, must needs culminate in that world catastrophe out of which the consciousness of world citizenship will be born, a consciousness that can alone provide an adequate basis for the organization of world unity, on which a lasting world peace must necessarily depend, the peace itself inaugurating in turn that world civilization which will mark the coming of age of the entire human race.

Shoghi Effendi

20. The Guardian has also read with deep interest all the enclosed papers. He is firmly convinced that through perseverance and concerted action the cause of Peace will eventually triumph over all the dark forces which threaten the welfare and

progress of the world today. But such purely human attempts are undoubtedly ineffective unless inspired and guided by the power of faith. Without the assistance of God, as given through the message of Bahá'u'lláh, peace can never be safely and adequately established. To disregard the Bahá'í solution for world peace is to build on foundations of sand. To accept and apply it is to make peace not a mere dream, or an ideal, but a living reality. This is the point which the Guardian wishes you to develop, to emphasize again and again, and to support by convincing arguments. The Bahá'í peace program is, indeed, not only *one* way of attaining that goal. It is not even relatively the best. It is, in the last resort, the *sole* effective instrument for the establishment of the reign of peace in this world. This attitude does not involve any total repudiation of other solutions offered by various philanthropists. It merely shows their inadequacy compared to the Divine Plan for the unification of the world. We cannot escape the truth that nothing mundane can in the last resort be enduring, unless supported and sustained through the power of God.

Shoghi Effendi

21. The world is in great turmoil, and what is most pathetic is that it has learned to keep away from God, Who alone can save it and alleviate its sufferings. It is our duty, we who have been trusted with the task of applying the divine remedy given by Bahá'u'lláh, to concentrate our attention upon the consummation of this task, and not rest until the peace foretold by the Prophets of God is permanently established.

On behalf of Shoghi Effendi

22. Whatever our shortcomings may be, and however formidable the forces of darkness which besiege us today, the unification of mankind as outlined and ensured by the World Order

of Bahá'u'lláh will in the fullness of time be firmly and permanently established. This is Bahá'u'lláh's promise, and no power on earth can in the long run prevent or even retard its adequate realization. The friends should, therefore, not lose hope, but fully conscious of their power and their role they should persevere in their mighty efforts for the extension and the consolidation of Bahá'u'lláh's universal dominion on earth.

On behalf of Shoghi Effendi

Social and Economic Development

23. If ye meet the abased or the downtrodden, turn not away disdainfully from them, for the King of Glory ever watcheth over them and surroundeth them with such tenderness as none can fathom except them that have suffered their wishes and desires to be merged in the Will of your Lord, the Gracious, the All-Wise. O ye rich ones of the earth! Flee not from the face of the poor that lieth in the dust, nay rather befriend him and suffer him to recount the tale of the woes with which God's inscrutable Decree hath caused him to be afflicted. By the righteousness of God! Whilst ye consort with him, the Concourse on high will be looking upon you, will be interceding for you, will be extolling your names and glorifying your action.

Bahá'u'lláh

24. O My Servant! The best of men are they that earn a livelihood by their calling and spend upon themselves and upon their kindred for the love of God, the Lord of all worlds.

Bahá'u'lláh

25. Man is he who forgets his own interests for the sake of others. His own comfort he forfeits for the well-being of all. Nay, rather, his own life must he be willing to forfeit for the life

of mankind. Such a man is the honor of the world of humanity. Such a man is the glory of the world of mankind. Such a man is the one who wins eternal bliss. Such a man is near to the threshold of God. Such a man is the very manifestation of eternal happiness. Otherwise, men are like animals, exhibiting the same proclivities and propensities as the world of animals. What distinction is there? What prerogatives, what perfections? None whatever! Animals are better even—thinking only of themselves and negligent of the needs of others. . . .

We ask God to endow human souls with justice so that they may be fair, and may strive to provide for the comfort of all, that each member of humanity may pass his life in the utmost comfort and welfare. Then this material world will become the very paradise of the Kingdom, this elemental earth will be a heavenly state and all the servants of God will live in the utmost joy, happiness and gladness. We must all strive and concentrate all our thoughts in order that such happiness may accrue to the world of humanity.

'Abdu'l-Bahá

26. The administrative machinery of the Cause having now sufficiently evolved, its aim and object fairly well grasped and understood, and its method and working made more familiar to every believer, I feel the time is ripe when it should be fully and consciously utilized to further the purpose for which it has been created. It should, I strongly feel, be made to serve a twofold purpose. On one hand, it should aim at a steady and gradual expansion of the Movement along lines that are at once broad, sound and universal; and on the other it should insure the internal consolidation of the work already achieved. It should both provide the impulse whereby the dynamic forces latent in the Faith can unfold, crystallize, and shape the lives and con-

duct of men, and serve as a medium for the interchange of thought and the coordination of activities among the divers elements that constitute the Bahá'í community.

Shoghi Effendi

27. The matter of Teaching, its direction, its ways and means, its extension, its consolidation, essential as they are to the interests of the Cause, constitute by no means the only issue which should receive the full attention of these Assemblies. A careful study of Bahá'u'lláh's and 'Abdu'l-Bahá's Tablets will reveal that other duties, no less vital to the interests of the Cause, devolve upon the elected representatives of the friends in every locality. . . .

They must do their utmost to extend at all times the helping hand to the poor, the sick, the disabled, the orphan, the widow, irrespective of color, caste and creed.

They must promote by every means in their power the material as well as the spiritual enlightenment of youth, the means for the education of children, institute, whenever possible, Bahá'í educational institutions, organize and supervise their work and provide the best means for their progress and development.

Shoghi Effendi

28. The friends must never mistake the Bahá'í administration for an end in itself. It is merely the instrument of the spirit of the Faith. This Cause is a Cause which God has revealed to humanity as a whole. It is designed to benefit the entire human race, and the only way it can do this is to re-form the community life of mankind, as well as seeking to regenerate the individual. The Bahá'í Administration is only the first shaping of what in future will come to be the social life and laws of community living.

On behalf of Shoghi Effendi

29. The inordinate disparity between rich and poor, a source of acute suffering, keeps the world in a state of instability, virtually on the brink of war. Few societies have dealt effectively with this situation. The solution calls for the combined application of spiritual, moral and practical approaches. A fresh look at the problem is required, entailing consultation with experts from a wide spectrum of disciplines, devoid of economic and ideological polemics, and involving the people directly affected in the decisions that must urgently be made. It is an issue that is bound up not only with the necessity for eliminating extremes of wealth and poverty but also with those spiritual verities the understanding of which can produce a new universal attitude. Fostering such an attitude is itself a major part of the solution.

The Universal House of Justice

30. The soul-stirring events in Bahá'u'lláh's native land and the concomitant advance into the theater of world affairs of the agencies of His Administrative Order have combined to bring into focus new possibilities in the evolution of the Bahá'í world community. Our Riḍván message this year captured these implications in its reference to the opening before us of a wider horizon in whose light can dimly be discerned new pursuits and undertakings upon which we must soon embark. These portend our greater involvement in the development of the social and economic life of peoples. . . .

. . . although it has hitherto been impracticable for Bahá'í institutions generally to emphasize development activities, the concept of social and economic development is enshrined in the sacred Teachings of our Faith. The beloved Master, through His illuminating words and deeds, set the example for the application of this concept to the reconstruction of society. Witness, for instance, what social and economic progress the Iranian believers attained under His loving guidance and, subsequently, with the unfailing encouragement of the Guardian of the Cause.

Now, after all the years of constant teaching activity, the Community of the Greatest Name has grown to the stage at which the processes of this development must be incorporated into its regular pursuits; particularly is action compelled by the expansion of the Faith in Third World countries where the vast majority of its adherents reside. The steps to be taken must necessarily begin in the Bahá'í Community itself, with the friends endeavoring, through their application of spiritual principles, their rectitude of conduct and the practice of the art of consultation, to uplift themselves and thus become self-sufficient and self-reliant. Moreover, these exertions will conduce to the preservation of human honor so desired by Bahá'u'lláh. In the process and as a consequence, the friends will undoubtedly extend the benefits of their efforts to society as a whole, until all mankind achieves the progress intended by the Lord of the Age. . . .

We go forward confident that the wholehearted involvement of the friends in these activities will ensure a deeper consolidation of the community at all levels. Our engagement in the technical aspects of development should, however, not be allowed to supplant the essentials of teaching, which remains the primary duty of every follower of Bahá'u'lláh. Rather should our increased activities in the development field be viewed as a reinforcement of the teaching work, as a greater manifestation of faith in action. For, if expansion of the teaching work does not continue, there can be no hope of success for this enlarged dimension of the consolidation process.

Ultimately, the call to action is addressed to the individual friends, whether they be adult or youth, veteran or newly enrolled. Let them step forth to take their places in the arena of service where their talents and skills, their specialized training, their material resources, their offers of time and energy and, above all, their dedication to Bahá'í principles, can be put to work in improving the lot of man.

May all derive enduring inspiration from the following statement written in 1933 by the hand of our beloved Guardian:

> The problems which confront the believers at the present time, whether social, spiritual, economic or administrative will be gradually solved as the number and the resources of the friends multiply and their capacity for service and for the application of Bahá'í principles develops. They should be patient, confident and active in utilizing every possible opportunity that presents itself within the limits now necessarily imposed upon them. May the Almighty aid them to fulfill their highest hopes.
>
> *The Universal House of Justice*

31. Bahá'í communities in many lands have attained a size and complexity that both require and make possible the implementation of a range of activities for their social and economic development which will not only be of immense value for the consolidation of these communities and the development of their Bahá'í life, but will also benefit the wider communities within which they are embedded and will demonstrate the beneficial effects of the Bahá'í Message to the critical gaze of the world.

The Universal House of Justice

32. The upsurge of zeal throughout the Bahá'í world for exploration of the new dimension of social and economic development is both heartwarming and uplifting to all our hopes. This energy within the community, carefully and wisely directed, will undoubtedly bring about a new era of consolidation and

expansion, which in turn will attract further widespread attention, so that both aspects of change in the Bahá'í world community will be interactive and mutually propelling.

The Universal House of Justice

33. In its message of 20 October 1983 to the Bahá'í world, the Universal House of Justice called for the incorporation of social and economic development processes into the regular pursuits of the community of the Greatest Name. During the past ten years, many communities have responded to this call and a considerable number of projects—mostly in education but also several in health, agriculture and community development— are now being actively pursued. A few of these projects have achieved the stature of development organizations with reasonably complex programmatic structures and significant spheres of influence. Beyond the success of this collection of projects and organizations, however, the most valuable outcome of the devoted efforts of the believers in this field has been the accumulated knowledge on how to operationalize a distinctively Bahá'í approach to social and economic development. The October 1983 message set out some of the most noteworthy elements of this approach, among which are the following:

- The oneness of mankind, which is at once the operating principle and ultimate goal of Bahá'u'lláh's Revelation, implies the achievement of a dynamic coherence between the spiritual and practical requirements of life on earth.
- The challenge of engaging in social and economic development evokes the resourcefulness, flexibility and cohesiveness of the many communities composing the Bahá'í world.
- The first steps to be taken must necessarily begin in the Bahá'í community itself, with the friends endeavoring,

through their application of spiritual principles, their rectitude of conduct, and the practice of the art of consultation, to uplift themselves and thus become self-sufficient and self-reliant.

- Progress in the development field will depend largely on natural stirrings at the grass roots, and should receive its driving force from those sources rather than from an imposition of plans and programs from the top.
- All, irrespective of circumstances or resources, are endowed with the capacity to respond in some measure to this challenge, for all can participate in the joint enterprise of applying more systematically the principles of the Faith to raising the quality of human life.
- Activities in the development field should be viewed as a reinforcement of the teaching work, as a greater manifestation of faith in action.
- The wholehearted involvement of the friends in these activities will ensure a deeper consolidation of the community at all levels.
- The key to success is unity in spirit and in action.

The experience gained during the past ten years is now sufficiently broad to allow the Bahá'í community to systematically expand the number and range of its social and economic development activities in the years to come. In this respect, a number of ideas merit careful consideration.

1. Degrees of Complexity

In general, social and economic development projects at the grass roots best begin with a relatively simple set of actions. The friends should be allowed to gain experience from, and increase the range of, their activities naturally, without undue pressure from opinions that are often based solely on theoretical considerations. A tutorial school, for example, can in principle become a center for activities such as health education, family counseling and reforestation, but in most cases, it is advisable for it to start simply as a school focusing all its resources on the children it proposes to serve. Insistence on initial simplicity of action at the local level does not, of course, contradict the inherent complexity of the development process itself. In fact, to raise local action to a reasonable level of effectiveness it is necessary to gradually develop corresponding structures in the micro-region, the region, and the nation itself capable of dealing with increasing degrees of theoretical and administrative complexity. Otherwise social and economic development runs the danger of being reduced to a set of laudable activities lacking the coherence and integration which are indispensable for consistent progress.

2. Capacity Building

It has often been said that development is not a product to be delivered by the "developed" to the "underdeveloped." Rather, it is a process the main protagonists of which have to be the people themselves. The greatest concern of Bahá'í projects has to be the development of the friends' capacity to make decisions about their spiritual and material progress and then to implement them. In an ideal project, while concrete action is directed towards visible improvement of some aspect of life, success is measured by the impact these actions have on the capacity of the community and its institutions to address development issues at increasingly higher levels of complexity and effectiveness.

In this context, the relationship between development and delivery of services needs to be examined. For Bahá'ís, of course, service is a basic principle of human existence; every act, every personal or community project, is to be carried out in the spirit of service. It is impossible to imagine a Bahá'í social and economic development project that does not operate on the principle of service. Nonetheless, the delivery of services should not be viewed as the main purpose of Bahá'í development undertakings. Approaches to development centered on the donation of goods and services, so characteristic of traditional religious charity and the programs of the welfare state, are known to have debilitating effects and often lead to paralysis. In the villages of the world, the Bahá'í community should become the spearhead of spiritual, social and economic transformation. A village does not develop merely because it receives simple services in primary health and sanitation, in primary education or in agricultural extension structured around credit and technological packages.

3. Learning

Central to the capacity of a Bahá'í community to lead a process of transformation is the ability of its members and institutions to apply the Revelation of Bahá'u'lláh to various aspects of life and thereby establish consistent patterns of change. In fact, learning to apply the Teachings to achieve progress could be taken as the very definition of Bahá'í social and economic development. Such learning has to occur locally, regionally, nationally and internationally and become the axis around which our development efforts are organized at all levels.

Learning in this sense is not limited to study and evaluation. It comes about in combination with action. The believers must regularly engage in consultation, action, reflection—all in the light of the guidance inherent in the Teachings of the Faith. Such a learning process can occur in a very simple manner at the village and local level, but with greater sophistication by national agencies and institutions. At the international level, it calls for a higher degree of conceptualization, one that takes account of the broader processes of global transformation as described in the Writings and serves to adjust the overall direction of development activities in each country accordingly.

4. Development of Human Resources

Learning and the building of capacity are closely linked to the development of human resources. The development ideas and projects are not imposed from above, and that institutions are to respond to aspirations and initiatives at the grass roots, are established characteristics of Bahá'í development. However, the vigilant application of these principles does not imply that no initiative can be taken from the top. Proven and well-conceived programs and approaches to development can be promoted nationally or internationally, primarily through training. Training methods would, of course, have to foster participation and be carried out with a humble attitude towards learning. Otherwise, training tends to produce a cadre of individuals who are slaves to a given way of doing things.

Moreover, the need for development of human resources is not limited to the direct participants in the actual projects. Thousands of Bahá'í youth in colleges and universities throughout the world, as well as an increasing number of professionals working in fields related to social and economic development, should be encouraged to participate in a worldwide learning process designed to grow in size and range. Indeed, Bahá'í development projects may be seen as sites where training is provided for an increasing number of individuals from both materially poor and wealthy nations and from various sectors of society.

5. Influencing Society

Irrespective of whether or not an individual who has benefited from a period of collaboration with a development project finally becomes directly involved in such projects, the ability to apply the Teachings of Bahá'u'lláh to the affairs of society—

learned in action—constitutes a valuable asset for his or her future efforts to serve and influence society. Development projects in themselves offer great opportunities to the friends to become involved in the life of society in ways that far transcend efforts to improve the lot of a few people. Openness to collaboration with people of capacity and leaders of thought concerned with issues of progress, and willingness and ability to invite them to participate in applying the Teachings to specific problems, have to be created at all levels, if we are to fully exploit this dimension of our development endeavors.

6. Integration

Certain lessons that have been learned in the larger society need to be incorporated into Bahá'í thinking about social and economic development. Paramount among these is the inescapable need for integration. Experience has shown that fragmented activities in various fields such as health, education, agriculture, or industrial development do not lead to sustainable development. The knowledge that should be brought to bear on development problems of the communities of the world does not fit in a single discipline. Effective development unequivocally calls for coordinated interdisciplinary and multi-sectorial action.

The idea of integral development may seem to contradict the principle enunciated above that grass roots action must begin simply and in a way that can be managed by the community itself. However, this apparent contradiction disappears if local action is seen as a means for building capacity. In this case it does not matter with which activity the development of a community actually begins; complexity will arise naturally in an organic way. What is to be avoided is the artificial fragmentation created by separate programs set in motion in a given population by professionals in specific disciplines, each ignoring the knowledge and experience of other groups, each competing for resources and for the constant attention of the people they are to serve.

For Bahá'í programs integration poses an additional challenge. Within the Bahá'í framework, material progress cannot be separated from spiritual development. Social and economic development endeavors have to be carried out in the more general context of the expansion and consolidation of the Faith. When this does not occur, when the various institutions that serve the local community are not well aware of each others' efforts and do not consult on the nature and the range of their activities, development projects become difficult to manage. Divorced from the basic processes of the expansion and consolidation of the Faith, Bahá'í social and economic development cannot prosper and is prone to failure.

In our zeal to pursue social and economic development in the context of expansion and consolidation we should avoid a pitfall that leads to the dissipation of energy and confusion: impressed by the interconnectedness of all the factors that lead to community development, one may be tempted to define social and economic development as a synonym for the development of the Bahá'í community. According to such a definition, all efforts to develop the community, including the establishment of the Nineteen Day Feast, the holding of classes for the spiritual education of children, and the strengthening of Local and National Assemblies and their agencies, would have to be regarded as social and economic development projects. Such a broad definition overlooks the fact that the growth of the Bahá'í community is the result of a number of interacting processes, each directed by various institutions of the Administrative Order and their agencies in collaboration with one another. Social and economic development is only one component and must lay a particular role in the growth process.

Readings on Bahá'í Social and Economic Development

Environmentalism

34. The exaltation of the animal world is to possess perfect members, organs and powers, and to have all its needs supplied. This is its chief glory, its honor and exaltation. So the supreme happiness of an animal is to have possession of a green and fertile meadow, perfectly pure flowing water, and a lovely, verdant forest. If these things are provided for it, no greater prosperity can be imagined. For example, if a bird builds its nest in a green and fruitful forest, in a beautiful high place, upon a strong tree, and at the top of a lofty branch, and if it finds all it needs of seeds and water, this is its perfect prosperity.

But real prosperity for the animal consists in passing from the animal world to the human world, like the microscopic beings that, through the water and air, enter into man and are assimilated, and replace that which has been consumed in his body. This is the great honor and prosperity for the animal world; no greater honor can be conceived for it.

'Abdu'l-Bahá

35. Consider for instance how one group of created things constituteth the vegetable kingdom, and another the animal kingdom. Each of these two maketh use of certain elements in the air on which its own life dependeth, while each increaseth the quantity of such elements as are essential for the life of the other. In other words, the growth and development of the vegetable world is impossible without the existence of the animal kingdom, and the maintenance of animal life is inconceivable without the co-operation of the vegetable kingdom. Of like kind are the relationships that exist among all created things. Hence it was stated that co-operation and reciprocity are essen-

tial properties which are inherent in the unified system of the world of existence, and without which the entire creation would be reduced to nothingness.

'Abdu'l-Bahá

36. When we consider existence, we see that the mineral, vegetable, animal and human worlds are all in need of an educator.

If the earth is not cultivated, it becomes a jungle where useless weeds grow; but if a cultivator comes and tills the ground, it produces crops which nourish living creatures. It is evident, therefore, that the soil needs the cultivation of the farmer. Consider the trees: if they remain without a cultivator, they will be fruitless, and without fruit they are useless; but if they receive the care of a gardener, these same barren trees become fruitful, and through cultivation, fertilization and engrafting the trees which had bitter fruits yield sweet fruits. . . .

The same is true with respect to animals: notice that when the animal is trained it becomes domestic, and also that man, if he is left without education, becomes bestial, and, moreover, if left under the rule of nature, becomes lower than an animal, whereas if he is educated he becomes an angel.

'Abdu'l-Bahá

37. Briefly, it is not only their fellow human beings that the beloved of God must treat with mercy and compassion, rather must they show forth the utmost loving-kindness to every living creature. For in all physical respects, and where the animal spirit is concerned, the selfsame feelings are shared by animal and man. Man hath not grasped this truth, however, and he believeth that physical sensations are confined to human beings, wherefore is he unjust to the animals, and cruel.

And yet in truth, what difference is there when it cometh to physical sensations? The feelings are one and the same, whether ye inflict pain on man or on beast. There is no difference here whatever. And indeed ye do worse to harm an animal, for man hath a language, he can lodge a complaint, he can cry out and moan; if injured he can have recourse to the authorities and these will protect him from his aggressor. But the hapless beast is mute, able neither to express its hurt nor take its case to the authorities. If a man inflict a thousand ills upon a beast, it can neither ward him off with speech nor hale him into court. Therefore is it essential that ye show forth the utmost consideration to the animal, and that ye be even kinder to him than to your fellow-man.

Train your children from their earliest days to be infinitely tender and loving to animals. If an animal be sick, let the children try to heal it, if it be hungry, let them feed it, if thirsty, let them quench its thirst, if weary, let them see that it rests.

'Abdu'l-Bahá

38. We cannot segregate the human heart from the environment outside us and say that once one of these is reformed everything will be improved. Man is organic with the world. His inner life moulds the environment and is itself also deeply affected by it. The one acts upon the other and every abiding change in the life of man is the result of these mutual reactions.

No movement in the world directs its attention upon both these aspects of human life and has full measures for their improvement, save the teachings of Bahá'u'lláh. And this is its distinctive feature. If we desire therefore the good of the world we should strive to spread those teachings and also practise them in our own life. Through them will the human heart be changed, and also our social environment provides the atmosphere in which we can grow spiritually and reflect in full the light of God shining through the revelation of Bahá'u'lláh.

On behalf of Shoghi Effendi

10

Youth Can Move the World

Messages from the Universal House of Justice

TO THE BAHÁ'Í YOUTH OF THE WORLD, JUNE 10, 1966

1. In country after country the achievements of Bahá'í youth are increasingly advancing the work of the Nine Year Plan and arousing the admiration of their fellow believers. From the very beginning of the Bahá'í Era, youth have played a vital part in the promulgation of God's Revelation. The Báb Himself was but twenty-five years old when He declared His Mission, while many of the Letters of the Living were even younger. The Master, as a very young man, was called upon to shoulder heavy responsibilities in the service of His Father in Iraq and Turkey, and His brother, the Purest Branch, yielded up his life to God in the Most Great Prison at the age of twenty-two that the servants of God might "be quickened, and all that dwell on earth be united." Shoghi Effendi was a student at Oxford when called to the throne of his guardianship, and many of the Knights of Bahá'u'lláh, who won imperishable fame during the Ten Year Crusade, were young people. Let it, therefore, never be imagined that youth must await their years of maturity before they can render invaluable services to the Cause of God.

A TIME OF DECISION

For any person, whether Bahá'í or not, his youthful years are those in which he will make many decisions which will set the course of his life. In these years he is most likely to choose his life's work, complete his education, begin to earn his own living, marry and start to raise his own family. Most important of all, it is during this period that the mind is most questing and that the spiritual values that will guide the person's future behavior are adopted. These factors present Bahá'í youth with their greatest opportunities, their greatest challenges, and their greatest tests—opportunities to truly apprehend the Teachings of their Faith and to give them to their contemporaries, challenges to overcome the pressures of the world and to provide leadership for their and succeeding generations, and tests enabling them to exemplify in their lives the high moral standards set forth in the Bahá'í Writings. Indeed the Guardian wrote of the Bahá'í youth that it is they "who can contribute so decisively to the virility, the purity, and the driving force of the life of the Bahá'í community, and upon whom must depend the future orientation of its destiny, and the complete unfoldment of the potentialities with which God has endowed it."

AN OPPORTUNITY UNIQUE IN HUMAN HISTORY

Those who now are in their teens and twenties are faced with a special challenge and can seize an opportunity that is unique in human history. During the Ten Year Crusade—the ninth part of that majestic process described so vividly by our beloved Guardian—the Community of the Most Great name spread with the speed of lightning over the major territories and islands of the globe, increased manifoldly its manpower and resources, saw the beginning of the entry of the peoples by troops into the Cause of God, and completed the structure of the Administrative Order of Bahá'u'lláh. Now, firmly established in the world, the Cause, in the opening years of the tenth part of that same process, is perceptibly emerging from the obscurity that has, for the most part, shrouded it since its inception, and is arising to challenge the outworn concepts of a corrupt society and proclaim the solution for the agonizing problems of a disordered humanity. During the lifetime of those who are now young the condition of the world, and the place of the Bahá'í Cause in it, will change immeasurably, for we are entering a highly critical phase in this era of transition.

THREE FIELDS OF SERVICE

Three great fields of service lie open before young Bahá'ís, in which they will simultaneously be remaking the character of human society and preparing themselves for the work that they can undertake later in their lives.

First, the foundation of all their other accomplishments is their study of the teachings, the spiritualization of their lives and the forming of their characters in accordance with the standards of Bahá'u'lláh. As the moral standards of the people around us collapse and decay, whether of the centuries-old civilizations of the East, the more recent cultures of Christendom and Islam; or of the rapidly changing tribal societies of the world, the Bahá'ís must increasingly stand out as pillars of righteousness and forbearance. The life of a Bahá'í will be characterized by truthfulness and decency; he will walk uprightly among his fellowmen, dependent upon none save God, yet linked by bonds of love and brotherhood with all mankind; he will be entirely detached from the loose standards, the decadent theories, the frenetic experimentation, the desperation of present-day society, will look upon his neighbors with a bright and friendly face and be a beacon light and a haven for all those who would emulate his strength of character and assurance of soul.

The second field of service, which is linked intimately with the first, is teaching the Faith, particularly to their fellow-youth, among whom are some of the most open and seeking minds in the world. Not yet having acquired all the responsibilities of a family or a long-established home and job, youth can the more easily choose where they will live and study or work. In the world at large young people travel hither and thither seeking amusement, education and experiences. Bahá'í youth, bearing the incomparable treasure of the Word of God for this Day, can harness this mobility into service for mankind and can choose their places of residence, their areas of travel and their types of work with the goal in mind of how they can best serve the Faith.

The third field of service is the preparation by youth for their later years. It is the obligation of a Bahá'í to educate his children; likewise it is the duty of the children to acquire knowledge of the arts and sciences and to learn a trade or a profession whereby they, in turn, can earn their living and support their families. This, for a Bahá'í youth, is in itself a service to God, a service, moreover, which can be combined with teaching the Faith and often with pioneering. The Bahá'í community will need men and women of many skills and qualifications; for, as it grows in size the sphere of its activities in the life of society will increase and diversify. Let Bahá'í youth, therefore, consider the best ways in which they can use and develop their native abilities for the service of mankind and the Cause of God, whether this be as farmers, teachers, doctors, artisans, musicians or any one of the multitude of livelihoods that are open to them.

When studying at school or university Bahá'í youth will often find themselves in the unusual and slightly embarrassing position of having a more profound insight into a subject than their instructors. The Teachings of Bahá'u'lláh throw light on so many aspects of human life and knowledge that a Bahá'í must learn, earlier than most, to weigh the information that is given to him rather than to accept it blindly. A Bahá'í has the advantage of the divine Revelation for this Age, which shines like a searchlight on so many problems that baffle modern thinkers; he must therefore develop the ability to learn everything from those around him, showing proper humility before his teachers, but always relating what he hears to the Bahá'í teachings, for they will enable him to sort out the gold from the dross of human error.

BAHÁ'Í CONSULTATION—TRACING NEW PATHS OF HUMAN CORPORATE ACTION

Paralleling the growth of his inner life through prayer, meditation, service and study of the teachings, Bahá'í youth have the opportunity to learn in practice the very functioning of the Order of Bahá'u'lláh. Through taking part in conferences and summer schools as well as Nineteen Day Feasts, and in service on committees, they can develop the wonderful skill of Bahá'í consultation, thus tracing new paths of human corporate action. Consultation is no easy skill to learn, requiring as it does the subjugation of all egotism and unruly passions, the cultivation of frankness and freedom of thought as well as courtesy, openness of mind and wholehearted acquiescence in a majority decision. In this field Bahá'í youth may demonstrate the efficiency, the vigor, the access of unity which arise from true consultation and, by contrast, demonstrate the futility of partisanship, lobbying, debate, secret diplomacy and unilateral action which characterize modern affairs. Youth also take part in the life of the Bahá'í community as a whole and promote a society in which all generations—elderly, middle-aged, youth, children—are fully integrated and make up an organic whole. By refusing to carry over the antagonisms and mistrust between the generations which perplex and bedevil modern society they will again demonstrate the healing and life-giving nature of their religion.

The Nine Year Plan has just entered its third year. The youth have already played a vital part in winning its goals. We now call upon them, with great love and highest hopes and the assurance of our fervent prayers, to consider, individually and in consultation, wherever they live and whatever their circumstances, those steps which they should take now to deepen themselves in their knowledge of the divine message, to develop their characters after the pattern of the Master, to acquire those skills, trades and professions in which they can best serve God and man, to intensify their service to the Cause of Bahá'u'lláh and to radiate its message to the seekers among their contemporaries.

TO THE NATIONAL SPIRITUAL ASSEMBLY OF THE BAHÁ'ÍS OF THE UNITED STATES, JUNE 26, 1968

2. WARMLY ACKNOWLEDGE CONFIDENT JOYOUS MESSAGE FROM BAHÁ'Í YOUTH GATHERED PRECINCTS MOTHER TEMPLE WEST. MOVED THEIR DETERMINATION SEIZE OPPORTUNITIES SERVE BELOVED FAITH CALL ON THEM BOLDLY CHALLENGE INVITE CONFUSED CONTEMPORARIES ENTRAPPED MORASS MATERIALISM TO EXAMINE PARTAKE LIFEGIVING POWER CAUSE JOIN ARMY BAHÁ'U'LLÁH CONFRONT NEGATIVE FORCES OF A SOCIETY SADLY LACKING SPIRITUAL VALUES. ASSURE YOUTH ARDENT PRAYERS HOLY SHRINES GUIDANCE CONFIRMATION THEIR COURAGEOUS EFFORTS.

TO THE BAHÁ'Í YOUTH OF THE WORLD, OCTOBER 9, 1968

3. In the two years since we last addressed the youth of the Bahá'í world many remarkable advances have been made in the fortunes of the Faith. Not the least of these is the enrollment under the banner of Bahá'u'lláh of a growing army of young men and women eager to serve His Cause. The zeal, the enthusiasm, the steadfastness and the devotion of the youth in every land has brought great joy and assurance to our hearts.

During the last days of August and the first days of September, when nearly two thousand believers from all over the world gathered in the Holy Land to commemorate the Centenary of Bahá'u'lláh's arrival on these sacred shores, we had an opportunity to observe at first hand those qualities of good character, selfless service and determined effort exemplified in the youth who served as volunteer helpers, and we wish to express our gratitude for their loving assistance and for their example.

Many of them offered to pioneer, but one perplexing question recurred: Shall I continue my education, or should I pioneer, now? Undoubtedly this same question is in the mind of every young Bahá'í wishing to dedicate his life to the advancement of the Faith. There is no stock answer which applies to all situations; the beloved Guardian gave different answers to different individuals on this question. Obviously circumstances vary with each individual case. Each individual must decide how he can best serve the Cause. In making this decision, it will be helpful to weigh the following factors:

- Upon becoming a Bahá'í one's whole life is, or should become devoted to the progress of the Cause of God, and every talent or faculty he possesses is ultimately committed to this overriding life objective. Within this framework he must consider, among other things, whether by continuing his education now he can be a more effective pioneer later, or alternatively whether the urgent need for pioneers, while possibilities for teaching are still open, outweighs an anticipated increase in effectiveness. This is not an easy decision, since oftentimes the spirit which prompts the pioneering offer is more important than one's academic attainments.
- One's liability for military service may be a factor in timing the offer of pioneer service.
- One may have outstanding obligations to others, including those who may be dependent on him for support.
- It may be possible to combine a pioneer project with a continuing educational program. Consideration may also

be given to the possibility that a pioneering experience, even though it interrupts the formal educational program, may prove beneficial in the long run in that studies would later be resumed with a more mature outlook.

- The urgency of a particular goal which one is especially qualified to fill and for which there are no other offers.
- The fact that the need for pioneers will undoubtedly be with us for many generations to come, and that therefore there will be many calls in future for pioneering service.
- The principle of consultation also applies. One may have the obligation to consult others, such as one's parents, one's Local and National Assemblies, and the pioneering committees.
- Finally, bearing in mind the principle of sacrificial service and the unfailing promises Bahá'u'lláh ordained for those who arise to serve His Cause, one should pray and meditate on what his course of action will be. Indeed, it often happens that the answer will be found in no other way.

We assure the youth that we are mindful of the many important decisions they must make as they tread the path of service to Bahá'u'lláh. We will offer our ardent supplications at the Holy Threshold that all will be divinely guided and that they will attract the blessings of the All-Merciful.

To the Bahá'í Youth Conferences in Costa Rica and Honduras, March 17, 1983

4. WARMLY WELCOME OCCASION SIMULTANEOUS CONFERENCES COSTA RICA AND HONDURAS TO GREET VIBRANT BAHÁ'Í YOUTH CENTRAL AMERICA. YOUR ENTHUSIASTIC EXERTIONS IN SERVICE CAUSE BAHÁ'U'LLÁH AS SHOWN BY SUBSTANTIAL INCREASE YOUR NUMBERS BRING GLADNESS TO OUR HEARTS AND INSPIRE EXHILA-

RATING THOUGHT THAT BRIGHT PROSPECTS SUCCESS LIE IMMEDI-
ATELY BEFORE YOU.

YOU MEET AT HIGHLY CRITICAL MOMENT HISTORY WHEN TURMOIL
ASSOCIATED WITH THIS ERA OF TRANSITION INTENSIFIES. WITHIN CAUSE
ITSELF CAN BE SEEN ON ONE HAND UNPRECEDENTED CAMPAIGN PER-
SECUTION LONG-SUFFERING IRANIAN BRETHREN AND ON OTHER HAND
RESOUNDING TRIUMPHS SEVEN YEAR PLAN INDUCED BY THEIR SACRI-
FICES AND SYMBOLIZED BY OCCUPANCY PERMANENT SEAT UNIVERSAL
HOUSE OF JUSTICE. MANKIND RAPIDLY APPROACHES RECKONING WITH
BAHÁ'U'LLÁH'S INJUNCTION THAT IT BE UNITED. FROM FAR AND NEAR
ANGUISHED MULTITUDES CRY FOR PEACE BUT BEING LARGELY IGNO-
RANT HIS LIFE-REDEEMING MESSAGE THEY FEEL NO HOPE. SITUATION
THUS PRESENTS BAHÁ'Í YOUTH WITH GREAT OPPORTUNITIES INESCAP-
ABLE CHALLENGE TO RESCUE THEIR PEERS FROM SLOUGH DESPONDENCY
POINTING THEM TOWARDS HOPE-RESTORING BANNER MOST GREAT
NAME. HOW FITTING THEN THAT YOU SHOULD CONSIDER AT THESE
CONFERENCES BEST MEANS EQUIP YOURSELVES SPIRITUALLY TO FULFILL
TEACHING MISSION PARTICULARLY SUITED TO YOUR CAPACITIES FOR
SERVICE, YOUR ABOUNDING ZEAL AND ENERGY.

ARDENTLY SUPPLICATING AT HOLY THRESHOLD ON YOUR BEHALF
THAT IN ADDITION TO PRAYING, ABSORBING HOLY PRINCIPLES AND
TEACHING FAITH, YOU WILL BE SO IMBUED BY BELOVED MASTER'S EX-
AMPLE SERVICE TO HUMANITY AS TO BE ABLE THROUGH YOUR INDI-
VIDUAL AND COLLECTIVE DEEDS TO DEMONSTRATE CIVILIZING POWER
OUR SACRED CAUSE AND CONVEY VISION ITS SPIRITUAL AND SOCIALLY
CONSTRUCTIVE BENEFITS TO YOUR COMPATRIOTS OF ALL AGES.

To the Bahá'í Youth of the World, June 23, 1983

5. RECENT MARTYRDOMS COURAGEOUS STEADFAST YOUTH IN SHIRAZ,
SCENE INAUGURATION MISSION MARTYR-PROPHET, REMINISCENT ACTS
VALOR YOUTHFUL IMMORTALS HEROIC AGE. CONFIDENT BAHÁ'Í YOUTH
THIS GENERATION WILL NOT ALLOW THIS FRESH BLOOD SHED ON

VERY SOIL WHERE FIRST WAVE PERSECUTION FAITH TOOK PLACE RE-
MAIN UNVINDICATED OR THIS SUBLIME SACRIFICE UNAVAILING. AT
THIS HOUR OF AFFLICTION AND GRIEF, AND AS WE APPROACH ANNI-
VERSARY MARTYRDOM BLESSED BÁB CALL ON BAHÁ'Í YOUTH TO RE-
DEDICATE THEMSELVES TO URGENT NEEDS CAUSE BAHÁ'U'LLÁH. LET
THEM RECALL BLESSINGS HE PROMISED THOSE WHO IN PRIME OF
YOUTH WILL ARISE TO ADORN THEIR HEARTS WITH HIS LOVE AND
REMAIN STEADFAST AND FIRM. LET THEM CALL TO MIND EXPECTA-
TIONS MASTER FOR EACH TO BE A FEARLESS LION, A MUSK-LADEN
BREEZE WAFTING OVER MEADS VIRTUE. LET THEM MEDITATE OVER
UNIQUE QUALITIES YOUTH SO GRAPHICALLY MENTIONED IN WRIT-
INGS GUARDIAN WHO PRAISED THEIR ENTERPRISING AND ADVENTUR-
OUS SPIRIT, THEIR VIGOR, THEIR ALERTNESS, OPTIMISM AND EAGER-
NESS, AND THEIR DIVINELY APPOINTED, HOLY AND ENTHRALLING
TASKS. WE FERVENTLY PRAY AT SACRED THRESHOLD THAT ARMY OF
SPIRITUALLY AWAKENED AND DETERMINED YOUTH MAY IMMEDIATELY
ARISE RESPONSE NEEDS PRESENT HOUR DEVOTE IN EVER GREATER
MEASURE THEIR VALUED ENERGIES TO PROMOTE, BOTH ON HOME-
FRONTS AND IN FOREIGN FIELDS, CAUSE THEIR ALL-WATCHFUL AND
EXPECTANT LORD. MAY THEY MANIFEST SAME SPIRIT SO RECENTLY
EVINCED THEIR MARTYR BRETHREN CRADLE FAITH, SCALE SUCH
HEIGHTS OF ENDEAVOR AS TO BECOME PRIDE THEIR PEERS CONSOLA-
TION HEARTS PERSIAN BELIEVERS, AND DEMONSTRATE THAT THE
FLAME HIS OMNIPOTENT HAND HAS KINDLED BURNS EVER BRIGHT
AND THAT ITS LIFE-IMPARTING WARMTH AND RADIANCE SHALL SOON
ENVELOP PERMEATE WHOLE EARTH.

TO THE EUROPEAN YOUTH CONFERENCE IN INNSBRUCK, AUSTRIA, JULY 4, 1983

6. With high hopes we greet the representatives of the Bahá'í youth of Europe gathered in conference in Innsbruck. This generation of Bahá'í youth enjoys a unique distinction. You will

live your lives in a period when the forces of history are moving to a climax, when mankind will see the establishment of the Lesser Peace, and during which the Cause of God will play an increasingly prominent role in the reconstruction of human society. It is you who will be called upon in the years to come to stand at the helm of the Cause in face of conditions and developments which can, as yet, scarcely be imagined.

European Bahá'í youth in particular face tremendous and challenging tasks in the immediate future. Can one doubt that the manner in which the governments of the European nations have rallied to the defense of the persecuted Bahá'ís in Iran will draw down blessings from on high upon this continent? And who among the people of Europe are more likely to be kindled by the challenge and hope of the Message of Bahá'u'lláh than the youth? Now is an opportunity to awaken the interest, set afire the hearts and enlist the active support of young people of every nation, class and creed in that continent. The key to success in this endeavor is, firstly, to deepen your understanding of the Teachings of the Cause so that you will be able to apply them to the problems of individuals and society, and explain them to your peers in ways that they will understand and welcome; secondly, to strive to model your behavior in every way after the high standards of honesty, trustworthiness, courage, loyalty, forbearance, purity and spirituality set forth in the Teachings; and, above all, to live in continual awareness of the presence and all-conquering power of Bahá'u'lláh, which will enable you to overcome every temptation and surmount every obstacle.

A vibrant band of Bahá'í youth on the European continent, committed to the promotion of the Cause of Bahá'u'lláh and the upholding of His laws and principles, determined to work in harmony and unity with their fellow believers of all ages and classes, can revolutionize the progress of the Cause. With a rapid increase in the size of the Bahá'í communities in Europe, the believers of that continent, the cradle of Western civilization, will be the better able to serve as a fountainhead of pioneers, traveling teachers and financial assistance to the Bahá'í communities of the Third World.

When deciding what course of training to follow, youth can consider acquiring those skills and professions that will be of benefit in education, rural development, agriculture, economics, technology, health, radio and in many other areas of endeavor that are so urgently needed in the developing countries of the world. You can also devote time in the midst of your studies, or other activities, to travel teaching or service projects in the Third World.

A particular challenge to the Bahá'í youth of Europe is the vast eastern half of the continent that is as yet scarcely touched by the light of the Faith of Bahá'u'lláh. It is not easy to settle in those lands, but with ingenuity, determination and reliance upon the confirmations of Bahá'u'lláh it is certainly possible both to settle and to persevere in service in goals which demand a spirit of self-sacrifice, detachment and purity of heart worthy of those who would emulate the shining example set by the martyrs in Iran, so many of whom are youth, who have given their lives rather than breathe one word that would be a betrayal of the trust of God placed upon them.

With love and utmost longing we call upon you to immerse yourselves in the divine Teachings, champion the Cause of God and His law, and arise for the quickening of mankind.

To Selected National Spiritual Assemblies,
December 13, 1983

7. The Universal House of Justice has been consulting upon aspects of youth service in pioneering throughout the Bahá'í

world, and has requested that we convey its views on service in other lands undertaken by Bahá'í youth with voluntary non-sectarian organizations.

In the past, the policy adopted by some National Assemblies was to discourage young Bahá'ís from enrolling to serve in activities sponsored by non-Bahá'í voluntary organizations, as the Assemblies were under the impression that these young people would not be able to engage in direct teaching, nor participate, for the most part, in Bahá'í activities while serving abroad in such programs. Perhaps in some instances the Bahá'ís involved were not sure how to function as members of the Bahá'í community in order to give each aspect of their lives its proper due.

In the light of experience, however, it is now clear that we should have no misgivings in encouraging young Bahá'ís to enroll in such voluntary service organization programs as the United Nations Volunteers, United States Peace Corps, Canadian University Services Overseas (CUSO) and similar Canadian agencies, the British Volunteer Program (BVP) of the United Kingdom, and other voluntary service organizations. Other countries such as Germany, the Netherlands, and the Scandinavian lands are understood to have similar service organizations which are compatible with Bahá'í development goals as now tentatively envisaged.

Some of the advantages of such service to the Faith are worth mentioning. Volunteers will receive thorough orientation and sometimes will be taught basic skills which will enable them to help the Bahá'í community in projects undertaken in developing countries. Wherever they serve, these volunteers should be able to participate in Bahá'í activities and contribute to the consolidation of the Bahá'í community. The freedom to teach is to a large extent dependent upon the local interpretation of the group leader, but even if volunteers do not engage in direct teaching, being known as Bahá'ís and showing the Bahá'í spirit and attitude towards work and service should attract favorable attention and may, in many instances, be instrumental in attracting individuals to the Faith of Bahá'u'lláh. And finally, the period of overseas service often produces a taste for such service, and volunteers may well offer to directly promote the pioneer work either in the same country or in another developing country.

It is well known that a considerable number of Bahá'ís have already gone abroad to serve with these agencies and that others have espoused the Faith while serving in foreign lands with voluntary service organizations. . . .

National Spiritual Assemblies which hold orientation courses for pioneers may benefit from including the subject of rural development in their program, and, as in the past, from inviting people who have served in voluntary service organizations to participate in the planning of orientation programs and in having them share their experiences as volunteer workers in developing countries.

The House of Justice expresses the hope that the information contained in this letter will dispel the misunderstandings that have in the past surrounded the question of participation of Bahá'í youth in projects sponsored by non-Bahá'í voluntary organizations.

To the Bahá'í Youth of the World, January 3, 1984
8. The designation of 1985 by the United Nations as International Youth Year opens new vistas for the activities in which the young members of our community are engaged. The hope of the United Nations in thus focusing on youth is to encourage their conscious participation in the affairs of the world through their involvement in international development and such other undertakings and relationships as may aid the realization of their aspirations for a world without war.

These expectations reinforce the immediate, vast opportunities begging our attention. To visualize, however imperfectly, the challenges that engage us now, we have only to reflect, in the light of our sacred Writings, upon the confluence of favorable circumstances brought about by the accelerated unfolding of the Divine Plan over nearly five decades, by the untold potencies of the spiritual drama being played out in Iran, and by the creative energy stimulated by awareness of the approaching end of the twentieth century. Undoubtedly, it is within your power to contribute significantly to shaping the societies of the coming century; youth can move the world.

How apt, indeed how exciting, that so portentous an occasion should be presented to you, the young, eager followers of the Blessed Beauty, to enlarge the scope of your endeavors in precisely that arena of action in which you strive so conscientiously to distinguish yourselves! For in the theme proposed by the United Nations—"Participation, Development, Peace"— can be perceived an affirmation that the goals pursued by you, as Bahá'ís, are at heart the very objects of the frenetic searchings of your despairing contemporaries.

You are already engaged in the thrust of the Seven Year Plan, which provides the framework for any further course of action you may now be moved by this new opportunity to adopt. International Youth Year will fall within the Plan's next phase; thus the activities you will undertake, and for which you will wish to prepare even now, cannot but enhance your contributions to the vitality of that Plan, while at the same time aiding the proceedings for the Youth Year. Let there be no delay, then, in the vigor of your response.

A highlight of this period of the Seven Year Plan has been the phenomenal proclamation accorded the Faith in the wake of the unabating persecutions in Iran; a new interest in its Teachings has been aroused on a wide scale. Simultaneously, more and more people from all strata of society frantically seek their true identity, which is to say, although they would not so plainly admit it, the spiritual meaning of their lives; prominent among these seekers are the young. Not only does this knowledge open fruitful avenues for Bahá'í initiative, it also indicates to young Bahá'ís a particular responsibility so to teach the Cause and live the life as to give vivid expression to those virtues that would fulfill the spiritual yearning of their peers.

For the sake of preserving such virtues much innocent blood has been shed in the past, and much, even today, is being sacrificed in Iran by young and old alike. Consider, for example, the instances in Shíráz last summer of the six young women, their ages ranging from 18 to 25 years, whose lives were snuffed out by the hangman's noose. All faced attempted inducements to recant their faith; all refused to deny their Beloved. Look also at the accounts of the astounding fortitude shown over and over again by children and youth who were subjected to the interrogations and abuses of teachers and mullahs and were expelled from school for upholding their beliefs. It, moreover, bears noting that under the restrictions so cruelly imposed on their community, the youth, rendered signal services, placing their energies at the disposal of Bahá'í institutions throughout the country. No splendor of speech could give more fitting testimony to their spiritual commitment and fidelity than these pure acts of selflessness and devotion. In virtually no other place on earth is so great a price for faith required of the Bahá'ís. Nor could there be found more willing, more radiant bearers of the cup of sacrifice than the valiant Bahá'í youth of Iran. Might it, then, not be reasonably expected that you, the youth and young adults living at such an extraordinary time, witnessing such stirring examples of the valor of your Iranian fellows, and exercising such freedom of movement, would sally forth, "unrestrained as the wind," into the field of Bahá'í action?

May you all persevere in your individual efforts to teach the Faith, but with added zest, to study the Writings, but with greater earnestness. May you pursue your education and training for future service to mankind, offering as much of your free time as possible to activities on behalf of the Cause. May those of you already bent on your life's work and who may have already founded families, strive toward becoming the living embodiments of Bahá'í ideals, both in the spiritual nurturing of your families and in your active involvement in the efforts on the home front or abroad in the pioneering field. May all respond to the current demands upon the Faith by displaying a fresh measure of dedication to the tasks at hand.

Further to these aspirations is the need for a mighty mobilization of teaching activities reflecting regularity in the patterns of service rendered by young Bahá'ís. The native urge of youth to move from place to place, combined with their abounding zeal, indicates that you can become more deliberately and numerously involved in these activities as traveling teachers. One pattern of this mobilization could be short-term projects, carried out at home or in other lands, dedicated to both teaching the Faith and improving the living conditions of people. Another could be that, while still young and unburdened by family responsibilities, you give attention to the idea of volunteering a set period, say, one or two years, to some Bahá'í service, on the home front or abroad, in the teaching or development field. It would accrue to the strength and stability of the community if such patterns could be followed by succeeding generations of youth. Regardless of the modes of service, however, youth must be understood to be fully engaged, at all times, in all climes and under all conditions. In your varied pursuits you may rest assured of the loving support and guidance of the Bahá'í institutions operating at every level.

Our ardent prayers, our unshakable confidence in your ability to succeed, our imperishable love surround you in all you endeavor to do in the path of service to the Blessed Perfection.

To the Bahá'í Youth Conference in London, Ontario, August 23, 1984

9. WE HAIL WITH JOY AND HOPE THE ENNOBLING PURPOSES OF YOUR CONFERENCE IN LONDON, ONTARIO. YOU ARE GATHERED AT A MOMENT WHICH RESOUNDS WITH THE SIGNIFICANCES AND CHALLENGES POSED BY THE WORLD-SHAKING EVENTS ENVELOPING THE COMMUNITY OF THE GREATEST NAME IN BAHÁ'U'LLÁH'S NATIVE LAND. THE OUTPOURING GRACE PROVIDENTIALLY VOUCHSAFED THE ONWARD MARCH OF OUR HOLY CAUSE AS A CONSEQUENCE OF THESE EVENTS IS CLEARLY EVIDENT.

OUR HEARTS LEAP AT THE INNUMERABLE IMMEDIATE OPPORTUNITIES FOR THE FURTHER UNFOLDMENT OF THE ORDER OF BAHÁ'U'LLÁH TO WHICH UNDOUBTEDLY, YOU CAN AND WILL APPLY YOUR ABUNDANT TALENTS, YOUR ZEST FOR ACTION AND, ABOVE ALL, THE ENTHUSIASM OF YOUR DEVOTION. SURELY, YOU WILL SEE THAT THE HEROIC DEEDS OF SACRIFICE ON THE PART OF YOUR IRANIAN BRETHREN ARE MATCHED WITH CORRESPONDING EFFORTS ON YOUR PART IN THE VAST FIELDS OF TEACHING AND SERVICE LYING OPEN BEFORE YOU.

THE EXHORTATIONS ESPECIALLY ADDRESSED TO YOUTH BY OUR BELOVED MASTER AND THE GALVANIZING INFLUENCE OF THE GUARDIAN'S GUIDANCE WILL ECHO EVEN MORE LOUDLY IN YOUR HEARTS NOW. INDEED, WE WILL PRAY ARDENTLY AT THE HOLY SHRINES THAT YOU MAY REALIZE IN YOUR LIVES THE IDEALS THEY SO PERSISTENTLY UPHELD, THAT YOU MAY THUS "ACQUIRE BOTH INNER AND OUTER PERFECTIONS" AS YOU INCREASE YOUR STUDY OF THE HEAVENLY WRITINGS, STRIVE TOWARDS EXCELLENCE IN THE SCIENCES AND ARTS AND BECOME KNOWN FOR YOUR INDEPENDENCE OF SPIRIT, YOUR KNOWLEDGE AND YOUR SELF-CONTROL. MAY YOU, AS 'ABDU'L-BAHÁ WISHED, BE "FIRST AMONG THE PURE, THE FREE AND THE WISE."

To the Bahá'í Youth of the World, May 8, 1985

10. We extend our loving greetings and best wishes to all who will meet in youth conferences yet to be held during International Youth Year. So eager and resourceful have been the responses of the Bahá'í youth in many countries to the challenges of this special year that we are moved to expressions of delight and high hope.

We applaud those youth who, in respect of this period, have already engaged in some activity within their national and local communities or in collaboration with their peers in other countries, and call upon them to persevere in their unyielding efforts to acquire spiritual qualities and useful qualifications. For if they do so, the influence of their high-minded motivations will exert itself upon world developments conducive to a productive, progressive and peaceful future.

May the youth activities begun this year be a fitting prelude to and an ongoing, significant feature throughout the International Year of Peace, 1986.

The present requirements of a Faith whose responsibilities rapidly increase in relation to its rise from obscurity impose an inescapable duty on the youth to ensure that their lives reflect to a marked degree the transforming power of the new Revelation they have embraced. Otherwise, by what example are the claims of Bahá'u'lláh to be judged? How is His healing Message to be acknowledged by a skeptical humanity if it produces no noticeable effect upon the young, who are seen to be among the most energetic, the most pliable and promising elements in any society?

The dark horizon faced by a world which has failed to recognize the Promised One, the Source of its salvation, acutely affects the outlook of the younger generations; their distressing lack of hope and their indulgence in desperate but futile and even dangerous solutions make a direct claim on the remedial attention of Bahá'í youth, who, through their knowledge of that

Source and the bright vision with which they have thus been endowed, cannot hesitate to impart to their despairing fellow youth the restorative joy, the constructive hope, the radiant assurances of Bahá'u'lláh's stupendous Revelation.

The words, the deeds, the attitudes, the lack of prejudice, the nobility of character, the high sense of service to others—in a word, those qualities and actions which distinguish a Bahá'í must unfailingly characterize their inner life and outer behavior, and their interactions with friend or foe.

Rejecting the low sights of mediocrity, let them scale the ascending heights of excellence in all they aspire to do. May they resolve to elevate the very atmosphere in which they move, whether it be in the school rooms or halls of higher learning, in their work, their recreation, their Bahá'í activity or social service.

Indeed, let them welcome with confidence the challenges awaiting them. Imbued with this excellence and a corresponding humility, with tenacity and a loving servitude, today's youth must move towards the front ranks of the professions, trades, arts and crafts which are necessary to the further progress of humankind—this to ensure that the spirit of the Cause will cast its illumination on all these important areas of human endeavor. Moreover, while aiming at mastering the unifying concepts and swiftly advancing technologies of this era of communications, they can, indeed they must also guarantee the transmittal to the future of those skills which will preserve the marvelous, indispensable achievements of the past. The transformation which is to occur in the functioning of society will certainly depend to a great extent on the effectiveness of the preparations the youth make for the world they will inherit.

We commend these thoughts to your private contemplation and to the consultations you conduct about your future.

And we offer the assurance of our prayerful remembrances of you, our trust and confidence.

TO THE INTERNATIONAL YOUTH CONFERENCE IN COLUMBUS, OHIO, JULY 11, 1985

11. OUR HEARTS UPLIFTED HIGH SPIRIT, LOFTY PURPOSES, MULTI-FARIOUS FEATURES, REMARKABLE IMPACT INTERNATIONAL YOUTH CONFERENCE COLUMBUS, OHIO, PARTICULARLY DISTINGUISHED BY IMPRESSIVE EXAMPLES SELFLESS SERVICE ITS PARTICIPANTS. THEIR UPRIGHT BEHAVIOR, NOBLE DEEDS, CREATIVE VIGOR HEIGHTENED PRESTIGE OUR GLORIOUS CAUSE INSPIRED JOY HEARTS BELEA-GUERED BRETHREN CRADLE FAITH. OFFERING PRAYERS THANKS-GIVING, BESEECHING BLESSED BEAUTY GUIDE, PROTECT, CONFIRM YOUTH IN THEIR EARNEST ENDEAVORS MOVE WORLD TOWARDS UNITY PEACE.

TO THE BAHÁ'Í YOUTH OF AUSTRALIA, JANUARY 13, 1986

12. ENTRANCE FAITH FOURTH EPOCH FORMATIVE AGE HERALDS ADVENT NEW CHALLENGES OPPORTUNITIES FRIENDS EVERYWHERE EXEMPLIFY DIVINE QUALITIES FIRMLY ESTABLISH BAHÁ'Í COMMUNITY AS MODEL WORTHY EMULATION PEOPLES WORLD INEVITABLY MOV-ING TOWARD TRANSFORMATION HUMAN SOCIETY AND LAYING FOUN-DATIONS WORLD PEACE. CONFIDENT ENERGETIC SPIRIT MEMBERS YOUR GENERATION WILL INSPIRE FELLOW BELIEVERS ALL AGES DIS-CHARGE THEIR SHARE DUTIES OBLIGATIONS DURING YEAR PEACE AS ALL LABOR UNITEDLY FOR VICTORY SEVEN YEAR PLAN AND CONTEM-PLATE NEW LEVELS ACHIEVEMENT COURSE SIX YEAR PLAN.

OFFERING OUR PRAYERS SUPPLICATIONS YOUR BEHALF. MAY PROM-ISED BLESSINGS CONFIRMATIONS BAHÁ'U'LLÁH SUSTAIN YOU DURING YOUR DELIBERATIONS AND CROWN YOUR EFFORTS WITH OUTSTAND-ING VICTORIES.

To the Youth Conference
in Manchester, England, August 4, 1987

13. LOVING GREETINGS TO PARTICIPANTS OF THIS CONFERENCE CONVENED AT TIME WHEN EUROPEAN BAHÁ'ÍS HAVE UNPRECEDENTED OPPORTUNITY DEMONSTRATE POWER FAITH ERADICATE BARRIERS INTERNATIONAL COOPERATION AND INFUSE DYNAMIC OPTIMISTIC QUALITIES INTO COMMUNITY WHICH HAS ALREADY MADE SUCH HISTORIC CONTRIBUTION ADVANCEMENT MANKIND.

EUROPEAN BAHÁ'Í YOUTH DISTINGUISHED BY ENERGY VITALITY AND ENTHUSIASM CAN MAKE DISTINCTIVE CONTRIBUTION EMERGENCE FAITH AS PRIMARY AGENT PROMOTING WORLD ORDER AND CIVILISATION.

URGE CONFERENCE PARTICIPANTS CONSIDER MEANS BY WHICH YOU CAN SHOW TO PEERS EFFECT OF HIGH MORAL STANDARDS IN PROMOTING TRUE LIBERTY ABIDING HAPPINESS, AND CAN RESTORE TO MANKIND APPRECIATION SPIRITUAL BASIS PURPOSE HUMAN LIFE.

ESSENTIAL THAT YOUTH PROLONGED SYSTEMATIC STUDY WRITINGS BELOVED GUARDIAN ACQUIRE PROFOUND UNDERSTANDING OPERATION OF FORCES OF DECLINE AND GROWTH CREATING UNIVERSAL FERMENT IN WORLD TODAY AND LEADING MANKIND FORWARD TO GLORIOUS DESTINY.

BURGEONING TEACHING OPPORTUNITIES EUROPE NECESSITATE GREATER EFFORT BELIEVERS CORRELATE TEACHINGS WITH CURRENT THOUGHT AND NEEDS OF ALL PEOPLE, THUS SHOWING BAHÁ'Í REVELATION SOLE REMEDY INNUMERABLE ILLS AFFLICTING PRESENT SOCIETY.

EUROPEAN BAHÁ'Í COMMUNITY HAS DISTINGUISHED RECORD FORMATIVE AGE DEMONSTRATING STRENGTH AND ACTIVITY ITS ADMINISTRATIVE INSTITUTIONS WITH FIDELITY AND PERSEVERANCE ITS ADHERENTS. BY FULL PARTICIPATION IN BAHÁ'Í COMMUNITY LIFE YOUTH CAN FURTHER ENHANCE THIS ENVIABLE RECORD. FROM SEEDS SOWN DURING MANY DECADES DEVOTED EFFORTS TEACHING FAITH, YOUTH CAN NOW GATHER BOUNTIFUL HARVEST.

To the National Spiritual Assembly
of the Netherlands, July 12, 1988

14. We offer our best wishes and our loving greetings to the participants of the Youth School being held at De Poort Conference Center in the Netherlands, with the theme "Living in Europe . . . Our Choices to Serve."

The Bahá'ís of Europe are privileged to be the residents of a region described by the beloved Guardian as "a continent, occupying such a central and strategic position on the entire planet: so rich and eventful in its history, so diversified in its culture." For decades the Bahá'í communities in this region have labored with heroism and devotion, undeterred by the relatively meager response to their constant endeavors to propagate the message of Bahá'u'lláh.

The time has now come for the European believers, most especially the Bahá'í youth, to take full advantage of the growing receptivity to the Bahá'í teachings now evident in Europe. The people of this continent are yearning for the tranquility, harmony and peace which can be established on an enduring foundation only through the erection of the World Order of Bahá'u'lláh. Through well-conceived, energetically-pursued and sustained teaching campaigns the youth can hasten the advent of that day when their continent will be blessed with entry by troops and the foundation laid for the spiritual revolution in Europe, anticipated by Shoghi Effendi.

We look forward with eager anticipation to European Bahá'í youth arising with a renewed surge of energy and dedication to commit themselves fully in pursuit of the goals of the Six Year Plan. Exciting and challenging vistas are open before them, not only on the homefront of western Europe, but also in eastern Europe where the social changes now occurring must lead eventually to freedom to teach the Faith and establish its institutions. There are vital needs in Africa which the youth in Europe can assist in meeting, renewing and strengthening the historical links binding these two great continents.

TO THE FIVE REGIONAL BAHÁ'Í YOUTH CONFERENCES
IN EUROPE, MAY 17, 1994

15. During this past year, with the encouragement of the European Bahá'í Youth Council, a new movement among this generation of Bahá'í youth has been gathering momentum throughout the continent. Like the swelling of a tide, some waves may be but wavelets yet, but the time for such an upsurge is here. Surely the successive impulses of training seminars, of the Conference of the National Bahá'í Youth Committees held in April, and now of these five continent-wide conferences, will reinforce the eagerness of the youth to rise and seize the challenge to play their part in reshaping the life of the peoples of the European continent.

It is but a century and a half since two young men sat in an upper room of the city of Shíráz; one the Manifestation of God revealing the first Words of God for this era, the other His first disciple. Within the space of six years, both had laid down their lives so that this outpouring of Divine Revelation might quicken all humankind. By that time, hundreds and thousands of eager hearts, men and women, old and young, rich and poor, learned and illiterate, had arisen to welcome the breaking of the Dawn of Divine Guidance and champion the truth before the world.

Now we see that the world has become another world. As Bahá'u'lláh has written: "Mankind's ordered life hath been revolutionized through the agency of this unique, this wondrous System—the like of which mortal eyes have never witnessed."

You have come together from lands which are troubled by many different ills: ecological, economic, political, social, intellectual and, above all, moral and spiritual. You are aware that some of your peers are desperately seeking solutions and, too often alas, are driven to violent means to combat those immediate evils which fill their vision. Others turn aside, despairingly or cynically from any thought that a remedy is possible. You know the solution, you have the vision, you have the guidance and you are the recipients of the spiritual power which can enable you to triumph over all the adversities and bring new life to the youth of Europe.

To be young is not easy. There are so many calls on one's time and energy because, not only are you summoned to perform the duties of the day, but also to prepare yourselves for the tasks which will be yours during the remainder of your lives. In weighing how to apportion your time and energy to such a multitude of activities you can call upon the power of consultation with your parents, your friends, and the divinely created institutions of the Bahá'í administration.

Those of you who are at a point in your studies or careers where you can devote a special period of service to the Cause of God, may be able to respond to the call of the Youth Council for an army of youth-year-of-service volunteers to go out after these conferences to accelerate the winning of the goals of the Three Year Plan in Europe. Those who cannot serve in this way, have other avenues of service in their own countries and abroad. For all of you there is the opportunity and the need to present the Teachings of Bahá'u'lláh to all whom you meet, through your character, your behavior, your unity, your deeds and your words, and to win their allegiance to the Faith.

To the U.S. National Youth Conference, Phoenix, Arizona, December 22, 1994

16. We are thrilled that you have gathered in Phoenix to reinforce your efforts during a rising tide of youth activities across your country. The news of the numerous Army of Light projects

and Bahá'í Youth Workshops fills us with delight and high expectations. May this conference generate a further mobilization of your energies, such as to break the past records of your individual and collective endeavors to spread the Teachings of Bahá'u'lláh and to conform your lives to His divine purpose. So desired an outcome is necessary if the youth are to contribute decisively to the victory of the Three Year Plan not only in your country but throughout the world in the precious, short time remaining to it.

Relevant also to this necessity is the fact that the period of youth is a fleeting moment; in this brief span, much of what is decided and done by each generation profoundly influences the future of society. Hence, there is no time like now, when the idealism, zeal and enthusiasm which are particular characteristics of youth can be employed to far-reaching benefit. Do not tarry, then, in the steps you must take to shape your future; the current state of humanity imposes too many challenges and opportunities for you to hesitate. The urgency to act is further increased by a looming reality: the youth of today will inherit the responsibilities of the rapidly approaching twenty-first century with all the hopeful prospects foreshadowed in our Writings for the near future.

The foundation of your preparation to meet the many unforeseeable changes that will come about rests with your determination and ability to internalize and act upon the divine principles expounded in the literature of our Faith—principles which direct one's inner development and private character, and which guide one's active life of teaching and service. These make for a righteous life—the wellspring of progress for the individual and society as a whole, the harbinger of the very triumph of the Cause of God.

By righteous life is not meant an excessive puritanism, but rather a sensible habit of living which, as guided by the Teachings and by the example of 'Abdu'l-Bahá, offers a sure path to attaining the noble purpose for which human beings were created by the Almighty. At this time of trouble and confusion, who can offer a greater demonstration than the Bahá'í youth of the power of righteous living to restore hope to the hopeless and confidence to the fearful among their disillusioned peers?

"Cleave unto righteousness, O people of Bahá!" is Bahá'u'lláh's resounding exhortation. "This," He affirms, "is the commandment which this Wronged One hath given unto you, and the first choice of His unrestrained Will for every one of you." The Blessed Beauty's promises in this regard are clear and compelling: "Valiant acts will ensure the triumph of this Cause, and a saintly character will reinforce its power."

Have no fears or doubts. Your opportunities are great, the confirmations of God abundant. Sally forth, therefore, to seize your moment, to make your mark on the destiny of humankind.

To the National Bahá'í Youth Conference in Dallas, Texas, December 25, 1995

17. Your conference coincides with the Counselors' Conference which has drawn 78 Counselors from the five continents to the Holy Land for discussions with the International Teaching Center concerning the provisions of the next global teaching and consolidation plan to be launched at Riḍván 1996. You may well draw inspiration from this coincidence as you take advantage of your togetherness to contemplate during the next few days the opportunities available to the Bahá'í youth both to bend their efforts towards great achievements in the teaching field during the remaining months of the Three Year Plan and to ensure through such achievements a fitting initiation for the new Plan, which will be in operation during the closing years of the unique Twentieth Century.

The threat of disintegration and chaos, on the one hand, and the promise of unity and peace, on the other, flash intermittently as prospects at this time of great transition for the entire human race. Unity and peace will triumph, we know; but until then humanity will surely experience trials and turmoil. Amid these can be found the countless opportunities to teach those, especially among your peers, who seek understanding and hope. The perspective which enables us to see clearly during this time of great perplexity is provided in the Sacred Writings of our Faith and in the life and deeds of our true Exemplar, 'Abdu'l-Bahá; these are abundant resources to which the followers of the Blessed Beauty, young and old alike, can turn time and time again for knowledge, inspiration and assurance.

May your collective and individual capacity for action increase as you take occasions such as this conference both to obtain a deeper understanding of your purpose and goal in life and to mobilize your efforts, in word and deed, to spread the glad tidings and demonstrate the revolutionizing effects of the appearance of the Lord of Hosts. Being among the ones who will increasingly be shouldering the responsibilities for the evolution of the Order of Bahá'u'lláh, the very pattern of future society, you, like the Bahá'í youth in every other land, can do no less than consider seriously what each and all of you will do now towards victoriously meeting the challenges and opportunities of these troubled but dynamic times.

TO THE YOUTH CONGRESS IN CHILE, JANUARY 6, 1998

18. As the Cause of God advances resistlessly along the path traced out for it by its Divine Founder, each stage of the process opens up to a new generation of Bahá'í youth challenges unique to the historical moment. Building on the accomplishments of the generation before, youth must devise ways to take

advantage of the opportunities presented to them. A discourse in consonance with the requirements of the time has to be refined, and activities aimed at transforming society have to be pursued with vigor.

To accomplish such tasks during the brief span of time afforded youth requires resolve, spiritual discipline, energy, reliance on the power of divine assistance, and constant immersion in the Word of God. These efforts, which constitute an integral part of the growth processes of the Bahá'í Community itself, nevertheless possess characteristics distinctly their own. In recent years, and in many parts of the world, Bahá'í youth have referred to their collective endeavors as a "youth movement," a reminder that the energy being generated will not only bring new recruits from among their peers, but will move an entire generation one step closer to the World Order of Bahá'u'lláh.

Over the next few days you will be contemplating the special opportunities which the Hand of Providence has laid before you. An essential component of any strategy you devise is training. In all your countries, this question is being enthusiastically addressed as institutes learn to operate with increasing effectiveness. You yourselves are participating, as students and as teachers, in building capacity in your communities to train thousands and thousands of believers, many of whom will be young people. With this vision in mind, you should devise actions, characteristic of your youth movement, in which your swelling numbers will engage. How will you teach the Cause and advance the process of entry by troops? How will you contribute to the establishment of a distinctly Bahá'í life? And how will you accelerate the transformation of Latin American society to achieve its high destiny? As you contemplate these questions, be assured that our prayers will surround you.

To the Youth Congress in Paraguay, January 8, 2000

19. You have come together to examine the progress of a youth movement which embraces larger and larger numbers of participants from generation to generation. As you deliberate on the issues before you, you can take pride in the accomplishments of the community of the Greatest Name in your continent. Youth have played a key role in the impressive unfoldment of the Four Year Plan throughout Latin America, and you can look forward with confidence to the harvest you are destined to reap.

As we recently stated, advancing the process of entry by troops will remain the focus of the global Plans that will carry the Bahá'í community to the end of the first century of the Formative Age. You and those who will be attracted to the Faith through your teaching efforts will bring about signal developments that will mark this twenty-one year period. As a result of recent endeavors to consolidate the work of institutes, your communities are now endowed with the capacity to address the training needs of your rapidly growing ranks. This training will help you exploit the opportunities offered you at this crucial moment in history. In the face of these opportunities, you need to examine and shape the discourse in which you will engage.

At the end of the twentieth century, the majority of the population of Latin America is under the age of 30. As this generation of youth assumes the responsibilities of conducting the affairs of society, it will encounter a landscape of bewildering contrast. On the one hand, the region can justly boast brilliant achievements in the intellectual, technological and economic spheres. On the other, it has failed to reduce widespread poverty or to avoid a rising sea of violence that threatens to submerge its peoples. Why—and the question needs to be asked plainly—has this society been impotent, despite its great wealth, to remove injustices that are tearing its fiber apart?

The answer to this question, as amply evidenced by decades of contentious history, cannot be found in political passion, conflicting expressions of class interest, or technical recipes. What is called for is a spiritual revival, as a prerequisite to the successful application of political, economic and technological instruments. But there is a need for a catalyst. Be assured that, in spite of your small numbers, you are the channels through which such a catalyst can be provided.

Be not dismayed if your endeavors are dismissed as utopian by the voices that would oppose any suggestion of fundamental change. Trust in the capacity of this generation to disentangle itself from the embroilments of a divided society. To discharge your responsibilities, you will have to show forth courage, the courage of those who cling to standards of rectitude, whose lives are characterized by purity of thought and action, and whose purpose is directed by love and indomitable faith. As you dedicate yourselves to healing the wounds with which your peoples have been afflicted, you will become invincible champions of justice.

We assure you of our loving prayers for the success of your deliberations.

To THE YOUTH CONFERENCE IN VANCOUVER,
BRITISH COLOMBIA, JULY 20, 2000

20. You come together at a time of immense promise for the national community to which you belong. It would be difficult to exaggerate the strengths that the Cause in Canada has developed, at the threshold of a new century.

The level of unity that has been achieved, the energy and competence being displayed by your Regional Councils, the financial sacrifices that the Canadian believers are so wholeheartedly making to support the work of the Cause internationally, the trust and respect that the community's collective efforts have won from governmental and non-governmental institutions alike, its extraordinary record of service in both the teaching and pioneering fields overseas, and most recently the dramatic mobilization of human resources across your vast country through the Canadian believers' embrace of the institute program being promoted by your National Assembly—such a brilliant demonstration of spiritual power must excite the admiration of any fair-minded observer.

In all of these great advances, Canadian Bahá'í youth have taken an increasingly vital role. In doing so you have developed capacities that distinguish you in Canadian society, however progressive, however highly trained, however materially well-endowed various segments of that society may be. You need to ask yourselves how these impressive capacities can best be used.

One evening, in the home of Mr. and Mrs. Sutherland Maxwell in Montreal, 'Abdu'l-Bahá summed up in a few intensely poignant words both the crisis He saw engulfing humankind and the sole means of deliverance:

> Today the world of humanity is walking in darkness because it is out of touch with the world of God. That is why we do not see the signs of God in the hearts of men. . . . When a divine spiritual illumination becomes manifest in the world of humanity, when divine instruction and guidance appear, then enlightenment follows, a new spirit is realized within, a new power descends, and a new life is given. It is like the birth from the animal kingdom into the kingdom of man. When man acquires these virtues, the oneness of the world of humanity will be revealed. . . . Then will the justice of God become manifest, all humanity will appear as the members of one family, and every member of that family will be consecrated to cooperation and mutual assistance.

It is to this divine illumination that you have turned your hearts. It is the force of this spiritual enlightenment—sharply focused in the institute process—that is opening your minds even wider to the possibilities of the Cause of God. And it is not surprising that, for those who are exposed to such influences, the experience does indeed seem like the birth from an old condition to an entirely new one.

With hearts filled with admiration for all that your community is accomplishing and with the brightest hopes for the contributions that you as youth will particularly bring to the great adventure ahead, we urge you to make a wholehearted commitment to this vision of 'Abdu'l-Bahá. Like the rest of the world, Canadian society stands in urgent need of moral transformation. Such transformation, as amply evidenced by decades of contentious history, cannot be achieved through political passion, the conflict of vested interests, or technical recipes. What is called for is a spiritual revival, as a prerequisite to the successful application of political, economic and technological instruments. But there is a need for a catalyst. Be assured that, in spite of your small numbers, you are the channels through which such a catalyst can be provided.

Be not dismayed if your endeavors are dismissed as utopian by the voices that would oppose any suggestion of fundamental change. Trust in the capacity of this generation to disentangle itself from the embroilments of a divided world. To discharge your responsibilities, you will have to show forth courage, the courage of those who cling to standards of rectitude, who champion the cause of justice, whose lives are characterized by purity of thought and action, and whose purpose is directed by love and indomitable faith.

As one of the co-executors of the Divine Plan, your community's mandate is not, of course, limited to Canada.

It is worldwide, and this global perspective must frame both your deliberations and your endeavors. Be confident that, as you turn your hearts and minds to the challenge facing you, you will be surrounded by our ardent prayers at the Holy Threshold that Bahá'u'lláh will empower you to realize your highest aspirations.

TO THE YOUTH CONFERENCE
OF THE INDIAN SUB-CONTINENT, DECEMBER 25, 2000

21. Since the outset of the Four Year Plan we have observed with great pleasure the steadily increasing tempo of activity in the Indian sub-continent and are well aware of the contribution that the youth have made to the advances achieved in recent years. We now see an able corps of devoted youth in each of your countries, touched by the spirit of the Faith and fired by the noble vision enshrined in the Writings, ready to play a significant role in the strengthening of the foundations of Bahá'í communities and in the spiritual regeneration of the society to which they belong.

Developing distinctive Bahá'í communities is a challenge you share with the rest of your fellow believers in that vast and promising region. You need to exert every effort to align your thoughts and actions with the Teachings and become the source of inspiration and encouragement to others. When you come across passive acceptance of the Faith, respond with passion for teaching. When you see compromise of principles in the name of expediency, demonstrate an even greater sense of spiritual discipline. When you notice traces of tendencies that lead to division, show forth your ability to act as builders of unity. Aspire to the station of servitude at His Threshold.

Your national institute programs will help you develop your capabilities of service, which will need to be directed not only to your own communities but to the society around you. The current generation of youth in the region is experiencing social change at a phenomenal rate. This change presents your peers with a host of unprecedented challenges, and the great majority finds itself in a state of utter confusion. Yet among them are many who aspire to create a new society in which justice prevails. Who but you, the dedicated servants of the Blessed Beauty, inspired and moved by His all-embracing vision of the new World Order, can show these youth the direction they seek? In your deliberations you will need to think of ways to attract your fellow youth to the Faith and persuade them to join you in your systematic study of the Teachings so that, galvanized by the same vision that spurs you to action, they can become active participants in your movement. Be assured of our loving prayers in the Holy Shrines that your efforts may be reinforced by the Supreme Concourse.

To THE YOUTH CONFERENCE
IN SHERBROOKE, QUEBEC, JUNE 28, 2001
22. The rising momentum of the series of youth conferences in the Americas has been a source of great joy to us, and we welcome the opportunity to speak directly to your gathering this weekend in the heart of French Canada.

As you are all certainly aware, the Bahá'í World Center has just been the scene of a series of extraordinary events marking the successful completion of the great building projects on Mount Carmel, events whose impact on public consciousness throughout the world has far surpassed the brightest hopes of the Bahá'í community. At the conclusion of the conference accompanying the inauguration, we addressed a message to the friends assembled from every part of the world and virtually every segment of humanity. Its central theme, and the perspectives in which that theme is set forth, hold special implications for the youth of the Bahá'í world, and we are therefore moved to forward you a copy of the statement, in the confidence that it will assist in focusing your consultations this weekend.

Historical circumstances have endowed people of North America—and particularly its youth—with opportunities and resources denied to the great majority of the rest of the human family. While the immediate focus of your deliberations must be the needs of the ambitious area growth programs underway throughout Canada and the United States, it is vital that you keep ever in the forefront of your minds the fact that your two communities have been singled out by the unerring pen of 'Abdu'l-Bahá for a mission that embraces the entire planet. Far from being inhibited by investment of your energies in other parts of the world, the work of the Cause in North America will derive fresh vision and vitality from such contributions.

Be confident of our ardent prayers at the Holy Shrines that Bahá'u'lláh will inspire the minds and hearts and confirm the resolutions you make to advance His Cause.

To the Eighth ASEAN Youth Conference in Thailand, December 22, 2001

23. We send our loving greetings to all those gathered at the Eighth ASEAN Youth Conference.

The Five Year Plan, which will undoubtedly be the focus of your consultations over the next few days, requires concentrated and sustained attention to two essential movements. The first is the steady flow of believers through the sequence of courses offered by training institutes, for the purpose of developing the human resources of the Cause. The second, which receives its impetus from the first, is the movement of geographic clusters from one stage of growth to the next. That Bahá'í youth must be intensely involved in both of these—indeed, that they must be a driving force behind them–goes without saying. We urge you, then, to cast your deliberations in the framework of these two pressing requirements. Ask yourselves how, as individuals, as members of your local and national communities, and as the vanguard of an entire generation in your region, you can ensure that the advancement in the process of entry by troops, called for by the Five Year Plan, is achieved in each of your countries.

We shall remember you in our prayers in the Holy Shrines.

TO THE FRIENDS GATHERED AT THE YOUTH CONGRESS
IN BRAZIL, JANUARY 17, 2002

24. We have followed with keen interest the series of youth conferences conducted across the American continent since the beginning of 2000. The enthusiasm generated among the youth by those events, and the spirit of devotion evoked, were noteworthy. This latest gathering is being held at a time when the initial stages of the Five Year Plan have unfolded, giving rise to well conceived plans of action, formulated on the basis of the geographic clusters into which each of your countries has been divided. To move these clusters from one stage of development to the next is the challenge being addresses by your institutions.

As you deliberate in the coming days on your experiences and aspirations, you should keep in mind that the success of the Five Year Plan in your continent will depend, in no small measure, on the wholehearted and sacrificial participation of the youth. You know well that the driving force behind growth in every cluster is the training institute. An enormous task lies ahead of these centers of learning as they strive to help large contingents of people pass through the sequence of courses they offer. Participating in their programs must rank high among the endeavours you undertake for the Faith. Your contribution to the efforts to multiply the number of study circles will be significant if you constantly seek out receptive souls in your schools, at your universities, and in the workplace and invite them to join you in your exploration of the Writings. But your concern should not end with your own place of residence. You should take advantage of every opportunity to meet the needs of clusters throughout the continent by offering periods of service as short-term pioneers or as traveling teachers. As you do so, you will be able to forge bonds of fellowship with people of diverse backgrounds and bring them together in unified action.

We pray ardently that Bahá'u'lláh will bless and confirm your every effort to serve His Cause.

To the Bahá'í Youth of the Northeastern United States, December 21, 2003

25. The news of the Festival and Conference at which you will be assembling in February has brought great joy to our hearts. Throughout the entire Bahá'í world, there is today a wave of confidence and commitment that is transforming the life of the Bahá'í community and winning extraordinary victories in the teaching work. Without question, the believers in North America have the capacity to make a vital contribution of their own to this common effort.

These advances are the fruit of the Five Year Plan. As the institute process steadily consolidates itself, it is demonstrating everywhere its ability to mobilize and empower all aspects of the teaching work. Central to the effort are, of course, the priority activities of devotional meetings, study groups and children's classes. With every passing day, the circle of non-Bahá'í friends and acquaintances who are affected by the cumulative power of these initiatives progressively widens. From community after community, heartwarming reports reach the

Bahá'í World Center of the way in which persons who are not yet officially registered as members of the Faith are nevertheless coming to identify themselves with Bahá'í programs and beliefs.

In the forefront of this spiritual adventure are the Bahá'í youth. Taking advantage of their relatively greater freedom and energy, they demonstrate their effectiveness as teachers of children's classes, serve as institute tutors, stimulate study of the Writings among their peers and provide convincing examples of the inner resources released by the devotional life. Not surprisingly, the spirit of joy that characterizes these services is expressing itself in an unprecedented explosion of music and other arts.

Merely to contemplate such developments brings to mind the words of the Master to the friends in your region of North America, a region on which He lavished so great a portion of His time, His energy and His love:

Praise be to God, that the Northeastern States are in the utmost capacity. Because the ground is rich, the rain of the divine outpouring is descending. Now you must become heavenly farmers and scatter pure seeds in the prepared soil. The harvest of every other seed is limited, but the bounty and the blessing of the seed of the divine teachings is unlimited.

In response to the guidance of your National Spiritual Assembly, you have committed yourselves to "blazoning the Name of Bahá'u'lláh" before the eyes of the people of your country, the strategy for which is set out in the Five Year Plan. The productivity of the forthcoming Festival will be enormously enhanced by the extent to which you are able to make use of the intervening weeks to gain firsthand experience of the Plan and its core activities.

Be sure of our prayers in the Holy Shrines that Bahá'u'lláh will guide and confirm your efforts.

Messages Written on Behalf of
the Universal House of Justice

To Two Individual Bahá'ís, October 28, 1992

26. The Universal House of Justice has considered the concerns expressed in your letter of 15 September 1992 regarding the manner of appealing to the youth and of involving them in Bahá'í activities, particularly with respect to the youth year of service, and we have been directed to convey the following.

The House of Justice sympathizes with your view that undue pressure should not be put on the youth to induce them to engage in activities of a youth year of service, and it certainly would not be in accord with the purposes of the Faith to require youth to abandon their academic training so as to teach or otherwise serve the Faith. Many factors bear on the various points you have raised; these must be understood by both youth and parents, and of course by members of Bahá'í institutions. For example, every Bahá'í, whether youth or adult, has spiritual duties and obligations in common; among these is the duty prescribed by Bahá'u'lláh to the individual to teach His Faith, a duty which He describes as the "meritorious of all deeds" and in which He urges us to be "unrestrained as the wind." Even so, the youth must be knowledgeable of the emphasis which Bahá'u'lláh places on the education and the acquisition of skills, and they should regard the pursuit of these objectives as a service to God.

Particular challenges must be met by the youth, parents, and the Bahá'í institutions in relation to their respective responsibilities. For instance:

• The youth face the pressing obligation of completing their education so as to acquire a profession or trade while at the same time observing their other spiritual obligations and duties to God.

- Parents have the responsibility of ensuring that their children are educated and, to the extent possible, must provide the material support for their academic or vocational training up through their youthful years; parents also continue during this period to offer them moral and practical guidance as befit their parental duties and with respect to the spiritual obligations which they share in common with their Bahá'í children.
- The Bahá'í institutions have not only to administer the affairs of the community and protect its interests but also to stimulate and exhort the friends to fulfill their spiritual duties and obligations. These same institutions, while encouraging the friends to teach the Cause of God and to make sacrifices in so doing, also have the clear responsibility laid upon them by Bahá'u'lláh to promote education of the human race, both spiritual and academic.

So fundamental are these duties and obligations that to some degree all entities—youth, parents, Bahá'í institutions—share in them, acting in accordance with their respective functions and responsibilities. There is a sphere in which each must make independent judgments and take independent action. A youth must decide on what professional training to pursue and keep a balance between such pursuit and his spiritual obligations; the parents must assist the youth, through material support and moral guidance, to achieve his goal, and must also encourage the youth in the observance of his spiritual obligations; the institutions must promote the Cause of God, endeavor to stimulate action on the part of individual believers in the teaching and consolidation of the Faith, with the full realization that if such action is neglected there can be no hope for the peace of mankind and the future growth of civilization. The institutions cannot, therefore, fail to urge the friends to service and to call their attention to the critical situation of the times and to point out the crucial importance of the action of the individual to the fortunes of the Faith and humanity as a whole.

Along with all these considerations is the factor of the special role which the youth, with their particular qualities of enthusiasm and idealism, play in the development of the Cause. This has been evident from the earliest days of the Faith and is indispensable to its ultimate triumph. A cursory review of Bahá'í history provides many examples of the heroic deeds of youth, and today's Bahá'í youth cannot help but be inspired by such heroism to also play their part in their own time before they become burdened with the cares of adult life.

In some circumstances, however much a youth may wish to respond to a call to Bahá'í service of a particular kind, he may not be able to do so because he may be in the midst of important academic training that cannot and should not be postponed, he may be dependent on parents who cannot afford to assist him materially both to take time out to engage in a year of service and to return to his academic pursuits later on, or there may be other obstacles. Then there are circumstances in which a youth may find that by postponing his academic training for a time, he is better able to determine exactly what to do with his life, if during this time he can make some useful contribution to the Faith or to society. There are numerous examples of such circumstances among Bahá'í youth who have found that by engaging in activities of the youth year of service, they were able not only to make valuable contributions to the teaching of the Faith or to development projects, but were also able to make up their minds about their life's work. There are also many youth who prefer to complete their education before offering special services to the Faith, and this is entirely in order.

The pre-eminent point drawn from your letter is the importance of balance in judgment and action. The members of Bahá'í institutions cannot escape their duty to urge and stimulate the friends, adult and youth, to serve the Cause, especially in the field of teaching, and in this they are inevitably enthusiastic. Of course, individuals differ in their approach and may in some cases be injudicious in their speech; this is to be regretted and dealt with as instances arise. But those who hear such persons, however much they may be stimulated by them, do also have the individual obligation to make judgments based upon their understanding of the Teachings, of the particular challenge at the moment, and of their circumstances, and should make their decisions accordingly.

As important as it is for parents to exercise their moral authority in assisting the youth not to make unwise decisions, it is also incumbent on the parents as Bahá'ís to give due consideration to the significance of the spiritual impact of the Faith upon the youth and recognize that the youth must have some latitude to respond to the stirring of their hearts and souls, since they, beginning at the age of 15, must assume serious spiritual obligations and duties and are themselves alone ultimately responsible to God for the progress of their own souls. The capacity for mature thinking on the part of youth differs from one to the other and according to age; some attain this ability earlier than others; for some it is delayed. Parents are generally in a position to judge these matters more acutely than others and must consider them in their attempt to guide the youth in their families, but the parents must strive to do so in such a way as not to stifle their children's sense of spiritual responsibility.

The House of Justice has written numerous letters to the youth which aim at guiding them to achieve a proper balance in their plans and activities. One of these, which was addressed to the Bahá'í youth in every land on 10 June 1966, may be of particular interest to you and is enclosed herewith.

With deep empathy for you as parents challenged with the onerous task of raising your children in a world beset with unprecedented problems and difficulties, the House of Justice assures you of its ardent prayers in the Holy Shrines on your behalf.

To the European Bahá'í Youth Council, December 7, 1992

27. The Universal House of Justice received a copy of your letter of 31 October 1992 addressed to selected Bahá'ís in Europe seeking their input on the development of a vision for the activities of the European Bahá'í Youth in the Three Year Plan. Accompanying this letter was a very interesting analysis of the current situation of the European Bahá'í youth community.

The House of Justice notes that you have shared this correspondence with all the European Counsellors. It feels that it would also be of considerable interest to the National Spiritual Assemblies and suggests that you send copies to them, if you have not already done so.

There is one comment that the Universal House of Justice has asked us to make in relation to a number of points made in the analysis, since this may assist in overcoming the problem of the bewildering range of alternatives that lie before youth in these days. This is the importance of conveying to the youth the awareness that every aspect of a person's life is an element of his or her service to Bahá'u'lláh: the love and respect one has for one's parents; the pursuit of one's education; the nurturing of good health; the acquiring of a trade or profession; one's behavior towards others and the upholding of a high moral standard; one's marriage and the bringing up of one's children; one's activities in teaching the Faith and the building up the strength of the Bahá'í community, whether this be in such simple matters as attending the Nineteen Day Feast or the observance of the Bahá'í Holy Days, or in more demanding tasks required by service in the administration of the Faith; and, not least, to take time each day to read the Writings and say the Obligatory Prayer, which are the source of growing spiritual strength, understanding, and attachment to God. The concept of the Youth Year of Service should be viewed in this context, as a special service that the youth can devote to the Cause, and which should prove to be a highly valuable element in their own spiritual and intellectual development. It is not an alternative to, or in conflict with, the carrying out of the other vital tasks enumerated above, but rather a unique service and privilege which should be combined with them in the way that is best suited to each individual case.

The House of Justice hopes that the discussion you have launched will produce highly significant insights into the current situation and provide you with potent ideas for the activities of the youth in the Three Year Plan.

Appendix:
Selected Prayers for Spiritual Growth

Obligatory Prayers

1. The daily obligatory prayers are three in number. . . . The believer is entirely free to choose any one of these three prayers, but is under the obligation of reciting one of them, and in accordance with any specific directions with which it may be accompanied.

On behalf of Shoghi Effendi

2. By "morning," "noon" and "evening," mentioned in connection with the Obligatory Prayers, is meant respectively the intervals between sunrise and noon, between noon and sunset, and from sunset till two hours after sunset.

The Kitáb-i-Aqdas

3. *Short obligatory prayer, to be recited once in twenty-four hours, at noon*

I bear witness, O my God, that Thou has created me to know Thee and to worship Thee. I testify, at this moment, to my powerlessness and to Thy might, to my poverty and to Thy wealth.

There is none other God but Thee, the Help in Peril, the Self-Subsisting.

Bahá'u'lláh

4. *Medium obligatory prayer, to be recited daily, in the morning, at noon, and in the evening*

Whoso wisheth to pray, let him wash his hands, and while he washeth, let him say:

Strengthen my hand, O my God, that it may take hold of Thy Book with such steadfastness that the hosts of the world shall have no power over it. Guard it, then, from meddling with whatsoever doth not belong unto it. Thou art, verily, the Almighty, the Most Powerful.

And while washing his face, let him say:

I have turned my face unto Thee, O my Lord! Illumine it with the light of Thy countenance. Protect it, then, from turning to anyone but Thee.

Then let him stand up, and facing the Qiblih (Point of Adoration, i.e., Bahjí, 'Akká), let him say:

God testifieth that there is none other God but Him. His are the kingdoms of Revelation and of creation. He, in truth, hath manifested Him Who is the Dayspring of Revelation, Who conversed on Sinai, through Whom the Supreme Horizon hath been made to shine, and the Lote-Tree beyond which there is no passing hath spoken, and through Whom the call hath been proclaimed unto all who are in heaven and on earth: "Lo, the All-Possessing is come. Earth and heaven, glory and dominion are God's, the Lord of all men, and the Possessor of the Throne on high and of earth below!"

Let him, then, bend down, with hands resting on the knees, and say:

Exalted art Thou above my praise and the praise of anyone beside me, above my description and the description of all who are in heaven and all who are on earth!

Then, standing with open hands, palms upward toward the face, let him say:

Disappoint not, O my God, him that hath, with beseeching fingers, clung to the hem of Thy mercy and Thy grace, O Thou Who of those who show mercy art the Most Merciful!

Let him, then, be seated and say:

I bear witness to Thy unity and Thy oneness, and that Thou art God, and that there is none other God beside Thee. Thou hast, verily, revealed Thy Cause, fulfilled Thy Covenant, and opened wide the door of Thy grace to all that dwell in heaven and on earth. Blessing and peace, salutation and glory, rest upon Thy loved ones, whom the changes and chances of the world have not deterred from turning unto Thee, and who have given their all, in the hope of obtaining that which is with Thee. Thou art, in truth, the Ever-Forgiving, the All-Bountiful.

(If anyone choose to recite instead of the long verse these words: "God testifieth that there is none other God but Him, the Help in Peril, the Self-Subsisting," it would be sufficient. And likewise, it would suffice were he, while seated, to choose to recite these words: "I bear witness to Thy unity and Thy oneness, and that Thou art God, and that there is none other God beside Thee.")

Bahá'u'lláh

5. Long obligatory prayer, to be recited once in twenty-four hours

Whoso wisheth to recite this prayer, let him stand up and turn unto God, and, as he standeth in his place, let him gaze to the right and to the left, as if awaiting the mercy of his Lord, the Most Merciful, the Compassionate. Then let him say:

O Thou Who art the Lord of all names and the Maker of the heavens! I beseech Thee by them Who are the Daysprings of Thine invisible Essence, the Most Exalted, the All-Glorious, to make of my prayer a fire that will burn away the veils which have shut me out from Thy beauty, and a light that will lead me unto the ocean of Thy Presence.

Let him then raise his hands in supplication toward God—blessed and exalted be He—and say:

O Thou the Desire of the world and the Beloved of the nations! Thou seest me turning toward Thee, and rid of all attachment to anyone save Thee, and clinging to Thy cord, through whose movement the whole creation hath been stirred up. I am Thy servant, O my Lord, and the son of Thy servant. Behold me standing ready to do Thy will and Thy desire, and wishing naught else except Thy good pleasure. I implore Thee by the Ocean of Thy mercy and the Daystar of Thy grace to do with Thy servant as Thou willest and pleasest. By Thy might which is far above all mention and praise! Whatsoever is revealed by Thee is the desire of my heart and the beloved of my soul. O God, my God! Look not upon my hopes and my doings, nay rather look upon Thy will that hath encompassed the heavens and the earth. By Thy Most Great Name, O Thou Lord of all nations! I have desired only what Thou didst desire, and love only what Thou dost love.

Let him then kneel, and bowing his forehead to the ground, let him say:

Exalted art Thou above the description of anyone save Thyself, and the comprehension of aught else except Thee.

Let him then stand and say:

Make my prayer, O my Lord, a fountain of living waters whereby I may live as long as Thy sovereignty endureth, and may make mention of Thee in every world of Thy worlds.

Let him again raise his hands in supplication, and say:

O Thou in separation from Whom hearts and souls have melted, and by the fire of Whose love the whole world hath been set aflame! I implore Thee by Thy Name through which Thou hast subdued the whole creation, not to withhold from me that which is with Thee, O Thou Who rulest over all men! Thou seest, O my Lord, this stranger hastening to his most exalted home beneath the canopy of Thy majesty and within the precincts of Thy mercy; and this transgressor seeking the ocean of Thy forgiveness; and this lowly one the court of Thy glory; and this poor creature the orient of Thy wealth. Thine is the authority to command whatsoever Thou willest. I bear witness that Thou art to be praised in Thy doings, and to be obeyed in Thy behests, and to remain unconstrained in Thy bidding.

Let him then raise his hands, and repeat three times the Greatest Name.* Let him then bend down with hands resting on the knees before God—blessed and exalted be He—and say:

---

* Alláh-u-Abhá.

Thou seest, O my God, how my spirit hath been stirred up within my limbs and members, in its longing to worship Thee, and in its yearning to remember Thee and extol Thee; how it testifieth to that whereunto the Tongue of Thy Commandment hath testified in the kingdom of Thine utterance and the heaven of Thy knowledge. I love, in this state, O my Lord to beg of Thee all that is with Thee, that I may demonstrate my poverty, and magnify Thy bounty and Thy riches, and may declare my powerlessness, and manifest Thy power and Thy might.

Let him then stand and raise his hands twice in supplication, and say:

There is no God but Thee, the Almighty, the All-Bountiful. There is no God but Thee, the Ordainer, both in the beginning and in the end. O God, my God! Thy forgiveness hath emboldened me, and Thy mercy hath strengthened me, and Thy call hath awakened me, and Thy grace hath raised me up and led me unto Thee. Who, otherwise, am I that I should dare to stand at the gate of the city of Thy nearness, or set my face toward the lights that are shining from the heaven of Thy will? Thou seest, O my Lord, this wretched creature knocking at the door of Thy grace, and this evanescent soul seeking the river of everlasting life from the hands of Thy bounty. Thine is the command at all times, O Thou Who art the Lord of all names; and mine is resignation and willing submission to Thy will, O Creator of the heavens!

Let him then raise his hands thrice, and say:

Greater is God than every great one!

Let him then kneel and, bowing his forehead to the ground, say:

Too high art Thou for the praise of those who are nigh unto Thee to ascend unto the heaven of Thy nearness, or for the birds of the hearts of them who are devoted to Thee to attain to the door of Thy gate. I testify that Thou hast been sanctified above all attributes and holy above all names. No God is there but Thee, the Most Exalted, the All-Glorious.

Let him then seat himself and say:

I testify unto that whereunto have testified all created things, and the Concourse on high, and the inmates of the all-highest Paradise, and beyond them the Tongue of Grandeur itself from the all-glorious Horizon, that Thou art God, that there is no God but Thee, and that He Who hath been manifested is the Hidden Mystery, the Treasured Symbol, through Whom the letters B and E (Be) have been joined and knit together. I testify that it is He Whose name hath been set down by the Pen of the Most High, and Who hath been mentioned in the Books of God, the Lord of the Throne on high and of earth below.

Let him then stand erect and say:

O Lord of all being and Possessor of all things visible and invisible! Thou dost perceive my tears and the sighs I utter, and hearest my groaning, and my wailing, and the lamentation of my heart. By Thy might! My trespasses have kept me back from drawing nigh unto Thee; and my sins have held me far from the court of Thy holiness. Thy love, O my Lord, hath enriched me, and separation from Thee hath destroyed me, and remoteness from Thee hath consumed me. I entreat Thee by Thy footsteps in this wilderness, and by the words "Here am I. Here am I" which Thy chosen Ones have uttered in this immensity, and by the breaths of Thy Revelation, and the gentle winds of the Dawn of Thy Manifestation, to ordain that I may gaze on Thy beauty and observe whatsoever is in Thy Book.

Let him then repeat the Greatest Name thrice, and bend down with hands resting on the knees, and say:

Praise be to Thee, O my God, that Thou hast aided me to remember Thee and to praise Thee, and hast made known unto me Him Who is the Dayspring of Thy signs, and hast caused me to bow down before Thy lordship, and humble myself before Thy Godhead, and to acknowledge that which hath been uttered by the Tongue of Thy grandeur.

Let him then rise and say:

O God, my God! My back is bowed by the burden of my sins, and my heedlessness hath destroyed me. Whenever I ponder my evil doings and Thy benevolence, my heart melteth within me, and my blood boileth in my veins. By Thy Beauty, O Thou the Desire of the world! I blush to lift up my face to Thee, and my longing hands are ashamed to stretch forth toward the heaven of Thy bounty. Thou seest, O my God, how my tears prevent me from remembering Thee and from extolling Thy virtues, O Thou the Lord of the Throne on high and of earth below! I implore Thee by the signs of Thy Kingdom and the mysteries of Thy Dominion to do with Thy loved ones as becometh Thy bounty, O Lord of all being, and is worthy of Thy grace, O King of the seen and the unseen!

Let him then repeat the Greatest Name thrice, and kneel with his forehead to the ground, and say:

Praise be unto Thee, O our God, that Thou hast sent down unto us that which draweth us nigh unto Thee, and supplieth us with every good thing sent down by Thee in Thy Books and Thy Scriptures. Protect us, we beseech Thee, O my Lord, from the hosts of idle fancies and vain imaginations. Thou, in truth, art the Mighty, the All-Knowing.

Let him then raise his head, and seat himself, and say:

I testify, O my God, to that whereunto Thy chosen Ones have testified, and acknowledge that which the inmates of the all-highest Paradise and those who have circled round Thy mighty Throne have acknowledged. The kingdoms of earth and heaven are Thine, O Lord of the worlds!

Bahá'u'lláh

Detachment

6. O Lord! Unto Thee I repair for refuge, and toward all Thy signs I set my heart.

O Lord! Whether traveling or at home, and in my occupation or in my work, I place my whole trust in Thee.

Grant me then Thy sufficing help so as to make me independent of all things, O Thou Who art unsurpassed in Thy mercy!

Bestow upon me my portion, O Lord, as Thou pleasest, and cause me to be satisfied with whatsoever Thou hast ordained for me.

Thine is the absolute authority to command.

The Báb

Firmness in the Covenant

7. O my Lord and my Hope! Help Thou Thy loved ones to be steadfast in Thy mighty Covenant, to remain faithful to Thy manifest Cause, and to carry out the commandments Thou didst set down for them in Thy Book of Splendors; that they may become banners of guidance and lamps of the Company above, wellsprings of Thine infinite wisdom, and stars that lead aright, as they shine down from the supernal sky.

Verily, art Thou the Invincible, the Almighty, the All-Powerful.

'Abdu'l-Bahá

Marriage

8. Glory be unto Thee, O my God! Verily, this Thy servant and this Thy maidservant have gathered under the shadow of Thy mercy and they are united through Thy favor and generosity. O Lord! Assist them in this Thy world and Thy kingdom and destine for them every good through Thy bounty and grace. O Lord! Confirm them in Thy servitude and assist them in Thy service. Suffer them to become the signs of Thy Name in Thy world and protect them through Thy bestowals which are inexhaustible in this world and the world to come. O Lord! They are supplicating the kingdom of Thy mercifulness and invoking the realm of Thy singleness. Verily, they are married in obedience to Thy command. Cause them to become the signs of harmony and unity until the end of time. Verily, Thou art the Omnipotent, the Omnipresent and the Almighty!

'Abdu'l-Bahá

9. O my Lord, O my Lord! These two bright orbs are wedded in Thy love, conjoined in servitude to Thy Holy Threshold,

united in ministering to Thy Cause. Make Thou this marriage to be as threading lights of Thine abounding grace, O my Lord, the All-Merciful, and luminous rays of Thy bestowals, O Thou the Beneficent, the Ever-Giving, that there may branch out from this great tree boughs that will grow green and flourishing through the gifts that rain down from Thy clouds of grace.

Verily, Thou art the Generous. Verily, Thou art the Almighty. Verily, Thou art the Compassionate, the All-Merciful.

'Abdu'l-Bahá

Parents

10. O God, my God! I implore Thee by the blood of Thy true lovers who were so enraptured by Thy sweet utterance that they hastened unto the Pinnacle of Glory, the site of the most glorious martyrdom, and I beseech Thee by the mysteries which lie enshrined in Thy knowledge and by the pearls that are treasured in the ocean of Thy bounty to grant forgiveness unto me and unto my father and my mother. Of those who show forth mercy, Thou art in truth the Most Merciful. No God is there but Thee, the Ever-Forgiving, the All-Bountiful.

Bahá'u'lláh

11. O Lord! In this Most Great Dispensation Thou dost accept the intercession of children in behalf of their parents. This is one of the special infinite bestowals of this Dispensation. Therefore, O Thou kind Lord, accept the request of this Thy servant at the threshold of Thy singleness and submerge his father in the ocean of Thy grace, because this son hath arisen to render Thee service and is exerting effort at all times in the pathway of Thy love. Verily, Thou art the Giver, the Forgiver and the Kind!

'Abdu'l-Bahá

Protection and Assistance

12. O God, my God! I have set out from my home, holding fast unto the cord of Thy love, and I have committed myself wholly to Thy care and Thy protection. I entreat Thee by Thy power through which Thou didst protect Thy loved ones from the wayward and the perverse, and from every contumacious oppressor, and every wicked doer who hath strayed far from Thee, to keep me safe by Thy bounty and Thy grace. Enable me, then, to return to my home by Thy power and Thy might. Thou art, truly, the Almighty, the Help in Peril, the Self-Subsisting.

Bahá'u'lláh

13. I adjure Thee by Thy might, O my God! Let no harm beset me in times of tests, and in moments of heedlessness guide my steps aright through Thine inspiration. Thou art God, potent art Thou to do what Thou desirest. No one can withstand Thy Will or thwart Thy Purpose.

The Báb

Spiritual Awakening

14. I have wakened in Thy shelter, O my God, and it becometh him that seeketh that shelter to abide within the Sanctuary of Thy protection and the Stronghold of Thy defense. Illumine my inner being, O my Lord, with the splendors of the Dayspring of Thy Revelation, even as Thou didst illumine my outer being with the morning light of Thy favor.

Bahá'u'lláh

15. My God, my Adored One, my King, my Desire! What tongue can voice my thanks to Thee? I was heedless, Thou didst awaken me. I had turned back from Thee, Thou didst graciously aid me to turn towards Thee. I was as one dead, Thou didst quicken me with the water of life. I was withered, Thou didst revive me with the heavenly stream of Thine utterance which hath flowed forth from the Pen of the All-Merciful.

O Divine Providence! All existence is begotten by Thy bounty; deprive it not of the waters of Thy generosity, neither do Thou withhold it from the ocean of Thy mercy. I beseech Thee to aid and assist me at all times and under all conditions, and seek from the heaven of Thy grace Thine ancient favor. Thou art, in truth, the Lord of bounty, and the Sovereign of the kingdom of eternity.

Bahá'u'lláh

Spiritual Qualities

16. Create in me a pure heart, O my God, and renew a tranquil conscience within me, O my Hope! Through the spirit of power confirm Thou me in Thy Cause, O my Best-Beloved, and by the light of Thy glory reveal unto me Thy path, O Thou the Goal of my desire! Through the power of Thy transcendent might lift me up unto the heaven of Thy holiness, O Source of my being, and by the breezes of Thine eternity gladden me, O Thou Who art my God! Let Thine everlasting melodies breathe tranquillity on me, O my Companion, and let the riches of Thine ancient countenance deliver me from all except Thee, O my Master, and let the tidings of the revelation of Thine incorruptible Essence bring

me joy, O Thou Who art the most manifest of the manifest
and the most hidden of the hidden!

Bahá'u'lláh

17. O Thou Lord of wondrous grace! Bestow upon us new
blessings. Give to us the freshness of the spring. We are saplings
which have been planted by the fingers of Thy bounty and
have been formed out of the water and clay of Thy tender affection. We thirst for the living waters of Thy favors and are dependent upon the outpourings of the clouds of Thy generosity. Abandon not to itself this grove wherein our hopes aspire,
nor withhold therefrom the showers of Thy loving-kindness.
Grant that from the clouds of Thy mercy may fall copious rain
so that the trees of our lives may bring forth fruit and we may
attain the most cherished desire of our hearts.

'Abdu'l-Bahá

Teaching and Service

18. Glorified be Thou, O my God! Behold Thou my head
ready to fall before the sword of Thy Will, my neck prepared to
bear the chains of Thy Desire, my heart yearning to be made a
target for the darts of Thy Decree, mine eyes expectant to gaze
on the tokens and signs of Thy wondrous Mercy. For whatsoever may befall me from Thee is the cherished desire of them
who thirst to meet Thee, and the supreme aspiration of such as
have drawn nigh unto Thy court.

By the glory of Thy might, O Thou my Well-Beloved! To
have sacrificed my life for the Manifestations of Thy Self, to have
offered up my soul in the path of the Revealers of Thy wondrous
Beauty, is to have sacrificed my spirit for Thy Spirit, my being for
Thy Being, my glory for Thy glory. It is as if I had offered up all
these things for Thy sake, and for the sake of Thy loved ones.

Though my body be pained by the trials that befall me from Thee, though it be afflicted by the revelations of Thy Decree, yet my soul rejoiceth at having partaken of the waters of Thy Beauty, and at having attained the shores of the ocean of Thine eternity. Doth it beseem a lover to flee from his beloved, or to desert the object of his heart's desire? Nay, we all believe in Thee, and eagerly hope to enter Thy presence.

Bahá'u'lláh

19. Praise be to Thee, O Lord my God! I implore Thee, by Thy Name which none hath befittingly recognized, and whose import no soul hath fathomed; I beseech Thee, by Him Who is the Fountainhead of Thy Revelation and the Dayspring of Thy signs, to make my heart to be a receptacle of Thy love and of remembrance of Thee. Knit it, then, to Thy most great Ocean, that from it may flow out the living waters of Thy wisdom and the crystal streams of Thy glorification and praise.

The limbs of my body testify to Thy unity, and the hair of my head declareth the power of Thy sovereignty and might. I have stood at the door of Thy grace with utter self-effacement and complete abnegation, and clung to the hem of Thy bounty, and fixed mine eyes upon the horizon of Thy gifts.

Do Thou destine for me, O my God, what becometh the greatness of Thy majesty, and assist me, by Thy strengthening grace, so to teach Thy Cause that the dead may speed out of their sepulchers, and rush forth towards Thee, trusting wholly in Thee, and fixing their gaze upon the orient of Thy Cause, and the dawning-place of Thy Revelation.

Thou, verily, art the Most Powerful, the Most High, the All-Knowing, the All-Wise.

Bahá'u'lláh

20. O my God, aid Thou Thy servant to raise up the Word, and to refute what is vain and false, to establish the truth, to spread the sacred verses abroad, reveal the splendors, and make the morning's light to dawn in the hearts of the righteous.

Thou art, verily, the Generous, the Forgiving.

'Abdu'l-Bahá

21. O God, my God! Aid Thou Thy trusted servants to have loving and tender hearts. Help them to spread, amongst all the nations of the earth, the light of guidance that cometh from the Company on high. Verily, Thou art the Strong, the Powerful, the Mighty, the All-Subduing, the Ever-Giving. Verily, Thou art the Generous, the Gentle, the Tender, the Most Bountiful.

'Abdu'l-Bahá

22. O Thou kind Lord! Grant that these trees may become the adornment of the Abhá Paradise. Cause them to grow through Thy celestial bounty. Make them fresh and verdant, and besprinkle them with heavenly dewdrops. Attire them with robes of radiant beauty, and crown their heads with gorgeous blossoms. Adorn them with goodly fruit, and waft over them Thy sweet savors.

Thou art the Bestower, the All-Loving, the Most Radiant, the Most Resplendent.

'Abdu'l-Bahá

Unity

23. O my God! O my God! Unite the hearts of Thy servants, and reveal to them Thy great purpose. May they follow Thy commandments and abide in Thy law. Help them, O God, in their endeavor, and grant them strength to serve Thee. O God! Leave them not to themselves, but guide their steps by the light

of Thy knowledge, and cheer their hearts by Thy love. Verily, Thou art their Helper and their Lord.

Bahá'u'lláh

24. O my God! O my God! Verily, I invoke Thee and supplicate before Thy threshold, asking Thee that all Thy mercies may descend upon these souls. Specialize them for Thy favor and Thy truth.

O Lord! Unite and bind together the hearts, join in accord all the souls, and exhilarate the spirits through the signs of Thy sanctity and oneness. O Lord! Make these faces radiant through the light of Thy oneness. Strengthen the loins of Thy servants in the service of Thy kingdom.

O Lord, Thou possessor of infinite mercy! O Lord of forgiveness and pardon! Forgive our sins, pardon our shortcomings, and cause us to turn to the kingdom of Thy clemency, invoking the kingdom of might and power, humble at Thy shrine and submissive before the glory of Thine evidences.

O Lord God! Make us as waves of the sea, as flowers of the garden, united, agreed through the bounties of Thy love. O Lord! Dilate the breasts through the signs of Thy oneness, and make all mankind as stars shining from the same height of glory, as perfect fruits growing upon Thy tree of life.

Verily, Thou art the Almighty, the Self-Subsistent, the Giver, the Forgiving, the Pardoner, the Omniscient, the One Creator.

'Abdu'l-Bahá

Women

25. O God! The trials Thou sendest are a salve to the sores of all them who are devoted to Thy will; the remembrance of Thee is a healing medicine to the hearts of such as have drawn nigh unto Thy court; nearness to Thee is the true life of them

who are Thy lovers; Thy presence is the ardent desire of such as yearn to behold Thy face; remoteness from Thee is a torment to those that have acknowledged Thy oneness, and separation from Thee is death unto them that have recognized Thy truth!

I beseech Thee by the sighs which they whose souls pant after Thee have uttered in their remoteness from Thy court, and by the cries of such of Thy lovers as bemoan their separation from Thee, to nourish me with the wine of Thy knowledge and the living waters of Thy love and pleasure. Behold Thy handmaiden, O my Lord, who hath forgotten all else except Thee, and who hath delighted herself with Thy love, and lamented over the things that have befallen Thee at the hands of the wicked doers among Thy creatures. Do Thou ordain for her that which Thou didst ordain for such of Thy handmaidens as circle round the throne of Thy majesty, and gaze, at eventide and at dawn, on Thy beauty.

Thou art, verily, the Lord of the Judgment Day.

Bahá'u'lláh

26. O God, although I am sitting concealed behind the screen of chastity and am restricted by the veil and exigencies of modesty, my cherished hope is to raise the banner of service and to become a maidservant at Thy Holy Threshold; to ride on a charger and penetrate the army of the ignorant, defeat the mighty regiments and subvert the foundations of error and violation. Thou art the Helper of the weak, Thou art the Sustainer of the poor, Thou art the Succourer of the handmaidens. Verily, Thou art the Almighty and All-Powerful.

'Abdu'l-Bahá

27. O Thou kind Lord! Bestow heavenly confirmation upon this daughter of the Kingdom and graciously aid her that she

may remain firm and steadfast in Thy Cause and that she may, even as a nightingale of the rose garden of mysteries, warble melodies in the Abhá Kingdom in most wondrous tones, thereby bringing happiness to everyone. Make her exalted among the daughters of the kingdom and enable her to attain life eternal.

Thou art the Bestower, the All-Loving.

'Abdu'l-Bahá

28. O Lord! Help this daughter of the Kingdom to be exalted in both worlds; cause her to turn away from this mortal world of dust and from those who have set their hearts thereon and enable her to have communion and close association with the world of immortality. Give her heavenly power and strengthen her through the breaths of the Holy Spirit that she may arise to serve thee.

Thou are the Mighty One.

'Abdu'l-Bahá

Youth

29. Glorified art Thou, O Lord my God! I give Thee thanks inasmuch as Thou hast called me into being in Thy days, and infused into me Thy love and Thy knowledge. I beseech Thee, by Thy name whereby the goodly pearls of Thy wisdom and Thine utterance were brought forth out of the treasuries of the hearts of such of Thy servants as are nigh unto Thee, and through which the Day-Star of Thy name, the Compassionate, hath shed its radiance upon all that are in Thy heaven and on Thy earth, to supply me, by Thy grace and bounty, with Thy wondrous and hidden bounties.

These are the earliest days of my life, O my God, which Thou hast linked with Thine own days. Now that Thou hast conferred upon me so great an honor, withhold not from me the things Thou hast ordained for Thy chosen ones.

I am, O my God, but a tiny seed which Thou hast sown in the soil of Thy love, and caused to spring forth by the hand of Thy bounty. This seed craveth, therefore, in its inmost being, for the waters of Thy mercy and the living fountain of Thy grace. Send down upon it, from the heaven of Thy loving-kindness, that which will enable it to flourish beneath Thy shadow and within the borders of Thy court. Thou art He Who watereth the hearts of all that have recognized Thee from Thy plenteous stream and the fountain of Thy living waters.

Praised be God, the Lord of the worlds.

Bahá'u'lláh

30. O Lord! Make this youth radiant, and confer Thy bounty upon this poor creature. Bestow upon him knowledge, grant him added strength at the break of every morn and guard him within the shelter of Thy protection so that he may be freed from error, may devote himself to the service of Thy Cause, may guide the wayward, lead the hapless, free the captives and awaken the heedless, that all may be blessed with Thy remembrance and praise. Thou art the Mighty and the Powerful.

'Abdu'l-Bahá

31. Praise and glory be to Thee, O Lord my God! This is a choice sapling which Thou hast planted in the meads of Thy love and hast nurtured with the fingers of Thy Lordship. Thou hast watered it from the wellspring of everlasting life which streameth forth from the gardens of Thy oneness and Thou hast caused the clouds of Thy tender mercy to shower Thy favors upon it. It hath now grown and developed beneath the

shelter of Thy blessings which are manifest from the Dayspring of Thy divine essence. It hath burst forth into leaves and blossoms, is laden with fruit through the providence of Thy wondrous gifts and bounties and is stirred by the fragrant breeze wafting from the direction of Thy loving-kindness.

O Lord! Cause this sapling to become verdant, fresh and flourishing by the outpourings of Thy special bounty and favor, wherewith Thou hast endued the tabernacles of holiness in Thy eternal kingdom and hast adorned the essences of unity in the arena of reunion.

O Lord! Assist him through Thy strengthening grace which proceedeth from Thine invisible kingdom, aid him with such hosts as are hidden from the eyes of Thy servants and grant that he may have a sure footing in Thy presence. Unloose his tongue to make mention of Thee and gladden his heart to celebrate Thy praise. Illumine his face in Thy kingdom, prosper him in the realm above and graciously confirm him to serve Thy Cause.

Thou art the All-Powerful, the All-Glorious, the Omnipotent.

'Abdu'l-Bahá

Special Tablets

32. These daily obligatory prayers, together with a few other specific ones, . . . have been invested by Bahá'u'lláh with a special potency and significance, and should therefore be accepted as such and be recited by the believers with unquestioning faith and confidence, that through them they may enter into a much closer communion with God, and identify themselves more fully with His laws and precepts.

On behalf of Shoghi Effendi

TABLET OF AḤMAD

33. He is the King, the All-Knowing, the Wise!

Lo, the Nightingale of Paradise singeth upon the twigs of the Tree of Eternity, with holy and sweet melodies, proclaiming to the sincere ones the glad tidings of the nearness of God, calling the believers in the Divine Unity to the court of the Presence of the Generous One, informing the severed ones of the message which hath been revealed by God, the King, the Glorious, the Peerless, guiding the lovers to the seat of sanctity and to this resplendent Beauty.

Verily this is that Most Great Beauty, foretold in the Books of the Messengers, through Whom truth shall be distinguished from error and the wisdom of every command shall be tested. Verily He is the Tree of Life that bringeth forth the fruits of God, the Exalted, the Powerful, the Great.

O Aḥmad! Bear thou witness that verily He is God and there is no God but Him, the King, the Protector, the Incomparable, the Omnipotent. And that the One Whom He hath sent forth by the name of 'Alí* was the true One from God, to Whose commands we are all conforming.

Say: O people be obedient to the ordinances of God, which have been enjoined in the Bayán by the Glorious, the Wise One. Verily He is the King of the Messengers and His Book is the Mother Book did ye but know.

Thus doth the Nightingale utter His call unto you from this prison. He hath but to deliver this clear message. Whosoever desireth, let him turn aside from this counsel and whosoever desireth let him choose the path to his Lord.

---

* The Báb.

O people, if ye deny these verses, by what proof have ye believed in God? Produce it, O assemblage of false ones.

Nay, by the One in Whose hand is my soul, they are not, and never shall be able to do this, even should they combine to assist one another.

O Aḥmad! Forget not My bounties while I am absent. Remember My days during thy days, and My distress and banishment in this remote prison. And be thou so steadfast in My love that thy heart shall not waver, even if the swords of the enemies rain blows upon thee and all the heavens and the earth arise against thee.

Be thou as a flame of fire to My enemies and a river of life eternal to My loved ones, and be not of those who doubt.

And if thou art overtaken by affliction in My path, or degradation for My sake, be not thou troubled thereby.

Rely upon God, thy God and the Lord of thy fathers. For the people are wandering in the paths of delusion, bereft of discernment to see God with their own eyes, or hear His Melody with their own ears. Thus have We found them, as thou also dost witness.

Thus have their superstitions become veils between them and their own hearts and kept them from the path of God, the Exalted, the Great.

Be thou assured in thyself that verily, he who turns away from this Beauty hath also turned away from the Messengers of the past and showeth pride towards God from all eternity to all eternity.

Learn well this Tablet, O Aḥmad. Chant it during thy days and withhold not thyself therefrom. For verily, God hath ordained for the one who chants it, the reward of a hundred martyrs and a service in both worlds. These favors have We bestowed upon thee as a bounty on Our part and a mercy from Our presence, that thou mayest be of those who are grateful.

By God! Should one who is in affliction or grief read this Tablet with absolute sincerity, God will dispel his sadness, solve his difficulties and remove his afflictions.

Verily, He is the Merciful, the Compassionate. Praise be to God, the Lord of all the worlds.

Bahá'u'lláh

FIRE TABLET

34. In the Name of God, the Most Ancient, the Most Great.

Indeed the hearts of the sincere are consumed in the fire of separation: Where is the gleaming of the light of Thy Countenance, O Beloved of the worlds?

Those who are near unto Thee have been abandoned in the darkness of desolation: Where is the shining of the morn of Thy reunion, O Desire of the worlds?

The bodies of Thy chosen ones lie quivering on distant sands: Where is the ocean of Thy presence, O Enchanter of the worlds?

Longing hands are uplifted to the heaven of Thy grace and generosity: Where are the rains of Thy bestowal, O Answerer of the worlds?

The infidels have arisen in tyranny on every hand: Where is the compelling power of Thine ordaining pen, O Conqueror of the worlds?

The barking of dogs is loud on every side: Where is the lion of the forest of Thy might, O Chastiser of the worlds?

Coldness hath gripped all mankind: Where is the warmth of Thy love, O Fire of the worlds?

Calamity hath reached its height: Where are the signs of Thy succor, O Salvation of the worlds?

Darkness hath enveloped most of the peoples: Where is the brightness of Thy splendor, O Radiance of the worlds?

The necks of men are stretched out in malice: Where are the swords of Thy vengeance, O Destroyer of the worlds?

Abasement hath reached its lowest depth: Where are the emblems of Thy glory, O Glory of the worlds?

Sorrows have afflicted the Revealer of Thy Name, the All-Merciful: Where is the joy of the Dayspring of Thy Revelation, O Delight of the worlds?

Anguish hath befallen all the peoples of the earth: Where are the ensigns of thy gladness, O Joy of the worlds?

Thou seest the Dawning Place of Thy signs veiled by evil suggestions: Where are the fingers of Thy might, O Power of the worlds?

Sore thirst hath overcome all men: Where is the river of Thy bounty, O Mercy of the worlds?

Greed hath made captive all mankind: Where are the embodiments of detachment, O Lord of the worlds?

Thou seest this Wronged One lonely in exile: Where are the hosts of the heaven of Thy Command, O Sovereign of the worlds?

I have been forsaken in a foreign land: Where are the emblems of Thy faithfulness, O Trust of the worlds?

The agonies of death have laid hold on all men: Where is the surging of Thine ocean of eternal life, O Life of the worlds?

The whisperings of Satan have been breathed to every creature: Where is the meteor of Thy fire, O Light of the worlds?

The drunkenness of passion hath perverted most of mankind: Where are the daysprings of purity, O Desire of the worlds?

Thou seest this Wronged One veiled in tyranny among the Syrians: Where is the radiance of Thy dawning light, O Light of the worlds?

Thou seest Me forbidden to speak forth: Then from where will spring Thy melodies, O Nightingale of the worlds?

Most of the people are enwrapped in fancy and idle imaginings: Where are the exponents of Thy certitude, O Assurance of the worlds?

Bahá is drowning in a sea of tribulation: Where is the Ark of Thy salvation, O Savior of the worlds?

Thou seest the Dayspring of Thine utterance in the darkness of creation: Where is the sun of the heaven of Thy grace, O Light-Giver of the worlds?

The lamps of truth and purity, of loyalty and honor, have been put out: Where are the signs of Thine avenging wrath, O Mover of the worlds?

Canst Thou see any who have championed Thy Self, or who ponder on what hath befallen Him in the pathway of Thy love? Now doth My pen halt, O Beloved of the worlds.

The branches of the Divine Lote-Tree lie broken by the onrushing gales of destiny: Where are the banners of Thy succor, O Champion of the worlds?

This Face is hidden in the dust of slander: Where are the breezes of Thy compassion, O Mercy of the worlds?

The robe of sanctity is sullied by the people of deceit: Where is the vesture of Thy holiness, O Adorner of the worlds?

The sea of grace is stilled for what the hands of men have wrought: Where are the waves of Thy bounty, O Desire of the worlds?

The door leading to the Divine Presence is locked through the tyranny of Thy foes: Where is the key of Thy bestowal, O Unlocker of the worlds?

The leaves are yellowed by the poisoning winds of sedition: Where is the downpour of the clouds of Thy bounty, O Giver of the worlds?

The universe is darkened with the dust of sin: Where are the breezes of Thy forgiveness, O Forgiver of the worlds?

This Youth is lonely in a desolate land: Where is the rain of Thy heavenly grace, O Bestower of the worlds?

O Supreme Pen, We have heard Thy most sweet call in the eternal realm: Give Thou ear unto what the Tongue of Grandeur uttereth, O Wronged One of the worlds!

Were it not for the cold, how would the heat of Thy words prevail, O Expounder of the worlds?

Were it not for calamity, how would the sun of Thy patience shine, O Light of the worlds?

Lament not because of the wicked. Thou wert created to bear and endure, O Patience of the worlds.

How sweet was Thy dawning on the horizon of the Covenant among the stirrers of sedition, and Thy yearning after God, O Love of the worlds.

By Thee the banner of independence was planted on the highest peaks, and the sea of bounty surged, O Rapture of the worlds.

By Thine aloneness the Sun of Oneness shone, and by Thy banishment the land of Unity was adorned. Be patient, O Thou Exile of the worlds.

We have made abasement the garment of glory, and affliction the adornment of Thy temple, O Pride of the worlds.

Thou seest the hearts are filled with hate, and to overlook is Thine, O Thou Concealer of the sins of the worlds.

When the swords flash, go forward! When the shafts fly, press onward! O Thou Sacrifice of the worlds.

Dost Thou wail, or shall I wail? Rather shall I weep at the fewness of Thy champions, O Thou Who hast caused the wailing of the worlds.

Verily, I have heard Thy Call, O All-Glorious Beloved; and now is the face of Bahá flaming with the heat of tribulation and with the fire of Thy shining word, and He hath risen up in faithfulness at the place of sacrifice, looking toward Thy pleasure, O Ordainer of the worlds.

O 'Alí-Akbar, thank thy Lord for this Tablet whence thou canst breathe the fragrance of My meekness, and know what hath beset Us in the path of God, the Adored of all the worlds.

Should all the servants read and ponder this, there shall be kindled in their veins a fire that shall set aflame the worlds.

Bahá'u'lláh

Notes

1 / Relationship with God and Bahá'u'lláh

1. Bahá'u'lláh, Kitáb-i-Aqdas, ¶1–2.
2. Bahá'u'lláh, *Prayers and Meditations,* p. 275.
3. The Báb, *Selections from the Writings of the Báb,* 3.12.2.
4. 'Abdu'l-Bahá, *Tablets of the Divine Plan,* no. 8.8.
5. Bahá'u'lláh, *Gleanings,* no. 34.1.
6. Bahá'u'lláh, Hidden Words, Arabic, no. 3.
7. Bahá'u'lláh, *Gleanings,* no. 27.2.
8. Bahá'u'lláh, Hidden Words, Arabic, no. 4.
9. Ibid., no. 38.
10. The Báb, *Selections from the Writings of the Báb,* 3.15.2–3.
11. 'Abdu'l-Bahá, *The Secret of Divine Civilization,* p. 71.
12. Shoghi Effendi, *God Passes By,* pp. 93–94.
13. Ibid., p. 194.
14. Bahá'u'lláh, Kitáb-i-Íqán, ¶208.
15. Baha'u'llah, *Epistle to the Son of the Wolf,* pp. 76–77.
16. 'Abdu'l-Bahá, quoted in J. E. Esslemont, *Bahá'u'lláh and the New Era,* p. 24.
17. Shoghi Effendi, *God Passes By,* p. 94.
18. Nabíl-i-A'ẓam, *The Dawn-Breakers,* pp. 119–20.
19. Bahá'u'lláh, *Epistle to the Son of the Wolf,* p. 52.
20. Bahá'u'lláh, *Gleanings,* no. 45.1.
21. Bahá'u'lláh, *Prayers and Meditations,* pp. 20–21.
22. Ibid., pp. 111–12.
23. Shoghi Effendi, *World Order of Bahá'u'lláh,* p. 100.
24. Shoghi Effendi, *God Passes By,* pp. 100–101.

25. Bahá'u'lláh, *Gleanings,* no. 136.2.

26. 'Abdu'l-Bahá, in *Bahá'í World Faith,* p. 368.

27. 'Abdu'l-Bahá, in "Prayer, Meditation, and the Devotional Attitude," *The Compilation of Compilations,* 2:1745.

28. Shoghi Effendi, in ibid., 2:1762.

29. On behalf of Shoghi Effendi, in Helen Hornby, ed., *Lights of Guidance,* no. 247.

30. Bahá'u'lláh, Kitáb-i-Íqán, ¶214.

31. Bahá'u'lláh, "Questions and Answers," in *Kitáb-i-Aqdas,* p. 111.

32. 'Abdu'l-Bahá, *Tablets of Abdul-Baha Abbas,* p. 186.

33. 'Abdu'l-Bahá, *Selections from the Writings of 'Abdu'l-Bahá,* no. 172.1.

34. The Universal House of Justice, *Messages from The Universal House of Justice 1963–1986,* no. 110.9.

35. On behalf of Shoghi Effendi, in *Bahá'í Prayers,* p. 3.

36. On behalf of Shoghi Effendi, in Helen Hornby, ed., *Lights of Guidance,* no. 1523.

37. Ibid., no. 2160.

38. On behalf of Shoghi Effendi, in "Prayer, Meditation, and the Devotional Attitude," *The Compilation of Compilations,* 2:1769.

39. The Universal House of Justice, in *Principles of Bahá'í Administration,* p. 8.

40. "A Synopsis and Codification of the Kitáb-i-Aqdas," in *Kitáb-i-Aqdas,* p. 144.

41. 'Abdu'l-Bahá, in "Prayer, Meditation, and the Devotional Attitude," *The Compilation of Compilations,* 2:1746.

42. On behalf of Shoghi Effendi, in Helen Hornby, ed., *Lights of Guidance,* no. 1489.

43. On behalf of Shoghi Effendi, in "Prayer, Meditation, and the Devotional Attitude," *The Compilation of Compilations,* 2:1776.

44. On behalf of the Universal House of Justice, in Helen Hornby, ed., *Lights of Guidance,* no. 1487.

45. 'Abdu'l-Bahá, in *Spiritual Foundations,* p. 9.

46. The Universal House of Justice, *Messages from the Universal House of Justice 1963–1986,* no. 110.9.

47. 'Abdu'l-Bahá, *Selections from the Writings of 'Abdu'l-Bahá,* no. 35.2.

48. Shoghi Effendi, letter to Amelia E. Collins, in *Bahá'í News* 167 (January 1944): 2.

49. On behalf of Shoghi Effendi, in *Principles of Bahá'í Administration*, p. 9.

50. Bahá'u'lláh, *Kitáb-i-Aqdas*, p. 179, note 32.

51. Bahá'u'lláh, *Gleanings*, no. 114.4.

52. 'Abdu'l-Bahá, *Tablets of Abdul-Baha Abbas*, p. 552.

53. 'Abdu'l-Bahá, *Selections from the Writings of 'Abdu'l-Bahá*, no. 174.2–3.

54. On behalf of Shoghi Effendi, in "Bahá'í Funds and Contributions," *The Compilation of Compilations*, 2:1295.

55. On behalf of Shoghi Effendi, in Helen Hornby, ed., *Lights of Guidance*, no. 386.

2 / The Distinctive Bahá'í Life

1. The Báb, in Nabíl-i-A'zam, *The Dawn-Breakers*, pp. 92–94.

2. 'Abdu'l-Bahá, in *O God, My God . . .* , no. 36.

3. 'Abdu'l-Bahá, *The Promulgation of Universal Peace*, p. 190.

4. On behalf of Shoghi Effendi, in *The Bahá'í World*, 12:562.

5. On behalf of Shoghi Effendi, in Helen Hornby, ed., *Lights of Guidance*, no. 2157.

6. The Universal House of Justice, in Helen Hornby, ed., *Lights of Guidance*, no. 2138.

7. Bahá'u'lláh, *Tablets of Bahá'u'lláh*, p. 36.

8. 'Abdu'l-Bahá, in Shoghi Effendi, *The Advent of Divine Justice*, ¶40.

9. On behalf of Shoghi Effendi, "Living the Life," *The Compilation of Compilations*, 2:1300.

10. On behalf of Shoghi Effendi, in Helen Hornby, ed., *Lights of Guidance*, no. 2263.

11. 'Abdu'l-Bahá, in "Youth," *The Compilation of Compilations*, 2:2234.

12. Shoghi Effendi, in ibid., 2:2255.

13. On behalf of Shoghi Effendi, in "Youth," *The Compilation of Compilations*, 2:2272.

14. Ibid., 2:2251.

15. Ibid., 2:2247.

16. Ibid., 2:2294.

17. Ibid., 2:2269.

18. On behalf of Shoghi Effendi, in "Deepening," *The Compilation of Compilations,* 1:492.

19. The Universal House of Justice, *Messages from the Universal House of Justice,* no. 37.2.

20. Bahá'u'lláh, *Gleanings,* no. 43.3.

21. 'Abdu'l-Bahá, *Paris Talks,* no. 28.19.

22. On behalf of Shoghi Effendi, in "Excellence in All Things," *The Compilation of Compilations,* 1:808.

23. Bahá'u'lláh, *Gleanings,* no. 130.1.

24. 'Abdu'l-Bahá, *Selections from the Writings of 'Abdu'l-Bahá,* no. 8.7–8.

25. Ibid., no. 16.5.

26. Shoghi Effendi, in "Living the Life," *The Compilation of Compilations,* 2:1267.

3 / Youth on the Forefront

1. The Universal House of Justice, *Messages from the Universal House of Justice,* no. 37.1.

2. Ibid., no. 365.1.

3. H. M. Balyuzi, *'Abdu'l-Bahá,* pp. 9–12.

4. Bahíyyih Khánum, in *Bahíyyih Khánum,* pp. 142–43.

5. Shoghi Effendi, in ibid., 32–35.

6. Lady Blomfield, *The Chosen Highway,* pp. 68–69.

7. Adib Taherzadeh, *The Revelation of Bahá'u'lláh,* 3:205.

8. Shoghi Effendi, *God Passes By,* p. 188.

9. Adib Taherzadeh, *The Revelation of Bahá'u'lláh,* 3:211.

10. Bahá'u'lláh, *Prayers and Meditations,* pp. 34–35.

11. Bahá'u'lláh, quoted in Shoghi Effendi, *This Decisive Hour,* no. 46.10.

12. 'Abdu'l-Bahá, *Memorials of the Faithful,* no. 69.1.

13. 'Abdu'l-Bahá, *A Traveler's Narrative,* pp. 19–20.

14. 'Abdu'l-Bahá, *Memorials of the Faithful,* no. 69.30–33.

15. Nabíl-i-A'zam, *The Dawn-Breakers,* pp. 265–66, 267.

16. Ibid., pp. 379–82.

17. Ibid., pp. 410–13.

18. 'Abdu'l-Bahá, *A Traveler's Narrative,* pp. 58–59.

19. Shoghi Effendi, *God Passes By,* p. 199.

20. Gloria Faizi, *Fire on the Mountain-Top,* pp. 86, 88–91.

21. Nabíl-i-A'ẓam, *The Dawn-Breakers,* pp. 549–52.

22. On behalf of the Universal House of Justice, letter dated January 10, 1985, to all National Spiritual Assemblies.

23. Ibid.

24. Olya Ruhizadegan, "Extract from an Account Concerning the Interrogation of Mona Mahmudnezhad, One of the Ten Bahá'í Women Hanged in Shiraz on June 18, 1983," in *World Order* 18 (Winter 1983–84): 28–29.

25. Olya Ruhizadegan, "Extracts from an Account of the Life and Activities of Zarrin Moqimi, One of the Ten Bahá'í Women Hanged in Shiraz on June 18, 1983," in *World Order* 18 (Winter 1983–84): 27–28.

26. On behalf of the Universal House of Justice, letter dated January 10, 1985, to all National Spiritual Assemblies.

27. Jáviddukht Khádím, "In Memoriam," *The Bahá'í World* 20:785.

28. Roger White, "In Memoriam," *The Bahá'í World* 14:313–15.

29. Mehru S. Rowhani, "In Memoriam," in *The Bahá'í World* 19:689.

30. O. Z. Whitehead, *Some Early Bahá'ís of the West,* pp. 65–68, 69, 70, 72.

31. 'Abdu'l-Bahá, *Selections from the Writings of 'Abdu'l-Bahá,* no. 158.1–15.

32. Hooper C. Dunbar, "In Memoriam," in *The Bahá'í World* 18:733–38.

33. O. Z. Whitehead, *Some Early Bahá'ís of the West,* pp. 15, 16.

34. O. Z. Whitehead, *Some Bahá'ís to Remember,* pp. 176, 179.

35. Dorothy Gilstrap, *From Copper to Gold,* pp. 410–11.

36. Sadeh Hakiman and Abdul Karim Sillah, "In Memoriam," *The Bahá'í World* 20:875–77.

37. M. Samandari and K. H. Payman, "In Memoriam," *The Bahá'í World* 20:827–29.

38. Medhi and Ursula Samandari, "In Memoriam," *The Bahá'í World* 13:925–26.

39. Robert Walker, "In Memoriam," *The Bahá'í World* 20:935–37.

40. Aaron Emmel, "Culture Crash," in Heather Brandon and Aaron Emmel, *On the Front Lines,* pp. 84–90.

41. Interviewer, "Transformation," ibid., pp. 100–106.

42. Kalim Armstrong, "Recite Ye the Verses," ibid., pp. 136–41.

4 / Education and a Life of Service

1. Bahá'u'lláh, *Tablets of Bahá'u'lláh,* pp. 161–62.

2. 'Abdu'l-Bahá, *Some Answered Questions,* p. 236.

3. Ibid., p. 8.

4. 'Abdu'l-Bahá, *The Secret of Divine Civilization,* p. 33.

5. 'Abdu'l-Bahá, *Selections from the Writings of 'Abdu'l-Bahá,* no. 118.1–2.

6. Ibid., no. 119.1–2.

7. Ibid., no. 128.1.

8. On behalf of Shoghi Effendi, in "Youth," *The Compilation of Compilation,* 2:2246.

9. On behalf of Shoghi Effendi, in "Deepening," *The Compilation of Compilations,* 1:511.

10. Ibid., 1:497.

11. On behalf of the Universal House of Justice, *Messages from the Universal House of Justice, 1963–1986,* no. 217.1.

12. Bahá'u'lláh, Kitáb-i-Íqán, ¶16.

13. 'Abdu'l-Bahá, *The Promulgation of Universal Peace,* p. 459.

14. Ibid., p. 293.

15. Shoghi Effendi, in "Deepening," *The Compilation of Compilations,* 1:432.

16. Shoghi Effendi, quoted in the Universal House of Justice, *Messages from the Universal House of Justice,* no. 35.13.

17. On behalf of Shoghi Effendi, in "Deepening," *The Compilation of Compilations,* 1:488.

18. The Universal House of Justice, letter dated 6/10/66 to the Bahá'í youth in every land, *Messages from the Universal House of Justice,* no. 37.5.

19. 'Abdu'l-Bahá, in "Deepening," *The Compilation of Compilations,* 1:395.

20. On behalf of Shoghi Effendi, ibid., 1:507.

21. Ibid., 1:485.

22. Ibid., 1:521.

23. Ibid., 1:487.

24. Ibid., 1:464.

25. Ibid., 1:463.

26. Ibid., 1:501.

27. Bahá'u'lláh, *Tablets of Bahá'u'lláh,* pp. 141–42.

28. 'Abdu'l-Bahá, *The Promulgation of Universal Peace,* p. 50.

29. 'Abdu'l-Bahá, *The Secret of Divine Civilization,* pp. 2–3.

30. Bahá'u'lláh, *Tablets of Bahá'u'lláh,* pp. 51–52.

31. Bahá'u'lláh, Hidden Words, Persian, no. 82.

32. Bahá'u'lláh, *Tablets of Bahá'u'lláh,* p. 26.

33. 'Abdu'l-Bahá, *Paris Talks,* no. 11.12–13.

34. 'Abdu'l-Bahá, *The Secret of Divine Civilization,* p. 106.

35. 'Abdu'l-Bahá, *Selections from the Writings of 'Abdu'l-Bahá,* no. 126.1.

36. On behalf of Shoghi Effendi, in "Deepening," *The Compilation of Compilations,* 1:477.

37. The Universal House of Justice, *Messages from the Universal House of Justice,* no. 37.7.

38. 'Abdu'l-Bahá, *The Secret of Divine Civilization,* pp. 35–36.

39. 'Abdu'l-Bahá, *Tablets of Abdul-Baha Abbas,* 3:501–2.

40. Shoghi Effendi, letter dated December 25, 1931, to an individual believer, in *Bahá'í News* 64 (July 1932): 4.

41. Shoghi Effendi, *Unfolding Destiny,* p. 445.

42. On behalf of Shoghi Effendi, in "Youth," *The Compilation of Compilations,* 2:2276.

43. On behalf of Shoghi Effendi, in "Bahá'í Education," *The Compilation of Compilations,* 1:658.

44. The Universal House of Justice, *Messages from the Universal House of Justice,* no. 369.4.

45. Bahá'u'lláh, in "Extracts from the Writings Concerning Arts and Crafts," *The Compilation of Compilations,* 1:10.

46. 'Abdu'l-Bahá, in *Developing Distinctive Bahá'í Communities,* no. 11.13.

47. 'Abdu'l-Bahá, *Selections from the Writings of 'Abdu'l-Bahá,* no. 102.3.

48. On behalf of Shoghi Effendi, in "Extracts from the Writings Concerning Arts and Crafts," *The Compilation of Compilations,* 1:25.

49. On behalf of Shoghi Effendi, *The Importance of the Arts in Promoting the Faith,* no. 27.

50. 'Abdu'l-Bahá, in *Bahá'í World Faith,* p. 377.

51. 'Abdu'l-Bahá, *Selections from the Writings of 'Abdu'l-Bahá,* no. 72.1–4.

52. On behalf of Shoghi Effendi in "Deepening," *The Compilation of Compilations,* 1:457.

53. Ibid., 1:496.

5 / Teaching

1. Bahá'u'lláh, *Gleanings,* no. 53.1.

2. Ibid., no. 128.10.

3. Ibid., no. 154.2.

4. 'Abdu'l-Bahá, *Selections from the Writings of 'Abdu'l-Bahá,* no. 1.6.

5. Ibid., no. 216.1.

6. Ibid., no. 212.1.

7. Shoghi Effendi, *The Advent of Divine Justice,* ¶66.

8. Shoghi Effendi, *Citadel of Faith,* p. 148.

9. The Universal House of Justice, *A Wider Horizon,* pp. 58–59.

10. Bahá'u'lláh, *Gleanings,* no. 43.4.

11. Ibid., no. 139.8.

12. 'Abdu'l-Bahá, *The Secret of Divine Civilization,* p. 46.

13. Ibid., p. 103.

14. Shoghi Effendi, in "Youth," *The Compilation of Compilations,* 2:2240.

15. On behalf of Shoghi Effendi, in "Living the Life," *The Compilation of Compilations,* 2:1276.

16. The Universal House of Justice, *Messages from the Universal House of Justice,* no. 73.3.

17. Ibid., no. 19.5.

18. Bahá'u'lláh, *Gleanings,* no. 132.5.

19. 'Abdu'l-Bahá, in "Guidelines for Teaching," *The Compilations of Compilations,* 2:1924.

20. 'Abdu'l-Bahá, *Selections from the Writings of 'Abdu'l-Bahá,* no. 200.8–9.

21. Shoghi Effendi, in *A New Way of Life,* p. 13.

22. On behalf of Shoghi Effendi, in "Guidelines for Teaching," *The Compilation of Compilations,* 2:1951.

23. Ibid., 2:1955.

24. On behalf of Shoghi Effendi, in Helen Hornby, ed., *Lights of Guidance,* no. 829.

25. On behalf of Shoghi Effendi, in "Guidelines for Teaching," *The Compilation of Compilations,* 2:2009.

26. The Universal House of Justice, *Messages from the Universal House of Justice,* no. 19.6.

27. Shoghi Effendi, in "Youth," *The Compilation of Compilations,* 2:2253.

28. On behalf of Shoghi Effendi, *Arohanui,* p. 33.

29. On behalf of Shoghi Effendi, in "Centers of Bahá'í Learning," *The Compilation of Compilations,* 1:102.

30. On behalf of Shoghi Effendi, in "Youth," *The Compilation of Compilations,* 2:2301.

31. The Universal House of Justice, *Messages from the Universal House of Justice,* nos. 321.5–5a.

32. Ibid., no. 37.6.

33. Ibid., no. 369.1–2.

34. Bahá'u'lláh, in "Guidelines for Teaching," *The Compilation of Compilations,* 2:1898.

35. Bahá'u'lláh, quoted in Shoghi Effendi, *The Advent of Divine Justice,* ¶77.

36. Bahá'u'lláh, quoted in Shoghi Effendi, *The World Order of Bahá'u'lláh,* p. 106.

37. 'Abdu'l-Bahá, *Tablets of the Divine Plan,* no. 7.5.

38. Ibid., no. 8.13.

39. 'Abdu'l-Bahá, in "Guidelines for Teaching," *The Compilation of Compilations,* 2:1920.

40. On behalf of Shoghi Effendi, *Messages of Shoghi Effendi to the Indian Subcontinent,* p. 206.

41. Bahá'u'lláh, *Tablets of Bahá'u'lláh,* p. 138.

42. 'Abdu'l-Bahá, Tablet appended to His Tablet to the Central Organization for a Durable Peace, The Hague, in *The Bahá'í World,* 15:36.

43. On behalf of Shoghi Effendi, in "Guidelines for Teaching," *The Compilation of Compilations,* 2:1987.

44. Ibid., 2:1991.

45. Bahá'u'lláh, quoted in Shoghi Effendi, *The Advent of Divine Justice,* ¶39.

46. 'Abdu'l-Bahá, in *Selections from the Writings of 'Abdu'l-Bahá,* no. 213.

47. Shoghi Effendi, *The Advent of Divine Justice,* ¶36.

48. Shoghi Effendi, *Citadel of Faith,* p. 149.

49. Bahá'u'lláh, *Gleanings,* no. 128.6.

50. Shoghi Effendi, *The Advent of Divine Justice*, ¶75.

51. Shoghi Effendi, in "Centers of Bahá'í Learning," *The Compilation of Compilations*, 1:100.

52. On behalf of Shoghi Effendi, in Helen Hornby, ed., *Lights of Guidance*, no. 2129.

53. On behalf of Shoghi Effendi, *Dawn of a New Day*, p. 180.

54. Bahá'u'lláh, *Gleanings*, no. 171.1.

55. 'Abdu'l-Bahá, in *The Individual and Teaching*, p. 10.

56. On behalf of Shoghi Effendi, in "Guidelines for Teaching," *The Compilation of Compilations*, 2:1993.

57. Ibid., 2:1983.

58. Ibid., 2:1984.

59. Ibid., 2:1989.

60. Ibid., 2:2012.

61. Ibid., 2:1952.

62. Ibid., 2:2011.

63. Ibid., 2:1948.

64. Ibid., 2:1947.

65. Bahá'u'lláh, in *The Advent of Divine Justice*, ¶114.

66. Bahá'u'lláh, in *Bahá'í World Faith*, p. 206.

67. 'Abdu'l-Bahá, in *Bahá'í Prayers*, p. 200–201.

68. 'Abdu'l-Bahá, *Selections from the Writings of 'Abdu'l-Bahá*, no. 184.2.

69. Bahá'u'lláh, *Gleanings*, no. 161.2.

70. 'Abdu'l-Bahá, *Selections from the Writings of 'Abdu'l-Bahá*, no. 1.6.

71. On behalf of Shoghi Effendi, in "Guidelines for Teaching," *The Compilation of Compilations*, 2:1950.

72. The Universal House of Justice, *Messages from the Universal House of Justice*, no. 52.2.

73. Shoghi Effendi, *The Advent of Divine Justice*, ¶101.

74. On behalf of Shoghi Effendi, in Helen Hornby, ed., *Lights of Guidance*, no. 2127.

75. On behalf of Shoghi Effendi, in "Youth," *The Compilation of Compilations*, 2:2284.

76. On behalf of Shoghi Effendi, *Dawn of a New Day*, p. 199.

77. On behalf of Shoghi Effendi, in Helen Hornby, ed., *Lights of Guidance*, no. 2133.

78. On behalf of Shoghi Effendi, in "Youth," *The Compilation of Compilations,* 2:2295.

79. On behalf of the Universal House of Justice, in Helen Hornby, ed., *Lights of Guidance,* no. 1408.

80. On behalf of Shoghi Effendi, in "Guidelines for Teaching," *The Compilation of Compilations,* 2:1945.

81. On behalf of Shoghi Effendi, in "Youth," *The Compilation of Compilations,* 2:2244.

82. Ibid., 2:2245.

83. Ibid., 2:2250.

84. On behalf of Shoghi Effendi, in Helen Hornby, ed. *Lights of Guidance,* no. 338.

85. On behalf of Shoghi Effendi, in "Extracts from the Bahá'í Writings on the Subject of Writers and Writing," *The Compilation of Compilations,* 2:2224.

86. The Universal House of Justice, in Helen Hornby, ed., *Lights of Guidance,* no. 1831.

87. The Universal House of Justice, *The Importance of the Arts in Promoting the Faith,* no. 69.

88. The Universal House of Justice, Riḍván letter, April 21, 2002.

89. The Universal House of Justice, letter dated January 17, 2003, to the Bahá'ís of the world.

90. The Universal House of Justice, letter dated January 9, 2001, to the conference of the Continental Board of Counsellors.

91. The Universal House of Justice, Riḍván letter, April 21, 2000.

92. On behalf of the Universal House of Justice, letter dated May 31, 2001, to an individual Bahá'í.

93. The International Teaching Center, "Training Institutes and Systematic Growth," February, 2000.

94. On behalf of Shoghi Effendi, in *Scholarship,* p. 12.

95. On behalf of Shoghi Effendi, in "Youth," *The Compilation of Compilations,* 2:2292.

96. The Universal House of Justice, *Messages from the Universal House of Justice,* no. 357.2.

97. 'Abdu'l-Bahá, *Tablets of the Divine Plan,* no. 7.8.

98. Ibid., no. 6.13.

99. Bahá'u'lláh, *Gleanings,* no. 157.1–3.

100. 'Abdu'l-Bahá, *Tablets of the Divine Plan,* no. 4.4.

101. Shoghi Effendi, *Unfolding Destiny,* p. 35.

102. On behalf of Shoghi Effendi, ibid., p. 187.

103. On behalf of Shoghi Effendi, in *Dawn of A New Day,* p. 121.

104. On behalf of Shoghi Effendi, in Helen Hornby, ed., *Lights of Guidance,* no. 2124.

105. The Universal House of Justice, *Messages from the Universal House of Justice,* no. 67.3–4.

106. On behalf of the Universal House of Justice, ibid., no. 382.2–4.

107. Raḥmatu'lláh Muhájir, in *The Quickeners of Mankind,* no. 206.

108. The Universal House of Justice, *Messages from the Universal House of Justice,* no. 142.16.

109. Ibid., no. 162.33–34.

110. Ibid., no. 386.1–3.

111. On behalf of the Universal House of Justice, in *The Mission of this Generation,* pp. 98–99.

6 / Personal Conduct

1. Bahá'u'lláh, quoted in *The Advent of Divine Justice,* ¶48.

2. Ibid.

3. Bahá'u'lláh, *Gleanings,* no. 147.2.

4. Bahá'u'lláh, *Tablets of Bahá'u'lláh,* p. 23.

5. The Báb, *Selections from the Writings of the Báb,* no. 3.5.1–2.

6. 'Abdu'l-Bahá, *Selections from the Writings of 'Abdu'l-Bahá,* no. 129.1–4.

7. 'Abdu'l-Bahá, *The Secret of Divine Civilization,* pp. 59–60.

8. Shoghi Effendi, *The Advent of Divine Justice,* ¶39.

9. Ibid., ¶41.

10. Ibid., ¶50.

11. 'Abdu'l-Bahá, *Selections from the Writings of 'Abdu'l-Bahá,* no. 129.6–9.

12. On behalf of Shoghi Effendi, in Helen Hornby, ed., *Lights of Guidance,* no. 1189.

13. Bahá'u'lláh, Hidden Words, Persian, no. 62.

14. Bahá'u'lláh, in *The Compilation of Compilations,* 2:1785.

15. 'Abdu'l-Bahá, tablet to an individual believer, in *The Compilation of Compilations,* 2:1790.

16. 'Abdu'l-Bahá, quoted in Shoghi Effendi, *The Advent of Divine Justice,* ¶49.

17. On behalf of Shoghi Effendi, in "Prohibition on Drinking Alcohol," *The Compilation of Compilations,* 2:1791.

18. On behalf of Shoghi Effendi, ibid., 2:1793.

19. On behalf of Shoghi Effendi, in Helen Hornby, ed., *Lights of Guidance,* no. 1175.

20. Ibid., no. 1173.

21. The Universal House of Justice, in "Prohibition on Drinking Alcohol," *The Compilation of Compilations,* 2:1810.

22. On behalf of the Universal House of Justice, in Helen Hornby, ed., *Lights of Guidance,* no. 1177.

23. 'Abdu'l-Bahá, *Selections from the Writings of 'Abdu'l-Bahá,* no. 129.10–11.

24. The Universal House of Justice, in Helen Hornby, ed., *Lights of Guidance,* no. 1184.

25. Ibid., no. 1183.

26. Ibid., no. 1185.

27. 'Abdu'l-Bahá, *Paris Talks,* no. 14.2.

28. The Universal House of Justice, in Helen Hornby, ed., *Lights of Guidance,* no. 1202.

29. Ibid., no. 1203.

30. 'Abdu'l-Bahá, *Selections from the Writings of 'Abdu'l-Bahá,* no. 129.14.

31. Ibid., no. 129.12.

7 / Interpersonal Relationships

1. Bahá'u'lláh, in "Family Life," *The Compilation of Compilations,* 1:821.

2. Ibid., 1:824.

3. The Báb, *Selections from the Writings of the Báb,* 3.22.1.

4. 'Abdu'l-Bahá, in "Family Life," *The Compilation of Compilations,* 1:843.

5. Ibid., 1:849.

6. 'Abdu'l-Bahá, *Some Answered Questions*, pp. 231–32.

7. On behalf of Shoghi Effendi, in "Family Life," *The Compilation of Compilations*, 1:682.

8. The Universal House of Justice, in "Family Life," *The Compilation of Compilations*, 1:915.

9. Bahá'u'lláh, in *Bahá'í Prayers*, p. 118.

10. 'Abdu'l-Bahá, in *Bahá'í Prayers*, pp. 118–19.

11. 'Abdu'l-Bahá, *Selections from the Writings of 'Abdu'l-Bahá*, no. 84.2–5.

12. Ibid., no. 92.1–3.

13. On behalf of Shoghi Effendi, quoted in *Messages from The Universal House of Justice*, no. 126.7d.

14. On behalf of Shoghi Effendi, in "Family Life," *The Compilation of Compilations*, 1:866.

15. The Universal House of Justice, *Messages from the Universal House of Justice*, no. 126.9.

16. 'Abdu'l-Bahá, *Selections from the Writings of 'Abdu'l-Bahá*, no. 86.1–2.

17. Ibid., no. 85.1.

18. 'Abdu'l-Bahá, newly translated tablet attached to a letter written on behalf of the Universal House of Justice dated April 15, 1985, to the Bahá'í Publishing Trust of the United States.

19. On behalf of Shoghi Effendi, in Helen Hornby, ed., *Lights of Guidance*, no. 1268.

20. The Universal House of Justice, ibid., no. 1231.

21. 'Abdu'l-Bahá, in *Bahá'í Prayers*, p. 117.

22. The Universal House of Justice, in Helen Hornby, ed., *Lights of Guidance*, no. 1257.

23. Ibid., no. 1256.

24. On behalf of Shoghi Effendi, ibid., no. 1235.

25. Ibid., no. 1240.

26. On behalf of Shoghi Effendi, *Messages to Canada*, pp. 205–6.

27. The Universal House of Justice, *Messages from the Universal House of Justice*, no. 126.5.

28. The Universal House of Justice, in Helen Hornby, ed., *Lights of Guidance*, no. 1237.

29. *Bahá'í Prayers*, p. 117.

30. On behalf of Shoghi Effendi, in *Principles of Bahá'í Administration*, p. 14.

31. Shoghi Effendi, *Directives from the Guardian*, pp. 40–41.

32. Bahá'u'lláh, Kitáb-i-Aqdas, ¶70.

33. 'Abdu'l-Bahá, in "Preserving Bahá'í Marriages," *Compilation of Compilations*, 2:443.

34. 'Abdu'l-Bahá, *Selections from the Writings of 'Abdu'l-Bahá*, no. 88.1–2.

35. On behalf of Shoghi Effendi, in Helen Hornby, ed., *Lights of Guidance* (1983 ed.), no. 695.

36. On behalf of Shoghi Effendi, in Helen Hornby, ed., *Lights of Guidance*, no. 1160.

37. Ibid., no. 1162.

38. The Universal House of Justice, in *Developing Distinctive Bahá'í Communities*, p. 867.

39. The Universal House of Justice, in Helen Hornby, ed., *Lights of Guidance*, no. 1161.

40. On behalf of the Universal House of Justice, in *Lights of Guidance* (1983 ed.), no. 702.

41. On behalf of the Universal House of Justice, in Helen Hornby, ed., *Lights of Guidance*, no. 1166.

42. Ibid., no. 1155.

43. Ibid., no. 1169.

44. Ibid., no. 1163.

45. 'Abdu'l-Bahá, *The Promulgation of Universal Peace*, p. 168.

46. 'Abdu'l-Bahá, *Selections from the Writings of 'Abdu'l-Bahá*, no. 103.1–3.

47. Ibid., no. 102.3.

48. The Universal House of Justice, in "Family Life," *The Compilation of Compilations*, 1:916.

49. On behalf of the Universal House of Justice, ibid., 1:916.

50. 'Abdu'l-Bahá, ibid., 1:845.

51. 'Abdu'l-Bahá, in *Paris Talks*, no. 9.21.

52. 'Abdu'l-Bahá, *The Promulgation of Universal Peace*, pp. 144–45.

53. 'Abdu'l-Bahá, *Selections from the Writings of 'Abdu'l-Bahá*, no. 221.9.

54. On behalf of Shoghi Effendi, in "Family Life," *The Compilation of Compilations,* 2:2156.

55. On behalf of Shoghi Effendi, in Helen Hornby, ed., *Lights of Guidance,* no. 252.

56. Ibid., no. 744.

57. Ibid., no. 729.

58. Bahá'u'lláh, *Tablets of Bahá'u'lláh,* p. 168.

59. 'Abdu'l-Bahá, in "Consultation," *The Compilation of Compilations,* 1:180.

60. 'Abdu'l-Bahá, in Helen Hornby, ed., *Lights of Guidance,* no. 588.

61. The Universal House of Justice, ibid., no. 589.

62. Ibid., no. 734.

63. 'Abdu'l-Bahá, *The Compilation of Compilations,* 1:1042.

64. On behalf of the Universal House of Justice, letter dated January 24, 1993, to an individual Bahá'í, printed in *The American Bahá'í,* November 23, 1993, pp. 10–11.

65. Bahá'u'lláh, *Gleanings,* no. 96.3.

66. Ibid., no. 60.3.

67. Bahá'u'lláh, in "A Chaste and Holy Life," *The Compilation of Compilations,* 1:148.

68. Shoghi Effendi, *The Advent of Divine Justice,* ¶47.

69. Ibid., ¶50.

70. Shoghi Effendi, in Helen Hornby, ed., *Lights of Guidance,* no. 1210.

71. On behalf of Shoghi Effendi, in "A Chaste and Holy Life," *The Compilation of Compilations,* 1:145.

72. On behalf of Shoghi Effendi, in Helen Hornby, ed., *Lights of Guidance,* no. 1212.

73. On behalf of Shoghi Effendi, *Dawn of a New Day,* p. 153.

74. On behalf of Shoghi Effendi, in "Youth," *The Compilation of Compilations,* 2:2285.

75. On behalf of Shoghi Effendi, in Helen Hornby, ed., *Lights of Guidance,* no. 2155.

76. Ibid., no. 2126.

77. The Universal House of Justice, ibid., no. 1209.

78. The Universal House of Justice, in "A Chaste and Holy Life," *The Compilation of Compilations,* 1:118.

79. The Universal House of Justice, in Helen Hornby, ed., *Lights of Guidance*, no. 1220.

80. On the behalf of the Universal House of Justice, letter dated September 11, 1995, in *The American Bahá'í*, November 23, 1995, p. 11.

81. On behalf of the Universal House of Justice, "A Chaste and Holy Life," *The Compilation of Compilations*, 1:119.

82. Bahá'u'lláh, *Gleanings*, no. 146.1.

83. 'Abdu'l-Bahá, *Tablets of the Divine Plan*, no. 10.10.

84. 'Abdu'l-Bahá, *Tablets of Abdul-Baha Abbas*, 1:45.

85. 'Abdu'l-Bahá, *'Abdu'l-Bahá in London*, p. 91.

86. 'Abdu'l-Bahá, *Paris Talks*, no. 9.21.

8 / Social Relationships

1. The Universal House of Justice, *Individual Rights and Freedoms in the World Order of Bahá'u'lláh*, p. 7.

2. Ibid., p. 21.

3. Ibid., pp. 21–22.

4. Bahá'u'lláh, *Tablets of Bahá'u'lláh*, pp. 22–23.

5. 'Abdu'l-Bahá, *Tablets of Abdul-Baha Abbas*, 2:343.

6. Shoghi Effendi, in Helen Hornby, ed., *Lights of Guidance*, no. 1463.

7. Bahá'u'lláh, *Gleanings*, no. 115.2.

8. 'Abdu'l-Bahá, *Selections from the Writings of 'Abdu'l-Bahá*, no. 53.2.

9. Shoghi Effendi, *Directives from the Guardian*, p. 56.

10. Shoghi Effendi, *The World Order of Bahá'u'lláh*, p. 65.

11. Ibid., pp. 41–42.

12. Bahá'u'lláh, *Gleanings*, no. 128.

13. Bahá'u'lláh, quoted in Shoghi Effendi, *God Passes By*, p. 198.

14. 'Abdu'l-Bahá, *Some Answered Questions*, p. 267.

15. The Universal House of Justice, *Messages from the Universal House of Justice*, no. 69.3–4.

16. Bahá'u'lláh, *Epistle to the Son of the Wolf*, p. 25.

17. 'Abdu'l-Bahá, *The Promulgation of Universal Peace*, p. 123.

18. Shoghi Effendi, *Directives from the Guardian*, p. 48.

19. On behalf of Shoghi Effendi, in *Principles of Bahá'í Administration*, pp. 95–96.

20. The Universal House of Justice, letter dated September 20, 1965, to the National Spiritual Assembly of the Bahá'ís of the United States.

21. On behalf of the Universal House of Justice, in Helen Hornby, ed., *Lights of Guidance*, no. 1357.

22. On behalf of the Universal House of Justice, letter dated July 27, 1987, to an individual believer.

23. On behalf of Shoghi Effendi, in Helen Hornby, ed., *Lights of Guidance*, no. 1396.

24. Ibid., no. 1391.

25. National Spiritual Assembly of the Bahá'ís of the United States, "Criteria for Membership in Non-Bahá'í Organizations," in *Bahá'í News* 108 (March 1967), U.S. Supplement, p. 2.

26. Shoghi Effendi, *Bahá'í Administration*, pp. 125–26.

27. On behalf of Shoghi Effendi, *Unfolding Destiny*, p. 91.

28. On behalf of Shoghi Effendi, in *Principles of Bahá'í Administration*, p. 26.

29. Shoghi Effendi, in Helen Hornby, ed., *Lights of Guidance*, no. 2.

30. Shoghi Effendi, *World Order of Bahá'u'lláh*, p. 145.

31. 'Abdu'l-Bahá, *Selections from the Writings of 'Abdu'l-Bahá*, no. 193.7.

32. 'Abdu'l-Bahá, quoted by Shoghi Effendi, *Bahá'í Administration*, p. 21.

33. Shoghi Effendi, *Bahá'í Administration*, p. 37.

34. The Universal House of Justice, *Messages from the Universal House of Justice*, no. 141.13.

35. Shoghi Effendi, *Bahá'í Administration*, p. 67.

36. On behalf of Shoghi Effendi, in "Youth," *The Compilation of Compilations*, 2:2259.

37. The Universal House of Justice, *Messages from the Universal House of Justice*, no. 141.16–17.

38. Ibid., no. 37.9.

39. Ibid., no. 37.9.

40. Ibid., no. 63.5.

41. 'Abdu'l-Bahá, *Selections from the Writings of 'Abdu'l-Bahá*, no. 201.2.

42. 'Abdu'l-Bahá, *The Promulgation of Universal Peace*, p. 156.

43. 'Abdu'l-Bahá, *Selections from the Writings of 'Abdu'l-Bahá*, no. 36.3.

44. Shoghi Effendi, *Bahá'í Administration*, pp. 130–31.

45. Shoghi Effendi, in Helen Hornby, ed., *Lights of Guidance*, no. 321.

46. On behalf of Shoghi Effendi, in "Youth," *The Compilation of Compilations*, 2:2252.

47. The Universal House of Justice, *Messages from the Universal House of Justice*, no. 34.16.

48. On behalf of Shoghi Effendi, in "Youth," *The Compilation of Compilations*, 2:2270.

49. The Universal House of Justice, in *Developing Distinctive Bahá'í Communities*, p. 607.

50. 'Abdu'l-Bahá, in *Bahá'í Prayers*, p. 84.

51. Shoghi Effendi, *The World Order of Bahá'u'lláh*, p. 6.

52. Shoghi Effendi, in "Bahá'í Funds and Contributions," *The Compilation of Compilations*, 1:1232.

53. On behalf of Shoghi Effendi, ibid., 1:1212.

54. Ibid., 1:1218.

55. Ibid., 1:1240.

56. Ibid., 1:1229.

57. The Universal House of Justice, *Messages from the Universal House of Justice*, no. 385.10.

58. 'Abdu'l-Bahá, *Selections from the Writings of 'Abdu'l-Bahá*, nos. 207.8–9.

59. 'Abdu'l-Bahá, *Tablets of the Divine Plan*, no. 13.5.

60. Shoghi Effendi, *Bahá'í Administration*, p. 62.

61. Ibid., p. 132.

62. Shoghi Effendi, *The World Order of Bahá'u'lláh*, p. 48.

63. Shoghi Effendi, in *Citadel of Faith*, p. 58.

64. The Universal House of Justice, *Messages from the Universal House of Justice*, no. 55.5–6.

65. The Universal House of Justice, *A Wider Horizon*, pp. 25–26.

66. The Universal House of Justice, *Messages from the Universal House of Justice*, no. 321.6.

9 / Social Issues

1. 'Abdu'l-Bahá, *Selections from the Writings of 'Abdu'l-Bahá*, no. 202.2–3.

2. Ibid., no. 1.4–7.

3. Shoghi Effendi, *The World Order of Bahá'u'lláh*, pp. 42–43.

4. The Universal House of Justice, *The Promise of World Peace*, p. 25.

5. The National Spiritual Assembly of the Bahá'ís of the United States, *The Vision of Race Unity*, pp. 5–12.

6. 'Abdu'l-Bahá, *Selections from the Writings of 'Abdu'l-Bahá*, no. 38.3.

7. 'Abdu'l-Bahá, in *Peace: More Than an End to War*, p. 139.

8. 'Abdu'l-Bahá, *The Promulgation of Universal Peace*, p. 375.

9. 'Abdu'l-Bahá, in "Women," *The Compilation of Compilations*, 2:2099.

10. Ibid., 2:2100.

11. 'Abdu'l-Bahá, *Selections from the Writings of 'Abdu'l-Bahá*, no. 92.1–3.

12. 'Abdu'l-Bahá, *The Promulgation of Universal Peace*, pp. 76–77.

13. The Universal House of Justice, *The Promise of World Peace*, pp. 26–27.

14. The Universal House of Justice, in "Women," *The Compilation of Compilations*, 2:2121.

15. The National Spiritual Assembly of the Bahá'ís of the United States, *Two Wings of a Bird*, pp. 2, 8–11.

16. Bahá'u'lláh, in "Peace," *The Compilation of Compilations*, 2:1587.

17. Bahá'u'lláh, quoted in Shoghi Effendi, *The World Order of Bahá'u'lláh*, pp. 38–39.

18. 'Abdu'l-Bahá, *Selections from the Writings of 'Abdu'l-Bahá*, no. 201.1–2.

19. Shoghi Effendi, *This Decisive Hour*, no. 55.5.

20. Shoghi Effendi, in "Peace," *The Compilation of Compilations*, 2:1619.

21. On behalf of Shoghi Effendi, ibid., 2:1615.

22. Ibid., 2:1620.

23. Bahá'u'lláh, *Gleanings*, no. 145.1.

24. Bahá'u'lláh, Hidden Words, Persian, no. 82.

25. 'Abdu'l-Bahá, in *Peace: More Than an End to War*, pp. 118–19.

26. Shoghi Effendi, *Bahá'í Administration*, p. 109.

27. Ibid., p. 37–38.

28. On behalf of Shoghi Effendi, in "Local Spiritual Assemblies," *The Compilation of Compilations*, 2:1405.

29. The Universal House of Justice, *The Promise of World Peace*, p. 25.

30. The Universal House of Justice, *Messages from the Universal House of Justice*, no. 379.1–10a.

31. Ibid., no. 385.6.

32. Ibid., *Messages from the Universal House of Justice*, no. 394.6.

33. A statement approved by the Universal House of Justice, *Readings on Bahá'í Social and Economic Development,* no. 2.1–22.

34. 'Abdu'l-Bahá, *Some Answered Questions,* pp. 78–79.

35. 'Abdu'l-Bahá, in "Conservation of the Earth's Resources," *The Compilation of Compilations,* 1:71.

36. 'Abdu'l-Bahá, *Some Answered Questions,* p. 7.

37. Ibid., pp. 158–59.

38. On behalf of Shoghi Effendi, in "Conservation of the Earth's Resources," *The Compilation of Compilations,* 1:85.

10 / Youth Can Move the World

1. The Universal House of Justice, *Messages from the Universal House of Justice,* no. 37.1–10.

2. Ibid., no. 61.1.

3. Ibid., no. 67.1–4.

4. Ibid., no. 357.1–3.

5. Ibid., no. 365.1.

6. Ibid., no. 369.1–6.

7. Ibid., no. 384.1–7.

8. Ibid., no. 386.1–9.

9. Ibid., no. 408.1–3.

10. Ibid., no. 428.1–10.

11. Ibid., no. 431.1.

12. Ibid., no. 449.1–2.

13. The Universal House of Justice, *The Mission of This Generation,* pp. 53–54.

14. Ibid., pp. 57–58.

15. Ibid., pp. 65–67.

16. Ibid., pp. 69–71.

17. The Universal House of Justice, letter dated December 25, 1995.

18. The Universal House of Justice, in *To Champion the Cause of Justice,* no. 1.1–3.

19. Ibid., no. 2.1–6.

20. The Universal House of Justice, letter dated July 20, 2000, to a youth conference in Vancouver, British Colombia.

21. The Universal House of Justice, letter dated December 25, 2000, to a youth conference in the Indian Sub-Continent.

22. The Universal House of Justice, in *To Champion the Cause of Justice,* no. 7.1–4.

23. Ibid., no. 16.1–3.

24. Ibid., no. 9.1–3

25. The Universal House of Justice, letter dated December 21, 2003, to the Bahá'í youth of the Northeastern United States.

26. On behalf of the Universal House of Justice, letter dated October 28, 1992.

27. On behalf of The Universal House of Justice, in *The Mission of This Generation,* pp. 61–62.

Appendix:
Selected Prayers for Spiritual Growth

1. On behalf of Shoghi Effendi, in *Bahá'í Prayers,* p. 3.

2. Bahá'u'lláh, *Kitáb-i-Aqdas,* p. 146.

3. Bahá'u'lláh, in *Bahá'í Prayers,* p. 4.

4. Ibid., pp. 4–7.

5. Ibid., pp. 7–16.

6. The Báb, in *Bahá'í Prayers,* p. 56.

7. 'Abdu'l-Bahá, in *Bahá'í Prayers,* pp. 71–72.

8. Ibid., p. 120.

9. Ibid., p. 121.

10. Bahá'u'lláh, *Tablets of Bahá'u'lláh,* pp. 24–25.

11. 'Abdu'l-Bahá, in *Bahá'í Prayers,* p. 64.

12. Bahá'u'lláh, in *Bahá'í Prayers,* p. 147.

13. The Báb, in *Bahá'í Prayers,* p. 227.

14. Bahá'u'lláh, in *Bahá'í Prayers,* pp. 123–24.

15. Ibid., pp. 19–20.

16. Ibid., pp. 164–65.

17. 'Abdu'l-Bahá, in *Let Thy Breeze Refresh Them,* pp. 27–28.

18. Bahá'u'lláh, *Prayers and Meditations,* 95–96.

19. Bahá'u'lláh, in *Bahá'í Prayers,* pp. 195–96.

20. 'Abdu'l-Bahá, in *Bahá'í Prayers,* pp. 200–201.

21. Ibid., p. 201.

22. 'Abdu'l-Bahá, *O God, My God . . . ,* no. 18.

23. Bahá'u'lláh, in *Bahá'í Prayers,* p. 238.

24. 'Abdu'l-Bahá, in *Bahá'í Prayers,* pp. 238–39.

25. Bahá'u'lláh, *Prayers and Meditations,* pp. 78–79.

26. 'Abdu'l-Bahá, in "Women," *The Compilation of Compilations,* 2:2187.

27. 'Abdu'l-Bahá, in *Bahá'í Prayers for Women,* p. 78.

28. Ibid., p. 18.

29. Bahá'u'lláh, in *Bahá'í Prayers,* pp. 171–72

30. 'Abdu'l-Bahá, in *Bahá'í Prayers,* p. 254.

31. Ibid., pp. 254–55.

32. On behalf of Shoghi Effendi, in *Bahá'í Prayers,* p. 307

33. Bahá'u'lláh, in *Bahá'í Prayers,* pp. 307–11.

34. Ibid., pp. 312–18.

Bibliography

Works of Bahá'u'lláh

Epistle to the Son of the Wolf. Translated by Shoghi Effendi. 1st pocket-sized ed. Wilmette, Ill.: Bahá'í Publishing Trust, 1988.

Gleanings from the Writings of Bahá'u'lláh. Translated by Shoghi Effendi. New ed. Wilmette, Ill.: Bahá'í Publishing, 2005.

The Hidden Words of Bahá'u'lláh. Translated by Shoghi Effendi. Wilmette, Ill.: Bahá'í Publishing, 2002.

Kitáb-i-Aqdas: The Most Holy Book. 1st pocket-sized ed. Wilmette, Ill.: Bahá'í Publishing Trust, 1993.

Kitáb-i-Íqán: The Book of Certitude. Translated by Shoghi Effendi. Wilmette, Ill.: Bahá'í Publishing, 2003.

Prayers and Meditations. Translated by Shoghi Effendi. 1st pocket-sized ed. Wilmette, Ill.: Bahá'í Publishing Trust, 1987.

Works of the Báb

Selections from the Writings of the Báb. Compiled by the Research Department of the Universal House of Justice. Translated by Habib Taherzadeh et al. 1st pocket-sized ed. Wilmette, Ill.: Bahá'í Publishing Trust, 2006.

Works of 'Abdu'l-Bahá

Memorials of the Faithful. New ed. Translated by Marzieh Gail. Wilmette, Ill.: Bahá'í Publishing Trust, 1996.

Paris Talks: Addresses Given by 'Abdu'l-Bahá in Paris in 1911. Wilmette, Ill.: Bahá'í Publishing, 2006.

The Promulgation of Universal Peace: Talks Delivered by 'Abdu'l-Bahá during His Visit to the United States and Canada in 1912. Compiled by Howard MacNutt.Wilmette, Ill.: Bahá'í Publishing Trust, 2007.

The Secret of Divine Civilization. Translated by Marzieh Gail and Ali-Kuli Khan. 1st pocket-sized ed. Wilmette, Ill.: Bahá'í Publishing Trust, 1990.

Selections from the Writings of 'Abdu'l-Bahá. Compiled by the Research Department of the Universal House of Justice. Translated by a Committee at the Bahá'í World Center and by Marzieh Gail. 1st pocket-sized ed. Wilmette, Ill.: Bahá'í Publishing Trust, 1996.

Some Answered Questions. Compiled and translated by Laura Clifford Barney. 1st pocket-sized ed. Wilmette, Ill.: Bahá'í Publishing Trust, 2004.

Tablets of Abdul-Baha Abbas. 3 vols. New York: Bahai Publishing Society, 1909–16.

Tablets of the Divine Plan: Revealed by 'Abdu'l-Bahá to the North American Bahá'ís. 1st pocket-sized ed. Wilmette, Ill.: Bahá'í Publishing Trust, 1993.

A Traveler's Narrative Written to Illustrate the Episode of the Báb. Translated by Edward G. Browne. New and corrected ed. Wilmette, Ill.: Bahá'í Publishing Trust, 1980.

Works of Shoghi Effendi

The Advent of Divine Justice. New ed. Wilmette, Ill.: Bahá'í Publishing Trust, 2006.

Bahá'í Administration: Selected Messages, 1922–1932. 7th ed. Wilmette, Ill.: Bahá'í Publishing Trust, 1974.

Citadel of Faith: Messages to America, 1947–1957. Wilmette, Ill.: Bahá'í Publishing Trust, 1965.

Dawn of a New Day: Messages to India, 1923–1957. New Delhi: Bahá'í Publishing Trust, n.d.

This Decisive Hour: Messages from Shoghi Effendi to the North American Bahá'ís, 1932–1946. Wilmette, Ill.: Bahá'í Publishing Trust, 2002.

Directives from the Guardian. New Delhi: Bahá'í Publishing Trust, 1973.

God Passes By. Rev. ed. Wilmette, Ill.: Bahá'í Publishing Trust, 1974.

Messages to Canada. 2nd ed. Thornhill, Ont.: Bahá'í Canada Publications, 1999.

Messages of Shoghi Effendi to the Indian Subcontinent 1923–1957. Compiled by Írán Fúrútan Muhájir. Revised and enlarged ed. New Delhi: Bahá'í Publishing Trust, 1995.

Principles of Bahá'í Administration: A Compilation. 4th ed. London: Bahá'í Publishing Trust, 1973.

The Unfolding Destiny of the British Bahá'í Community: The Messages from the Guardian of the Bahá'í Faith to the Bahá'ís of the British Isles. London: Bahá'í Publishing Trust, 1981.

The World Order of Bahá'u'lláh: Selected Letters. New ed. Wilmette, Ill.: Bahá'í Publishing Trust, 1991.

Works of the Universal House of Justice

Messages from the Universal House of Justice, 1963–1986: The Third Epoch of the Formative Age. Compiled by Geoffry Marks. Wilmette, Ill.: Bahá'í Publishing Trust, 1996.

The Mission of This Generation: Messages from the Universal House of Justice to Bahá'í Youth. Compiled by the European Bahá'í Youth Council. London: Bahá'í Publishing Trust, 1996.

The Promise of World Peace: To the Peoples of the World. Wilmette, Ill.: Bahá'í Publishing Trust, 1985.

To Champion the Cause of Justice: Messages from the Universal House of Justice to the Youth Congresses in the Americas 1998–2002. Compiled by the Continental Board of Counselors in the Americas. West Palm Beach, FL: Palabra Publications, 2002.

A Wider Horizon: Selected Messages of the Universal House of Justice 1983–1992. Compiled by Paul Lample. Riviera Beach, FL: Palabra Publications, 1992.

Compilations from the Bahá'í Writings

Bahá'u'lláh and 'Abdu'l-Bahá. *Bahá'í World Faith: Selected Writings of Bahá'u'lláh and 'Abdu'l-Bahá,* 2nd ed. Wilmette, Ill.: Bahá'í Publishing Trust, 1976.

———. *Let Thy breeze refresh them: Bahá'í Prayers and Tablets for Children.* Oakham, England: Bahá'í Publishing Trust, 1976.

————. *O God, My God . . . : Bahá'í Prayers and Tablets for Children and Youth.* Text in English and Persian. Wilmette, Ill.: Bahá'í Publishing Trust, 1984.

————. *The Individual and Teaching: Raising the Divine Call.* Compiled by the Research Department of the Universal House of Justice. Wilmette, Ill.: Bahá'í Publishing Trust, 1977.

————. *Spiritual Foundations: Prayer, Meditation, and the Devotional Attitude: Extracts from the Writings of Bahá'u'lláh, 'Abdu'l-Bahá, and Shoghi Effendi.* Compiled by the Research Department of the Universal House of Justice. Wilmette, Ill.: Bahá'í Publishing Trust, 1980.

Bahá'u'lláh, 'Abdu'l-Bahá, Shoghi Effendi, and Bahíyyih Khánum. *Bahíyyih Khánum: The Greatest Holy Leaf.* Compiled by the Research Department at the Bahá'í World Centre. Haifa: Bahá'í World Centre, 1982.

Bahá'u'lláh, 'Abdu'l-Bahá, Shoghi Effendi, and the Universal House of Justice. *The Compilation of Compilations: Prepared by the Universal House of Justice, 1963–1990.* 2 vols. Australia: Bahá'í Publications Australia, 1991.

————. *Scholarship: Extracts from the Writings of Bahá'u'lláh and 'Abdu'l-Bahá and from the letters of Shoghi Effendi and the Universal House of Justice.* Mona Vale: Bahá'í Publications Australia, 1995.

Bahá'u'lláh, the Báb, and 'Abdu'l-Bahá. *Bahá'í Prayers: A Selection of Prayers Revealed by Bahá'u'lláh, the Báb, and 'Abdu'l-Bahá.* New ed. Wilmette, Ill.: Bahá'í Publishing Trust, 1991.

Hayes, Terrill, comp. *Peace: More than an End to War: Selections from the Writings of Bahá'u'lláh, the Báb, 'Abdu'l-Bahá, Shoghi Effendi, and the Universal House of Justice.* Wilmette, Ill.: Bahá'í Publishing, 2007.

Hornby, Helen, comp. *Lights of Guidance: A Bahá'í Reference File.* 6th ed. New Delhi, India: Bahá'í Publishing Trust, 1999.

Marks, Geoffry W., comp. *Call to Remembrance: Connecting the Heart to Bahá'u'lláh.* Wilmette, Ill.: Bahá'í Publishing Trust, 1992.

The National Spiritual Assembly of the Bahá'ís of Canada, comp. *The Importance of the Arts in Promoting the Faith.* Thornhill, Ont.: Bahá'í Publications Canada, 1999.

Other Works

'Abdu'l-Bahá in London: Addresses and Notes of Conversations. London: Bahá'í Publishing Trust, 1982.

The Bahá'í World: A Biennial International Record. vol. 12, (1950–1954). Compiled by the National Spiritual Assembly of the Bahá'ís of the United States. Wilmette, Ill.: Bahá'í Publishing Committee, 1956.

The Bahá'í World: An International Record, vols. 13–20 (1954–1992). Compiled by the Universal House of Justice. Haifa: The Universal House of Justice, 1970, 1974, 1975, 1978, 1986, 1994, 1998.

Balyuzi, H. M. *'Abdu'l-Bahá: The Centre of the Covenant of Bahá'u'lláh.* London: Bahá'í Publishing Trust, 1971.

Blomfield, Lady (Sitárih Khánum). *The Chosen Highway.* Wilmette, Ill.: Bahá'í Publishing Trust, n.d.; repr. 1975.

Brandon, Heather, and Aaron Emmel, eds. *On the Front Lines: Bahá'í Youth in Their Own Words.* Oxford: George Ronald, 2002.

Developing Distinctive Bahá'í Communities: Guidelines for Spiritual Assemblies. Evanston, Ill.: Office of Assembly Development, 2007.

Esslemont, J. E. *Bahá'u'lláh and the New Era: An Introduction to the Bahá'í Faith.* 5th ed. Wilmette, Ill.: Bahá'í Publishing Trust, 1980.

Gilstrap, Dorothy Freeman. *From Copper to Gold: The Life of Dorothy Baker.* Wilmette, Ill.: Bahá'í Publishing Trust, 1999.

Faizi, Gloria. *Fire on the Mountain-Top.* London: Bahá'í Publishing Trust, 1973.

Nabíl-i-A'zam (Muhamman-i-Zarandí). *The Dawn-Breakers: Nabíl's Narrative of the Early Days of the Bahá'í Revelation.* Translated and edited by Shoghi Effendi. Wilmette, Ill.: Bahá'í Publishing Trust, 1999.

National Spiritual Assembly of the Bahá'ís of the United States. *Two Wings of a Bird: The Equality of Women and Men, A Statement by the National Spiritual Assembly of the Bahá'ís of the United States.* Wilmette, Ill.: Bahá'í Publishing Trust, 1997.

———. *The Vision of Race Unity: America's Most Challenging Issue.* Wilmette, Ill.: Bahá'í Publishing Trust, 1991.

National Spiritual Assembly of the Bahá'ís of the United States, comp. *A New Way of Life: What It Means to Be a Bahá'í Youth.* Rev. ed. Wilmette, Ill.: Bahá'í Publishing Trust, 1971.

Quickeners of Mankind: Pioneering in a World Community. Wilmette, Ill.:
   Bahá'í Publishing Trust, 1998.

Readings on Bahá'í Social and Economic Development. Riviera Beach, FL:
   Palabra Publications, 2000.

Taherzadeh, Adib. *The Revelation of Bahá'u'lláh: 'Akká, the Early Years
   1868–77.* Vol. 3. Oxford: George Ronald, 1983.

Whitehead, O. Z. *Some Bahá'ís to Remember.* Oxford: George Ronald,
   1983.

———. *Some Early Bahá'ís of the West.* Oxford: George Ronald, 1977.

Index

Most Great Spirit, 11
   see also Holy Spirit
mothers, rights and duties of,
   231, 233, 234, 240,
   304, 307
movements, non-Bahá'í, 132,
   193–94, 275–78,
   343–44
Mubarak, 100–102
Muḥammad, 7, 11, 27, 115–16
Mullá Ḥusayn, 54–57, 354
music, 147, 369
Muslims, teaching Bahá'í Faith
   to, 179–80
Muther, Elizabeth, 96n

N

Nakhjavání, 'Alí, 97–98
Náṣiri'd-Dín Sháh, Bahá'u'lláh's
   Tablet to, 59–60, 61
nations, unity of, 310, 311
Navváb (wife of Bahá'u'lláh),
   43, 46, 47–48
Naw-Rúz, 21
neighbors, teaching Bahá'í Faith
   to, 184
Netherlands, Bahá'í youth in,
   353–54
New World Order, 278–89,
   352, 363, 365
   see also World Order of
   Bahá'u'lláh
Nine Year Plan, 79, 331–36
nobility, 39, 250, 357
North America, Bahá'í youth
   in, 366, 368–69

O

obedience
   examples of, 82, 84, 85

   to God, 20, 120, 149,
     228, 259
   to government, 267–68,
     269, 273
   to laws of Bahá'u'lláh, 1,
     3–4, 14, 16–17, 28–29,
     31, 177, 203, 223, 228,
     252–53
   to parents, 216, 233
   to Spiritual Assemblies,
     279
obligatory prayers, 16–18, 19,
   21, 123–24, 125, 375,
   397
   texts of, 377–85
occupations. *See* professions,
   choice of
Old World Order, 265–78,
   282, 335, 339, 363
opium, 209–10, 213
oppression, freedom from, 240,
   241, 265
organizations
   Bahá'í, 188–89
   ecclesiastical, 203, 275
   non-Bahá'í, 132, 193–94,
     275–78, 343–44

P

Paraguay, Bahá'í youth in, 360
parental rights, loss of, 244, 246
parents
   children's relationship
     with, 215–17, 227–39,
     245–46
   prayers for, 387
   responsibilities of, 371,
     373, 374
   see also consent, parental;
     fathers, rights and